DAUGHTERS OF THUNDER

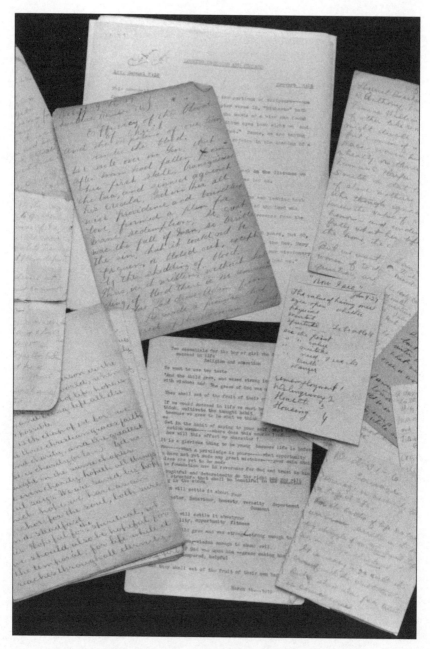

Source: *Florence Spearing Randolph Collection, Center for African American History and Culture, Temple University.*
Photograph by Zohrab Kazanjian.

WOMAN'S RIGHTS

There's neither Jew nor Gentile,
To those Who've paid the price;
'Tis neither Male nor Female,
But one in Jesus Christ.

I am going to tell you friends
Without the slightest doubt,
A day is coming very soon,
When your sins will find you out.

A day is coming very soon,
When sin you cannot hide:
Then you will wish you'd taken,
The Bible for your guide.

You'll wish you had let women alone
When they were trying to teach.
You'll be sorry you tried to hold them down,
When God told them to preach.

Come, dear brothers, let us journey,
Side by side and hand in hand;
Does not the Bible plainly tell you
Woman shall co-ordinate the man?

The hand that rocks the [cradle]
Will rule the world, you know;
So lift the standard high for God,
Wherever you may go.

Some women have the right to sing,
And some the right to teach;
But women, called by Jesus Christ,
Surely have the right to preach.

Some men will call you anti-Christ,
And some would rather die:
Than have the Spirit poured out,
When women prophesy.

To prophesy is to speak for God,
Wherever man is found;
Although lots of hypocrites,
Still try to hold them down.

So be steadfast in the Word of God,
Though fiery darts be hurled;
If Jesus Christ is on your side,
He is more than all the world.

—Lillia M. Sparks, *Latter Day Messenger,* 1934
adapted from a sermon by Ida B. Robinson

DAUGHTERS
OF THUNDER

Black Women Preachers and Their Sermons,
1850–1979

Bettye Collier-Thomas

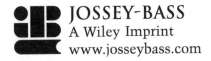
JOSSEY-BASS
A Wiley Imprint
www.josseybass.com

Published by Jossey-Bass
A Wiley Imprint
989 Market Street, San Francisco, CA 94103-1741   www.josseybass.com

Jossey-Bass books and products are available through most bookstores. To
contact Jossey-Bass directly call our Customer Care Department within the U.S. at
(800) 956-7739, outside the U.S. at (317) 572-3986 or fax (317) 572-4002.

Jossey-Bass also publishes its books in a variety of electronic formats. Some content that
appears in print may not be available in electronic books.

Credits are on p. 346

Library of Congress Cataloging-in-Publication Data

Collier-Thomas, Bettye.
    Daughters of thunder : Black women preachers and their
    sermons, 1850–1979 / Bettye Collier-Thomas.
        p. cm.
    Includes bibliographical references and indexes.
    ISBN 0–7879–0918–1 (alk. paper)
        1. Afro-American women clergy. 2. Sermons, American—
    Afro-American authors. 3. Sermons, American—Women authors.
    4. United States—Church history. 5. Black theology.
    6. Afro-Americans—Religion. I. Title.
    BR563.N4C64   1997
    251'.0082—dc21   97–4850

Printed in the United States of America
FIRST EDITION
HB Printing 10 9 8 7 6 5 4

CONTENTS

For my mother, grandmothers,
and great-grandmother

Katherine Bishop Collier

Luzella Veal Collier

Maria Bishop

Minnie Dillard Veal

PREFACE

I DID NOT BEGIN this work by looking for sermons by black women preachers. Rather, I discovered many of the sermons while researching topics as varied as black entertainment, race designation, black biography, and African American women's roles in black Church history. In the case of Florence Spearing Randolph, the sermons were delivered to me in a suitcase by her granddaughter, Anise Johnson Ward. There were several large manila envelopes with hundreds of small loose sheets of paper. It took me three years to match the pieces and assemble what became the sermons. I spread the sheets out on my basement floor and tried to match them by the ink or pencil and size and color of paper. Out of this disorganized mass has emerged the first major sermon collection of an early African American preacher woman. The sermons of Florence Spearing Randolph and Pauli Murray are the only known collections of black women's sermons in a repository: Randolph's sermons are at the Center for African American History and Culture at Temple University, and Murray's are at the Schlesinger Library, Radcliffe College.

This book results from the research I have done on African American churchwomen for more than twenty years. During the early 1970s, while engaged in doctoral research on the Baltimore black community, 1865 to 1910, I became acutely aware of the absence of black women in published histories about the African American community. I could not understand why their names did not grace the pages of scholarly books and other monographs. Reading secular and nonsecular publications, I discovered that black women wrote extensively. There was no dearth of sources to document their individual and collective histories, explore their intellectual thought, and trace their community work and activism.

I also learned that there was a great deal of discussion during the late nineteenth century about the proper role and place for women in the Church and in society. In 1972, with great excitement, I found the handwritten records of black Methodist preachers' meetings of the Washington Annual Conference between 1872 and 1890. This conference included Methodist Episcopal ministers in the District of Columbia, Maryland, and Virginia. I spent four months indexing these records to

determine the ministers' concerns. In addition to discussing Church rit-
ual, sermon development, and community issues, the ministers raised a
number of questions about women's proper role in the Church polity and
their deportment in church. In 1890, after eighteen years of meetings, the
ministers addressed the question, "Is woman inferior to man?" The chairman of the meeting stated, "Sad as it may be, woman is as inferior to man
as man is to God." This one statement summed up their beliefs about
women's status in the Church and in society.

In 1977, I became the founding director of the Bethune Museum and
Archives, the first U.S. institution to focus on documenting and preserv-
ing African American women's history. That November, I was invited to
speak at the national meeting of the National Council of Negro Women
(NCNW) and to lead a black women's collection development workshop
for their members. It was thought that the NCNW Sections would be a
perfect vehicle for identifying the individual and collective records of black
women throughout the country.

One of the people in that workshop was Shirley Herd of Indianapolis.
When Shirley returned home, she involved her Section in a statewide project to collect black women's papers. I was impressed with the extent to
which she followed the directions I gave in the workshop, right down to
asking local banks and businesses to support the project financially. She
succeeded in developing an impressive collection and raising quite a bit
of money, including $10,000 from a bank to write and publish a history.
Shirley asked me to write the history of black women in Indiana. I said I
was too busy developing the Bethune Museum and Archives, but recom-
mended that she contact Darlene Clark Hine, a professor of history at
Indiana University at Lafayette. As a result of this project, Hine wrote
When the Truth Is Told and launched the Black Women in the Midwest
Project.

In 1978, I developed plans and wrote a proposal for the first national
conference on black women's history. The National Endowment for the
Humanities provided funding for "Black Women: A Research Priority—
The First National Scholarly Research Conference on Black Women."
What a memorable occasion! The Bethune Museum and Archives opened
with great fanfare on November 11, 1979, followed by a two-day conference. Held in conjunction with the NCNW's convention, the conference attracted more than two thousand people, including university
scholars, organizational leaders, representatives of federal agencies, and
laypersons. The program included diverse sessions that reflected the status of the scholarship at the time. At one of the sessions, "Black Women in
the Church," Evelyn Brooks Barnett [Higginbotham] delivered a paper on

black Baptist women, and I spoke about black women in the African Methodist Episcopal Church.

During the 1980s, I aggressively pursued my research agenda on black women and sought research funding. In 1987, I submitted a grant proposal to the Lilly Endowment to research and write the first comprehensive history of black churchwomen. The agency expressed interest, but questioned whether there were enough data to pursue such a project. The Lilly Endowment decided to fund a planning grant to document the nature of the sources. When I completed the planning grant, the Lilly Endowment funded the project in 1990.

In 1992, I learned that there were no published sermons of pioneering black women preachers and that there was only one two-volume publication of contemporary women's sermons. Moreover, I discovered that there were no published histories of black women preachers, few scholarly articles, and no books on this topic. I possessed over four hundred sermons by the Reverend Florence Spearing Randolph, as well as sermons for many of the early preacher women who appear in this work. It was then that I decided to undertake this book.

My purpose in *Daughters of Thunder* is to explore the history of African American preaching women and the issues and struggles they confronted in their efforts to function as ministers and to become ordained. The book also presents for the first time the sermons of pioneering black women preachers.

Who were these women? What were their experiences? What impact did they have on the black Church, and how did they pursue careers as ministers? Are there denominational differences or similarities in terms of how much they have been allowed to function as preaching women? In what ways do the sermons of black preaching women compare with those of white preaching women and black male clergy? Although the papers of most black preaching women remain uncollected, and it is difficult to document their lives consistently, it is possible to reconstruct and identify their careers across denominational lines and to trace their development during the nineteenth and twentieth centuries.

With the exception of a very few women such as Jarena Lee, Julia Foote, Sojourner Truth, and Amanda Berry Smith, most black preaching women who pursued a ministry between 1800 and 1970 are virtually unknown. Those few who have been rescued from obscurity have survived primarily because they wrote spiritual autobiographies that have been recovered and published. However, there are legions of women who enjoyed great visibility and had long careers in the ministry. Whether they were ordained or whether they functioned as local preachers, evangelists, missionary preachers, or worked in other capacities, many women had active careers in the ministry. They often traveled extensively and crossed denominational lines as they preached throughout the United States.

The names of any number of these women have appeared in the black press. Some of their sermons were reproduced in the secular and nonsecular press, and a few have survived in private collections. Some wrote letters and articles that appeared in diverse media. Their obituaries, both sketchy and detailed, are frequently recorded in black newspapers. But rarely do women preachers appear in books, either as subjects or as a part of the text, nor do their names grace the buildings of the denominational colleges or other edifices.

In *The Black Church in the African American Experience,* C. Eric Lincoln and Lawrence H. Mamiya use "daughters of thunder" to refer to African American female preachers. The authors explain that "while the folk idiom 'son of thunder' was used to designate the booming voiced, fiery preacher, the origin of the term may also be related to 'Shango,' the West African god of thunder and lightning, whose symbol was the axe. Many African American folk customs are related to thunder." Impressed by the term and what it signifies, I chose it as the title of this book, because I felt that it reflected the power, authority, charisma, and confidence that black women preachers often evoked in their personas and sermons.

This book will be useful for scholars and others interested in religion, preaching, and the history of African American women ministers; teachers and students of Women's Studies and Black Studies; and those looking for hermeneutical models. For those concerned about the struggle of women to preach and to be ordained over most of the last two centuries, it provides a historical context for understanding the issues that engaged black and white preaching women.

Daughters of Thunder offers a unique and revealing collection of sermons, allowing the reader to sample the intellectual content and social, moral, and theological concerns of black women preachers for almost 150 years. As to the choice of sermons, with the exception of the Reverend Florence Spearing Randolph and the Reverend Pauli Murray, there was no choice to be made, because these are all of the sermons by black women preachers that have been unearthed to date.

Unfortunately, the records of black women, particularly those of many pioneering women, are still uncollected. In the last few years, there have been important publication breakthroughs in African American women's history, most prominently a biographical dictionary, *Notable Black American Women* (1992, 1996), edited by Jessie Carney Smith, and *Black*

Women in America: A Historical Encyclopedia (1993), edited by Darlene Clark Hine, Elsa Barkley Brown, and Rosalyn Terborg Penn. However, many prominent preaching women, such as Harriet Baker, Mary Small, Ida Robinson, Rosa Horn, Mary G. Evans, Elder Lucy Smith, and any number of other important women preachers, are not mentioned in these sources. They do include traditional figures such as Jarena Lee, Amanda Berry Smith, and Julia Foote, and more recent twentieth-century notables such as Pauli Murray.

Although the sermons in *Daughters of Thunder* differ widely in hermeneutical style, content, and target audience, when viewed as a whole, they reveal a unifying theme. They seek to present their audience with strategies for understanding and living with the tension between what *is*—human imperfection, injustice, suffering—and what *God calls creation to be*—a creation in which humans live righteous, harmonious lives in their relations with God and with other human beings. While never denying the reality of human suffering, these black preaching women offer powerful messages that all humans *can* overcome the imperfections of the world, and, moreover, that all humans are *called* by God to overcome imperfections, both spiritual and temporal. Thus, these sermons offer their audience hope that one has power, through Christ, to defeat worldly evils by overcoming either personal shortcomings or oppressive political, economic, and social structures.

Cherry Hill, New Jersey   BETTYE COLLIER-THOMAS
July 1997

ACKNOWLEDGMENTS

I AM INDEBTED TO a number of persons for their support and assistance in developing this work. First and foremost, I want to thank Jacqui Burton, program director for religion at the Lilly Endowment, Inc., for her unstinting encouragement and support. The Lilly Endowment generously awarded the Temple University Center for African American History and Culture a multiyear grant to research "African American Women and the Church, 1787–1970." The grant has made it possible to complete this work and has provided for the development of a forthcoming comprehensive history of black churchwomen. A special thanks to Temple University, especially President Peter Liacouras, former provost Barbara Brownstein, and Vice President Rich Joslyn, for providing the "African American Women and the Church" project and me with space and continual support. I wish to thank the New Jersey Historical Commission, especially Giles Wright, director of the Afro-American History Program, for the grant to do beginning research on the Reverend Florence Spearing Randolph.

There are a small but growing number of scholars in black churchwomen's history and mainstream women's religious history whose work and conversations have helped me formulate thoughts and develop analytical approaches to preaching women. I have benefited greatly from the pioneering work of Jacquelyn Grant, Cheryl Townsend Gilkes, Jualynne Dodson, Jean McMahon Humez, William L. Andrews, Ella Pearson Mitchell, Donald Dayton, Lucille Sider Dayton, Nancy Hardesty, Delores S. Williams, Barbara Brown Zikmund, Cheryl J. Sanders, Evelyn Brooks Higginbotham, and Katie G. Cannon.

I owe a huge debt of gratitude to Anise Johnson Ward, Florence Randolph's granddaughter, for her extraordinary efforts in locating and making available Randolph's papers and sermons; and to both Elder Minerva Bell, historian for Mount Sinai Holy Church of America, Inc., and Bishop Betty M. Middleton of the Pentecostal Faith Church, for graciously providing sermons and photographs for Bishop Ida Robinson and Bishop Rosa Horn. I thank Phil Lapsansky, director of the Philadelphia Library Company, for thoughtfully bringing to my attention sources on black preaching women. I received especially valuable assistance from William

N. Flemister Sr. and his staff at the Atlanta University Archives, especially
Minnie H. Clayton and Mamie Williams; the Reverend Willie Aldridge,
director of Heritage House, and Elizabeth Mosby, director of the Carnegie
Library, both at Livingstone College; Marvin Dulaney and his staff at the
Avery Research Center for African American History and Culture; and
the archivists and staff members at Radcliffe College's Schlesinger Library.
I also want to thank Lawrence Reddick, editor of the *Christian Index*; Karen
Watson, the executor of Pauli Murray's estate; Michael Brown of the
Chicago Defender; and Frances M. Draper of the *Baltimore Afro-American*.

I want to thank my Temple University staff researchers on the Church
project—Debbie Skoh, Patricia Parkman, and Fatima Aliu—for their
research assistance. I am grateful to Karen Seat, a doctoral candidate in
the Department of Religion, for assistance in evaluating the sermons. I am
particularly indebted to Debbie Skoh for her indispensable organizing and
supervisory skills in transcribing Randolph's sermons. I am extremely
grateful to Fatima Aliu for her persistence in following up leads and locating sermons for Rosa Horn and Ida Robinson and for her critical statis-
tical research on women clergy. I also want to thank Richard Woodland
and Alice Wingert, staff researchers at the Center for African American
History and Culture, for unearthing key information related to Ruth Dennis and other churchwomen. And of course, I thank Joanne Hawes
Speakes, my administrative assistant, for the many chores she performed,
which helped launch this project. I also appreciate the support of Marie
McCain in rendering diverse services.

Were it not for the loving support and continual encouragement I have
received from my husband, Charles J. Thomas, these materials would still
be in my files. Of equal importance are the continued prodding and the
intellectual sustenance provided by some of my dearest friends, who are
among the most supportive scholars I have known. I am especially grateful to John Hope Franklin, C. Eric Lincoln, V. P. Franklin, James Turner,
Genna Rae McNeil, Sharon Harley, Rosalyn Terborg-Penn, Janet Sims
Wood, Alexia B. Henderson, Gloria Dickinson, Lillian Williams, and Bettye J. Gardner, who have spent years patiently listening to me talk inces-
santly about my research and publication plans. The continued
encouragement and prodding of my editors, Darren Hall and Joanne
Clapp Fullagar, helped me flesh out many issues and make this work read-
able and accessible to a broad audience, and for this I am grateful. Finally,
my deepest appreciation goes to V. P. Franklin, Cheryl Townsend Gilkes,
Samuel Proctor, and C. Eric Lincoln for their very careful reading of the
manuscript.

DAUGHTERS OF THUNDER

INTRODUCTION:
THE POWER OF BLACK
WOMEN PREACHERS

ACKNOWLEDGMENT OF THE SIGNIFICANCE of African American women in black religious history is one of the most prominent advances in recent African American scholarship. The study of black women and religion is crucial to our understanding of American and black religion. A focus on black churchwomen's experiences changes the nature of African American history and introduces new dimensions to the discourse on religious tradition and authority, which have been traditionally defined as male history.

The sermons and personalities in *Daughters of Thunder* highlight the enduring significance of religion and spirituality in American life and history. The book reveals the importance of pioneering women in particular denominations whose ministries frequently advanced the development of the African American Church. It provides a unique opportunity to hear the eloquent voices of pioneering African American women as they address issues of historical yet surprisingly contemporary relevance. The voices of these preaching women are representative of a great American tradition heretofore largely unknown and untapped. To both men and women, these powerful sermons bring messages of hope and faith that God hears and answers prayers.

Organization of the Book

Daughters of Thunder includes a historical overview of African American women preachers, a chapter on pioneering black preaching women for whom no sermons have been found, a chapter for each of the women whose sermons appear in this book, and a concluding chapter or epilogue.

The overview "Rising Above Adversity: The Struggle to Preach" provides a context for understanding the nineteenth- and twentieth-century experiences of black preaching women and the religious traditions they represent. It explores the importance of the holiness tradition to the empowerment of black preaching women and its place in the African American community. It then traces the history of black women's struggle to preach and to be ordained.

Part One, containing four chapters, examines the lives and sermons of nineteenth-century black women preachers. Unfortunately, no sermons have been recovered for many of these early preaching women. Chapter One, "Women Who Paved the Way," features six women for whom this is true: Elizabeth, Jarena Lee, Zilpha Elaw, Rebecca Cox Jackson, Amanda Smith, and Sojourner Truth. We do have access to the sermons of Julia Foote, Harriet Baker, and Mary Small, however, so we can hear the voices of nineteenth-century preaching women and explore their feminist theology. By analyzing these sermons in the remainder of Part One, we can look at the roots of the preaching tradition among African American women.

In Part Two, Chapters Five through Fifteen, we will hear the voices of Florence Randolph, Mary Evans, Ella Whitfield, Ruth Dennis, Mrs. Raiff, Rosa Horn, Ida Robinson, Rosa Edwards, Quinceila Whitlow, F. E. Redwine, and Pauli Murray. These preaching women represent diverse traditions within the Methodist, Baptist, Episcopal, and Pentecostal Holiness groups. The women included in Part Two pursued all avenues in order to preach. Although they represent many twentieth-century black women preachers and provide both a sermonic model and a profile of women's struggle to preach in this century, there are many more preaching women whose sermons and papers need to be collected and whose stories should be told.

The black preaching women in this anthology represent several different time periods and traditions. I have organized *Daughters of Thunder* around two groupings—nineteenth-century women and twentieth-century women. Although the two centuries of women's struggle to preach certainly have continuities, one pivotal event divides them clearly: the 1897 ordination of Mary Small as an elder in the AME Zion Church is a defining point in the history of black preaching women. This event symbolizes how, in most black religious traditions, women won the battle to preach. Small's ordination heralded new opportunities for women to advance in the Church polity.

Examining the six distinct time periods and traditions reflected in the lives and sermons of these preaching women, we are able to trace the changes that occurred in the status of churchwomen and the issues that they addressed and to recognize the similarities and differences that resonate across time and tradition.

- Julia Foote, Harriet Baker, and Mary Small represent black female preachers of the mid- to late nineteenth century from African Methodist Episcopal (AME) and African Methodist Episcopal Zion (AME Zion) denominations.

- Florence Randolph, whose sermons date from 1898 to 1945, represents early- to mid-twentieth-century AME Zion black preaching women.

- While the careers of Mary Evans, Ella Whitfield, Ruth Dennis, and Mrs. Raiff overlapped that of Randolph, their sermons particularly represent 1920s black preaching women's sermons in the AME and Baptist denominations.

- Rosa Horn, Ida Robinson, and Rosa Edwards reveal the preaching styles and concerns of 1920s and 1930s black preaching women involved in the Holiness, Pentecostal, and Spiritual movements. The sermons of women such as Robinson remind us that, contrary to popular thought, the Pentecostals also preached on social and political issues.

- Quinceila Whitlow and Mrs. F. E. Redwine represent Colored Methodist Episcopal (CME) black preaching women of the 1940s.

- Pauli Murray, an Episcopalian priest ordained in 1977, represents black preaching women who have been influenced by the black theology and feminist theology that have developed since the civil rights and women's movements.

We will now look at each of the groupings more closely.

Nineteenth Century

Foote, Baker, and Small empower their congregations by revealing that God's call and Christ's example provide all Christians' lives with a higher purpose. Like many nineteenth-century preachers, Foote, Baker, and Small primarily emphasize the importance of conversion and salvation in their sermons, rather than directly addressing social ills. While stressing the importance of eternal salvation, however, all three preachers also accentuate the importance of doing God's work here on earth. All three call their audience to serve their fellow human beings with perfect Christian love—a love that is attained only through sanctification in Christ.

Revealing a formidable knowledge of Scripture, as well as Protestant Reformation theology, Foote employs a wide variety of sources for arguing that humans must be transformed through sanctification in order to lead others to the holy process of conversion, sanctification, and salvation. Like many African American preachers, she interprets God's words to the people of Israel, recorded in the Old Testament, in a way that applied to black Christians of her day. The Old Testament prophecies that God's people will be filled with God's spirit, Foote asserts, are now coming to fruition within the lives of modern black women and men. Empowering herself and her audience by claiming a place of legitimacy in the Christian tradition, Foote aligns herself and other black preachers with the great preachers and reformers of the past, including the apostle Paul, Martin Luther, and John Wesley.

Like Foote, Baker asserts that all Christians are called to do God's holy work, as she paints a colorful picture of Christ's passion and crucifixion to serve as an example for Christians to follow. Just as Christ laid down his life for humanity, Baker declares, so should Christians lay down their lives for their "brethren."

Reflecting the burgeoning American missionary movement of the late nineteenth century, Small emphasizes the importance of black Christians who are relatively privileged, spiritually and materially, to serve the less privileged by bringing them the Christian message of salvation. She asserts that Christ died for the salvation of all people, even those individuals who might seem unappealing because of their class and character.

While emphasizing sanctification and salvation, therefore, all three of these nineteenth-century black preaching women also empower their audience by imbuing each person's life with an earthly purpose of Christian service and leadership. Although none of these nineteenth-century sermons directly addresses gender issues, their content also indirectly empowers women to do God's work, as they (Foote and Baker) refer to biblical women and as they (Small) emphasize the importance of doing God's work in addition to prescribed domestic tasks. Most important, they all stress the inclusiveness of God's call.

Early Twentieth Century: AME Zion

While emphasizing the importance of sanctification and salvation just as nineteenth-century preaching women did, Randolph represents the shift that occurred in twentieth-century sermons from primarily emphasizing issues of conversion and salvation to addressing social problems directly. Thus, Randolph stresses the importance of sanctification by connecting this process of inner purification with the process of overcoming social ills. She asserts that it is only by relying on Christ's transformative power that Christians will be able to work for a more just society. As Randolph asserts in "Hope," through Christ African Americans can overcome the seemingly impossible obstacle of racism. Randolph also argues that for God's will to be done on earth, the African American community must value women by putting resources into girls' upbringing ("Hope") and by accepting female preachers ("Antipathy to Women Preachers").

Thus, while nineteenth-century black preaching women implicitly affirmed women's ministerial work by emphasizing the inclusiveness of God's call, Randolph reflects how twentieth-century black preaching women began to identify specific strategies for social change that would actually make it possible for women to follow God's call. While affirming women's ministries, Randolph and a number of other preaching women (for example, Whitfield and Redwine) attest to prevailing gender ideologies of "true womanhood" and domesticity, stressing that it is women's virtue and moral sway in the home that constitute much of women's value to society.

1920s: AME and Baptist

Evans, Dennis, Raiff, and Whitfield preached during the 1920s. They primarily sought to provide specific guidelines for righteous living to audiences faced with the chaos of the Great Migration of southern blacks to northern cities, as well as the general social chaos that new modern challenges generated in a rapidly changing world. Like Randolph, these preachers connect the importance of salvation and sanctification with specific social issues. Their sermons reveal a practical, no-nonsense awareness of the precarious nature of life. Righteous Christian living is not only necessary for eternal life, they suggest, but is absolutely necessary for survival in a chaotic world.

Aware of the far-reaching social crises of her day, as evidenced in her reference to the problematic "trusts of Wall Street," Evans harshly denounces specific forms of corruption in the Church (for example, adultery and gambling), revealing the urgent need for Christian purification in an age of iniquity.

Whitfield connects salvation and sanctification with everyday life by giving specific advice on how to live a sanctified Christian life, such as how to dress, study, and act on the job.

Dennis stresses the importance of children's religious education for their salvation as well as for the advancement of the race, stating that this is a matter of such urgency that parents should follow King Solomon's advice to use the "rod" in driving corruption from the lives of their children. Dennis also warns that unless all Christians take to heart the Church's guidelines for moral living and involve themselves in God's work, the Church will sink into oblivion.

Finally, Raiff asserts that mere outward acts of Christian living are not acceptable, but that Christians must be truly transformed through Christ. Thus, in the sermons of 1920s AME and Baptist preaching women, we see a powerful call to moral order and inner purification as a means of individual and racial survival in a chaotic society.

1920s and 1930s: Holiness and Pentecostal Movements

Horn, Robinson, and Edwards reveal the same urgency in their sermons as did their contemporaries discussed previously. While addressing the importance of moral order and inner purification in an age of chaos, these Pentecostal and Holiness preachers were also intent on clarifying their distinct theological and social position as black preaching women who had broken off from mainline African American denominations.

Horn most clearly reveals the attempt of Pentecostal black preaching women to define and legitimize this alternate path to the ministry. Many black preaching women left the mainline denominations because of the obstacles these denominations posed for women in the ministry, and Horn reflects the commitment of these women to reject those who would stand in the way of female preachers. As she explicates the biblical warrants for women to preach ("Was a Woman Called to Preach? Yes!"), she reveals her conviction that Christians are living in an era when people do not have the luxury to split hairs over who should or should not preach, but that all of God's people are desperately needed to bring others to salvation. She also attempts to unify Pentecostals by critiquing the theology of other Pentecostal groups with opposing theologies ("Is Jesus God the Father or Is He the Son of God?"). Finally, she distinguishes her holiness theology from that of mainline preachers by critiquing those who focus merely on sanctification and stressing the importance of the baptism of the Holy Spirit ("What Is Holiness? A Complete Life in Christ").

While Robinson does address the importance of having each church member master the Church's theology in order to avoid outside criticism ("And a Little Child Shall Lead Them"), she had established a secure Pentecostal church and denomination and was presumably not as concerned as Horn with legitimizing Pentecostalism. She often resembles the mainline preachers of the 1920s as she addresses specific social and political issues of concern to contemporary black Christians. Robinson stresses the importance of inner purification by paralleling Ezekiel's vision of the "dry bones" of Israel with her vision of the African American community ("Can

These Bones Live?"), a hermeneutic popularly employed by black preachers. Like other 1920s preachers, Robinson asserts that the black Church will only survive if corruption (such as gambling, fornication, and adultery) is completely stamped out; the dry bones can only be transformed through the reviving power of sanctification. Robinson also addresses the problem of white supremacy and denounces the racist practices and theology of white America ("The Economic Persecution"). She asserts the importance of sanctification for surviving a racist world. Black Christians (with whom she contrasts white America's "modern pagans," who persecute modern-day black Christians) must rely on Christ's transformative power rather than their own power to survive in the present world and the afterlife.

Edwards's sermon aims to ensure the strength of Robinson's denomination. In "Ministers Are Examples," she urges Pentecostal preachers to follow the tenets of the Church carefully in order to represent Robinson and the Mount Sinai Holy Church of America denomination positively.

1940s: CME

As new economic opportunities began to open up for some women in the 1940s, black preaching women such as Whitlow and Redwine asserted women's value to the community in terms of their economic contributions, among other things. Whitlow contends that just as women are needed in the labor force, they are needed to work in the Church. Redwine maintains that women are valuable not only for their domestic contributions and moral virtues, but also for their financial contributions to the family and to the Church; the Church would in fact close down, Redwine declares, if not for the economic reliability of churchwomen.

Modern Times: The Legacy of Liberation Movements

Murray represents the transformation in theological discourse that resulted from the upheaval of the 1960s and 1970s—most significantly, the radical social and ideological changes that took place as a result of the civil rights and women's movements. While black preaching women from every era supported radical social change, many of the earlier preaching women directed their energy toward denouncing individual sins and stressing the importance of salvation in the life to come. Murray systematically articulates the need to rethink such traditional Christian theology and biblical interpretation in order to reorient Christianity to be a true force of liberation in an oppressive world.

Murray states that Christian tenets only have value to the extent that they further the goal of justice for all human beings. The liberation theology to which Murray adheres, and which she most extensively discusses in "Salvation and Liberation," focuses more on the present life than the afterlife; thus, salvation comes to be understood as the liberation of the oppressed. Unlike preaching women of earlier eras, Murray believes that the Church should not focus on individuals' so-called sins as much as on the fight to overcome social structures that perpetuate evil in the form of mass oppression. Despite the magnitude of the world's systematic, institutionalized evil, Murray asserts, Christians are nevertheless called on to dismantle these structures, relying on the strength of a loving and powerful God.

Significance of the Sermons and the Book

The sermons in this book reveal how black preaching women of the past century and a half have strategically addressed their congregations' spiritual and temporal needs. As present-day women continue meeting obstacles to taking full leadership in the church, these sermons provide hermeneutical strategies of legitimizing women in the ministry.

One of the most formidable obstacles to women's claiming their rightful place as full members of society is the invisibility of historical women who rose to positions of leadership. Thus, illuminating the lives of these women is of utmost importance. Shining a light on their pasts provides a model for today's women and reveals that even in the face of the most oppressive obstacles, women leaders have been powerful forces to reckon with, asserting their brilliance as theologians, orators, and spiritual leaders.

Any attempt to understand American religious history, the black Church, or American women's history without an adequate grasp of the groundbreaking work of these black preaching women will be incomplete. Not only did they open doors in the ministry that had been closed to women of all races, but they also represented the best of the African American preaching tradition, providing their audience with spiritual and practical tools for living in and fighting against a chaotic and unjust society. As these women struggled to follow God's call to preach, they taught by example as well as by their words how to negotiate the reality of what the world is with the Christian vision of what the world should be: a world that reflects God's justice and love.

All theology, including that espoused in sermons, is on some level autobiographical. In analyzing sermons to find the underlying autobiographical content, one can see the unique value of these black women's sermons. No other group of Americans has experienced multiple oppressions based on race, sex, and often class and color, as much as black women have. Furthermore, though black men experienced racism and white women experienced sexism, racism affected black women differently than it did black men, and sexism affected black women differently than it did white women. The autobiographical window of black women's sermons offers a glimpse of the particular issues of race, gender, and class that black women have faced in the past century and a half.

Many white women of the late nineteenth and early twentieth centuries revealed overt or implicit racist and classist assumptions. Drawing on the Victorian era's notion of "true womanhood" or on classical liberalism's notion of "individual rights" to argue for elite white women's advancement in society, these women frequently suggested that black women and lower-class women were the very antitheses of the "true woman" or the "rational individual." At the same time, black men who denounced racism often conceived of racial progress in terms of black males' advancement, and often uncritically accepted or even supported the existing sexism in both white and black cultures.

It is crucial to understand the widespread racism in white feminism and the widespread sexism in black male progressivism to understand the uniqueness of black preaching women like those in *Daughters of Thunder*. Whereas the arguments employed by these black women may seem to resemble those of black male progressives or white feminists, they reveal a primary commitment to the advancement of black women, something which is largely absent in the rhetoric and work of their contemporaries who are concerned with racism and sexism.

Black preaching women may argue for racial advancement as black male preachers do, by comparing the suffering of African Americans with that of Old Testament Israelites or Christ. These women do so, however, by emphasizing biblical women and the importance of black women's contributions and leadership for the advancement of the race as a whole. For example, in sermons such as "Hope" and "What Woman Is," Randolph and Redwine assert that women are indispensable to racial advancement, for they are the ones who instill morality in future generations of African Americans. While many of these black preaching women may resemble white women of their time by employing prevailing notions of "true womanhood" in their arguments for women's advancement, their being African American women alters the significance of their use of this ideology. Black preaching women who employ the "true woman" ideology to reveal black women's value to the African American community also challenge white supremacist assumptions about African American moral degeneracy, particularly that of African American women.

TEXTUAL NOTE

IN EACH OF THE SERMONS, the original spelling, punctuation, paragraphing, and section divisions have been preserved, except for some inconsistencies in spelling or obvious typographical mistakes that apparently resulted from printer's errors. In a few instances, letters have been added to complete the spelling of a word, or a word has been inserted to render a sentence more comprehensible. The author made changes to some biblical citations in the sermons, to standardize either the format or the placement within the sentence. Although there are a few silent punctuation changes, most alterations are indicated with brackets. All endnotes in the sermons have been added by the author.

RISING ABOVE ADVERSITY: THE STRUGGLE TO PREACH

We may be debarred entrance to many pulpits (as some of us now are) and stand at the door or on the street corner in order to preach to men and women. No difference when or where, we must preach a whole gospel.

—Julia A. J. Foote, "Christian Perfection"

If a man may preach, because the Saviour died for him, why not the woman? seeing he died for her also. Is he not a whole Saviour, instead of a half one? as those who hold it wrong for a woman to preach, would seem to make it appear.

—Jarena Lee

BLACK WOMEN WHO PREACH have not been as scarce as the historical literature on women, religion, and African Americans has suggested. Although women who preach have not been and still are not widely recognized in mainstream Christianity as the equals of male preachers, they have continued to come forth and to pursue the prize—the pulpit. In doing so, they have been singular heroes and powerful actors in the struggle for black empowerment, especially the empowerment of black women.

The voices of black women preachers have not been heard in the pages of history. When and where the names of black women preachers have appeared, their stories have been told primarily in excerpts that render them exceptional and isolated from the very people they sought to elevate. Most nineteenth- and many twentieth-century black women preachers have gained little except scorn. They have often been viewed as different, strange, and in some cases crazed simply because they chose to preach.

That they have pursued a ministry at all attests to their personal strength and their belief in themselves and in the Holy Ghost.

Churchwomen are the spiritual sisters of preaching women. It is the power of their voices and those of their spiritual sisters "within the public discourse of racial and gender self determination" that helped fuel the efforts of black women's secular organizations, such as the National Association of Colored Women (NACW), and to empower many of its leaders. Scholars have not always identified these secular leaders as Christian feminist activists belonging to specific religious traditions.[1] In fact, many women who were prominent in the NACW were also leaders in their own denominations.[2] Many preaching women, as well as Christian feminist activists such as Sarah A. Pettey, Katherine Davis Tillman, and Alice Felts, actively confronted the male clergy on the issue of participatory democracy and equality for women in the Church and society.[3]

Holiness Tradition Among African Americans

The holiness tradition played a central part in the struggle of women, particularly black women, to preach. Believing in holiness was the basic source of these women's empowerment. It provided them with a strategy to overcome the barriers of the Church, which contended that the Bible does not sanction women to preach. Preaching women who embraced the holiness doctrine asserted that they did not need the Church's sanction, because their ministry was authorized by a power beyond the Church, namely God, who spoke to them through the Holy Spirit. The feminist activism of most of the preaching women derived from religious inspiration, particularly their belief in the holiness doctrine of spiritual sanctification.

To be sanctified was to be free from sin. Sanctification was the result of Christian commitment after conversion. Spiritual sanctification meant that one could purify "one's inner disposition to willful sin, a liberation of the soul to follow the indwelling voice of Christ," or the Holy Spirit.[4] Many preaching women spoke freely about the Holy Spirit's power to remove all obstacles and to speak through them. They believed that the Holy Spirit empowered them to act, think, speak, and simply be.

The holiness tradition among African Americans has received little treatment from scholars. Although sanctification and holiness are quite prevalently discussed in nineteenth-century African American Church history and are mentioned in the autobiographies and biographies of religious figures, the holiness tradition has remained obscure. Given the prevalence of this doctrine among African American preaching women, it is essential to understand its impact and practice.

In the nineteenth century, both white and black women embraced the Holiness movement, because they perceived its power to liberate. Historically, the movement has maintained a consistent feminist thrust, due to both the definition and practice of holiness.

The Holiness movement embraced six essential tenets. Its doctrine (1) centered around experience, (2) had roots in Scripture, (3) emphasized the work of the Holy Spirit, (4) created an aura of freedom that encouraged experimentalism, (5) had a reformist and even revolutionary nature, and (6) encouraged the formation of sects.[5]

The Holy Spirit or Holy Ghost has been central to African American Christianity, particularly as it relates to the slave community. The Holiness movement's emphasis on the holiness doctrine and the Holy Spirit owes a debt to Blacks in particular, because it was essentially the gift of African American slaves. In *Working the Spirit,* Joseph Murphy states: "There is a distinctive spirituality that can be identified and appreciated in a variety of cultural settings throughout the Americas. This spirituality has its roots in Africa and was developed in the slave and emancipated societies of the Western hemisphere."[6] As to the holiness doctrine's special relevance to issues of race and color, in the introduction to Julia Foote's spiritual autobiography in 1879, Thomas Doty asserted, "Holiness takes the prejudice of color out of both the white and the black, and declares that 'The [heart's] the standard of the man.'"[7]

Although a few African Americans were active in some of the prominent holiness groups prevalent during the nineteenth century, and there is evidence of black participation in the great revivals and camp meetings associated with white religionists, most never affiliated with or took part in the movement. Some African Americans resented the way Whites used them as a drawing card for the meetings, presenting them as exotic novelties. Although nineteenth-century black preacher Amanda Berry Smith comments on this, she was pleased that her ministry was gaining visibility. Also, like other black women preachers, she recognized the value of white validation, which frequently helped to raise a ministry's status in the black community.

Camp Meetings

In 1867, the "National Camp Meeting Association for the Promotion of Holiness" was formed by holiness advocates who wished to keep the movement within the Methodist Church. By 1887, the organization had held over sixty interdenominational camp meetings.[8] In spite of the concern about Methodism, the camp meetings were ecumenical in scope.

Indeed, these meetings, which included holiness revivals, differed from other revivals in their ecumenical attendance and in their outdoor locations, which made them accessible to people of all walks of life and all faiths. The egalitarianism of the holiness camp meetings provided a stimulus for women and Blacks to speak, shout, and testify. Although the meetings began as local and regional events, they became more formalized in national camp meetings.[9]

Rebecca Cox Jackson, Amanda Berry Smith, and Julia Foote participated in the National Holiness Association Camp Meetings. In "Christian Perfection," Foote refers to the "Burned Over District," an area in New York City where there was so much religious fervor that it was considered to be "on fire."[10] Her reference points to the importance and popularity of the nineteenth-century holiness revivals and camp meetings.

African Americans appear to have been less attracted to the Holiness movement than Whites, in the sense that most African Americans were not interested in affiliating with predominantly white religious sects. Although some attended the national camp meetings, they spoke about the resentment their presence engendered in some Whites and the segregation that prevailed in housing patterns and meetings.[11] However, their interest in the holiness doctrine after 1850 is evident in the African American religious discourse, which occurs most often in the nonsecular press and in feminist spiritual autobiographies. The first known evidence of black feminist consciousness of the holiness doctrine and its power to subvert religious sexism is articulated by Jarena Lee in her spiritual autobiography, published in 1836.[12]

Although there is no antebellum black groundswell for the Holiness movement, and African Americans appeared solidly wed to a strict interpretation of Christianity and reluctant to give credence to holiness even tacitly, some embraced sanctification. In part, their relationship to Christianity was defined by what they perceived as acceptable to mainstream white America, whose religion they had adopted, even though they chose to separate themselves from the segregated pews of the Methodist Church. Their religious disciplines and the structure of their polity differed little from that of white Methodists.

Methodism: History and Role in the Holiness Movement

I refer almost exclusively to Methodists because the majority of antebellum African American religionists engaged in the holiness discourse were Methodist and Baptist. With the exception of Ella Whitfield, who was a

Baptist missionary, all of the preaching women in this book were associated at some point with Methodism. Census figures for denominational memberships are available from 1890 to the present. Although no statistics exist for the antebellum and Reconstruction periods, prescriptive literature and denominational Church development patterns seem to indicate that prior to 1870, a preponderance of African Americans were Methodist, maintaining memberships in the Methodist Episcopal, the AME, and AME Zion Churches. The CME Church was founded in 1872. Between 1870 and 1890, black Baptists expanded their base, particularly in the rural South among former slaves, many of whom were attracted to the Baptist Church's more emotional religious services and less restrictive structure and rituals.[13]

The Methodist Episcopal Church espoused sanctification and holiness from the beginning. John Wesley embraced the canon, articulating and defining its principles in his speeches and writings. In *A Plain Account of Christian Perfection,* Wesley posited sanctification as a process that unfolded over time and probably reached completion at or near death. In time, many of Wesley's followers asserted that they had attained sanctification. Some felt it was an instant process. Most of the early black preaching women, at least those who wrote spiritual autobiographies, believed in instant sanctification.[14]

Wesley did not approve of the formal ordination of women but allowed them to function as local preachers and itinerant evangelists. In 1739, he appointed women as class leaders. He later granted women permission to preach. His flexibility about women's roles in the Church helped women gain some prominence in the Evangelical Revival that his preaching generated, a revival infused with the holiness doctrine.[15]

Methodist differences regarding the significance of holiness led to tensions and a schism in the Church. Although Wesley endorsed the holiness doctrine, not all Methodists accepted it. Orthodox holiness adherents, otherwise known as Sanctified Christians, repudiated slavery, labeling it a sin in society and an evil to be ferreted out of the Methodist Church. Ideological differences over slavery led to a split in the Church. In 1843 and 1844, the Wesleyan Methodist Church was developed in New York and in New England, and in 1844 the Methodist Episcopal Church South was formed. The Wesleyan Methodist Church, embracing the doctrine of holiness, was a veritable breeding ground for woman's rights advocates and abolitionists. In 1848, the first woman's rights convention was convened in a Wesleyan Methodist Church in Seneca Falls, New York.[16]

Nineteenth-Century Practice of Holiness

The Methodist Church's split over the issue of slavery caused some black Methodists to reconsider the doctrine of holiness. Although they sometimes differed over the proper nature of worship, fewer black Christians labeled holiness practitioners as heretics by 1870. Rather, the doctrine gradually permeated Church theory and practice. Black Christians, particularly Methodists, liberally sprinkled their writings with references to the Holy Ghost, the Holy Spirit, sanctification, and regeneration. Moreover, after 1850, the black clergy actively debated aspects of sanctification, justification, and regeneration, and ways to determine their manifestation.[17] Regeneration refers to spiritual renewal or revival. Justification is the act or process of being forgiven for one's sins by God. Unfortunately, there is no known published discourse on these issues prior to 1850, during the period when Elizabeth, Jarena Lee, Rebecca Cox Jackson, and Julia Foote were converted to the holiness doctrine and became active exponents of its tenets. Of course, as the spiritual autobiographies of Foote and others illustrate, during the early nineteenth century, many black religionists did not understand what it meant to be sanctified or the relationship of holiness to Christianity.[18]

Holiness doctrine issues discussed in the black Christian Church after 1850 related primarily to questions of sanctification and regeneration. The discourse frequently focused on questions of who was saved (the regenerate) and who was not (the unregenerate), whether sanctification was immediate or gradual, and how one could determine that it had occurred. Ministers, as well as laypeople, articulated their views.

In 1864, the Reverend Jabez P. Campbell, a minister and later bishop in the AME Church, spoke of the importance of the sanctification doctrine. He felt that it was a fundamental principle of Christianity. For him, its importance was defined in the Scriptures, which made clear that salvation could not exist without sanctification. Therefore, Campbell reasoned, the subject was of great practical importance, particularly because there was such a great diversity of views, and little clarity or agreement, on its meaning.[19]

The African American discourse on holiness was highlighted in black nonsecular publications that published original essays by African American ministers and laypeople and reprinted articles published in the white religious press. The *Christian Recorder* exposed black Methodists to holiness tenets and discussions published in the *Wesleyan*, the organ of the Methodist Episcopal Church, whose views and practices held considerable sway with nineteenth-century black Methodists.

The most detailed treatise on the belief in and practice of holiness among African Americans appears in Amanda Berry Smith's spiritual autobiography. Although Smith confirms that by the late 1850s, African Americans, at least in the Northeast, were familiar with religious conversion and holiness, they were less knowledgeable about sanctification. In her autobiography, Smith reveals that by 1869, the holiness doctrine and practice had a recognized presence in the AME Church and that weekly holiness meetings were held in private homes, at camp meetings, and even in churches where the doctrine was taught. She also indicates that it was no longer considered a heresy to proclaim that one had experienced religious conversion. Most of the holiness activities Smith cites occurred in New York City during the late 1860s.[20] Although holiness was openly practiced, Smith, like Foote, complained: "I had much to suffer, in and with my own people—for human nature is the same in black and white folks. They oppose the doctrine of personal holiness, so do white people; but God has a remnant among the old, and some of the young, both preachers and laymen, that believe and know the truth of this doctrine from the bible standpoint experimentally, which is the top stone of all. Hath not God declared it that without holiness no man shall see the Lord?"[21]

Some black and white women understood the validation powers that the holiness doctrine conferred on churchwomen, particularly spiritual sanctification. In the spiritual autobiographies and sermons of Elizabeth, Jarena Lee, Julia Foote, Amanda Smith, Florence Randolph, Rosa Horn, Ida Robinson, and Pauli Murray, we hear eloquent testimonies to holiness and the power of the Holy Spirit. Women imbued with the doctrine of holiness believed that no man or institution could sanction their right to preach, that this was the sole prerogative of God. Taken literally, this meant that holiness freed them from the intercession of man and society, that they were required to answer only to God. Belief in the doctrine of holiness empowered them to set aside denominational law and practice and to repudiate elements of the polity that inveighed against their freedom to preach. Women who adhered to this tradition emphasized that they were called to preach by God. Of course, the black male clergy disagreed with and rejected their interpretation of sanctification as an authorization to preach.[22]

During the early nineteenth century, many pioneering black and white women contended for the right to preach. Early women preachers such as Elizabeth, Jarena Lee, Zilpha Elaw, Amanda Smith, and Julia Foote succeeded in developing ministries without ordination. However, the "new woman" of the late nineteenth century, influenced by the woman's rights and suffrage movements and the rhetoric of woman's equality, sought greater recognition and equality in the Church. As women continued to struggle to preach, they also demanded recognition as preachers and equality with men in the polity. Thus, the latter half of the nineteenth century was dominated by the struggle of women for rights in the Church polity, especially for ordination.

Struggle for Ordination

Ordination is the process by which a preacher's ministry is officially legitimated by a religious tradition. It is a credentialing process that enables one to participate fully in a tradition, to acquire certain rights, and to assume certain responsibilities denied to an unordained minister. It provides authorization for a minister to pastor a church and to ascend to other positions in a religious organization's hierarchy. However, authorization does not ensure that a ministerial appointment will be forthcoming. Historically, for many preaching women, ordination was a major step toward attaining recognition and acceptance in the polity. Ordination might be viewed as another level in women's struggle to preach; it allowed them to preach with authorization.

White denominations and sects, particularly the early Quakers, Universalists, Unitarians, Congregationalists, and Methodists, were not as rigid as most early denominations on the issue of women's preaching. In the seventeenth century, the Quakers were the only Christian denomination or sect to accept women as preachers. Quakers neither restricted the ministry to men nor stressed ordination. Because of this policy, there were many Quaker women preachers.[23] Some of the earliest black women preachers, such as Elizabeth and Zilpha Elaw, received their first orientation to preach while attending Quaker meetings.

The increasing number of women preachers in the nineteenth century created quite a stir. The majority of preaching women, particularly white women, were not members of mainline denominations, and most were not ordained. Most white preaching women were affiliated with the Quakers, Freewill Baptists, Free Methodists, and a variety of holiness and spiritual associations. All these groups stressed direct communication with God, the primacy of the Holy Spirit, and the call to ministry above the authority of the Church. The emphasis on a philosophy that made spiritual gifts a priority opened the door for women ministers. Few women served as pastors. Most were evangelists. The fact that they preached was enough to draw the ire of the established denominations.

The growing presence of preaching women was in part related to the political activism of women such as Lucretia Mott, a Quaker preacher and the leader of the movement for equal rights for women ministers, and Elizabeth Cady Stanton, a leading figure in the woman's rights movement. At the 1848 woman's rights convention, Mott drafted the Seneca Falls Declaration of Sentiments, which stressed that women had been denied freedom and were oppressed in all areas of American life, including religion. She proposed "the overthrow of the monopoly of the pulpit."[24]

In 1853, amid the struggle for woman's rights, Luther Lee, a Wesleyan Methodist minister, preached the ordination sermon for Antoinette Brown, a white woman and the first of her sex to receive "full ordination." Brown was ordained by a local congregation, the First Congregational Church of South Butler, New York. In 1863, Olympia Brown, another white woman, was ordained by the Northern Universalist Association in Canton, New York. She was the first woman to be ordained at a level beyond the local congregation. In 1864, the Wesleyan Methodist Church's General Conference rejected a resolution against licensing women preachers, leaving the issue to local conferences. Although local conferences did not ordain women, they licensed them as local preachers. By 1880, a number of white women had been ordained. Anna Howard Shaw, M.D., was the first woman ordained in the Methodist Protestant Church. In that same year, the Methodist Episcopal General Conference denied ordination to women and revoked all previously granted licenses to preach. By 1888, approximately twenty women served as pastors of churches in the United States and there were an estimated three hundred fifty Quaker women preachers and at least five hundred women evangelists. The Baptists and Unitarians joined the ranks of those churches ordaining women.[25]

In the nineteenth century, most black denominations were unwilling to license women to preach, even as local preachers, and with the exception of the AME Zion Church, none were inclined to ordain them. A few women were licensed to preach, and the AME Zion Church began ordaining women in 1895.

Evangelists

Through persistent protest, women opened up opportunities to be exhorters and evangelists and to assume a variety of ex-officio preaching roles. Exhortation was an intermediate stage between testimony and preaching. It included testifying to one's experience and holding prayer meetings. In these meetings, exhorters admonished sinners and pleaded with them to repent. As a religious public speaker, licensed by the church, an exhorter might speak to an assembled group, pray or testify, speak informally at a class meeting, or in some cases substitute for an itinerant minister.[26] Many women who began as exhorters later became evangelists.

By 1920, most mainline black denominations (with the exception of the Baptists) had a number of women whom they acknowledged and actively supported as evangelists. Many male clergy welcomed the services of women evangelists, recognizing their value in building church membership and raising funds. Unlike preachers assigned to pastor a single local congregation, evangelists preached the gospel wherever they were invited or chose to go. Many preaching women gained great visibility in their work as evangelists. Their ministry included preaching at church revivals, camp meetings, Woman's Day programs, and many other events where they could garner the public's attention and attract a large audience. Unlike itinerant ministers, they did not travel on a designated route. In some denominations, such as the AME and AME Zion Churches, however, evangelists were appointed to specific Annual Conferences that covered a defined territory or represented an Episcopal district. Their primary responsibility was to preach. A conference could have one assigned evangelist or more, depending on its geographical range and the demand for their services.[27]

The tradition of black female evangelists appears to have developed first in the AME Church. This may have occurred because the Church became prominent during the early nineteenth century in northern cities with large free black populations. Before the Civil War, the black female evangelist phenomenon was particularly prevalent in Pennsylvania, New York, and New Jersey, and was concentrated in the Philadelphia area to some extent. Jarena Lee, Sophie Murray, Amanda Berry Smith, Harriet Baker, and Rebecca Cox Jackson are among the most salient examples of preaching women who began in the Philadelphia area and who, with the exception of Baker, had some connection with Mother Bethel AME Church. Sophie Murray gained a reputation for her evangelistic activities throughout the Philadelphia area long before the 1816 founding of the AME denomination. In 1881, Joseph Thompson, a chronicler of the history of Mother Bethel AME Church, characterized Murray as its "first" evangelist.[28]

In some denominations, such as the AME Church, the evangelist's role was specifically authorized in church law. Although this position was legislated in 1884, women unofficially functioned as evangelists before that date. In fact, the denomination legislated the position because the AME women demanded ordination and assumed preaching functions without authorization.[29] In the AME and AME Zion Churches, the position was not defined by gender.

In the nineteenth century, there were few, if any, black male evangelists. However, by the end of the second decade of the twentieth century, their presence was felt. Although some men pursued careers as evangelists, prior to the advent of famous white male evangelists such as Billy Sunday, few black men chose to work as evangelists. Given that the nineteenth-century authorization of the position was designed to accommodate women who wished to preach, the position was viewed primarily as a feminine domain.

Nineteenth-Century Debates

Whether they were evangelists or were ordained, most white preaching women and all of the nineteenth-century black preaching women pressed on with their need to preach. Empowered by their beliefs in holiness and sanctification, they overlooked their own hesitations about the matter. They professed that they did not believe in having women preach, and agonized over how to preserve their marital relations and attend to their duties as wives and mothers, but then they all decided that they had to dedicate their lives to preaching the gospel.

Through the power of their testimony and their dedication to their mission, these women not only empowered themselves in ways that few have understood but also empowered other churchwomen to continue confronting the male clergy on the issue of participatory equality and the ordination of women. Unlike their sisters in the 1880s and 1890s, many of the early black preaching women did not aggressively seek ordination, but they provided the model for what a woman preacher could be and helped accelerate the growth of women as evangelists.

The nineteenth century ended with a national debate on issues related to female voting and participation in the local and national Church polity. The debate also concerned female ordination. This debate set the tone and defined the issues that black churchwomen would face in the twentieth century. Although the ordination and gender equality debate surfaced in the AME Church as early as 1844, it did not become pronounced in black denominations until the late 1880s, and not full-blown until the mid-1890s.

Deliberations on women's roles in black and white denominations occurred during a time of great reform and discussion about the equality of women. The woman's rights, suffrage, and temperance movements were in full swing. Although few black women were active in the first two movements, they were affected by the public discourse. They were influenced by what they read in the black and white secular and nonsecular press, as well as by the lectures of black feminist activists who spoke at their churches. Literary associations held debates in local churches about woman's rights and woman suffrage. The impact of these movements, as well as the larger public discourse on gender issues, can be seen in the increased number of men and women writing in black secular and non-secular media about women's equality and gender discrimination in the black Church.[30]

Although the record is incomplete, it appears that among African Americans, the official debate over women's ordination began in the AME polity during the antebellum period. It is noteworthy that the first black women preachers appeared in the AME and AME Zion denominations. The discourse began with Jarena Lee. The presence of Lee, Foote, and other black preaching women at AME General Conferences, as well as their attempt to set up a clergywomen's group in the 1850s, precedes a proposal to license women to preach. On May 3, 1852, the AME General Conference voted against licensing women to preach.[31]

In 1876, the AME Zion Church became the first black denomination to grant women suffrage, which meant that they could vote on Church issues in their local churches and have a voice in the Quarterly and Annual Conferences.[32] In 1884, the Church passed legislation that opened the way for women to be elected as lay delegates to the General Conference, the national legislating body. As lay delegates, they could attend the meeting and discuss and vote on legislation affecting all churches in the denomination.[33]

In the last decade of the nineteenth century, two events occurred that changed Church history irrevocably. In 1895, Julia A. J. Foote and Mary Small were ordained as deacons; this gave the AME Zion Church the additional distinction of being the first black denomination to ordain women to the ministry officially. In 1898, the AME Zion Church ordained Mary Small as an elder, thereby becoming the first Methodist church, black or white, to ordain a woman as an elder. Small's ordination triggered a major debate about the propriety and scriptural authority for ordaining women as ministers. The controversy and the discourse involving her ordination are important for understanding the black Church's position on the ordination and role of women.[34]

Until Julia Foote was ordained as a deacon in the AME Zion Church, no black preaching woman had received denomination authorization to clergy rights. Foote's elevation to the diaconate drove the debate over women's right to ordination to a new level and opened the door for Mary Small's ordination as an elder.[35]

In the beginning of the nineteenth century, women sought equality in the Church and society. By the end of the century, although their right to preach was still controversial, many actively pursued their calling. In

1898, few people realized the full significance of Small's elevation to the position of elder, or recognized the impact that this precipitous shift in traditional religious practice would have on the national black and white religious discourse about women's position in the Church.

Impact of AME Zion Ordination Controversy

The AME Zion's granting of elder's orders to a woman—Mary Small—thundered through the nation. It was a watershed event in the struggle of preaching women, black and white; the impact of this ordination transcended Church boundaries. Among African Americans, the ordination's effects might be seen in the opening up of new opportunities for women in the Church and in the expansion of preaching positions for women. Small's ordination also empowered churchwomen. To ascertain the ordination's meaning and impact, we will explore the issues that dominated the public discourse and the changes that occurred as a result. First, however, we must understand why the discourse was so bitter in the Small case as opposed to the Foote ordination.

Foote's ordination caused some concern, but it did not receive major attention or become the subject of national controversy. It was Small's ordination as an elder that created great consternation and engendered bitter denominational debate within the AME Zion Church and among black and white male clergy nationally. The Small ordination threatened the male clergy in ways that the Foote ordination did not. Julia Foote was seventy-one years old at the time of her ordination. Having preached for over fifty years by 1894, she was well known among white and black Methodists and revered by many for her intellect and the power of her preaching. Foote's ordination was more a form of recognition than empowerment, because her career was in its twilight. It was not expected that she would be appointed to pastor a church. Her primary gain was official denominational recognition of her ministry and admittance to equality with males in the polity.[36]

Although many male clergy knew that Julia Foote's ordination was unprecedented, they did not expect the floodgates to open and women to be allowed unlimited access to the pulpit. In fact, many viewed Foote's ordination with pride and celebrated the fact that the AME Zion Church was the first black Methodist denomination to grant women suffrage, the right to be lay delegates, and the rights of full ordination. With the exception of suffrage, these accomplishments were directly related to the 1884 General Conference revision of the Church discipline, which eliminated the word *male* from its laws. This action, at least on paper, effectively removed every obstacle to women's unconditional work in the Church. However, it seems likely that the male clergy expected a continued token recognition of women in the Church. Clearly, they did not anticipate a rapid movement toward full equality.[37]

The notion was unspoken among men at first, but was later clearly articulated, that although some few women might be ordained to the diaconate, they would not be appointed to pastor major churches and would not be considered for elder's orders or the bishopric. They would still serve as conference evangelists and missionaries. Those few women who received ministerial appointments were usually appointed to missions or to churches with only a few members. Moreover, for many male clergy, women receiving full ordination rights were still women; they had the same rights, privileges, and roles as other women. Put simply, they were not the intellectual or physical equals of males but were the "weaker sex."

AME Zion women, on the other hand, perceived the acquisition of ordination rights as a step toward equality in the polity and as a force for liberation from the historically prescribed roles for churchwomen. Within two decades, every legal obstacle preventing the advancement of women in the Church was removed. Before obtaining religious suffrage and eliminating the word *male* from the discipline, women were limited to a narrow, prescribed boundary in their church work. Following Small's ordination, Sarah Pettey, editor of the *Star of Zion* women's column, summed up what many women felt. She said, "Christian generosity, keeping pace with the advanced ideas of to-day, has overleaped the once insurmountable barriers, and to-day, to the called female churchworker there is no majestic Shasta looming up before her, with sexual prejudicial peaks and impregnable sentimental buttes saying 'thus far shalt thou come and no farther.'"[38]

Small's ordination as an elder cut the ground out from under the black male clergy's feet. In the view of many males, a woman elder was functioning out of her sphere. Unlike an unordained preacher or an ordained deacon, an elder possesses power and authority over other ordained clergy. Historically, ordained ministers in the AME Zion polity have been of two orders—deacon and elder. Deacons preach, assist in the administration of Holy Communion, baptize, administer matrimony, and try disorderly members in the absence of the elder. The eldership represents the highest of holy orders. An elder assumes all of the deacon's perquisites. An elder is one step removed from the bishop. Only an elder can consecrate the Eucharist in the church. Elders possess judicial prerogatives, which are demanded wherever a lay member appeals a pastoral decision.

The elder mitigates disputes between the minister and lay member. As the general missionary and superintendent of a district, a presiding elder possesses even greater powers.[39]

For a woman to be an elder challenged the natural order of society that males had come to expect. On this issue, black males differed little from white males. In fact, patriarchal views and practices were well respected among black leaders.[40] In many ways, women's gaining access to the male religious hierarchy was comparable to Blacks' advancing in a white world. In other words, under pressure, token equality could be granted, but there was no expectation that the minority group would receive open access based simply upon objective criteria. The arguments black and white men voiced to justify exclusionary religious practices were based on scriptural authority and gender assumptions. In addition, black males had few professional occupational choices available to them, and therefore felt duty bound to challenge Small's ordination.

The Small debate, ostensibly over women's right to preach, expanded to encompass women's rights in the Church and society. As important as this debate was in raising social consciousness about gender equality, it did not lead to widespread legislative changes granting full ordination rights to women in other denominations.

Small's ordination and the continuing debate over women's right to preach created interdenominational and gender tension that caused other denominations to reconsider legislative restrictions on women's roles. Despite the vigorous debate, changes in women's status would come much later in the twentieth century. However, the possibility of changing rules encouraged many women to seek careers in the ministry. These shifts occurred at a time when suffrage and other rights of women were being strongly contested throughout American society. Moreover, the debate about Small's 1898 ordination came on the heels of the 1896 organization of the National Association of Colored Women. Many important NACW leaders were also influential religious figures. Eliza Gardner, a powerful and well-respected leader in the AME Zion Church, was an NACW founder and officer. Similarly, AME women such as Katherine Davis Tillman and Hallie Quinn Brown were forces to be reckoned with in the Church and were prominent in the NACW. These women supported the ordination of women and the granting of laity rights. Moreover, they used the NACW as a platform to undergird the efforts of women like Small and to articulate a national black female agenda for equality. Their efforts fueled the debate taking place in the denominations and sustained the black feminist view in the public discourse.[41]

Ordination Traditions Among Churches

The AME Zion Church was the leader in the African American movement to ordain and grant laity rights to women. Black women were first ordained by the AME Zion Church, which was one of the few denominations to grant women of any race ordination rights in the nineteenth century. The AME Zion Church was not, however, the only site of struggle for black preaching women. It is also important to look at the ordination traditions among the AME, CME, Baptist, Holiness, Pentecostal, and Spiritual Churches. Women's struggle for equality in one religious tradition was not isolated from that of others. Undoubtedly, women and men were influenced and empowered to act by the information they obtained in the larger public discourse, where the issues and events occurring in all black and white religious traditions were explicated.

Although there are similarities among the traditions, there are also large differences between them. For this reason, it makes sense to look at how women gained ordination rights in each tradition, rather than looking at the various gains along one time line. Women made progress in each denomination at different times, but they confronted similar problems. These problems included gaining the right to ordination, gaining acceptance in the polity, and pursuing traditionally defined careers as ministers with regularized church appointments.

For most black preaching women seeking ordination, the goal was inclusion in the Church polity. Though some saw the need for transformation of the patriarchal Church, few were willing to pursue such a course. Their struggle for ordination was in some ways defined by the need for a strong Church that could act as a bulwark against racism.

AME Church

Women in the AME Church were among the first to contend for ordination actively. The struggle for full ordination by black women in the AME Church was protracted and difficult. In 1884, the General Conference approved the licensing but not the ordination of preaching women. Licensing could occur only under the strict control of the Quarterly Conference of the church to which the women belonged. Many male ministers viewed women preachers as a threat and feared job competition from female ministers. To restrict women preachers further, the General Conference forbade the appointment of women to pastorates.

In 1885, at the North Carolina Annual Conference, Sarah Ann Hughes was ordained a deaconess in the AME Church. This unauthorized ordination caused extensive debate and protest among male ministers. Hughes began her ministry in 1881 as an evangelist of the North Carolina Conference, and received an appointment in 1882 to pastor a church in Fayetteville, North Carolina. This was a rare occurrence in the AME Church and seemingly resulted from her superior preaching skills as an evangelist. However, Hughes's assignment to Fayetteville, along with similar advances made by a few other AME women (most notably Margaret Wilson of New Jersey), prompted the AME Church to pass legislation restricting the advance of women preachers. Moreover, the North Carolina Annual Conference of 1887 deordained Sarah Hughes, a move that the 1888 AME General Conference ratified.[42]

In 1900, in response to escalating internal and external pressure, the AME Church established the position of deaconess without ordination. In doing so, they adopted the pattern that the northern and southern white Methodist bodies had established. Although AME women consistently petitioned and argued for ordination rights, it was not until 1948 that favorable legislation was passed.[43]

CME Church

The extent to which women pressed for full ordination in the CME Church is not known. Organized in 1870, the CME Church was largely concentrated in the South. It was extremely traditional and conservative and dominated by a male clergy that maintained a consistently hostile attitude to the advancement of women.

During the late nineteenth century, when other black Methodist women were expanding their leadership base and roles in meaningful ways, the CME Church refused women the right to organize missionary societies. For many years, CME women fought this ruling. In 1918, the Women's Connectional Missionary Council received approval as an organization. In 1926, legislation was passed granting women the right to serve as lay delegates to the General Conference.[44]

Despite the CME Church's conservatism, between 1895 and 1960, some CME women established careers as evangelists, were licensed to preach, and were ordained. In 1897, Mary Mims of Kentucky was the first woman licensed to preach in the CME Church. As an evangelist, she was favored for revivals and for her lectures to girls and women. In 1915, Ida E. Roberts and Georgia A. Mills were ordained at the North Carolina Annual Conference in Charlotte. Roberts had begun her preaching career in 1891. Until the 1940s, Roberts and Mills were the only CME women ordained to preach. In 1943, D. B. Whitehead of Williams Temple CME

Church in Philadelphia became the third known female to be ordained in that denomination.[45]

In 1948, the CME Church approved the licensing and ordination of women as local preachers, deacons, and elders. In 1966, following many years of defeat, a resolution was passed granting women "full clergy rights." In that year, Virgie Amanda Jackson Ghant became the first woman to be ordained as an elder in the CME Church.[46]

Baptist Denominations

In the three black Baptist denominations—National Baptist Convention, U.S.A., Inc.; National Baptist Convention of America, Unincorporated; and Progressive National Baptist Convention—the struggle for ordination has been extremely difficult. The independent Church polity of the Baptists guarantees the autonomy of individual congregations in matters of faith and practice. In deference to the power, authority, and autonomy of the local churches and associations, none of the Baptist Conventions has taken a formal position on the issue of ordination. Traditionally, Baptists have been extremely conservative and have consistently opposed women's ordination.[47]

Pentecostals

Although modern African American Pentecostals trace their origin to the early twentieth century and represent one of the seven historically black denominations, traditional scholarship has obscured the significance of the movement and the role of black preaching women in its early development.

Some of the most powerful black women preachers were what is commonly referred to as Pentecostal Holiness preachers. By strict definition, Pentecostalism and Holiness are discrete terms. In practice, however, it is frequently difficult to distinguish a church or minister as being one or the other. The lines between the two are obscured because of the blending of traditions. Both Pentecostalism and Holiness require conversion and sanctification for salvation. They also require baptism in the Holy Ghost, which might manifest itself in glossolalia (speaking in tongues), also known as personal holiness. Some Pentecostals insist that one must speak in tongues to be accepted into the faith; others are more flexible. Holiness advocates emphasize sanctification but are divided (or silent) on the issue of speaking in tongues.[48]

The roots of Pentecostalism are arguably in the nineteenth century, but the modern Pentecostal movement's acknowledged origin in the United States is the Azusa Street Revival, which occurred in Los Angeles between

1906 and 1909 under the leadership of William J. Seymour. Lucy Farrow and Neely Terry were among the pioneering women ministers at Azusa Street. Seymour's introduction to the idea of the baptism of the Holy Ghost was through Lucy Farrow. As one who had experienced complete sanctification, Seymour was able to enhance his experience through knowledge of the baptism of the Holy Ghost and the validating phenomenon of speaking in tongues.[49] The ministry of African American Pentecostal women may be traced from Farrow and Terry to Bishop Ida Robinson, Elder Lucy Smith, and Rosa Horn to numerous other twentieth-century black Pentecostal women. Robinson, Smith, and Horn did not have to contend for their ministries. Rather, they founded their own churches, a trend prevalent among the diverse Pentecostal denominations.

The Church of God in Christ (COGIC), which was founded in 1897 and which is the largest black Pentecostal denomination, opposes ordaining women as clergy. Although many male clergy have used the Scriptures to argue against ordaining women, traditional mainline denominations have been reluctant to define their predilection in writing. However, COGIC's *Official Manual* explicitly defines the prohibition against women's ordination as pastor, elder, or bishop while defining their roles as evangelists and teachers who can "have charge of a church in the absence of the pastor." COGIC women have exploited these restrictions and definitions as they continue to struggle for the right of the pulpit. In the process, they have maximized their power in the church by creating a Women's Department that is among the most powerful in any Christian denomination. COGIC women do what may be acknowledged as preaching, but it is under the guise of teaching the gospel. Cheryl Townsend Gilkes asserts that "teaching the Gospel involved setting forth biblical doctrine, Church polity, and duties; conducting revivals; [and] presenting teachings in the morning service in lieu of and in the style of a sermon." Gilkes points out that "often members of particular congregations have been hard pressed to distinguish between men's preaching and women's teaching."[50] Although they are neither ordained nor licensed, COGIC women do serve as pastors. Joseph M. Murphy notes that COGIC's main seminary is increasingly "training women for the post. Though it is still relatively unusual, the pastor of the 1978 Philadelphia church was a woman."[51]

Spiritualism

In addition to the Pentecostal Holiness women preachers, there are the women in the Spiritual churches. Spirituals believe that one can achieve financial success, love, prestige, and good health by practicing magical religious rituals or by obtaining confidential information. Many of the Spiritual churches stress self-reliance, positive thinking, and personal accountability for one's status in life. They assert that one can control one's status through magical religious practices. Spirituals' techniques include burning candles, using the occult, and employing mediums who participate in public and private divination. Some Spirituals develop complex metaphysical systems.[52]

During the late nineteenth century, women played a prominent role in organizing Spiritualism. Although research for this book unearthed no sermons by Spiritual women preachers, and although there has been a tendency to ignore Pentecostal, Holiness, and Spiritual women preachers, they played an important and little recognized role in socializing black migrants in urban areas after 1920. Like the Pentecostal and Holiness women preachers, the Spirituals gravitated to large northeastern and midwestern cities during the Great Migration. Historically, they have maintained a following among the poor and socially disinherited.[53] Among African American Spirituals and Pentecostals, women have had significance as private prayer practitioners. In their monumental work *Black Metropolis*, St. Clair Drake and Horace Clayton (1945) noted that "the ban on women pastors in the regular churches has increased the popularity of the Pentecostal, Holiness, and Spiritual churches where ambitious women may rise to the top."[54]

The right to preach was for many clergymen the last bastion of male privilege to be relinquished. Although women have made substantial gains in the twentieth century, they have not achieved full equality in the Church. The ascendancy and acceptance of black women clergy in the Church polity has been slow and painful.

Developments in Women's Preaching Status

The debate over women's ordination was central to the advancement of black women not only in the Church but also in the community. The 1898 ordination of Mary Small as an elder and the increasing number of female evangelists in most traditional denominations opened up new opportunities for black women preachers. The 1896 founding of the NACW expanded black feminists' base of power beyond the Church and provided a national venue for black female leadership. These events fueled an escalation of feminist rhetoric that called for black women to defend themselves and their image. Their rhetoric and agenda suggested new possibilities and became a clarion call for women to take charge of their lives, their communities, and their destinies. There was a revolution of rising black feminist expectations that undergirded black women's struggle for equality in the Church and society.[55]

While the Church became a site of contention for black women, America became a battleground for stripping African Americans of what little gains they had made after 1865. *Plessy* v. *Ferguson*, the 1896 Supreme Court decision upholding segregation under the "separate but equal" doctrine, sounded the death knell for black equality under the law. By 1900, disfranchisement, lynching, segregation, and rampant discrimination were the order of the day. As lynching became a national issue and as racism surged, black women continued to organize and become actively involved in the struggle to defend their race and gender.[56]

Ironically, in the face of the rising onslaught directed against African Americans, black women pressed even harder for their rights in the Church. In 1894, Fannie Barrier Williams gained notoriety at the Chicago World's Fair when she addressed the predominantly white World's Congress of Representative Women. She spoke on the moral progress of black women after slavery and alluded to the abuse—rape and forced seduction—to which they had been subjected as slaves. Black women, she said, recognized the double burden of race and gender, but they also bore the legacy of slavery, which had tainted the image of black womanhood. After slavery, the majority of these women, particularly southern black women, worked in the homes of Whites, former slave owners, as domestics. Many of the women of whom Williams spoke were churchwomen.[57]

As the twentieth century began, black and white women continued to struggle for recognition and equality in the Church and in society. As fundraisers and dispensers of community charity, women had indisputable equality in Church service but faced inequality in recognition. Historically, the Quakers are the only religious group to have ensured equality for both genders; they achieved this mainly by eliminating all gender distinctions and establishing a Spirit-conferred leadership, based on the belief that anyone who feels moved by the Spirit of God should be free to speak. Inequality continues to exist today in most of the Protestant and Catholic churches, whether in preaching, positions of leadership, ordination, or administration of sacraments.[58]

In the twentieth century, black churchwomen became more outspoken and began pressing for the right to preach and for equality in the polity. The number of women licensed and ordained to preach grew as the AME Zion Church continued to credential women and as the number of evangelists increased, particularly among black Methodist denominations. In fact, a few evangelists, such as Mary Evans (AME), gained fame and developed a national following among numerous denominations.

At the same time, women steadily left mainline black churches, moving into sects and founding their own churches. In these new churches, which were typically Pentecostal, Holiness, or Spiritualist Churches, women were no longer viewed as radical. They received full recognition for their spiritual gifts, and tradition restricted neither their pursuit of the ministry nor their mode of religious expression. Thus, we see the rise of women such as Bishop Rosa Horn (New York), Elder Lucy Smith (Chicago), and Ida Robinson (Philadelphia). These women became powerful and attracted thousands of followers, many of whom were Southern migrants seeking a better life in the North.

Evangelists' popularity grew during the early years of the century. The male clergy knew the value of having female evangelists available, especially for leading revivals. Bishops who would not approve of ordaining a woman would grant her a license to preach. This is evidenced by the number of evangelists appointed to preach in the different Episcopal districts. In 1919, at the Thirty-Seventh Annual Conference of the Chicago District of the AME Church, Bishop Coffin appointed nine female evangelists, including the well-known Reverend Nora Taylor, to the Keokuk district. In 1927, at the Northwest AME Conference meeting in St. Paul, Minnesota, Bishop A. L. Gaines appointed seven female evangelists to serve the district and appointed the Reverend Lillian A. P. Jones to pastor a church in Yankton, South Dakota. On that occasion, Mary Gould was licensed as a missionary preacher. Gaines also appointed nine women evangelists to the district in Des Moines, Iowa.[59]

It was not until 1948 that the AME General Conference voted to grant women ordination rights as local deacons. In 1960, women acquired full ordination rights as elders. Local deacons were eligible for temporary ministries, primarily in missionary churches, and they were subordinate to itinerant elders, an exclusively male position.[60]

In the twentieth century, at least on paper, African American women obtained the right to participate in the polity as voters and as lay delegates. Since 1975, they have had full clergy rights in most denominations. Some black Baptist churches and COGIC continue to deny women ordination, however, justifying their positions with traditional biblical arguments.[61] In the 1970s, black feminist theologians such as Pauli Murray emerged out of mainline white denominations such as the Episcopal Church. African American women still struggle to find a preaching role in traditional black churches. Many achieve the status, but they often never receive a regular pastoral appointment.

Secular Events Affecting Preachers' Status

As the twentieth century unfolded, many events affected the Church and the status of black preaching women. The developments that had perhaps the greatest impact were World War I, the Great Migration, the passage of the Nineteenth Amendment, World War II, and the civil rights movement.

World War I spurred African Americans to migrate out of the South. Between 1916 and the end of 1918, more than one million African Americans moved to the North and West. The concentration of migrants in cities created new needs and problems. Organized religion found it difficult to serve this new mass of humanity, which differed markedly from the urbane black population already in the city. Some churches were not interested in adding poor, unkempt migrants to their rolls. Storefront churches, cults, and sects literally popped up on every corner.

Hundreds of evangelists, such as Rosa Horn, Ida Robinson, Rosa Edwards, and Lucy Smith, profited from the migration. Evangelists with mainline black denominations, such as Ruth Dennis and Mary Evans, found themselves in demand as the black male clergy scrambled to sign up charismatic black women evangelists to conduct revivals and deliver sermons at the regular church services.[62]

Many black churchwomen celebrated the ratification of the Nineteenth Amendment to the U.S. Constitution, which granted female citizens the right to vote. Though most black women in the South were disfranchised, women fighting for equal rights and suffrage in the Church expected a trickle-down effect. The General Conference of the AME Church responded immediately to these rising expectations by granting women the right of representation on the Church boards of trustees, making them eligible for election as delegates to the General Conference. Some ministers, such as the Reverend Edward E. Tyler, pastor of Bridge Street AME Church in New York City, challenged the new law by refusing the petition of black female church members to nominate three women to the institution's board of trustees. He stated that the General Conference did not intend for women to hold office in larger churches.[63] The AME Church also decreed that female members were eligible to hold any office in the Church.

African American women began to receive more recognition in the Church—everything short of ordination. In 1924, Mary G. Evans, then pastor of the St. John AME Church in Indianapolis, received a doctor of divinity degree from Wilberforce University. She was the first black woman to enjoy this status. In that same year, the General Conference of the Methodist Episcopal Church granted women the right of ordination in local pastorates but denied them admission to Annual Conferences and the itinerant ministry, arguing that "the responsibilities of the itinerant ministry [are] too great for women, who might at any time have to assume the burden of motherhood."[64]

The 1920s and 1930s also witnessed an upsurge in individual black female achievement and political activism. In 1921, Georgiana R. Simpson, Sadie Tanner Mossell, and Eva Dykes were the first black women to earn Ph.D.'s in the United States. In 1922, Mary B. Talbert was the first woman to receive the Spingarn Medal from the National Association for the Advancement of Colored People. In 1924, Elizabeth Ross Haynes was the first black woman elected to the national board of the YWCA. In that same year, the National League of Republican Colored Women was organized. The organization included many leading black churchwomen, such as Nannie Burroughs, the Reverend Florence Randolph, and Hallie Quinn Brown, all of whom actively engaged in secular and nonsecular politics. In addition, for the first time in history, African American women were running for political office. In 1924, Randolph was nominated for New Jersey assemblywoman on the Republican ticket.[65]

World War II brought new opportunities for women to serve their country in the Women's Reserve of the United States Navy (WAVES) and Women's Army Corps (WAC). More women joined the labor force to meet wartime needs. This work affected the way women perceived themselves and were perceived by society. Women's organizations, secular and nonsecular, developed programs to address the human suffering so much in evidence throughout the country. As more women assumed leadership roles in the society, the demand for female equality in the Church rose.

Throughout the 1930s, 1940s, and 1950s, as churchwomen attended and participated in deliberations at their denominations' annual legislative meetings and as their missionary organizations and conventions forcefully argued for women's equality, the barriers began to collapse. In 1930, Presbyterian churches voted down the movement to permit the full ordination of women as ministers but voted in favor of women serving as local evangelists. In that same year, the first female lay delegates participated in the CME General Conference. In 1932, Irmah L. Moore, who held a doctor of divinity degree from Wilberforce University, became the pastor of St. Paul AME Church in Cedarville, Ohio. In 1936, Martha Jayne Keys of Louisville, Kentucky, who had been an evangelist and a preacher for thirty years, introduced legislation at the AME General Conference, with the support of the AME missionary society, asking that women with five years' training in an accredited theological school be ordained as elders and ministers, thus obtaining the rights to perform marriages and give communion. The legislation was voted down, but the women vowed to continue fighting. Also in 1936, Lillian Cannady was the first woman to be licensed to preach by the Metropolitan Methodist Episcopal Church, a prominent church in Baltimore.[66]

The AME Women's Missionary Society continued to push the ordination issue and finally got results. In 1948, the General Conference of the AME Church voted to ordain women as deacons in the local church. The legislation passed despite the protests of a small group of ministers who yelled, "They'll never serve as Deacons in my church!" Following the passage of this legislation, Rebecca M. Glover was ordained and appointed assistant pastor of the Metropolitan AME Church in Washington, D.C., an old-line church.[67]

During the 1950s and 1960s, churchwomen played an important, though little recognized, role in the civil rights movement. The impact of their activism, as well as the rise of the feminist movement, directly caused many denominations to reconsider their stance on women's rights and ordination. As the press for black and women's equality ensued, legislation for female ordination was passed. In 1956, the United Methodist Church, the Presbyterian Church in the United States of America (PCUSA), and the AME Church legislated the full ordination of women. In 1964, the Presbyterian Church in the United States (PCU) voted to permit the ordination of women as ministers.[68]

In the 1970s, women continued to gain rights in the religious sphere. In 1970, the Evangelical Lutheran Church in America admitted women to the clergy. In 1972, women were ordained as rabbis for the first time in Reform Judaism. In 1974, the Free Methodist Church granted women full ordination as elders. And in 1976, the Episcopal Church admitted women to the clergy.[69]

Missionary Associations

During the early twentieth century, churchwomen concentrated their leadership and power in the missionary associations and in women's conventions that developed in the Baptist and Methodist denominations and in COGIC. These associations had thousands of members in communities throughout the United States.[70] Such organizations represented a major fundraising arm for their affiliated denominations, and a central organizing force for black women in the Church and community.

The missionary association became an alternative path for women who wanted to bring their spiritual gifts to the pulpit. Missionary preachers, such as Ella Whitfield and F. E. Redwine, worked primarily within the national missionary societies attached to the major black denominations. They gained a following by preaching at the societies' local, state, regional, and national meetings, at annual anniversary celebrations, and at Woman's Day services held in all black churches.[71]

Lack of Support from the Pew

It is because of the support of the missionary associations and the women's conventions and their members who filled the pews at the revivals and Woman's Day programs that many women had a ministry at all. This is the arena in which the support of the pew was most important. In the twentieth century, in particular, women preachers have clearly enjoyed the support of the pew in their pursuit of a ministry.

In the critical area of ordination and in the appointment of pastors, however, the women in the pew have not been willing to challenge publicly the dominant male clergy leaders, particularly the Methodist bishops and the powerful leaders of the National Baptist Convention, Inc., and the National Baptist Convention of America. In the Methodist Church, the bishops, as corporate officers of their respective denominations, wield power at the general conferences and at the annual and district conferences. In deference to the power, authority, and autonomy of the local churches and associations, neither of the Baptist conventions has formally taken a position on ordination. Yet given their numerical dominance in the pew, if women determine that they want to change the church or denomination, they can strike, close the churches down, and force change. The majority of black women are not likely to choose this option, however. They have not been willing to hold their churches and denominations hostage to their pew power.

Why has the female pew been willing to support an evangelist or itinerant minister but been unwilling to demand that the Church ordain and appoint female pastors? One reason is that relationships—family ties and kinship networks—figure prominently in Church politics. Family stresses religion in a variety of ways that help shape Church policy and action. The existence of extensive friendship and kinship connections often means that loyalty to the leadership reaches deep into the pew, making it less likely that someone will be inclined to rock the boat. In all of the black religious traditions, powerful clergymen appoint their wives and other women in their friendship and kinship network to positions of power and authority, particularly in churchwomen's organizations. Some women preachers have been directly connected to the dominant male leadership by marriage or other familial links.

A second reason is that black women's racial ideologies have taken precedence over any feminist leanings. Black women continue to view the most critical issue in their lives as being racial oppression. In a white patriarchal society that has economically, politically, and socially oppressed Blacks, black women have largely been unwilling to side with white feminists, or even with black feminists who argue that women must fight for their freedom and equality. Many black women cannot see how their family's economic status would benefit materially from feminist protest.

Having had to support and protect themselves, many black women want a traditional family, one in which men do the supporting. Black women have historically outnumbered men and have frequently had no husbands. Given that the black Church has been a major entity for male recognition and achievement, black churchwomen have been ambivalent about challenging male authority.

On the other hand, black men who have bought into the American idea of masculine prerogatives have keenly felt that black women undercut them by seeking positions of power long identified as male. Although one could argue logically against this ideology, the reality is that many black men and women continue to accept these ideas and to resist change.

—————— o ——————

Whatever their struggle has been, the reality is that legions of black women have preached for almost two hundred years. Despite the Church's failure to recognize their spiritual gifts and their work, they have exercised leadership in Christian mission and have spoken out on the issues of race, sex, class, and color. They have embraced the Church and joined their sisters in the pew in defending and supporting it. Their faith has been strengthened and their wits sharpened by the struggle that they and their foremothers have endured. They have been eloquent in the articulation of their faith and constant in their belief in the Holy Spirit. They have left us a rich and inspiring legacy in their lives and in their writings. *Daughters of Thunder* provides an opportunity to hear the messages of the pioneers and to distill a part of their experience as African Americans, as women, and as believers in God.

PART ONE

PURSUING
A MINISTRY
ORDAINED
BY GOD

1850–1900

WOMEN WHO PAVED THE WAY

ALTHOUGH A NUMBER OF African American women preached in the nineteenth century, only fragments of their sermons have survived. Some scholars surmise that there were slave women preachers, and there are isolated references to women who styled themselves as prophetesses, but there is no substantive documentary evidence of them.[1] Sermons exist for only four of the more than twenty women known to have preached in the nineteenth century: Julia A. J. Foote, Harriet Baker, Mary J. Small, and Florence Spearing Randolph. Later chapters will explore these four women in depth. The present chapter will examine the life and work of those women about whom we know a great deal, although their sermons have not survived.

Elizabeth

The earliest black female preacher was a woman known simply as Elizabeth. Born a slave in Maryland in 1766, she was set free in 1796. Her parents were devout Methodists, and her father read the Bible aloud to his children every Sunday, instilling in them a fervent belief in the Scriptures and the power of prayer.

At the age of eleven, Elizabeth was sent to another farm. Although she was denied permission to visit her family, out of loneliness and despair she risked punishment and possibly death to see them. When she returned to the farm where she resided, the overseer tied her with a rope and lashed her. Recognizing the danger of Elizabeth's actions and her need for guidance and communion, her mother told her that she had "none in the world to look to but God."

Religion, particularly prayer, became her constant refuge. Every place became an altar. She mourned and moaned "in the corners of the field, and under the fences." For six months she prayed and wept, and gradually she lost her appetite and became extremely weak. It was in this state that she had her first vision and felt "the power of the Holy Ghost."[2]

Elizabeth's description of her conversion experience is remarkably similar to that described by other women preachers. She felt "sustained by some invisible power." Converted to Christ at the age of twelve, she continued to pray and wrestle with the divine invocation that she should live a life of prayer and devotion to Christian principles.

Although Elizabeth had visions of traveling and preaching, it was many years before she actually had these experiences. When she was forty-two, as she later related, it "was revealed to me that the message which had been given to me I had not yet delivered, and the time had come." Lacking sufficient reading skills, Elizabeth questioned whether or not she could deliver the message, because she did not know the Scriptures. She sought guidance from other Christians but was discouraged from pursuing her mission. She was told that the Scriptures did not sanction women's preaching and that women were not suited to the rigors of travel required of an itinerant minister. Thoroughly disheartened, she first resisted the Holy Spirit but then felt the Holy Spirit's urging her to take up her mission.[3]

In 1808, Elizabeth became a preaching woman, holding her first meeting in Baltimore.[4] She was rejected at every turn by the "elders and rulers," and harassed at every meeting she attempted to hold in a church. Some women supported her desire to preach, but they feared expulsion from the Church if they allowed her to hold meetings in their homes. As the persecution against Elizabeth increased, the elders argued more adamantly that because she was a woman, her meetings went against the Methodist Church's discipline.

Elizabeth's perseverance and her firm belief in the holiness doctrine of salvation empowered her to continue preaching. She began to travel in the South and North, preaching and lecturing wherever she could. Despite the risk to her life and the possibility of reenslavement, she held meetings in Virginia and remote places throughout the South. Once in Virginia, while speaking against slavery, she was challenged and threatened with imprisonment. When asked by what authority she spoke and if she were ordained, she answered, "Not by the commission of men's hands: if the Lord had ordained me, I needed nothing better." Her unprecedented answer, supreme confidence, conviction, and apparent godliness were enough to set aside many a threatening force. Elizabeth preached for almost fifty years before retiring to Philadelphia, where she lived among Quakers and spent her final years.[5]

Jarena Lee

Source: *Center for African American History and Culture, Temple University.*

Jarena Lee

Jarena Lee, the second black woman known to preach, was born free in Cape May, New Jersey, on February 11, 1783. Little is known of her childhood. Hired out by her parents to work as a servant at the age of seven, she was most likely apprenticed to a family for several years. During that time, she acquired domestic skills and learned to read and write.

During her tenure as a servant, Lee was introduced to religion. In 1804, at the age of twenty-one, she had a religious awakening when she heard the first verse of Psalms. As a Presbyterian preacher read the words "Lord, I am vile, conceived in sin, / Born unholy and unclean," she felt the weight of what she described as her "sins and sinful nature."[6]

After this experience, Lee went to Philadelphia and began attending a white Methodist church. Within three months, she started to feel distant from the congregation. Lee suggested that "there was a wall between me and a communion with that people, which was higher than I could possibly see over, and seemed to make this impression upon my mind, *this is not the people for you.*"[7] Lee wanted a fellowship with black Methodists. She attended a religious service conducted by the Reverend Richard Allen.[8] After hearing Allen preach, Lee joined the African Methodists.

Five years later, in 1809, she felt the call to preach and sought permission to do so from the black Methodist Church in Philadelphia that Allen directed. Allen denied her a license. Believing that she had been called by God, Lee entered a ministry.[9]

In 1811, at the age of twenty-eight, she married Joseph Lee. Within six years, her husband and five other family members had died, leaving her with two children to rear.[10]

In 1817, after the AME Church organized and Allen became a bishop, Lee renewed her request. Allen stated that there were no precedents for female preachers in the Methodist tradition, but because the church needed to increase its membership, Lee could hold prayer meetings outside the church and exhort congregations after licensed ministers had delivered their sermons.[11]

Three weeks after affiliating with the black Methodists, Lee was converted. She learned about sanctification, became deeply immersed in prayer, and eventually encountered the Holy Ghost. According to her account, the Holy Ghost implored her, "Go preach the Gospel!" When Lee responded, "No one will believe me," the Spirit answered, "Preach the Gospel; I will put words in your mouth, and will turn your enemies to become your friends."[12] She became sanctified almost three months after her conversion.

Experiencing sanctification and empowered by the Holy Ghost, Lee was not to be shunted aside by mere mortals who argued that women should not be preaching the gospel. Undaunted by Allen's decision, she reasoned, "If a man may preach, because the Saviour died for him, why not the woman? seeing he died for her also. Is he not a whole Saviour, instead of a half one? as those who hold it wrong for a woman to preach, would seem to make it appear."[13] With determination, Lee forged ahead in her ministry. She held many prayer meetings that included both genders, even though the prevailing attitude was that women should not address mixed-gender assemblies. Bishop Allen gave her speaking engagements in churches throughout Pennsylvania and permitted her to travel with him and other ministers to meetings in New Jersey and New York.[14]

Between 1818 and 1849, Lee had a very successful itinerant ministry. She launched her preaching career in Philadelphia and later expanded it as far south as Baltimore, as far north as Rochester, New York, and as far west as Dayton, Ohio. Speaking to white and black audiences, she established herself and broke down some of the earlier resistance that she encountered with the male clergy. She eventually gained a degree of acceptance in the Methodist Church. It is probable that once ministers discovered that she posed no threat to their ministry, they embraced her efforts. As a female itinerant minister and exhorter, she was a novelty and could be used to attract new members and financial support for the Church.[15]

In 1836, Lee published her autobiographical journal, *The Life and Religious Experience of Jarena Lee, A Coloured Lady, Giving an Account of Her Call to Preach the Gospel*. Between that year and 1849, when an updated and revised edition of the autobiography was issued, at least three thousand copies of the work were printed and distributed. The importance of this work cannot be overstated. In *Sisters of the Spirit*, William Andrews asserts that Lee's book "launched black women's autobiography in America with an argument for women's spiritual authority that plainly challenged traditional female roles as defined in both the free and the slave states, among whites as well as blacks."[16]

It is likely that contemporary black women preachers were familiar with Lee's book and the subsequent autobiographies of other preaching women. If so, then they were empowered by knowing the experiences of their preaching foremothers and peers. Moreover, their own publications were most likely influenced by these spiritual autobiographies, which may account for their similarity in format.

Ten years after the first publication of Lee's book, *Memoirs of the Life, Religious Experience, Ministerial Travels and Labours of Mrs. Zilpha Elaw, An American Female of Colour*, was published.[17] Although we know that Lee knew Elaw and shared the pulpit with her on at least one occasion, we do not know the extent of their relationship. It seems likely that Lee was a mentor to Elaw and that Lee's autobiography served as a model and source of encouragement as Elaw wrote her book.[18]

Zilpha Elaw

Born free in Pennsylvania around 1790, Zilpha Elaw appears to have grown up near Philadelphia in a religious family. When she was twelve, her mother died, and Zilpha was placed with a Quaker family. During her years with the Quakers, she attended their religious meetings but was little influenced by their teachings. Viewing herself as an unrepentant sinner, Zilpha was frequently filled with remorse. Through prayer and contrition, she grew closer to God. According to her, she was converted at this early age and her whole being became filled with the Holy Ghost.[19]

In 1810, Zilpha married Joseph Elaw, whom she has described as a "very respectable young man," but not a Christian. He was a worldly man who enjoyed music, dancing, and other "hedonistic" amusements available in Philadelphia. She later advised her "unmarried sisters" that it was a mistake to marry a nonbeliever, particularly since "woman is dependant on and subject to man." To be subordinate to an unregenerate non-Christian was deplorable and painful for her. According to Elaw, her husband tried persuading her to renounce her religion and to stop attending church. In 1815, the Elaws moved from Philadelphia to Burlington, New Jersey, a more provincial and less seductive environment, more suited to her tastes.[20]

Elaw flourished in Burlington and became immersed in her religious experiences. In 1817, she attended her first camp meeting. Awed by the camp meeting setting and the entire experience, she attended meetings as often as she could. The following year, Elaw visited her sister, who was gravely ill and was expected to die. According to Elaw, as death neared, her sister became possessed with the Holy Ghost. In a vision, she saw Jesus and was informed by an angel to "tell Zilpha that she must preach the gospel."[21]

For a few years, Elaw spurned any suggestion that she should preach. She was particularly sensitive to the impact that such a decision could have on her marriage.

In 1821, Elaw attended another camp meeting, one that attracted an estimated seven thousand people, including many African Americans. The black participants decided to stay together in one tent. Elaw described the gathering as being filled with evangelical energy, "heaving bursts of penitential emotion," and great weeping. A voice told her to go outside. To her amazement, when she stepped outside the tent, she began to exhort in a loud voice. It was there that she submitted to the Holy Ghost and the injunction that "thou must preach the gospel; and thou must travel far and wide."[22]

Having been divinely commissioned to preach, from that day on, Elaw put aside all concerns for husband, daughter, family, and friends and immersed herself in her mission, preaching wherever she could, fully empowered by the Holy Ghost. She was persecuted and ridiculed, and her husband was belittled for having a wife who chose to preach. He died in January 1823.

In 1827, after many years of reproach from friends, relatives, and the community and much soul searching, she decided to pursue an itinerant ministry. For the next thirteen years, she preached throughout the Northeast. Although she feared being arrested and sold into slavery, she also preached to black congregations in small Southern towns. The news of a black woman preacher spread far and wide. The curious and committed all came to see what such a specimen was like.[23]

In June 1840, Elaw sailed for England. She remained in England for six years, publishing her memoirs in London in 1846. Nothing is known of Elaw after this publication. It is possible that she died in England.

Rebecca Cox Jackson

Rebecca Cox Jackson was born free in Horntown, Pennsylvania, in 1795. She was raised by her mother, Jane, and her maternal grandmother. Cox later moved to Philadelphia, where she worked as a seamstress and lived with her brother, Joseph Cox, a tanner and local preacher at the Bethel AME Church. In 1830, at the age of thirty-five, Cox married Samuel S. Jackson.

Most of what we know about Jackson comes from her autobiographical writings, which were discovered more than two decades ago in the Shaker collections of the Case Western Reserve Historical Society in Cleveland, Ohio; the Library of Congress; and the Berkshire Athenaeum in Pittsfield, Massachusetts. Jackson began her autobiography around the time of her marriage and the start of her involvement in the Holiness movement.

An iconoclastic, highly motivated, and articulate leader of praying bands, and later a public preacher, Jackson attracted attention for advocating celibacy for those who chose a holy life. Her controversial career as a minister and her charge that the AME Church and its leaders were fostering "carnality" (sexual intercourse for pleasure) alienated her from her husband, family, and friends. Initially, her visibility was enhanced by her brother Joseph's prominence.

Like other feminist Holiness activists, Jackson's belief in spiritual sanctification made her rely on her inner voice. She declared that she had direct personal communication with the Holy Spirit, whom she promised at the time of her conversion to "obey in all things, in all places, and under all conditions."[24]

In the 1830s and early 1840s, Jackson was an itinerant preacher. She then joined the Shakers in Watervliet, New York. Initially attracted by the Shakers' religious celibacy, which focused on spiritualistic experience and advocated a non-gender-specific deity, she later became increasingly concerned about the Shakers' failure to proselytize among African Americans. She left Watervliet in 1851, returning briefly in 1857, at which time she was granted permission to found and lead a Shaker family group in Philadelphia. Jackson's group, primarily composed of Blacks and females, lasted for at least two decades after her death in 1871.[25]

Amanda Berry Smith

One of the best-known black preaching women during the late nineteenth century, Amanda Berry Smith won international acclaim as a leader in the Holiness movement. Born a slave in Long Green, Maryland, on January 23, 1837, she was the second of Samuel and Miriam Berry's thirteen children. Through hard work and extreme frugality, her father saved enough money to purchase his family's freedom. Many writers emphasize that Smith was born a slave, without explaining that she had little firsthand experience of the institution. In her autobiography, she asserted, "I was quite small when my father bought us, so [I] know nothing about the experience of slavery, because I was too young to have any trials of it."[26]

Like her counterparts, Smith had a charismatic and distinctive presence, partly due to dress. Smith modeled her sartorial style after that of her former mistress, whom she commented "dressed very much after the Friends' style." Bishop J. M. Thoburn noted that at a camp meeting in 1876, he spotted "a colored lady dressed in a very plain garb, which reminded me somewhat of that worn by the Friends in former days."[27]

Smith received only a few months of formal education but taught herself to read and write. In 1850, at the age of thirteen, she lived and worked as a domestic in Shrewsbury, a small town near York, Pennsylvania. During this period, Smith affiliated with the Methodist Episcopal Church. Although the church tolerated her attendance, there were unspoken

Amanda Berry Smith

Source: *Center for African American History and Culture, Temple University.*

understandings about the "place" of Blacks. Smith noted that a black person could not "be led in class before a white person, [and] must wait till the white ones were through."[28] It did not matter where she sat; the class leader would call on her last and thus cause her to be late in returning to her job as a domestic. Finally, she had to choose between attending church and keeping her job—she chose the job.

In 1854, at the age of seventeen, she married her first husband, Calvin Devine, and moved to Lancaster, Pennsylvania. She soon discovered that her husband was a heavy drinker. In 1855, she became very ill and was expected to die. One day during that period of illness, she fell into a deep sleep, which she later described as "a kind of trance or vision." In this state, she encountered an angel and saw herself preaching at a large camp meeting attended by several thousand people. A year later on March 17, 1856, after a lengthy period of spiritual turmoil, Smith was converted.[29]

For the next six years, Smith continued to work in Lancaster and Columbia, Pennsylvania, as a domestic for several families. At some point, she and her husband separated. He later joined the Union army and died during the Civil War.

In 1862, she went to Philadelphia, where she worked for several years before meeting her second husband, James Smith, a local preacher and an ordained deacon in the AME Church. They soon moved to New York and it was not long before Amanda Smith discovered that she had again married the wrong man.

Emotionally abused by her husband, she sought counsel from Mother Jones, a member of Sullivan Street AME Church and a staunch believer in holiness. Jones told her that prior to sanctification, she had undergone the same trials with her husband. Jones asserted that "when God sanctified my soul He gave me enduring grace, and that is what you need; get sanctified, and then you will have enduring grace."[30] Reflecting on Jones's advice, Smith thought, "Is that what sanctification means? Enduring grace? That is just what I need; I have always been planning to get out of trials, instead of asking God for grace to endure."[31]

In New York, Smith affiliated with the Sullivan Street AME Church. One Sunday morning in September 1868, however, she attended a predominantly white church and heard the Reverend John Inskip preach about "instantaneous sanctification."[32] On that day, she testified to being sanctified and distinctly heard the words, "There is neither Jew nor Greek, there is neither bond nor free, there is neither male nor female, for ye are all one in Christ Jesus" (Gal. 3:28). These words took on new meaning for her. For the first time in her life, she confronted her fear of Whites.

Smith said, "Somehow I always had a fear of white people—that is, I was not afraid of them in the sense of doing me harm . . . —but a kind of fear because they were white, and were there, and I was black and was here!"[33]

After her husband died in 1869, Smith began conducting revivals primarily, but not exclusively, at black churches in New York and New Jersey. She met great resistance from black ministers, who felt that a woman should not preach or participate in any public ceremonial Church rites. With the support of a few ministers, she eventually won support for work as an evangelist. In October 1870, she left home "at God's command" to begin her evangelistic work.[34] Traveling throughout the Northeast from 1870 to 1878, she built up a national following by speaking at churches, revivals, and camp meetings.

Smith formally began her evangelistic career in Salem, New Jersey. According to Smith, God gave her a message that indirectly suggested sanctification as the subject of her sermon. Informed of Smith's topic, the widow of a former Salem preacher advised her, "Don't you say a word about sanctification here. Honey, if you do, they will persecute you to death. My poor husband used to preach that doctrine, and for years he knew about this blessing. But, Oh! honey, they persecuted him to death. You must not say a word about it."[35] Smith considered and prayed over this admonition, but she felt that she must obey God and suffer the consequences. To her amazement, that sermon spawned a series of revivals that spread throughout the area and lasted for several weeks.[36]

At the beginning of her preaching career, Smith showed no concern about being ordained. God had ordained her mission, and she was simply responding to the call. She later wrote that God "knew that the thought of ordination had never once entered my mind, for I had received my ordination from Him, Who said, 'Ye have not chosen Me, but I have chosen you, and ordained you, that you might go and bring forth fruit, and that your fruit might remain.'"[37]

As she gained notoriety as an evangelist and was identified as a preaching woman, the black male clergy became concerned about her motives and ambitions. In 1872, several AME ministers ridiculed Smith when she expressed interest in attending an AME General Conference. Ignoring the ministers' criticism, Smith raised money and attended the conference. The black male clergy and their "high toned" wives snubbed her and gossiped about her plain dress and purpose for attending. Smith recalled, "I was eyed with critical suspicion [sic] as being there to agitate the question of the ordination of women."[38] However, the victory belonged to Smith; when she attended the major public conference event, she was recognized, brought to the stage, and introduced as an important figure by the director of the Fisk Jubilee Singers, who had shared the stage with her on other occasions and recognized her as a significant person.

In July 1870, Smith attended the "National Camp Meeting Association for the Promotion of Holiness" in Oakington, Maryland. The meeting exposed Smith to the power of the Holiness movement, its role in the lives of prominent Whites, and the possibilities it held for women and African Americans. At the meeting, a white missionary spoke about her experiences in India. This impressed Smith with the possibility that African American women could do missionary work.[39]

During the next eight years, Smith regularly attended and participated in national camp meetings. From the beginning, she was the subject of much white attention. She was followed, stared at, and finally requested to sing and speak of her holiness experience. The camp meeting experience helped to eliminate her sense of being inferior to Whites and her fear of discrimination.[40]

Although the camp meeting experience reinforced the egalitarian nature of the Holiness movement, Smith experienced prejudice when she attended some white holiness meetings in New York and Philadelphia. Once, in New York during the early 1870s, some white women invited her to attend a lecture by Sarah Smiley, a noted Quaker speaker. Approaching Smiley to thank her for an enlightening address, Smith found her "rather cool." Smiley's assistant confronted Smith, asking, "Who told you to come here?" The woman barraged a speechless Smith with further insults and asked her to leave. Crying out of humiliation, Smith turned to go but was besieged by "so much sympathy and pity for me that they almost killed me. I cried, almost to convulsions. I was nearly dead. If they had not pitied me and seemed to feel so sorry for me, I could have got on well enough."[41]

This rejection changed after Smith became popular. Addressing this shift, Smith said, "Now, . . . instead of Amanda Smith, the colored washwoman's presence having a bad effect on a meeting where ladies of wealth and rank are gathered to pray and sing His blessing, they think a failure more possible if the same Amanda Smith, the colored woman, cannot be present."[42]

During the 1870s, Smith launched a career as a holiness evangelist that spanned several decades and brought her international acclaim. In 1878, she went to England for a three-week stay that lasted for twelve years, and also took her to Africa and India. Returning to the United States in 1890, she preached for several years before settling down in Chicago, where she wrote her memoirs and established a home for black orphans.

In the 1890s, Amanda Berry Smith became quite popular among white feminist reformers in the woman's rights and suffrage movements, who frequently invited her to sing. They valued her spirituality and used her presence in their midst as a symbol of their liberality. Unlike many of the noted educated and sophisticated black feminist reformers of the time, with whom these white women felt a certain discomfort, Smith was unschooled and quaint. Among white feminist reformers, her presence reinforced their sense of superiority.

As an international holiness evangelist and social reformer, Smith established an accepted role for women in the AME Church and helped expand women's role in the Methodist Church. When she died in 1915, she was compared to antislavery activist and publisher Frederick Douglass. Admirers hailed her contributions and oratorical skills as superior to those of the venerated leader.

Sojourner Truth

For many years, Sojourner Truth has been celebrated as the foremost nineteenth-century black preaching woman. The reality, however, is that during her lifetime and particularly during the period of her greatest spiritual activism, she was not well known among black people, nor was she accepted among African Americans as one of the major black female preachers. Although in the twentieth century the AME Zion Church helped perpetuate her name as a member of their denomination and as one of the foremost preaching women, their publications in the nineteenth and early twentieth centuries hardly mention her.

Born Isabella Baumfree, a slave in Ulster County, New York, around 1797, she was free by 1826. By 1829, she moved to New York City, where she worked as a domestic in white households.

Baumfree affiliated with several Methodist churches, including the predominantly white John Street Church, known as the mother church of American Methodism. She later joined the Zion Church, which had split from the John Street Church in protest against its refusal to ordain black ministers. Zion Church is known as the mother church of the AME Zion denomination.

Although Baumfree was exposed to black abolitionists and other activists in the AME Zion Church and the larger black community, she did not participate in any black organizations or work on behalf of any black causes. Slavery left Baumfree with a deep sense of inferiority—she was, after all, a farm girl who spoke in broken Dutch-English dialect—and contact with the urbane free Blacks of New York City reinforced her sense of alienation from the black community. Secretly longing to be an evangelist, Baumfree recognized that she would not be acceptable to Blacks, whom, she surmised, wanted to hear great preachers, not ignorant, inarticulate ones such as herself.[43]

Instead, she placed her faith in Whites, whom she felt could do more for her. Casting her lot with white Methodists, Baumfree became "'zealous' among Methodists, her style being to preach and pray long and loud."[44] Among white Methodists, and later white women activists, she was viewed and accepted as a highly spiritual, exotic black woman and received a measure of respect for her quaintness and unique insights. However, few Whites saw her as an equal; rather, they recognized very early that she could be a useful, nonthreatening symbol of their liberalness toward Blacks. In time, African Americans and women would also embrace her as a useful, multipurpose symbol.[45]

By 1831, Baumfree became involved with Elijah Pierson. A respected white merchant, he was also a biblical scholar given to fasting, faith healing, and preaching in his house. Employed by Pierson as a domestic, Baumfree joined him in his efforts to evangelize prostitutes. This work was not to her liking, however, because some Whites identified her too closely with the prostitutes.

By 1832, she and Pierson affiliated with Robert Matthias's utopian community, the Kingdom, which was a small cult group. Matthias was a strict cult leader who demanded obeisance from his followers, advocated faith healing, and observed strict ceremonial practices, including the washing and kissing of members' feet and sex between "match spirits" because marriages performed by ministers other than Matthias were not considered binding. Matthias believed that women were inferior and should not be allowed to pray or preach. He gave orders to all his followers and whipped those who disobeyed him. Baumfree allowed Matthias to whip her. She believed he was God on earth. The only black member of the Kingdom, Baumfree also worked as an unpaid domestic for Matthias. The Kingdom disintegrated after Pierson died mysteriously and Matthias was investigated and tried for murder; he was eventually acquitted.[46]

Like other black preaching women, Baumfree believed in the Holy Spirit and asserted that she had conversed with the Spirit for many years. On June 1, 1843, the day of Pentecost, she was converted and could no longer ignore the dramatic call of the Holy Ghost, a call that propelled her to change her name and become Sojourner Truth. Historian Nell Irvin Painter states, "On one level, 'Sojourner Truth' means itinerant preacher, for a sojourner is someone not at home, and truth is what preachers impart. She saw her mission as lecturing to the people, testifying and exhorting them to embrace Jesus, and refrain from sin."[47]

Unlike any other black women evangelists of this period, Truth had no known church or organizational connection. In the 1840s, it was unusual for a woman to speak or preach. Moreover, women did not travel alone and speak at will. This was unorthodox, dangerous behavior. Truth felt, however, that she had to leave the "wicked life" in New York and become an evangelist speaking on behalf of God. Thus, as Sojourner Truth, she left behind her family and her job and began her new life.[48]

Traveling to New England, Truth became an antislavery lecturer, speaking wherever the "spirit" directed or opportunity offered. In the late 1840s and 1850s, she gained a national reputation for her work in the antislavery movement. Her sharp mind, shrewd judgment, and powerful presence frequently turned the tide of action and thought at antislavery and suffrage meetings.

During the Civil War, Truth went to Washington to work in the relief effort for wounded soldiers and recently emancipated slaves. After the war, she settled in Battle Creek, Michigan, where she died in 1883.[49]

Conclusion

Elizabeth, Jarena Lee, Zilpha Elaw, Rebecca Cox Jackson, Amanda Berry Smith, and Sojourner Truth overcame ridicule and rejection, penury, fears of reenslavement and discrimination, and unhappy marriages, among other obstacles. After experiences with conversion and sanctification, in which the Holy Spirit commissioned them to preach, they each set out to answer this call. Nothing could deter them—not laws and attitudes that opposed women's preaching, not even geographical limits. These women spread their message throughout the Northeast, the mid-Atlantic states, the South, the Midwest, and even across oceans. Most of them preserved their thoughts and experiences in autobiographies, which inspired other preacher women of that period and in times to come. It is fortunate that they had the foresight to record their words, as all of these women's sermons have been lost to us.

Julia Foote, another nineteenth-century preacher, eloquently articulated the argument that all of these women embraced, the argument for the right of Christian women to preach: "I could not believe that it was a short-lived impulse or spasmodic influence that impelled me to preach. . . . If the power to preach the Gospel is short-lived and spasmodic in the case of women, it must be equally so in that of men; and if women have lost the gift of prophecy, so have men."[50]

Like the women in this chapter, Julia A. J. Foote, Harriet Baker, and Mary J. Small succeeded in their missions to preach. Their lives and sermons are the subjects of the next three chapters. Because some of their sermons have been uncovered, we can hear the voices of nineteenth-century preaching women and explore their feminist theology. By analyzing these sermons, we can begin to understand the preaching tradition among African American women and to determine the thematic linkages between the different generations of these preaching women.

2

JULIA A. J. FOOTE

She was a great preacher, an uncompromising advocate
of holiness, and [one] who practiced the gospel she preached.

—AME Zion Bishop Alexander Walters, *My Life and Work.*

BORN IN SCHENECTADY, NEW YORK, in 1823, the fourth child of former slaves, Julia Foote was among the pioneering black women preachers who began their careers before the Civil War. From 1833 to 1836, she
lived with a prominent white family who enrolled her in an integrated
country school, where she received a rudimentary education. In 1836, she
moved with her family to Albany, New York. Married at age sixteen to
George Foote, Julia moved to Boston, where she joined the AME Zion
Church pastored by the Reverend Jehiel C. Beman, a leading antislavery
orator and president of the Massachusetts Temperance Society of Colored
People. It was there that she began her much contested ministry. The
members of this church, like Julia, were former members of the Methodist
Episcopal Church who withdrew and affiliated with a black denomination in pursuit of greater religious freedom.

Although Foote had experienced conversion several years earlier, it was
in Boston that she was moved to exhort and pray publicly, and she
became committed to preaching the gospel. Ironically, for most of her life,
she had been opposed to women preaching and had spoken against it. She
did not relish facing the difficulties she knew existed for women preachers. But, as she later recalled, she was obligated to respond to the call that
had come in God's name.

Julia A. J. Foote

Source: *Atlanta University Archives.*

Foote ignored the gender conventions of her day and insisted on her right to preach. Her decision placed her in conflict with her family, friends, and black ministers, who challenged the right of women to preach. Choosing to pursue a ministerial career meant that Foote would be in contention for most of her life. However, she possessed an inordinate faith in herself and an unyielding determination to speak the truth. Her faith, determination, and eloquence as an evangelist were attested to by legions, both black and white, who turned out to hear her preach wherever she spoke.[1]

For more than fifty years, she served as an itinerant evangelist and a Methodist holiness preacher, traveling and lecturing widely at camp meetings, revivals, and churches in California, the Midwest, the Northeast, and Canada. Like the spiritual autobiographies of Zilpha Elaw and Jarena Lee, Foote's spiritual autobiography, A Brand Plucked from the Fire (1879), presents a strong feminist argument for including women preachers in the Christian Church polity.[2]

In 1895, Foote became the first woman to be ordained a deacon and in 1899 was the second woman to be ordained an elder in the AME Zion Church. She was a role model for black women aspiring to be ministers and one of the most forceful advocates for participatory equality and ordination of women in the Church.[3]

Foote remained active as a minister until around 1900. From 1884 until her death in 1901, she resided with Bishop Alexander Walters and his family. Foote assisted Walters during his ministry at the Stockton Street AME Zion Church in San Francisco (1883–1886), forging bonds with the Walters family that would last the rest of her life.[4]

Foote was exposed to the early waves of revivalism in western New York's notorious "Burned Over District." This exposure predisposed her to the Holiness movement, launched by believers in perfectionist doctrines of sanctification in the Methodist Church and in society who during the 1830s and 1840s were active in New York and Ohio. Perfectionists sought to rid the world of corruption. Like other early-nineteenth-century feminists touched by perfectionism, Foote attacked the evils of racism and male authoritarianism, as well as other societal issues.[5]

With the exception of Foote, none of the early black preaching women appear to have spoken directly of Christian perfection. Most of the preaching women and some of the most outspoken earlier reformers, black and white, believed in perfectionist doctrines of sanctification.[6] Few, if any, of these women disputed spiritual sanctification, for it was the most essential element to their self-empowerment and functioning as ministers. This is not to imply that their beliefs in sanctification were the same; there are clear differences in how these women perceived and practiced sanctification.

While Foote accepted perfection as a tenet of holiness, she said, "Do not misunderstand me. I am not teaching absolute perfection, for that belongs to God alone. Nor do I mean a state of angelic or Adamic perfection, but Christian perfection—an extinction of every temper contrary to love."[7]

Foote's Sermons

Two of Foote's sermons, "A 'Threshing' Sermon" and "Christian Perfection," are presented here. These sermons were written forty-three years apart.

"A 'THRESHING' SERMON." Foote delivered "A 'Threshing' Sermon" in 1851 in Detroit at the behest of a prominent man in the community, a self-proclaimed sinner concerned about saving his soul. She was asked to speak from Mic. 4:13: "Arise and thresh, O daughter of Zion." Invoking the holiness doctrine, she discusses the need for inner purification, the need to "thresh" out the devil and let in the Holy Ghost.

Foote's feminist sentiments underpin the sermon's emphasis on inner purification. Foote maintains that *all* of God's people, men and women, "are commanded to arise and thresh." Not only are all people called to "thresh out" their own sins, but they are also called to convict others of their iniquities so that all may accept God's gift of purification.

While later preaching women such as Randolph and Horn argue more directly that God calls on women to preach, Foote subtly affirms women preachers by highlighting Joel 2:28–29, which emphasizes that both men and women will receive God's spirit in "the Gospel times," enabling them to do God's work. Foote's underlying message is that she, and women like her, are fulfilling this prophecy by following the call to "arise and thresh," despite the strong societal opposition to preaching women. She boldly thanks Jesus that this ancient prophecy—that God will lift up women as well as men to positions of spiritual leadership—has indeed become a reality.

Foote had no doubt heard the common argument that women's supposed spiritual, mental, and physical weaknesses made them inadequate and even dangerous religious leaders. In the "threshing" sermon, while never directly referring to these attacks on preaching women, Foote clearly undercuts any such sentiments. Foote argues that God will provide "supernatural aid to the faithful that they might perform for him those services for which their own feeble and unassisted powers were totally inadequate."

Her skillful analysis of Scripture reveals to her audience that it is unbiblical for anyone, male or female, to rely on human powers in performing God's work. Referring to the metaphorical oxen hooves and horns of Mic. 4:13 ("Arise and thresh, O daughter of Zion: for I will make thine horn iron, and I will make thy hoofs brass"), Foote argues that God provides strength beyond individuals' "natural" capacities, for "the text promised an addition to the natural horny substance on the feet of these animals, by making the horn iron and the hoof brass." Just as oxen with indestructible horns and hooves would be perfect for threshing corn, all of God's people will be unassailable threshers of the soul if only they "go to God, who alone is able to qualify them for their labors by making their horns iron and their hoofs brass."

Paralleling the hooves and horns with a more modern threshing instrument, the flail, Foote states that the flail "is one of the weapons which [God] employs in the hands of his people to carry his gracious designs into execution." Thus, while human beings may be weak, God has provided them, both male and female, with "weapons both offensive and defensive" for waging the spiritual battle against sin.

In order to rely on God's powers to become powerful threshers, men and women must die to their old selves. Here, Foote echoes the apostle Paul's message—which she directly addresses in her later sermon, "Christian Perfection"—that Christians must die to sin in order to live in Christ. The process of crucifying one's worldly self through threshing out the devil is painful to the "unhumbled soul." As Foote explains in another reference to Mic. 4:13, threshing "shall beat in pieces many people," as impurities are cast out of their souls. Thus, God's weapons for threshing "may seem contemptible in the eyes of the natural man."

However, Foote proclaims, Christ's atonement for sins "is the greatest weapon" against human beings' resistance to the painful process of purification. Quoting Rev. 12:11, which states that because of "the blood of the Lamb" God's people "loved not their lives unto the death," Foote argues that Christ transforms people so that they may die to their natural, sinful selves and live in a state of purity. The natural state of being pales in comparison with life in Christ. Thus, while the image of the flail may seem contemptible, threshing is nevertheless "a kind and loving" act, for it is only after one has had the devil cast out that one may hope "that Christ may live and reign in me without a rival."

Since both men and women must die to their natural selves to become purified in Christ, as God commands, both men and women may receive God's power work as God's threshers. Quoting Isa. 23:18 and 60:6–9, which describe the riches that "will be set apart for the Lord," in conjunction with her explanation of threshing, Foote reveals that it is only through the tireless work of all of God's people toward the goal of purification that the harvest may be gathered up for God's kingdom.

"CHRISTIAN PERFECTION." The second sermon, "Christian Perfection," was published in the *Star of Zion* in 1894. It expresses Foote's belief that perfection, a holiness tenet, was misunderstood and had become unpopular among Christians. She argues that the use of the term *perfection* and the practice of Christian perfectionism suffered greatly because of the beliefs and practices of various groups. In particular, she criticized the practitioners in the western New York Burned Over District, the Oneida Perfectionists, and the Roman Catholic Church for bringing the word "into disrepute."[8]

Foote's critique of these groups is indirectly a commentary on Rebecca Cox Jackson, who demanded celibacy for those who claimed sanctification; on Sojourner Truth, who joined the Kingdom of Matthias, led by a Prophet Matthias who represented himself as God and predicted that the world would end on a certain date; and on the Millerite movement, whose leader, "Father" William Miller, held beliefs similar to those of Prophet Matthias.[9]

Although Foote chose the Roman Catholic Church as the example of what she considered extremism in defining perfectionist practice, one can easily apply this interpretation to any number of lesser groups that at that time required vows of poverty, chastity and obedience to superiors as proof of Christian perfection.

By distancing herself from the perfectionist doctrines and practices of the Burned Over District's holiness adherents (one of the most prominent antebellum groups), the Oneida Perfectionists (perhaps the best known and one of the most successful perfectionist associations), and the Roman Catholic Church (one of the most powerful religious denominations, and one that, by 1890, was deemed a threat to Methodism), Foote casts the argument in such a way as to avoid offending black Methodists. She also aligns herself with the leaders of the Protestant Reformation—most significantly with John Wesley—in her attempt to encourage the AME and AME Zion ministers to incorporate the holiness doctrine into their preaching.[10]

She argues that the perfectionist doctrine is truly a part of the Protestant heritage, stating that even though Martin Luther broke away from the Catholics, "He did not throw overboard the idea of perfection, but insisted that it did not consist in celibacy, beggary and filthy clothing, but in utter self abnegation and love." She thus shows that her adherence to perfectionism, despite her critique of the Roman Catholic practice of perfectionism, is supported by the theology of John Wesley, the father of Protestantism.

In addition to drawing from Martin Luther's theology, her reference to John Wesley is key, for Methodism is based upon Wesleyan theology. She stresses that John Wesley's doctrine of perfectionism was "better" than even the doctrine of Martin Luther, stating that "Luther's idea of ardent love was not quite up to Wesley's perfect love." Wesley's doctrine of "perfect love" stresses sanctification (or the gift of moral perfection), which God offers to Christians when he justifies, or forgives, their sins. Christians' sins can be forgiven and sanctified because Christ died in their place for their iniquities. Wesley proclaims that God's saving grace, and the resulting sanctification of Christians, is freely offered to all people, a theological tenet that directly opposes John Calvin's teaching that grace is available only to the "select" few. In addition to Wesley's assertion that all people can be justified and made righteous through Christ, he argued that this gift of righteousness transforms Christians so that they will be able to love God and neighbor perfectly. Christian perfection is attained, therefore, through sanctification, which makes possible the lifelong work of loving others, just as God perfectly loves.

It was of utmost importance to preaching women such as Foote to ensure that the doctrine of Christian perfection did not fall into disrepute among the Methodists and other prominent denominations, for it was this doctrine—that all may be sanctified in order to do God's work of love— that legitimized the ministry of preaching women. Foote is thus meticulous in building her argument that the doctrine of perfection, which Luther and Wesley upheld, is central to the message of the gospel.

She states that even though the doctrine has fallen out of favor in modern times, it is crucial that "the nineteenth century should be adapted to the gospel" in this matter, for in Jesus' teachings it is clear that "perfection is not a privilege only, it is mandatory." Foote quotes Matt. 5:48 in which Jesus admonishes his followers, "Be ye therefore perfect, even as your Father which is in heaven is perfect." She asserts that this text makes clear that focusing on Christian perfection is the "duty of a true preacher." She argues that the apostle Paul, the quintessential preacher of the Christian faith, was so successful in his ministry because he took seriously the call of Christ to perfection, and sought "to present every man perfect in Christ Jesus" (Col. 1:28).

In this sermon, Foote strategically aligns the doctrine of perfection, as well as her ministry (which was based on this doctrine), with Christ's teachings, the apostle Paul's ministry, and Luther's and Wesley's theologies. The sermon therefore brilliantly poses a hefty challenge to those who would reject the preaching of perfection.

A 'THRESHING' SERMON

TEXT: Micah 4:13; Joel 2:28–29;
Isaiah 23:18, 60:6–9; Revelation 12:11

[In] 710 B.C. corn was threshed among the Orientals by means of oxen or horses, which were driven round an area filled with loose sheaves. By their continued tramping the corn was separated from the straw. That this might be done the more effectually, the text promised an addition to the natural horny substance on the feet of these animals, by making the horn iron and the hoof brass.

Corn is not threshed in this manner by us, but by means of flails, so that I feel I am doing no injury to the sentiment of the text by changing a few of the terms into which are the most familiar to us now. The passage portrays the Gospel times, though in a more restricted sense it applies to the preachers of the word. Yet it has a direct reference to all God's people, who were and are commanded to arise and thresh. Glory to Jesus! now is this prophecy fulfilled (Joel 2:28–29). They are also commanded to go to God, who alone is able to qualify them for their labors by making their horns iron and their hoofs brass. The Lord was desirous of imparting stability and perpetuity to his own divine work, by granting supernatural aid to the faithful that they might perform for him those services for which their own feeble and unassisted powers were totally inadequate. More than this, it is encouraging to the saints to know that they are provided with weapons both offensive and defensive.

The threshing instrument is of the former description. It is of the same quality as that which is quick and powerful and sharper than any two-edged sword. "For this purpose the Son of God was manifested, that he might destroy the works of the devil," and this is one of the weapons which he employs in the hands of his people to carry his gracious designs into execution, together with the promise that they shall beat in pieces many people [Mic. 4:13; Isa. 23:18; 60:6–9].

There are many instances of the successful application of the Gospel flail, by which means the devil is threshed out of sinners. With the help of God, I am resolved, O sinner to try what effect the smart strokes of this threshing instrument will produce on thy unhumbled soul. This is called the sword of the Spirit, and is in reality the word of God. Such a weapon may seem contemptible in the eyes of the natural man; yet, when it is powerfully wielded, the consequences are invariably potent and salutary.

Bless God! the Revelator says: "They overcame by the blood of the Lamb and by the word of their testimony; and they loved not their lives unto the death" (Rev. 12:11). The atonement is the greatest weapon. In making trial of its efficacy, little children have caused the parent to cry aloud for mercy; but, in every case, much of its heavenly charm and virtue depends upon the mode in which it is applied.

This Gospel flail should be lifted up in a kind and loving spirit. Many shrink at [the] sight of the flail, and some of us know, by blessed experience, that when its smart strokes are applied in the power and demonstration of the Holy Spirit, it causes the very heart to feel sore and painful. Penitent soul, receive the castigation, and you will feel, after it, like saying: "Now let me be crucified, and this work of the devil, inbred sin, put to death, that Christ may live and reign in me without a rival."

CHRISTIAN PERFECTION

Text: Matthew 5:48; Colossians 1:28;
1 Corinthians 3:13; Mark 8:38

Dear Editor of the Star:—Because I have but *one* talent I don't see why I should give it to your contributors that have ten. The Lord helping me I shall use it in offering a few thoughts on the all important subject of "Christian Perfection," etc.

(Matt. 5:48). "If a minister were as faithful in speaking the truth in these days, and in denouncing sin as Christ was in His day, he would sacrifice his life"—Dr. Parker, London, Eng[land].

The duty of a true preacher:—"Warning every man and teaching every man in all wisdom, that we may present every man perfect in Christ Jesus" (Col. 1:28).

"Every man's work shall be made manifest, for the day shall declare it because it shall be realized by fire and the fire shall try every man's work, of what sort it is" (1 Cor. 3:13).

The great object of the ministry of the Apostle Paul was to present every man perfect in Christ Jesus; this master purpose was the secret of his wonderful success.

I know it is said [that] the gospel is not adapted to the nineteenth century; men are different now from what they were. Yes, they may be different externally but essentially they are the same. What man was, man is; what man needed he needs still.

No, the Gospel is not adapted to any century; it wasn't intended to be. It was intended that the nineteenth century should be adapted to the gospel. Our work is not to make the truths of the Bible fit into all the crooks and crevices of the lives and beliefs of men. We are to stamp, not overlay; to coin, not gild. There are peculiarities of the times that will require special methods of delivering the truth and special truth. We may be debarred entrance to many pulpits (as some of us now are) and stand at the door or on the street corner in order to preach to men and women. No difference when or where, we must preach a whole gospel.

I think the words of the text are the greatest words that the Lord Jesus ever uttered: "Be ye therefore perfect, even as your Father in heaven is perfect." I think we may [emphasize] the word "ye"; every Greek scholar knows that is the emphatic word, for where the pronouns are used emphasis is always meant.

The revised version reads, "Ye shall be perfect." So perfection is not a privilege only, it is mandatory. There are two ways of commanding; one is to say "Do!" and the other "Thou shalt do." It is a little stronger to say, "John, you shall go to school!" than "John, go to school."

Most of the commandments use the emphatic "Thou shalt!" Jesus revised the law and put Himself on a par with the lawgiver: "I came not to destroy but to fulfill." He came to fill it full of meaning, to show its height and depth and breadth and length.

The "ye" must be put in contrast to what goes before, viz: the usages of the publicans and worldly men. The publicans are represented as loving those who love them. We conclude that the "therefore" is confined to the exposition of the law of love and hatred.

What is the meaning of perfect? It is a great word. We ought honestly to inquire what is meant by it. It is used very frequently in the New Testament, also in the Old, and is used more times in the Revised New Testament than in the King [James] version. Regeneration is used only twice in the New Testament, and only once with reference to the reconstruction of human character; the second being used with reference to the reconstruction of human society. If preachers would observe the same proportions in preaching that the Scriptures do, they would preach twenty-five sermons on Perfection to one on Regeneration. but if a man to-day reverses the order and preaches every twenty-fifth sermon on Christian Perfection, people [would] call him a hobbyist.

We are tempted to omit the use of the word perfection; then we turn to the Bible and read the 38th verse of the 8th chapter of Mark. The life blood of Jesus is in His words; cut them and they will bleed; neglect them and you neglect Him. We are to find out their meaning as well as we can by study and prayer, but not to reject or neglect them. Behind every word of Jesus is a doctrine—a meaning deep and high.

Preachers have been tempted to skip this word because it has been abused. We notice some sources of abuse.

First. The Human Conscience seems to rise up and object to the use of this word. We feel so imperfect.

Second. Because it has been treated as a specialty; special meetings have been held and special periodicals issued to promote it. I believe it is a better way for every pulpit to preach the whole gospel. But if this doctrine drops out of the pulpit, what is to be done? Dr. Curry says a doctrine dropped out of the pulpit is lost in a generation.[11] Preachers had better be specialists than go to judgement having neglected this doctrine.

Third. The word has been brought into disrepute by various parties. There was a people in Western New York who professed to get so near

God that they had no need of prayer; their whole life was a prayer. They did not use the sacraments or the Bible; every meal was a sacrament, the Holy Spirit was their teacher.

Then there were the Oneida Perfectionists. They became so perfect that they invented the monstrous idea of complex marriages. By such means the word perfection has been brought into disrepute.

The Roman Catholics have helped to make the word unpopular. They teach that we should withdraw from society to monasteries and nunneries if we would attain perfection; we must take the vows of poverty, chastity and obedience to superiors.

The devil is a good climber; brick and mortar can not keep him out.

Thank God when Martin Luther began he did not throw overboard the idea of perfection, but insisted that it did not consist in celibacy, beggary and filthy clothing, but in utter self abnegation and love.

John Wesley afterwards did better. Luther's idea of ardent love was not quite up to Wesley's perfect love.

Calvin threw the whole doctrine overboard by putting it off till death. His followers have been against the doctrine as attainable in the present life.

Arminius taught (article 6) that every believer may be certain or assured of his own salvation, and (7) it is possible for a regenerate man to live without sin.

The Westminster Catechism taught that in the moment of death men are sanctified. Their only proof text is "The spirits of just men made perfect." But the men, and not the spirits, were made perfect, and the time is not named in the proof text.

3

HARRIET A. BAKER

THE 1987 REPRINT OF *The Colored Lady Evangelist* reintroduced scholars to Harriet A. Baker, a once well-known late-nineteenth-century AME preacher. Appointed by the Philadelphia AME Conference in 1889 "to take charge of the St. Paul's Church on Tenth Street, in the city of Lebanon, Pa.," Baker, an evangelist, is perhaps the first black woman to be appointed to pastor a church.[1] In her spiritual biography, first published in 1892, Baker talks about her conversion experience; her struggle to answer the call to preach; overcoming bitter opposition from her husband, church, friends, and relatives; and her triumph in the ministry. The experiences she recounts are very similar to those related by Amanda Berry Smith, Julia Foote, and other preaching women during that era.

In 1829, Harriet A. Baker was born free to William and Harriet Cole in Havre de Grace, Maryland. William's death in 1840 left the mother with seven children to rear. To protect Harriet from kidnappers who actively stalked free black children to sell to southern slaveholders, her mother hired her out as a domestic. Although Harriet held many jobs, for several years she worked for a Mrs. Bailey, who was quite fond of her.

In 1845, at the age of sixteen, Harriet married William Baker, a fugitive slave. The Bakers settled in Columbia, Pennsylvania, a lumber region with a population of approximately eight thousand people. Harriet and her husband secured jobs at the local mill. Demand and wages for laborers were high. Within a year, the Bakers had built a home and purchased furnishings. Within three years, they retired the debt for the house.

Congress passed the Fugitive Slave Bill in 1850, giving slave owners the right to pursue and retrieve their "property." In 1851, Harriet's husband became the first slave to be captured and sent back to slavery under the law. William Baker was tried, found guilty, and returned to his master. With the help of friends, Harriet raised $750 to purchase her husband's freedom.

Harriet A. Baker

Source: *Center for African American History and Culture, Temple University.*

Although there is no written testimony of her fealty to the holiness doctrine, Harriet Baker described her conversion experience, which occurred in 1842. When Harriet was thirteen, her mother took her to a prayer meeting. About sixteen women were present in a small room, which they locked and barred. The women sang and prayed, and two of them fell to the dirt floor. The other women surrounded them and fell to their knees, singing and praying. Harriet, a fastidious girl who liked dancing and fine clothing, was very concerned about getting her dress dirty, so she avoided getting on her knees. She states that as she leaned against a fireplace and braced herself, "The power of God struck me down."[2] In that state, she experienced God and was converted. According to Harriet, she knew nothing about God or the Bible before 1842. Her exposure to religion had been very slight. On one occasion she had heard her mother and other women praying and talking to God. Harriet states that following her conversion, God "taught me by his spirit to read his holy Word, and not only to read it, but to understand it also."[3]

In the winter of 1872, Harriet announced that she intended to preach. The members of her church asserted that God did not intend women to preach. Her pastor spoke against her from the pulpit and spoke privately to her about the decision. Her friends and husband tried, to no avail, to dissuade her. Her husband said he would never forgive her if she left and something happened to their two daughters, ages eleven and thirteen.[4] Shortly afterward, the daughters became ill and died.

After the death of her daughters, Baker had a vision in which a voice "seemed to say, Go now or you shall die."[5] Although she experienced renewed opposition, was verbally abused by her class leader, and was told to leave the Church, Harriet determined that she had received "Divine commission" to preach the gospel.[6] The Church reeled in opposition and held an open discussion about her announcement, but she would not leave, for she had made a "solemn covenant" with God to hold fast to her decision. It was her perception that God stilled the opposition. Several years later, around 1874 or 1875, the Church authorized her to preach.[7]

At the time of the verbal abuse and the highly charged church discussion, as she sat with her head bowed, she had a vision of being carried away to Calvary, where she saw three crosses. She imagined that she was standing in a field and that Simon, the Cyrenian who bore Christ's cross, guided her to a mountain. There, she saw Jesus, who spoke to her and said he had come to deliver her. In ecstasy, she arose, praised God, and "shouted glory! glory! glory!" The church was filled with God's presence, which quelled the opposition. Her sister testified to seeing a light streaming through the church. And her husband and others not present in the church felt a shock throughout the town. Harriet later said that "the universal cry the next day was 'loose the woman, and let her go.'"[8]

Confirmed in her decision to preach, Harriet packed her clothing and left her husband and three children (ages four, six, and eight). When she boarded the train, she had no plan or particular destination in mind. Miraculously, she was befriended by a Mr. Getts, a white butcher who took her home, fed her, and introduced her to the Reverend Mr. Brown, pastor of the Evangelical Church in Brownstown, Pennsylvania. There, she began her ministry, preaching to white evangelicals who welcomed her with open arms. She held a revival that lasted for three weeks and witnessed the conversion of seventy-two people.[9]

Although we know little about Harriet Baker's beliefs in the holiness doctrine, and neither her spiritual biography nor the sermons "Behold the Man" and "Jesus Weeping over Jerusalem" speak directly to this issue, her biographer stated that she "firmly believes that she was directed by the Holy Spirit to enter upon her mission IN THIS MANNER AND IN THIS PLACE and wonderfully did the Lord show her the way."[10]

Baker returned home and reported her experience preaching in white churches and her success in converting sinners. Impressed that white religionists had graciously received her and that God approved of her ministry, as signified by the overwhelming number of conversions, the pastor and members of the all-black AME Church sanctioned her ministry.

Between 1874 and 1889, Harriet Baker served as an evangelist, speaking actively at camp meetings and conducting revivals. She developed quite a reputation among white and black ministers and spoke widely in the churches of both groups. This may partly explain how in 1889, the AME Conference appointed her to the pastorate of St. Paul's Church in Lebanon, Pennsylvania. This appointment followed the denomination's decision to license evangelists. There are no other known examples of a woman's pastoring a church at this early date. However, she may have been assigned this church because no man wanted it. Upon her arrival, she discovered a church with few members and encumbered by an overwhelming debt.

In 1897, Baker settled in Allentown, Pennsylvania. By that time, her fame had spread throughout the East Coast. Although she continued to travel and preach, she based her operations in Allentown, where she established the Bethel Mission. Built in 1900, the mission was housed in a two-story structure. The first floor included an auditorium with a pulpit and benches, and the second floor served as Baker's residence. Blacks and Whites traveled from as far away as New England to hear Baker preach and sing. Baker died in 1913 at the age of eighty-three.[11]

Baker's Sermons

Baker delivered the sermons "Behold the Man" and "Jesus Weeping over Jerusalem" between 1874 and 1892. As an extremely popular evangelist, especially among Whites, Baker was frequently invited to preach at camp meetings during the summer and at revivals during the winter.

"BEHOLD THE MAN." In "Behold the Man," Baker speaks of Jesus' betrayal and crucifixion. She admonishes her listeners to "look to Jesus" for deliverance, not to the preacher. The minister is only Jesus' mouthpiece, the bearer of the word. As Jesus hangs on the cross, his faith in God shows humans what is possible if they believe.

While Baker never directly refers to the holiness doctrine in her sermons, her belief that only God can sanction one to preach, and that sanctification frees one from the constraints of society's authorities, is clearly present in her sermons on Christ's passion and crucifixion. Her sermons reveal a social message beyond their obvious invitation to the audience to accept Christ's death for their salvation, for she brilliantly orchestrates powerful, if subtle, challenges to her audience's suspicions of female religious leaders.

In the beginning of "Behold the Man," Baker likens her call to preach to that of the apostle Paul, when she states, "But a cry for help came from Macedonia, and here I am in response to that cry." In this reference to Acts 16:9, in which the apostle Paul envisions a man who begs him to preach the gospel in Macedonia, Baker asserts not only the legitimacy of her role as a God-ordained preacher but also the importance of her message for the congregation's spiritual and social well-being. Immediately following her reference to Paul's vision, she again emphasizes the importance of her preaching role by likening herself to a horn. She evokes the image of the ram's horn in Exod. 19:13, with which God signaled for Moses to lead his people to Mount Sinai to receive the covenant.

Having asserted her authority as God's messenger, Baker vividly narrates the story of Christ's passion, or suffering, before and during his crucifixion. The challenge underlying Baker's message—that one may be called by God to be a religious leader, despite opposition from one's community, established religious superiors, and society—is powerfully present in her analysis of Christ's passion. She emphasizes how Jesus was rejected by the religious authorities of his day, despite the purity of his ministry and message. Affirming the superiority of God-given authority over worldly authority, she states that "when the priests and the scribes demanded his authority for what [Jesus] did, he put them to shame before all the people by the wisdom of his reply." Baker leaves the audience to remember Jesus' reply and that his authority came from God. Thus, Baker's holiness doctrine continually surfaces in her sermon.

To appreciate fully Baker's haunting, melancholy description of Christ's rejection and torture, one must understand the social context in which she and her black female peers lived. As Blacks, they were denied full human status in society, and as women, they were denied this status in their own communities. Baker's words echo the suffering this caused them when she states that Christ was "denied the protection of the three homes which [were] his by birth, by residence, and by adoption." Baker repeatedly describes how Jesus' selfless ministry to the world was "not enough to secure him acceptance." In this mournful incantation, one can see the tragic dimensions of black preaching women's lives refracted in Baker's retelling of Christ's passion.

In addition to emphasizing the tragic depths of Christ's suffering, Baker evokes a sense of awe about her pain. She states that "the betrayal, the arrest, the arraignment, the false accusation, the mockery, the denial, the scourging, the final sentence, and its execution, must all unite to make up the meaning of that most sacred and awful mystery, the cross of Christ."

As she concludes "Behold the Man," Baker reveals her conviction that the suffering of those who follow God's call is sacred. Baker declares that the actual place where Jesus was betrayed continues to be covered with olive trees, whose "bent and twisted" trunks reflect "the [tortures] of centuries," and are thus "undoubtedly the most fitting monuments, if any be needed to make the ground sacred." Though suffering may leave one bent and twisted like the trunks of olive trees, it is sacred when it reflects Christ's passion as he fulfilled God's divine plan.

In her last sentence, Baker deliberately affirms women's unique identification with this awesome and sacred passion of Christ as she states that Christ died not only amid "the mockery of the multitude who clamored for his death" but also amid "the wails of the daughters of Jerusalem." While tragic, the wails are also awesome as they reflect these women's devotion to God, despite all opposition from religious and social authorities.

"JESUS WEEPING OVER JERUSALEM." In "Jesus Weeping over Jerusalem," Baker describes Jesus' triumphant entry into Jerusalem, and his sorrow because he knows that within a short time, the same people who welcomed him will call for him to be crucified on the cross. He weeps because he knows that many have repudiated his appeal to humankind, and that their actions will bring them everlasting sorrow, shame, and suffering. Baker carefully analyzes why and how Jesus died. She presents his death as a "great crowning event" that contains specific messages for humankind.

In "Jesus Weeping over Jerusalem," Baker revisits several of the themes she addressed in "Behold the Man." Baker touched on the story of Jesus' weeping over Jerusalem in "Behold the Man," and she returns to the story in this later sermon to explore its full significance. Through her retelling of this story, she again illuminates the dual triumph and tragedy of Christ's passion, emphasizing Jesus' earthly rejection as well as the adulation that would be his in heaven. She deliberately focuses on biblical women's openness to God's call to faith and action. As she did in "Behold the Man," she thereby carefully presents her sermon in a way that will challenge any doubts about her presence at the pulpit.

She begins "Jesus Weeping over Jerusalem" by emphasizing that Jesus wept at his rejection not because "his work has failed," but because the people rejected him "to their own [destruction]." While in "Behold the Man" Baker reveals that earthly rejection does not invalidate God's call to religious leadership, in "Jesus Weeping over Jerusalem" Baker uses the story of Christ's passion to stress that earthly rejection does not, in the end, hurt the one who is rejected, only those who blindly spurn the messenger of salvation.

The significance of Jesus' story, as Baker presents it, is not only that he provides salvation for the life to come but also that he serves as a model for living a pure and godly life here on earth. Fully aware that he will experience utmost rejection and grave suffering on earth, Jesus nevertheless voluntarily goes forth with God's plan, for he knows that "sorrow . . . shall give place to joy when he shall look back upon the travail of his soul, and be satisfied, with the fruits of his toil and suffering." Baker meticulously makes her point that no one in her audience can use personal suffering, no matter how great, to shrink from God's work. Baker proclaims, "How light are all our crosses, what are they all compared with the sufferings of Christ! . . . Whatever may come upon us it is not fit to be spoken of on the same day on which we speak of our Saviour's death."

She extensively examines Christ's passion—the voluntary sacrifice, the shame, the pain, the solitude, the brutality. She argues that, after all that Christ suffered for the atonement of our sins, we should "hate our sins and put them all to death." Invoking the holiness doctrine here in a manner similar to Foote, Baker stresses the importance of attaining inner purification through accepting Christ—to die to sin and live in Christ. She asserts that the blood of Christ will make those who follow Christ indestructible. Evoking stories from the Old Testament—the story in Exod. 12 of how God spared the Israelites who sprinkled lamb's blood over their door, and the story in Josh. 2 of how the Israelites spared Rahab's family when she displayed a scarlet thread on her door—Baker interprets these red markers as symbols of Christ's atonement, just as the early Church did, and declares, "All is safe when the blood of remission is applied."

Clearly revealing her social message in the conclusion, Baker quotes 1 John 3:16: "Hereby perceive we the love of God because he laid down his life for us, and we ought to lay down our lives for the brethren." Christ's life should be an inspiration to follow God's call to holy living, despite all opposition, for "we need no fairer argument for love to our brethren, than is drawn from Christ's love in dying for us."

Baker's reference to Rahab in her conclusion is significant, for through this reference, she subtly affirms women as spiritual leaders. Just as she illuminates women's unique identification with Christ's passion by referring in "Behold the Man" to the "daughters of Jerusalem," she illuminates women's faith and action as followers of Christ in her reference to Rahab in "Jesus Weeping over Jerusalem." In the New Testament, Rahab—the Canaanite who, out of faith in God, risked her life to help the Israelites invade Jericho—is hailed as a model for followers of Christ, because of both her faith (Heb. 11:31) and actions (James 2:25). As only a women preacher could, Baker resurrects the honor the early Christians bestowed upon Rahab and states that just as the "scarlet thread in [Rahab's] house protected her from all harm at the fall of Jericho, so all the prisoners go forth by the blood of the covenant." Baker shows that Christians should not only *accept* that sanctified women fully participate in God's divine plan but should actually *follow* the examples of those women whose devotion to God has been unsurpassed.

BEIIOLD THE MAN

Text: John 19:5

I repeat the text "Behold the Man," and in order to give you an idea of what gave rise to it, it is necessary to read the foregoing chapter. . . . [She reads John 19:4.]

I now call attention to this man, mentioned in the text, and I wish you all to give special attention, as the constant labor of five months has almost broken me down. But a cry for help came from Macedonia, and here I am in response to that cry. I ask you all to pray. Do pray now as there is hard work to be done. Pray now if ever. Look to Jesus, and not to me; see him by faith as he hangs on the cross in the last act of atonement, and get the blessing of Jesus, the man of my text. I think of myself as resembling a horn; as nothing but a horn. You all know what a horn is and the uses that are made of it. The horn talks the sentiments of the person blowing it; it may sound the alarm of fire, of murder, or of danger; or it may give the glad sound of invitation to dinner to some half-starved soul who is hungering for the richness of the Master's table, where all may freely partake of the bread of everlasting life.

I will consider my text from three principal points:

1st. Jesus in his power and might.

2nd. Jesus in his meekness.

3rd. Jesus in his humiliation.

Jesus was the Immaculate Son of God. Look at him as he was before the world was. When the wonders of creation were taking place, Jesus was there. When the Lord divided the waters from the dry land, and gave to the ocean its "metes and bounds," Jesus was there. When the darkness was driven away, and the glorious light beamed forth upon a new born world, Jesus was there. When the stars and planets were given their positions, and orbits, in the immensity of space, Jesus was there. When God said "Let us make man in, our image, after our likeness," Jesus was there. When God created the fishes which swim in the mighty ocean, and the beautiful lakes, and the winding rivers, and the mountain streams, Jesus was there. When the beasts of the field were made, and the birds of the air sent forth their first notes of praise, Jesus was there. And dear friends I want you to hear to-day of his atonement for the sins of the world, and his ascension to heaven, where he has prepared a home for all his people. Glory to God for the atonement and for the resurrection.

On the sixth day of creation man was made in the image of God, male and female, and given the injunction to be fruitful, multiply, and replenish the earth. Upon the empty air this earth was well balanced, and with joy Jesus saw the mansion where the sons of men should dwell. Yes, this same Jesus was with the Father at the foundation of the world, and shall be with him until the last, for he is the first and the last. Truly when the morning stars sang together and the sons of God shouted for joy, this great Saviour of mine was there, and he was yet there when God made man, and when man fell from that happy sate of purity, and was driven from that beautiful garden, he was yet there with man in his unhappy condition, and promised him salvation. And when the angels made the search in heaven to find one that could open the book, and read the contents thereof, this same Jesus came forth as a lamb from under the altar. And when the question was asked "who is worthy to open the book?" Jesus was there, and as the angels listened, and John wept at the revelation, a voice was heard saying "weep not!" and the four and twenty elders sang a new song, saying, "Thou art worthy to take the book, and to open the seal thereof: for thou wast slain, and hast redeemed us to God by the blood, out of every kindred, and tongue, and people, and nation." And thank God, Jesus came, and redeemed us, and he has been with his church ever since, and he fights for her to-day.

Oh! how I do thank the Lord for the gift of his Son, and for the gift of the Holy Ghost, how he taught me to pray, and to read and understand his holy word. And as the poet says,

> Grace led my roving feet,
> To tread the heavenly road,
> And new supplies each hour I meet
> While pressing on to God.
>
> Grace found me when I was in my sins,
>   and I was led to realize, and
> Know that the Lord is God alone:
> He can create, and He [can] destroy.

He is the foundation of all wisdom, upon the plain of wisdom this world was founded, and by the wisdom of God the sun, and moon, and stars, were made, and keep their regular course, and do not run one against the other. It is by the wisdom of God that the sun revolves in his place. It is by the wisdom of God that we move and live. Oh! how I do thank him for his grace, and for his wisdom, that he has given unto me.

I can say in truth, all glory belongs to him. Wisdom cried aloud. It is the voice of God's eternal Son. And deserves it no regard? I hear the voice of Jesus saying,

> I was my Father's chief delight,
> His everlasting Son,
> Before the first of all his works,
> Or creation was begun;
> Before the flying clouds,
> Before the solid land,
> Before the fields, before the flood:
> I dwelt at his right hand.

When he adorned the skies, and built them; when he ordained the time for the sun to rise and set, and when he marshalled every star, I was there.

> When he poured out the sea,
> And spread the roaring deep,
> He gave the flood a firm decree,
> And its own bounds to keep,

But I want to speak of Jesus in his meekness.

Driven from Bethlehem by the wrath of a king, expelled from Nazareth by the violence of the people, received at Capernaum at first, only to be rejected at last, denied the protection of the three homes which was his by birth, by residence, and by adoption.

Jesus comes to Jerusalem to be betrayed, and to Calvary to die. Thirty years of retirement, and three years of public ministry, and yet all that the world will endure of its Messiah is not enough to secure him acceptance. It is not enough that he heals the sick, and feeds the hungry, and raises the dead. It is not enough that he speaks as never a man spake, and does the works which never a man did. It is not enough that he endures the contradiction of sinners with the meekness and majesty of infinite love. He must go down to a still lower depth of humiliation. He must take upon his soul the burden of a great agony, he must give his very life in sacrifice, before the strong walls of prejudice, and hatred, and unbelief will yield, and give him access to the hearts of men. We have something to learn from every step which he takes, as he approaches the great sacrifice of calvary. He had returned to Bethany for the night, the first decisive step towards the great sacrifice had been taken; he had showed himself the object of supreme interest to the multitude: and so had excited the envy and hatred of the customary leaders to the highest degree; he had come once more within their reach, they had already entered upon new plans to destroy him, it will take them yet four days to complete their dark counsel, and then when they demand the victim he will hold himself ready for the sacrifice.

Monday he comes back to the city, and made a still more striking exhibition of the power of his presence over men, by causing all that bought and sold in the temple to leave the holy place and take their tables and merchandise with them. At his command, hardened, selfish and calculating as they were, they could not withstand the authority with which he spake. The blind, the sick, and the lame, were brought to him in great numbers, and he healed them. The populace had been induced by threats or persuasions to hold their peace, but the children in the temple took up the songs and cries of the previous day, and sang [hosannas] to the son of David; When the priests and the scribes demanded his authority for what he did, he put them to shame before all the people by the wisdom of his reply. And when evening was come he went back to Bethany leaving them still more enraged, and intent upon seeking his life.

Tuesday he comes again to the city; This was the third and last successive day of his public teaching. His enemies assailed him in greater numbers, and with greater subtlety than ever before, when one was silenced, another would renew the assault, all alike endeavour to ensnare him in his words, and to draw from him some expression which could be used as an accusation against him, before the magistrate; But all in vain, they only induce him to set before the people by new parables, and in a more awful light, the dreadful doom which they would bring on themselves on the temple, and the holy city, by thus rejecting the Messiah, He pronounced in their hearing the most fearful woes upon the blind and bigoted leaders of the people, and then left them.

This is enough, the priests and scribes will see to it that the dreaded voice of their reprover shall not be heard in the courts of the temple, or in the streets any more. To-night the great councel will meet in secret session, at the palace of their high priest, and the betrayer will be there to bargain for the reward of his iniquity in delivering Jesus into their hands.

On his way out to Bethany Jesus paused before passing the ridge of Olives, and sat down with his disciples over against the temple, to look back upon Jerusalem for the last time. The sun was setting and the whole city, with the surrounding [valleys], and the hill-sides which were covered with camps of pilgrims, lay beneath him. In the evening light, the history of a thousand years, the divine oracles speaking by a thousand voices, the monuments of prophets, patriarchs, and Kings, the visitation of Angels, the [miraculous] interposition in judgement, and in blessing, by the offering of [Isaac], and the building of the temple, was presented to him, as he looked upon Moriah and Zion; and as he heard the murmur, and the evening song of a million people gathered within, and around the walls of the whole city.

Now my hearers, was it possible here on earth to find another scene of such commanding interest, as that which lay [before] the eyes of Jesus, when he turned to look upon Jerusalem for the last time[?] There he sat until the sun went down, and the stars shone, and the already risen moon grows bright over the mountain. There he poured forth in the most solemn and touching words, prophecy, and warning, and [instruction], concerning the desolation of Jerusalem, the depression of the jewish people, the preaching of the gospel to all nations, and his own final coming to judge the world in righteousness. And he closes this the most awful, and sublime of all his discourses with [a] distinct and solemn declaration that after two days he should be betrayed, and crucified. Then he resumes his walk to Bethany, and rested for the night.

The whole of the following day, Wednesday, he spent in retirement, at his chosen and quiet home in Bethany, his public work was done, and while his enemies [were] completing their plans, for his destruction, he would take a little time to gird up his soul for the trial of mockery and scourging, and for the crowning agony of the cross. He would need the repose of two quiet days to prepare himself for the last sleepless night, and for the long tortures of the last dreadful day. When he leaves the quiet village for the last time on Thursday, he goes to be betrayed and crucified. His whole body, and soul, and spirit will be [taxed] with the most exhausting intensity, until he bows his head in death at the ninth hour on Friday afternoon. As the evening of Thursday draws near, Jesus sets forth upon his last walk with his disciples, before his passover. We do not know what words of farewell were spoken when he parted with his beloved friends at Bethany, they fondly hoping to see him return to lodge with them as before, and he well knowing that his next resting place would be the grave. We are not told what he said to his disciples as he walked with them up the same steep, or down the same descent of Olives, where the multitudes hailed his coming with [hosannas], four days before. We do not know whether in silence, or with weeping, or with comfortable words. He passed Gethsemanie, and across the brook Kidron, and climb[ed] up the ascent to what is now called St. Stephen's gate. And for the moment of his arrival at the upper chamber in the city, where the passover was prepared, we may well imagine that his countenance wore an unwonted tenderness and solemnity, and that the wondering disciples saw the foreshadowing signs of the final agony upon him. The awful history of this last night, and the following day, will be studied with wonder and adoration, by angels and redeemed men forever. We can now only recite its most familiar facts, as a preparation for the lesson of the cross.

I want now to speak of Jesus in his humiliation.

He was just about to complete his earthly humiliation, and to return to the throne of heaven, with all power in his name, and all glory upon his head. Jesus teaches his disciples the greatest lesson of humiliation.

While they were contending with each other for the promise of the highest place in his kingdom, he girded himself as a servant, and washed the feet of them that called him Lord.

He was just about to offer himself, the pure and spotless Lamb of God, in the great and only sacrifice for sin; He finished the sacrifice of four thousand years, as he [ate] the passover with his [disciples]. This was one of the national festivals which the Jewish people observed from the days of Moses.

Jesus started a new dispensation and instituted a memorial service, to be kept by his followers of every nation, to the end of time. As he looks around upon the chosen company of his disciples, the dark shadow of coming treachery over shadows and troubles his soul, and groaning within himself, he nerves his heart, to make the sad declaration, "Verily, verily, I say unto you that one of you shall betray me." The disclosure makes the company of the disciples, and the presence of the Master, intolerable to the traitor, and he goes immediately out.

It is night in the streets of blinded and abandoned Jerusalem, night in the councels of the enemies of Jesus, night in the soul of the betrayer, night upon the path which he must tread, for no sooner had the dark shadow of the traitor left the room, than the troubled cloud passed from the face of Jesus, and he turns to his remaining disciples with the light of heaven in his look, and he pours forth his soul in words of love, of counsel, and of prayer, which shall outlive the languish of earth, and shall be sung by happy voices to the music of heaven. He himself joins with his disciples in singing the great Hallelujah song, with which Israel had closed the passover for a thousand years. Praise the Lord, all ye nations: praise him all ye people; for his merciful kindness is great towards us, his mercy endures forever.

He knows where the betrayer will expect to meet him, at the midnight hour, and there he goes that he may be ready, when the officers and soldiers come with Judas for their guide, to take him once more through their silent streets, and out of their eastern gate, and across the Kidron valley, beneath the shadows of the olive trees which are cast in the full light of the moon. Jesus goes to his place of prayer, the betrayer knows the spot, for Jesus had often been there before with his disciples.

To this day in spite of all intervening changes, the scene can be identified with reasonable accuracy. And it is the most solemn and affecting of all the holy places in palestine. The aged olive trees, with gnarled and distorted trunks, appearing as if bent and twisted by the [tortures] of centuries, are undoubtedly the most fitting monuments, if any be needed to make the ground sacred.

Whilst waiting for the armed band to appear, Jesus is again troubled in spirit, and his soul is bowed down under the weight of a more awful and mysterious agony than had ever come upon him before. He is overcome with a strange amazement, an inexplicable and shuddering dread, a horror of great darkness, and an exceeding great sorrow, embittered with more than the bitterness of death; the sweat wrung out by the inward torture, falls in blood drops to the ground. Thrice he prays in the same words, that the cup may pass from him.

When the armed band appears, and he goes forth to give himself up, his troubled countenance at once assumes so much of its serene and godlike majesty that the hardened soldiers, are struck to the ground with awe, but the delay is only momentary, he offers himself again, and they bind him, and lead him away. It is now past midnight, and from this time forward the course of the events in this awful history, ran swiftly on the closing scene on the cross.

Walking painfully with bound hands, amidst the rude and merciless mob, Jesus was hurried up the steep pass, through the city gates to the house of Annas, not for a formal trial did they bring him there, but only that the old father-in-law of the high priest[,] the man whose counsel was of the highest authority in the nation, might have the dreadful satisfaction of seeing Jesus of [Nazareth] a prisoner.

Then out again, into the dark, narrow streets, finding their way, only, by the uncertain light of lanterns and torches, they hurry their unresisting victim, with insult and mockery to the palace of Caiaphas. There he is questioned by the high priest, testified against by false witnesses, smitten by the officers, reviled by the whole assembly, condemned to death by the counsel, and still after the decision kept exposed to every form of [contemptuous] speech, and personal abuse, till the breaking of the day. The morning of Friday breaks, a day to be recognized as the greatest of all the days of time, a day to be remembered as long as redeemed souls can remember the sacrifice which purchased for them a blessed immortality. The sentence of the sanhedrin must now be confirmed and executed by the civil power, or it will be of no effect, and the enemies of Jesus hurry on their dreadful work, with such malignant and impetuous zeal, that the prisoner, who was seized in Gethsemanie, without the city, at midnight, has been led to and fro, through many streets, to four different places of tribunals, has been arranged before the high priest, twice before the sanhedrin, twice before Pilate, once before Herod, once robed and crowned in mockery, twice scourged, everywhere mocked and condemned, led outside of the city wall, and by nine o'clock, when the sun is looking over the ridge of Olivet, in the deep valley of Kidron, he is already nailed to the cross. In six hours more, the most momentous hours in the world's history, the awful tragedy is finished, and the Incarnate Son of God bows his head in death. It is all one act, one mysterious and [infinite] passion, from the agony in Gethsemanie, to the last bitter cry upon calvary.

The betrayal, the arrest, the arraignment, the false accusation, the mockery, the denial, the scourging, the final sentence, and its execution, must all unite to make up the meaning of that most sacred and awful mystery, the cross of Christ. The most sorrowful procession that ever moved on this earth, was that in which Jesus was led out of the city, to be crucified, amidst the wails of the daughters of Jerusalem, and the mockery of the multitude who clamored for his death.

JESUS WEEPING OVER JERUSALEM

Text: Luke 12:50, 19:41; Psalm 40:8;
John 10:17–18, 13:34, 15:12, 19:11; Matthew 26:53;
Acts 2:23; Galatians 3:13; Zechariah 13:7;
Isaiah 53:5–6; 1 John 3:16; Romans 16:3–4

And when he was come near,
he beheld the city, and wept over it.
—Luke 19:41

In the gardens and vineyards on all the hill-sides facing the city, are encamped thousands and thousands who had come up to the great national feast, all this vast population are moved at his coming: and the multitude around him lifted up their voices in cries of welcome so loud, that some within the city walls, hearing the sound, said, the world has gone after him. At this moment, of supreme triumph, Jesus weeps; not for himself, although he well knows, that before that week should close, the hosannas of the multitude would give place to the cry, "crucify him, crucify him." Not because his work has failed, and his mission must close in defeat, and disappointment, He weeps over doomed and blind Jerusalem, because she knows not the time of her visitation; He weeps, because, the last and utmost appeal which he can make, to the hearts of men, by his death on the cross, will still be rejected by many, to their own [destruction]; He weeps, because, many by continuance in impenitence and unbelief will bring on themselves wrath unto the uttermost, when they might have been saved with a full and everlasting salvation. And so Jesus began the great work of his passion, with triumph, and with tears, the earthly triumph will soon be passed, but it will give place to another, when he shall have led captivity captive, and the angelic host shall form the dazzling procession, and the everlasting gates of heaven, shall be lifted up, that the King of glory may come in. The sorrow with which Jesus wept over Jerusalem, shall give place to joy when he shall look back upon the travail of his soul, and be satisfied, with the fruits of his toil and suffering. From this time forward Jesus [pursued] the open and avowed course, which he knew must bring him to the cross. For a time he had avoided publicity, and had kept himself out of the reach, of those who were plotting together, at Jerusalem, to put him to death. But now the work of teaching is done, the evidences of his Divine Mission are complete, and he goes voluntarily, to put himself in the way of his enemies, that their malice may become the instrument, of completing the great sacrifice for the world's redemption. Descending the western slope of Olivet, and crossing the Kidron, Jesus entered the city by the gate of St. Stephens, and went and showed himself in the courts of the temple, with the singing and shouting multitude still around him. The whole city was moved, the scribes read the law with none to listen, and the priests were left alone with the evening sacrifice, for everybody had joined the eager crowd, that was swaying and singing to and fro, in their endeavor, to see, and to hear . . . the prophet of Nazareth. Having looked around silently upon all things, Jesus left the temple, and the city. His first entrance into Jerusalem on the solemn week of his passion, has the appearance of a triumph. He had walked up the wild and dreary road from [Jericho], and from the fords of the Jordan to Bethany, and had spent his last earthly sabbath at the house of his friends, in that mountain village. It was the week of the passover, and multitudes of pilgrims [were] on their way from Galilee, to keep the great festival in the holy city. Some remained with him at Bethany. On the day of rest many passed over the brow of Olivet, and encamped in the gardens, and orchards, on the western slope of the mountain, everywhere spreading the tidings that the prophet of Nazareth was but two miles off at Bethany, and would appear in the city, before the feast had closed. On the afternoon of [Sunday], the first day of the Jewish week, Jesus renewed his Journey, accompanied by a great multitude from Bethany, who were eager to witness his reception into the city. He set forth knowingly and willingly to meet his death. When the new life of the year had come, and the whole land was green and blossoming, with the glory of spring, taking the most traveled road, over the southern ridge of Olivet, he was joined by a still greater multitude, who had heard of his coming, and had gone forth from the camp on the hillside, and from the streets of Jerusalem, to meet him. When the two great processions met, the one which from the direction of the city turned and went before, and the other which started out from Bethany followed, with Jesus in the midst, and both united in rending the air with shouts of joy, which were heard in all the streets, and on all the hill-sides around and about Jerusalem. Branches were broken from the palms, by the way-side, and hastily braided into mattings to carpet the road, others still more enthusiastic, threw off their outer garments, and spread them in [the] way to be trodden upon by the beast that bore the Son of David. And so far were the excited multitudes from exaggerating the greatness of the occasion, by their shouts, and demonstrations of joy, that Jesus himself said, that the stones would immediately cry out, were the people to hold their peace.

Rounding the southern ridge of the mountain, and coming out upon a level platform of the rock, Jesus beheld across the deep [ravine] of the Kidron, the whole magnificent city in one full and instantaneous view. Conspicuous above everything else, the golden domes, and pinnacles, of the temple, rise before him, like the flame of a mighty sacrifice. The whole mass of compact streets, and stone houses, within the walls, are crowded with people, and while they shout hosannas, Jesus returns to Bethany for the night. And now the first decisive step towards the great sacrifice had been taken.

Christ died for our sins according to the Scriptures. Christ's death was not the beginning of his sufferings, it was the end of them. Without his death his work would not have been finished. It was the great crowning event of which much is said in the word of God. We ought to think much of it. Let us briefly look at a few things respecting it.

1st. *Christ's death was real.*

Some have contended that it was only apparent and shadowy, and that Jesus Christ did not actually die. His enemies said he was dead, the soldiers around his cross were so sure that he was dead that they [broke] not his legs, his friends and disciples so firmly believed that he was dead, that they were cast into the deepest gloom. Christ really died.

2nd. *Christ's death was anticipated by himself; in fact he himself foretold it.*

He knew it by his own omniscience. He well understood the prophets and they said he must die. He died for our sins according to the Scripture. He so fully anticipated his own death and the manner of it, that it cast a spell of sadness over his whole life. He says "I have a baptism to be baptized with, and how am I straitened until it be accomplished" (Luke 12:50).

From men, the time and manner of their death is concealed, they may commonly hope that it will not be in such torment as that, that our Lord endured. But he knew the time and manner in which he should die. He died his death as it were a thousand times.

3rd. *Christ's death was voluntary.*

This was a great point. Had Christ died unwillingly his blood would have availed nothing for us. On this point the Scriptures are very clear[;] in one of the Messianic prophecies, Christ speaking on the subject of the great sacrifice he was to offer, says; "I delight to do Thy will O God" (Ps. 40:8). And during his stay on earth he repeatedly said that if he chose he could avoid dying. When Pilate said, "knowest thou not that I have power to crucify thee?" Jesus answered: "Thou couldest have no power at all against me except it were given thee from above" (John 19:11).

Even before that he had said, "I lay down my life, that I may take it again, no man taketh it from me but I lay it down of myself" (John 10:17–18). Still later he said "thinkest thou that I cannot now pray to my Father and he shall presently give me more than twelve legions of angels?" (Matt. 26:53). Nothing is more clear than that our saviour died voluntarily, yet he died a violent death. In fact it was exceedingly violent. He was put to death in a manner expressive of the greatest hatred by his enemies. On the day of pentecost Peter proved that he had been murdered. "Him being delivered by the determinate counsel and foreknowledge of God ye have taken and by wicked hands have crucified and slain" (Acts 2:23). Christ had full power over his own life but he permitted his foes to crucify him.

4th. *Christ's death was shameful.*

Hanging has always been a death of [ignominy] and the death of the cross has always been the most shameful[;] no citizen nor even a liberated slave could be crucified in the Roman Empire. That kind of death was for servile criminals alone. This manner of putting criminals to death was continued until Constantine abolished it in honor of our Lord's death. Every mark of shame attended our Saviour's death. His raiment was taken from him, he was put to death between two thieves, one of whom confessed that they deserved death, no mark of respect was shown him, all was cold contempt, but he endured the cross despising the shame. The death of our Saviour was accursed, indeed he was made a curse for us, for it is written "cursed is every one that hangeth on the tree" (Gal. 3:13). It was only in this way that he could redeem us from the curse of the law, it rested on us till he bore it in our room and stead. We may never know the half or the thousandth part of what is meant by his being made a curse. In many respects his sufferings were the most mysterious ever witnessed, that awful wrath of God which was due to us fell on him.

5th. *Christ's death was inconceivably painful.*

The theory of death by crucifixion was to torture men to death by nervous distress[;] some blood indeed was shed, but not enough to take life. If ever there was such a thing as dying by inches it was when men hung upon the cross. There was no change of posture in that death[;] it was slow and lingering[;] there was never any death like it.

6th. *Christ's death was solitary.*

His friend John, his mother, and some other women, were there looking at the awful spectacle but they were filled with grief and dismay, not one of them seems to have said a word to cheer or comfort him. He saw what Simeon had foretold, a sword piercing the soul of his mother, everything like solace was withheld.

Often through life he had enjoyed the light of his Father's face, but in his agony, even that was taken and he cried out, "My God, my God, why hast thou forsaken me." Neither man or woman, nor angel nor God stood by him, he trod the wine-press alone.

7th. *Christ's death was without comfort.*

We have seen how he was forsaken, when he said "I thirst." They gave him vinegar, mingled with gall, a potion suited to increase his torment. After a while they offered him a stupefying dose, but he declined it. Usually the dying are left to die quickly but his murderers taunted him, and the soldiers who executed him went to gambling at the foot of the cross, all was coarse brutality in his foes. The pain of our Saviour's body was but a small part of his suffering, his agony was chiefly in his soul. The sufferings of his soul were the soul of his sufferings. Before the kiss of betrayal, before his arrest or trial, he said, "my soul is exceeding sorrowful even unto death." Jehovah had said, "Awake O sword against my shepherd and against the man that is my fellow" (Zech. 13:7). O that death! None but the Saviour who endured it, and God who inflicted it, knew what it was.

8th. *Christ's death was expiatory.*

He died for our sins, he had no sins of his own, he never displeased God, his soul was holy, but he took our place under the law which we had broken. The Bible is explicit on this point, "surely he hath borne our griefs and carried our sorrows. . . . He was wounded for our transgressions, he was bruised for our iniquities, the chastisement of our peace was upon him, and with his stripes we are healed" (Isa. 53:5–6). Blessed be God.

The wine-press has been trodden, the work of expiation is finished, justice is satisfied, the law is magnified, God is glorified, the Scriptures are true, the prophecies and histories of our Lord so fully agree, the types and the antitypes so perfectly correspond that if we had no proof of the Divine origin of the Bible but that furnished by the prophecies and life of our Lord, the argument would be clear and full. There are so many things of this sort and of so marked a kind that we know we have God's word when we read the Bible. How light are all our crosses, what are they all compared with the sufferings of Christ! If we believe in Jesus there is not a drop of wrath in any cup of bitterness ever put into our hands. Whatever may come upon us it is not fit to be spoken of on the same day on which we speak of our Saviour's death.

9th. *Christ's death is a great argument against sin.*

If it was of so malignant a nature as to bring on our surety and substitute such dreadful agonies surely we ought to crucify it. How shall we who are dead to sin live any longer therein[?] We need not accuse the Jews, Pilate or the Romans, it was our sins that caused the death of Christ. O let us hate our sins and put them all to death. Want of faith in Christ is a great sin, after all he has done and suffered for us to doubt his love and willingness to save, or to reject his grace is a wickedness that has few equals. If Christ has not proved his love and pity for men it cannot be proven that there is such a thing as love or pity. We cannot have, and we need no fairer argument for love to our brethren, that is drawn from Christ's love in dying for us. It is conclusive, "Hereby perceive we the love of God because he laid down his life for us, and we ought to lay down our lives for the brethren" (1 John 3:16; see also John 13:34 and 15:12, and Rom. 16:3–4). The confidence and composure of believers in Christ is well founded. Conscience as well as Scripture says that "without the shedding of blood there is no remission," and conscience as well as Scripture, says, "the blood of Christ cleanseth from all sin." The destroying angel never entered a house in Egypt where the blood of the paschal lamb was sprinkled on the lintels of the door. The scarlet thread in [Rahab's] house protected her from all harm at the fall of Jericho, so all the prisoners go forth by the blood of the covenant. In it, and in him who shed it, we may have the most abundant joy. All is safe when the blood of remission is applied. We need no more atonement than we find in the great sacrifice of [C]alvary. No wonder that he who believeth in Jesus and sees anything of the fullness of his grace and mercy seek no other Saviour, desires no other intercessor but Christ alone.

4

MARY J. SMALL

MARY JULIA SMALL was born to Agnes Blair on October 20, 1850, in Murfreesboro, Tennessee. Little is known of Small's background, and biographical sources do not mention her father. There is some indication that during the antebellum period she attended a Catholic school, perhaps the Oblate Sisters of Providence Academy in Baltimore.[1]

On October 23, 1873, she married the Reverend John Bryan Small, who became a distinguished AME Zion bishop.[2] Mary Small worked with her husband in pastoral fields, including parishes in Connecticut, North Carolina, Washington, D.C., and York, Pennsylvania. Bishop Small died in 1905.[3]

Licensed as an evangelist and missionary in 1892, and ordained to the diaconate in 1895, Mary Small was ordained an elder in 1898. She was the first woman, black or white, to achieve this honor. Her elevation to this status precipitated a bitter debate among male clergy, many of whom questioned the propriety of granting such a status to a woman.[4]

Although Small had the credentials, there is no evidence that she ever pastored a church. She appears to have continued her evangelistic activities and worked on behalf of the Women's Home and Foreign Missionary Society (WHFMS), in which she held many offices, and the Women's Christian Temperance Union in York, Pennsylvania. In 1912, Mary Small was elected president of the WHFMS, a position she held for four years.[5] During the first ten years after her ordination as a deacon, she was active in her role as the wife of Bishop John Bryan Small. Following his death, however, she was unencumbered and could have pursued a ministerial career. After 1905, except for occasional references to her work with the WHFMS, there is little discussion of her activities. Given the resentment and anger resulting from her ordination as elder and the jealousy that tended to surround her husband during his lifetime, it is likely that she

Mary J. Small

Source: *Center for African American History and Culture, Temple University.*

was simply passed over and ignored by the bishops, who were responsible for the appointment of ministers to charges. Mary Small and Sarah Pettey, the wife of one of the "feminist" bishops who engineered Mary Small's ordination, are excellent examples of how wives of controversial bishops are treated following the deaths of their husbands.[6]

Mary Small died in McKeesport, Pennsylvania, on September 11, 1945, at the age of ninety-four. Her funeral was held at York, Pennsylvania, in the AME Zion Church named after her husband. In his laudatory eulogy of Mary Small, Bishop C. C. Alleyne alluded to the difficulty she faced following her husband's death: "Not alone was she resplendent in wifehood, but she was glorious in widowhood. When one has virtually walked with kings, sharing the honors of exalted office and wielding the mace of ecclesiastical power, and suddenly finds oneself removed from the source of those honors and powers, and forced to accept the change which is inevitable—and does so with becoming modesty. Then goes on to live without complaint or rancor, the character of such a one has been severely tested; and in her case its grandeur and nobility became the more apparent."[7]

Small's Sermon

Small delivered "Zion's Mission Work" to the AME Zion Church's WHFMS at a General Conference in Mobile, Alabama, in January 1898. A symbol of successful womanhood and the first of her sex to break through the denominational sexist glass ceiling of ministerial recognition, she was much revered by black women, especially missionaries. A lifelong advocate for foreign missions, she speaks in this sermon of the importance of supporting domestic and foreign missionary work. She argues that "the only true service which can be rendered to God, can only be accomplished by serving our fellow creatures."

Just as Foote argues that Christian perfection must be attained to do the work of love, Small begins her sermon by asserting that Christians must be transformed through Christ in order to do the selfless work of missions. She states that "We are so sensitive and sensible of self and self-concern—self-interest—and as a general thing, so insensible to the interests of others, that a transformation scene is often necessary to arrive at facts in their true light." This transformation can only occur if people have "the connecting link of the spirit of Jesus Christ," for only then will they be able to live selflessly as Christ did.

Small's elite class status is evident in her sermon. Because Small was married to an AME Zion bishop and attained a unique position of power as a female elder herself, her sermon resembles the speeches of privileged white women of her day who were also active in missionary work. Foote and Baker use their sermons strategically to gain support for their ministries, which reflects their struggles to subsist while maintaining preaching careers. In contrast, Small appears relatively removed from the struggles of most preaching women. In her sermon, she speaks in the third person of those who struggle, and apparently assumes that her audience—the AME Zion Church's WHFMS—is not deprived of material and spiritual blessings. When beseeching her audience to look beyond their self-interests in order to support missionary work, she states that "when we are in our comfortable homes, surrounded with the blessings of life, by loving, kind and benevolent friends, we least think of our less fortunate brothers and sisters who are differently situated, in mission fields."

While she addresses the fact that some who struggle may not have had the opportunities to overcome their hardships, she primarily paints a picture of the lost souls in the mission field as "shiftless, unwilling and 'don't care' people" who have spurned "favorable opportunities." She argues that these people's low class and character are not good reasons to neglect the mission field, for Jesus "in His dying breath prayed that they may be forgiven—that they may be saved." She asserts that the shiftless nature of the heathen is in fact the very reason missionaries should be supported, or else "we will assist the heathen in opposing them," and thus, by implication, civilized Christians will be no different from the heathen. She concludes her sermon by asking from a missionary's perspective, "If our brethren who send us refuse to sustain us, what proof have we that our holy religion is better than the heathen's?"

Like many of her nineteenth-century contemporaries, Small believes that Asians, Africans, East Indians, and other people of color were backward and uncivilized and needed missionaries to bring the glorious message of Christianity. Her sermon to the WHFMS is designed to motivate them to raise the necessary funds to support the missionary cause abroad. Fundraising for missionary work in Africa is especially important to her, because her husband was the first AME Zion bishop appointed to Africa.

ZION'S MISSION WORK

One of the greatest drawbacks to a religious cause is, persons are likely to seek to carry the lightest end of a cross; and it is so much easier to tell than to do, that a great many excellent tellers are poor doers.

The way we have thought more advantageous to the advancement of home and foreign mission work, is, to make ourselves missionaries, individually. We are so sensitive and sensible of self and self-concern—self-interest—and as a general thing, so insensible to the interests of others, that a transformation scene is often necessary to arrive at facts in their true light.

It is not amiss to know (for very few so consider it) that the only true service which can be rendered to God, can only be accomplished by serving our fellow creatures. This is a striking evidence that there can be nothing selfish about true religion. Whenever we allow self to occupy the throne, the connecting link of the spirit of Jesus Christ has been broken. Persons are not likely to judge justly when self is in the way. The Prophet Nathan knew this fact, hence, when he would call from King David's lip a declaration which reflected on the integrity of the king himself, the prophet took up a parable, and putting in David's place a transgressor (instead of the king), he found it easy to kindle David's anger at the flagrant violator, and drew forth as judgment: "As the Lord liveth, the man that hath done this thing shall surely die." Had David known that the "Thou art the man," would follow in the next sentence[,] doubtless he had not rendered the severe though just judgment before quoted.

Speaking of missions and missionary work, when we are in our comfortable homes, surrounded with the blessings of life, by loving, kind and benevolent friends, we least think of our less fortunate brothers and sisters who are differently situated, in mission fields—home and foreign. It is not always necessary to go to foreign mission fields in order to find distress among a class of God's creature who are strangers to the inviting calls of the gospel—we may find them sometimes in our gospel land.

The way we think best to awaken our thoughts to the true interest of this important work, is, to put ourselves in the places where missionaries are employed—in the home and foreign mission fields. We will speak:

1. Of our home mission work. In this our land of boasted civilization and Christianity, there are millions of people who seem worse off than those of heathen countries. There may be those who have opportunities to assist themselves (while others may not) but have not the will nor

energy. Notwithstanding the neglect of favorable opportunities, for them Jesus lived, suffered, died; and in His dying breath prayed that they may be forgiven—that they may be saved. Of that class of individuals He declared: "I came not to call the righteous, but sinners to repentance." He sent His disciples to go into all the world and preach the gospel to every creature.

It is true some people are not eloquent in tongue, but they can use other means just as effectively, and which may speak more eloquently than tongues.

That sinful people are faulty, the reason they are not saved, does not relieve us of responsibility in trying to save them. Were it not for the efforts of others, directly and indirectly, we would be in their condition. The fact remains, they are unsaved, and it is plainly our duty to make every effort possible to save them. They cannot "Hear without a preacher"; neither can preachers preach unless they are sent. God has employed the efforts of man in sending messengers to preach the Gospel. It is our indispensable duty, our Christian duty, a duty that God demands of His people, to send missionaries to cultivate the waste places in His vineyard. Go into the vineyard and work, says the Master, and whatsoever is right I will give thee. Remember, pay-day is coming! Sometimes we send ministers into Christian communities and they suffer. Think of what is implied in sending them among a shiftless, unwilling and "don't care" people. Yet to that class of people Jesus not merely sends us, but came into the world to save. If that class of people cannot nor will not support themselves, it is useless to expect them to support ministers; yet, they must be saved, if possible. It is our duty to do our part in that direction. Is it not our duty to assist in the support of missionaries? Let us ask ourselves—ask ourselves individually—how much do I give annually to the mission cause, to aid in the conversion of my less fortunate brothers and sisters? Do I give for the salvation of my brothers and sisters, according to my ability, what God requires of me? These are searching questions, and worthy of our serious consideration.

2. The Foreign mission work—While it is our first duty to look out for home and its necessities, that is not our only duty; it is only a part of our obligations.

The following expression came from the sacred lips of our blessed Saviour during His earthly career: "The field is the world"; and so the world is our field of operation. If this were not so, we would be in darkness today. When the light of truth shone in the countenance of others, they made their way to their less fortunate brothers and sisters and succeeded in getting the word into their hands and hearts. If they were the means of bringing us to Christ, for this if for no other reason, we ought, also, to make or send the word of reconciliation to our brothers and sisters who are in the land of darkness and the shadow of death.

When we contemplate the cruelties and suffering of the heathen world, our [sorrowful] go out in pity for them but what will that avail, unless we give them a helping hand? When we see with our eyes the sufferings of those who are in darkness in civilized and Christianized countries, like our own, what must it be in China, Japan, Africa, India, Fiji and other heathen countries? Is it not our Christian duty to send them the Gospel? Yes, we feel it is—we know it is! Sometimes we send it with much [scarcity]—with apparent reluctance, and so the bearers suffer the consequence. Ought we to allow those we sent to heathen countries to suffer? Is it generous? Is it Christianlike to do so? The Lord pardon us for such dereliction.

When we send missionaries to heathen countries, we send them to contend with obstructions, to overcome great difficulties, and amid them all to spread the light of the blessed Gospel. They go to oppose heathenism and to dispel the darkness. We cannot expect the heathen to help them in so doing. Christ said himself that Satan is not likely to oppose himself; we ought not to expect it. When we send missionaries abroad, we must be prepared to render them some support, or we will assist the heathen in opposing them.

Let us put ourselves in their stead. We are in a strange land, among a strange people, contending with darkness and striving to spread the light of life. We tell them we are sent to give them the light of truth—that we are from the land of light, peace and righteousness. That the people of our country are enlightened, gracious, God fearing and benevolent. They doubt our good intention, as is natural, and look for evidence as in days of old we looked for miracles to establish the truth. They say to the missionary, if the people of your God send you, if they are gracious, God fearing and benevolent, we will see; let them supply your necessities. So saying they wait for the evidence, and lo! starvation looks us in the face. We write to our Christian friends, but receive no reply. It is natural this destroys the faith of the heathen. If our brethren who send us refuse to sustain us, what proof have we that our holy religion is better than the heathen's?

PART TWO

CLAIMING
THE POWER OF
THE PULPIT

1900–1979

5

FLORENCE SPEARING RANDOLPH

FLORENCE SPEARING RANDOLPH was among a small group of women evangelists who were licensed to preach and ordained as deacons and elders in the late nineteenth century. Like many "sisters of the Spirit," she defied gender conventions and went against the wishes of her husband, family, and friends to pursue a preaching career. Similar to Julia Foote and Mary J. Small, she was a member of the AME Zion Church, the first black denomination to grant women suffrage (1876) and full clergy rights (1894). Randolph was distinguished from most women preachers in that she received appointments to pastor a number of churches. Her crowning achievement was serving as minister of Wallace Chapel AME Zion Church in Summit, New Jersey (1925–1946).[1]

A renowned AME Zion minister, missionary, suffragist, lecturer, organizer, and temperance worker, Randolph was profoundly influenced by the holiness teachings of Julia Foote and the Reverend E. George Biddle. Beginning her ministry in the late 1880s, she was one of the first women in the AME Zion Church to receive a regular ordination and a regular appointment to a church. During the twentieth century, she would be one of a few women affiliated with a mainline black denomination to pastor a church consistently. Most of her contemporaries continued to function as evangelists or were appointed to small missions.[2]

Florence Spearing was born in Charleston, South Carolina, on August 9, 1866, to John and Anna Smith Spearing. She was born into a family whose free black lineage stretched back almost two generations before the Civil War. Florence's mother died when Florence was very young, leaving her father, a cabinetmaker and painter, with four children to rear. Florence, the youngest child, attended local public schools and graduated from the Avery Normal Institute. Though most of her classmates were studying to be teachers, Florence decided to become "an outstanding

Florence Spearing Randolph

Source: *Center for African American History and Culture, Temple University.*

modiste with dreams of travel and some sort of a career." Her family's economic status influenced this decision to become a dressmaker. By 1880, her father was ill and her three other sisters worked as seamstresses and domestic servants. Florence surveyed her sisters' condition and determined to develop a skill that could provide her with a decent living. After she graduated from the Avery Institute, Florence became a dressmaker and an instructor in a dressmaking school.[3]

In 1882, at the age of sixteen, Florence moved to New York and later to Jersey City, New Jersey. She stayed in Jersey City for economic reasons. There, she could earn as much as $1.50 a day as a dressmaker, compared with 50 cents a day in Charleston, and she could move and work in a freer environment. In Jersey City, she met Hugh Randolph of Richmond, Virginia, who worked on the railroad as a cook. They married in 1886. The marriage was very successful, lasting until his death in 1913.[4]

In 1886, Florence Spearing Randolph became a member of the Monmouth Street AME Zion Church, where she was appointed Sunday school teacher and class leader for the young people. As a child in Charleston, South Carolina, she had attended the Centenary Methodist Episcopal Church, where she was converted at the age of thirteen. She frequently accompanied her blind grandmother, who made house visits to pray with the sick and to explain the Scriptures. This experience left a deep impression on the young Florence, who later determined to pursue a career in the ministry. In the late 1880s, she began studying the Bible under the tutelage of Rev. E. George Biddle, an AME Zion Holiness minister and a Yale graduate known as a Greek and Hebrew scholar.[5]

Randolph received most of her early theological training from Rev. Biddle, who provided her first teacher's Bible, and allowed her to use his extensive library. Randolph became involved as an exhorter and assistant to Biddle in organizing holiness meetings. Shortly after he became her instructor, Biddle invited her to become a "helper" in his holiness class, along with Rev. Julia Foote. Randolph stated that Foote "preached and taught holiness in white and colored churches for many years."[6]

Working with Biddle and Foote, Randolph actively sought out and attended diverse holiness meetings. While attending one such meeting, she appears to have experienced instant sanctification. Speaking of this experience, Randolph related how she and a friend wandered into a white holiness mission one Sunday afternoon and heard the mission leader speak about a vision "she had the night before of someone coming into the mission whom God wanted all for himself and what would happen." Randolph wrote:

Well something did happen that afternoon and it happened to me. My friend and I were the only two colored persons in the building, so at the close of the sermon or message, the speaker invited all to come forward and unite in prayer and as she termed it "to wait on God." We were sitting near the door, my friend accepted the invitation and went forward, but I did not. Then the speaker came direct[ly] to me, and urged me to come forward and kneel with the rest, as I was the only one sitting alone near the door, I had been praying a long time for power for service[,] a real fire baptism, but seemingly could not get the answer, so reluctantly went forward. As soon as my knees touched the floor, I felt a burning desire to pray. I did, and how well I remember the words "Thou who knoweth all my weaknesses, thou who knoweth all my fears, while I plead each precious promise, hear, hear, and answer [my] prayer." With that I swooned to the floor and remained almost like dead for sometime, as the speaker would not allow anyone to touch me.[7]

Throughout the late 1880s and early 1890s, Florence Randolph operated a flourishing dressmaking business from her home in Jersey City. During this period, she began to exhort and do active temperance and church work. In 1888, she decided to spend one afternoon a week doing city missionary work, rather than attending to her business.[8]

During the unexpected illness of Rev. R. R. Baldwin, the pastor of the Jersey City AME Zion church, Florence was granted permission to start a meeting, which turned out to be one of the greatest revivals in the church's history. Her youth and sex attracted large crowds, increasing the membership of her church and others in the vicinity. Local press coverage and word of mouth increased her visibility and popularity. Small churches and missions, both white and black, invited her to speak and conduct revivals. Because of her success, she was officially named a class leader, an exhorter, and finally a local preacher. Randolph states at this time, "The ball of criticism, fault finding and persecution began rolling. In 1897 I was granted head preacher. Not that I wanted honors, nor sought them but pressure was brought to bear by the pastor."[9]

Like Lee, Elaw, Foote, Smith, and other earlier preaching women, Randolph professed distaste at the idea of a woman preacher. She became a Bible student and took regular Bible lessons in order to speak in the rescue missions and Christian Endeavor meetings, not to preach. However, her pastor and the presiding elder called it "preaching without proper license," so to keep the peace, she accepted a local preacher's license. As the demands for her services increased, she rebelled against becoming a preaching woman. She appealed to God to provide evidence of her call, asking that he let her dressmaking business fail that year. Her business failed and she prayed that if it were God's will for her to preach, he would let the next year be a spiritual success.

Convinced that God had called her to preach, she confronted an "unsaved husband" and a sister who objected strenuously. She was "bitterly opposed [by] false friends who had put out the rumor [that] I was losing my mind and [I received] the severe criticism of ministers." Randolph took the matter to God. Strengthened by reading about Abraham's willingness to offer up love, after a night of struggle in prayer she "gave up husband, home and baby and all[,] determined to go out homeless and [penniless] alone with Christ."[10]

In 1898, Randolph joined the New Jersey Conference of the AME Zion Church. Her acceptance followed a lengthy and somewhat bitter debate. The presiding bishop's opposition set the tone for other fellow ministers to argue against elevating women to positions of authority in the Church. This was just the beginning of many years of struggle before Randolph was accepted and treated as an equal in the AME Zion ministry. It must be remembered that Randolph's ministerial elevation followed the controversial ordination of Mary Small as an elder. The AME Zion Church was in an uproar over what many felt was an unauthorized ordination.[11]

Randolph became the New Jersey Conference evangelist. At the April 1901 New Jersey AME Zion Annual Church Conference meeting in Atlantic City, she was ordained a deacon, and in August 1903, she was ordained an elder. In August 1901, she was a delegate to the Ecumenical Conference meeting in London, where she received extensive publicity, preaching and lecturing in England, Scotland, France, and Belgium.[12]

Between 1897 and 1901, Randolph pastored several churches in New York City, Newark, and Poughkeepsie. During her career, she pastored five churches in New Jersey, working without a salary from 1897 to 1909. The churches to which she was assigned were small and poor and had few members. Once the churches became solvent, she would be replaced by a "nice young man" and reassigned to another problem church. Her last "problem" in her ministerial career was Wallace Chapel in Summit, New Jersey, where she served as pastor for twenty-one years, from 1925 until her retirement in 1946. She continued as pastor emeritus until her death in 1951.[13]

Randolph was well known by the African American educated social elite. An avid organizer, she was a Christian Endeavor worker, an official lecturer at the New Jersey WCTU, founder and first president of the New Jersey Federation of Colored Women's Clubs, a member of the executive board of the New Jersey State Suffrage Association, chaplain of the Northeastern Federation of Colored Women's Clubs (1918–1919), and chairman of the religion department of the NACW (1919–1927). She served as president of the New Jersey AME Zion WHFMS for seventeen years, and was elected national president in 1916 by the denomination's General Conference.[14]

Randolph's work with the WCTU as an organizer and lecturer against the liquor traffic influenced her ministerial thought and style. Working in this capacity until after the 1933 repeal of the Eighteenth Amendment, abolishing Prohibition, she reflected the fiery zeal of the WCTU reformers. As a young minister, she was described as "a militant herald of temperance and righteousness. She adopted the technique of the period and fought fiercely and furiously." Her lectures and speeches were frequently direct in their attacks on racism, colonialism, and sexism. Even though her public posture was strong and direct and she spoke and worked on behalf of woman suffrage, she was accepted and supported by a number of men because of her feminine demeanor. In 1905, one male writer stated: "Her sermons, lectures and public addresses are all the more attractive and impressive because of the modest womanly manner in which they are delivered. In the pulpit, or on the platform she is always a woman, and when she speaks [she] has something to say." This public persona served her well throughout her career.[15]

Randolph's Sermons

A foremost advocate and practitioner of the holiness doctrine, Randolph refers to holiness in many of her sermons. Although many changes occurred in the twentieth century, changes that led Methodists away from openly advocating holiness and that caused the development of independent Holiness and Pentecostal Churches, Randolph continued to identify with and stress the importance of the doctrine.

Although Randolph's ministry begins in the late nineteenth century, her career as a preacher takes place primarily in the twentieth century. Therefore, I have placed this chapter on Randolph in Part Two. The chapter includes the following Randolph sermons: "Hope" (1898 and 1945), "Antipathy to Women Preachers" (ca. 1930), "The Friends of Wickedness" (1909), "If I Were White" (1941), "Christian Perfection" (1926), "Conversion" (1931), "Woman, the Builder of Her House" (1909), "Looking Backward and Forward" (1943), and "Leaning the Wrong Way" (1934). These sermons represent some of the key themes Randolph emphasized during her long career.

"HOPE." In "Hope," the main theme focuses on a gender issue—the need for a home to protect African American girls. The subtheme is race advancement. "Hope" reflects a clear shift in the sermons of twentieth-century preaching women as they begin to bring social and spiritual issues to the pulpit overtly. In contrast to Foote and Baker, whose challenges to sexism are subtly intertwined with the overtly spiritual themes of their sermons, Randolph and other twentieth-century women devote much of their preaching to challenging social ills directly. Randolph is conscious and deliberate about making this shift, and eloquently makes a case in "Hope" for preaching social messages: "As hopeful for the spiritual, we should also be hopeful for the temporal; for life while it reaches throughout all eternity, begins in this world."

Randolph encourages her audience members, who face severe racial discrimination, to resist becoming "discouraged because things are not just as we would have them." She asserts that the only way to advance the African American community is through hopeful persistence, until "a [seeming] impossibility is made to give way." Persistently working for change is the responsibility of each member of the congregation. Randolph argues that the "assiduous labor" of each person is the only way that the entire race will "reach the top of the mountain" of racial equity.

An important step toward racial equity, Randolph asserts, is for the community to work together to ensure that all African American girls are reared properly in a nurturing, loving, Christian environment. Arguing that girls have a crucial role to play in the advancement of the African American community, Randolph echoes the prevailing discourse on gender that had developed during the social and economic changes of the nineteenth century.

As the base of the U.S. economy shifted from agriculture to industry during the nineteenth century, the home came to be described as the "woman's sphere," while the workplace was seen as the "man's sphere." Many nineteenth-century and early-twentieth-century feminists argued that the home—and thus, by extension, the woman—was the backbone of the advancing nation. Only the virtuous woman, these feminists argued, who properly rears her children and morally restrains her man as he goes out into the perilous work world will ensure that the nation continues to be civilized.

Given the prevalence of this gender ideology, racist discourses concerning the moral degeneracy of Blacks often focused on the corrupt nature of black women. The NACW was founded, in part, to address this issue. As founder and president of the New Jersey Federation, Randolph emphasized this issue. Fully aware of the prevailing white supremacist assumptions concerning black women's degeneracy, Randolph stresses in "Hope" that it is important for African American girls to grow up to be good mothers and wives, for "every virtue in women has its influence on the world." She challenges her audience by suggesting that they will never reach a state of racial equity as long as they do not support the "unfortunate" girls of the African American community, especially when there are several homes in their state "for girls of other races."

While many black women, including Randolph herself, had to spend much of their lives away from home in pursuit of an income, Randolph suggests in "Hope" that the greatest contribution African American women can make to their race is through their domestic activity as nurturers and moral safekeepers. The African American community, therefore, should support the effort to raise African American girls to be "true women." African American girls must be valued, Randolph argues, for "they are the future mothers" and "under their care will be reared the future men and women."

Randolph asserts that individualism will never pay off in the African American community, for as long as the race as a whole is looked down upon, each individual within that race will suffer. She therefore asserts that it is each person's responsibility to support the girls, and concludes her sermon by stating that "we promote our own happiness in the exact proportion we contribute to the comfort and happiness of others."

"THE FRIENDS OF WICKEDNESS." In "The Friends of Wickedness," Randolph states at the outset that her sermon is about "the hideousness of sin." While the text of the sermon is drawn from the biblical story of a "wicked" woman, Herodias, much of the sermon praises biblical women who were "good and tender and [perfectly] gentle." All too familiar with the overemphasis in male-dominated theology on the sinful women in the Bible, before discussing Herodias Randolph carefully shows that the vast majority of biblical women were upright followers of God. Having established the prevailing virtue of biblical women, Randolph depicts John the Baptist as a paragon of Christian perfection, mirroring his foremothers as it were. While establishing the righteousness of biblical women was most likely a feminist move to counter prevailing sexism in biblical interpretation, Randolph's description of virtuous women, in conjunction with the story of John the Baptist, also serves as an effective way to argue against sin, enabling Randolph to present the iniquities of Herodias in bold relief against the purity of the other biblical figures.

Significantly, Randolph begins her discussion of virtuous biblical women with Eve. In a sermon about sin, Randolph chooses to portray Eve not in her sinfulness but in her perfection. Randolph thus counters the centuries-old view of Eve as the symbol of the flawed, weak nature of womankind, and the related emphasis on Eve's role in the fall of humankind by taking the forbidden fruit from the tree of life. Rather than depicting Eve as a curse to humanity, Randolph emphasizes that Eve was "the mother of the human family." Only after God made Eve was creation complete and did God proclaim that "all was good." Through Eve, "perfection was stamped on everything." Thus, Randolph asserts a radical iconography for Eve in this sermon; deliberately rejecting the assumption that women are by nature morally degenerate, Randolph portrays Eve as the prototype for Christian perfection, a prototype which, she reveals, women have mirrored throughout history.

Randolph stresses the spiritual and social leadership provided by Miriam, Deborah, Ruth, the Queen of Sheba, Queen Vashti, Esther, Elizabeth, Hannah, Mary the mother of Jesus, and the women who were faithful to Jesus throughout his passion and crucifixion and who first saw him upon his resurrection. Because of the "pride and sacred devotion" that these women evoke, it is "with sorrow" that Randolph turns her audience's attention to that of a "wicked" biblical woman.

Randolph proceeds to tell the story of Herodias and John the Baptist. Herodias was the wife of Herod's brother Phillip. Herod took Herodias from Phillip and married her, although she was still Phillip's wife. This was adultery. John the Baptist (whom, according to Christian biblical interpretation, the prophets Isaiah and Malachi had predicted to be Jesus' forerunner) angered Herodias and Herod by chastising them for their sin.

Randolph's depiction of John the Baptist reveals her adherence to the holiness doctrine. She stresses that he was filled with the Holy Ghost, did not drink "wine nor strong drink" (alcohol signaled a sinful nature to many holiness Christians of Randolph's day), and spent his time "fearlessly pleading with men to repent." Living a life of perfection himself, he sought to bring others into a life of perfection in God.

The sin of rejecting such a person as John the Baptist is indeed grave, Randolph declares. Thus, Herodias's first sin was rejecting John's admonishment for her and Herod to stop living in sin. Randolph, revealing that one sin leads to another, shows how this stubborn refusal to repent of sin ultimately led to Herodias's greatest sin—telling her daughter Salome to ask Herod for John the Baptist's head. In contrast to Eve, the mother of the human family, and the other praiseworthy mothers that Randolph honored earlier in her sermon, Randolph asserts that Herodias was not fit to be called a mother for planting "the seed of murder in the heart of her innocent child." Randolph concludes her sermon by calling her audience to follow the lessons of the gospel, which calls Christians to turn "envy, hatred, strife to love and joy and peace."

"ANTIPATHY TO WOMEN PREACHERS." In "Antipathy to Women Preachers," Randolph illuminates the biblical warrants for women to participate in Christian ministry, a topic that Rosa Horn more extensively addresses in "Was a Woman Called to Preach? Yes!" While in "Hope" and "Woman, the Builder of Her House," Randolph stresses the importance of women's roles in the domestic sphere, in "Antipathy to Women Preachers" Randolph affirms the necessity and validity of women's doing God's work in the public sphere.

Randolph begins with words to strengthen the women of the audience, quoting the great biblical leaders who told God's people to "fear not" for those who follow God will be delivered from adversity. Springboarding from the powerful "fear nots" of Isaiah, Jeremiah, Ezekiel, and Daniel, as well as from the direct words of God and Jesus in the Old and New Testaments, Randolph declares, "Fear not, women, because you are about a great work for I know that ye seek *Jesus.*" Despite the adversity women face in preaching God's word, Randolph asserts, they can rest assured in the promises delivered by the prophets, and by Jesus himself, that they will be rewarded for their sacrifices.

In order to argue for women's capabilities as religious leaders, Randolph revisits several of the exemplary biblical women she highlighted in "The Friends of Wickedness." First, she states, of all Jesus' followers, it was the women who were unshakable in their faith despite Jesus' death. Thus, it was those women that the resurrected Jesus commanded to go "preach the first gospel sermon."

Randolph then expounds upon the lives of Miriam and Deborah. Quoting Mic. 6:4 ("I sent before thee *Moses, Aaron,* and *Miriam*"), Randolph reveals that Miriam was a prophetess whose importance classed her with the leading male "deliverers of Israel." Similarly, Randolph challenges, Deborah was "a great liberator." Just as Randolph stated in "The Friends of Wickedness" that Deborah "proved to the world woman's capacity for public affairs," in "Antipathy to Women Preachers" Randolph asserts that while Deborah was a capable wife and mother, she worked "both in and *outside.*" Whereas Randolph continues to affirm the importance of women's role in the domestic sphere, she also strongly affirms their presence in the "outside" world, including their public leadership as preachers. Randolph denounces the continual "antipathy to women preachers," when clearly the Bible shows that "God, with whom there is neither . . . male nor female, in His wonderful plan of salvation has called and chosen men and women according to His divine will as laborers together with Him for the salvation of the world" (Gal. 3:28).

"IF I WERE WHITE." "If I Were White" was delivered on Race Relations Sunday, February 14, 1941, at Wallace Chapel AME Zion Church. At the time, the sermon was considered very controversial and was widely reported in the local and state press. The sermon speaks of the need for racial justice, and the social responsibility white Americans should assume for Blacks' economic, political, and social conditions.

Randolph begins "If I Were White" by addressing the psychospiritual impact of World War II. She states that many people have been rapidly losing faith "not only in Christianity but even in God" during the war, a problem which she addresses again in "Looking Backward and Forward." The entire Christian community is in crisis, she asserts, as the rapidly changing world meets the human potential for evil exposed by the war. Having illuminated this problem, Randolph reveals what she would do if she were white. She maintains that white Christians bear great responsibility for bringing "the world into a just and durable peace."

Clearly, Randolph sees a connection between Euro-Americans' oppression of African Americans and the human injustices of the world at large. Returning to the theme of an earlier sermon, "Leaning the Wrong Way," Randolph reveals that Euro-Americans, who have the bulk of political and economic power domestically and worldwide, can use the "superior resources" available to them to create either human suffering or human well-being. If Whites want to work for world peace, Randolph asserts, they must begin by fighting racial injustices within the United States, for "charity must begin at home." Randolph highlights a number of social issues that must be addressed if racial injustice is to be overcome, including racial inequalities in housing, education, the media, and the professional world.

Evoking the holiness tenet that all Christians must strive to attain moral perfection, Randolph asserts that Whites must actively work to cast out their sins in order to be true Christians. She states, "If I were white and believed in God, in His Son Jesus Christ, and the Holy Bible, I would speak in no uncertain words against Race Prejudice, Hate, Oppression, and Injustice." Alluding to Euro-American Christians' heavy contribution to white supremacist discourses concerning Blacks' moral degeneracy, Randolph states that if she were to preach from the white pulpit, she would challenge her audience as Jesus did to "cast out the beam out of thine own eye" rather than considering "the mote that is in thy brother's eye" (Matt. 7:3–5).

She also refers to 1 John 4:20 to support her point that white Christians must overcome racism; Randolph states that if she were white, she would remember that "His word says 'If a man say, I love God, and hateth his brother, he is a liar.'" Finally, she reveals that when Whites inflict suffering on Blacks, they also inflict suffering on Christ, echoing the words of Jesus in Matt. 25:40 ("Inasmuch as you have done it unto one of the least of these my brethren ye have done it unto me"). Speaking as though she were a white person attempting to castigate a black man, she states, "I cried what right have you to stand beside me here? I paused, struck dumb with fear, For lo, the black man was not there, but Christ stood in his place. And Oh! the pain, the pain, the pain, that looked from that dear face."

Randolph's sermon posits that as long as Whites continue to perpetuate injustices, both domestically and abroad, they will be living in sin rather than in Christ. Whites must attend not only to the impurity of their own souls, but also to the material labor of making the world a better place for all.

"CHRISTIAN PERFECTION." Randolph's holiness doctrine is most evident in two sermons, "Christian Perfection," and "Conversion." Both of these sermons were preached at Wallace Chapel, in 1926 and 1931 respectively. Resembling Foote, Randolph emphasizes the transformative nature of true Christian conversion when one is made holy through God's grace.

In "Christian Perfection," Randolph elaborates on how Christians may reach a state of spiritual perfection. Whereas Foote uses her sermon of the same title to argue for the legitimacy of Christian perfection, Randolph attempts to explain in her sermon "what is requisite to a perfect life in Christ."

Even though Randolph's sermon does not primarily focus on legitimizing Christian perfection to her audience, she nevertheless begins the sermon by building an argument supporting the doctrine of Christian perfection. Randolph is clearly aware that many Christians of her day questioned the doctrine, and like Foote, she believes that it is crucially important, especially as a preaching woman, to uphold the doctrine. Although Randolph was one of the few women to have been called to pastor a church, she was no less concerned than many other preaching women about gaining support for her ministry by legitimizing the holiness doctrine and the related doctrine of Christian perfection.

Randolph begins "Christian Perfection" by arguing that all God's people cannot be angels, but they can all attain "such perfect conformity to His spiritual and moral image, that we will reflect, as it were, the very image of the Master." Referencing Matt. 5:48, as Foote did, ("Be ye therefore perfect, even as your Father which is in heaven is perfect"), Randolph argues that Christ would not have told his followers to be perfect if such a state were unattainable.

Having asserted the legitimacy of the doctrine of Christian perfection, she emphasizes that the perfection she speaks of is perfection according to Christ, not perfection "in the sight of man," for attaining perfection in the sight of humans, as Randolph well knows, "is impossible." Christian perfection is, first and foremost, an inner state of purity; thus, one is on the wrong track if one hopes to attain true perfection according to human standards, because, as Randolph reveals through quoting 1 Sam. 16:7, "man looketh on the out-ward appearance, but God looketh on the heart." Not only are human beings poor judges of Christian perfection, but their standards for perfection are often directly opposed to God's standards. Thus, persecution in this earthly life, Randolph suggests, is more a sign of Christian perfection than no persecution. Affirming human's struggles to follow God, including her own struggle to follow God's call to preach, Randolph quotes 2 Tim. 3:12: "All that will live godly in Christ Jesus shall suffer persecution." Again, we see a preaching woman carefully and deliberately undercut any notion that social opposition invalidates their call to be preachers.

Randolph proceeds to explain how one attains Christian perfection. The most important element of Christian perfection is faith in God. In addition to acknowledging God's existence, one must seek to accept and understand God's omnipotence, omnipresence, and omniscience. Just as Christian perfection may be invisible to the "natural eye," so are "the existence and attributes of God" difficult to discern without faith. However, one can strengthen one's faith in this invisible God by marveling at God's glory as revealed in the wonders of the world.

Even if one does reach a state where one is "quite willing to believe the existence and attributes of God," Randolph challenges, it is still difficult for Christians to accept that God will reward them for their faith. It is on this point, believing in the reward of Christian perfection, that the most faithful Christians may "fall into doubt." Randolph, resembling Harriet Baker, evokes the story of a biblical woman to illuminate her discussion of Christian faith. In order to challenge her audience members' doubts that God may reward them with Christian perfection, she refers to story in the Gospels of the woman "who had the issue of blood" for twelve years and who, by reaching out through faith to touch Jesus' cloak, was healed and made "whole." The woman, whose condition rendered her ritually impure for twelve years, serves as a metaphor for the unclean sinner. Even such a woman as this, Randolph reminds her audience, received the gift of wholeness and peace through her faith in Christ. Randolph's underlying message is that anyone, even the impure woman, may attain Christian perfection.

"CONVERSION." In "Conversion," Randolph further elaborates on the nature of the change that takes place when one has been truly converted to righteousness through faith in God. She stresses that the change that takes place through conversion is total; true conversion is a spiritual change, not an outward transformation. Randolph deems conversion "absolutely necessary" in order to be saved, and proposes that this conversion can only occur once one has faith and truly repents of one's sins.

To illuminate her discussion of conversion, Randolph primarily cites the biblical story of Simon Peter. Because her references rely on the audience's knowledge of the story of Peter, the connections between the biblical references and her discussion of the meaning of conversion may appear vague. She discusses Luke 22:31–33, in which Jesus warns Peter that "Satan hath desired to have you" (22:31), and in which Jesus promises that he will pray for Peter, so that Peter's faith will not fail and he will be "converted"(22:32). Randolph uses this story to show that "there is a great difference between a believer and a thoroughly converted person." Even though Peter is a follower of Jesus, and swears that he is ready "to go with thee [Jesus] both into prison, and unto death" (22:33), he is nevertheless susceptible to fall into sin, for he will deny Jesus after making these claims of loyalty. It is only after Peter is fully convinced of his susceptibility to sin, and repents of his weakness, that he is able to live as a thoroughly transformed follower of Christ.

Randolph emphasizes that even though Peter thought he had the faith to follow Christ unto death, it was apparently "easier to actually go to death or to prison than to stand up and face and contend with wicked men"; despite Peter's sincerity in following Jesus, he denied that he knew Jesus when he was accused of this after Jesus' arrest (Luke 22:56–60). Once Peter realized that he had denied Christ, he was no longer so confident in his human ability to avoid sin, and he "really repented." Randolph argues that this honest awareness of one's sinful, weak nature, as well as this true repentance for one's sins, constitutes "conversion or the change from a weak sinful life to a life in Christ Jesus."

Randolph further emphasizes that it is only through Christ, and not through one's own efforts, that one may be truly converted. She asserts that it was only through Christ's praying for Peter that Peter could ultimately repent and be transformed into a state of righteousness. Thus, Randolph asserts, the only way any person may be truly converted is through "simple childlike faith in Jesus Christ and the power of his shed blood," not by relying on one's own attempts at righteous living, as "the scientists and advanced thinkers" suggest.

Just as Peter became a new person once he was truly converted, so anyone who has faith in Christ will become "a new creature" (2 Cor. 5:17). Randolph concludes her sermon by stating that once the inner purification of conversion has taken place, the converted person, "man or woman," will reveal "a wonderful change" through "his walk[,] his conversation, his actions, his deportment" (Acts 16:30). Just as Peter was, everyone may be converted and live a new life of religious purity and leadership, in which they strengthen their "brethren."

"WOMAN, THE BUILDER OF HER HOUSE." In "Woman, the Builder of Her House," a sermon delivered in Newburgh, New York, in 1909, Randolph uses the construction of a house as a metaphor. Randolph contends that a woman is in control of her destiny. She can choose to succeed or fail. The most important element is her character. To build a house on a firm foundation, a woman must choose God and give up foolish pleasures. She is the chief model for her children and has a profound influence over her husband and everything in her sphere.

In "Woman, the Builder of Her House," Randolph elaborates on her domestic gender ideology, which she evoked in her earlier sermon "Hope." Randolph suggests that building a house entails "building up" the family within the domestic sphere. She expounds on Prov. 14: "Every wise woman buildeth her house: but the foolish plucketh it down with her hands."

Randolph stresses the importance of women's work in building homes, both "temporally" and "spiritually." Temporally, "home" is the domestic sphere in which the family unit seeks refuge from the trials and tribulations of the "outside" world. The woman is in charge of this sphere; she is "the real homemaker," even if she does not literally build the physical house. It is solely up to her to determine whether her home will be "a paradise or . . . the most miserable place on earth." The family depends on her to ensure "the welfare of the husband and children" within the home.

Temporal homemaking is intimately connected with spiritual home-making. The family's moral character is formed in the domestic sphere. Given that the woman is the anchor of this sphere, her moral character will determine the spiritual well-being of the rest of the family. The woman must "build" "knowledge, faith, [and] love" in her home, "cement and knit together spiritually" her family so that her home will be a "household of God," and place the household in God's hands. In order to accomplish this spiritual house building, a woman must have "true wisdom."

In her discussion of "true wisdom," Randolph's holiness doctrine is evident. Randolph asserts that the foolish woman of Prov. 14 is sinful. A woman can attain true wisdom not through her own understanding but rather through the transformative grace of God and inner purification through Christ—by attaining Christian perfection. This is the only way to become a good "homemaker," to learn to run a home "justly and fitly," both temporally and spiritually.

"LOOKING BACKWARD AND FORWARD." Randolph delivered "Looking Backward and Forward" in 1943 on the sixtieth anniversary of the WHFMS of the AME Zion Church. In this sermon, Randolph preached to the same missionary society that Mary Small addressed in her 1898 sermon "Zion's Mission Work." In "Looking Backward and Forward," Randolph honors Small, who was approaching ninety-three years old at the time, for her involvement in missionary work. Noting the men who began mission work within the AME Zion Church, Randolph celebrates that "in the fullness of time the women became inspired to do a greater foreign work." In addition to hailing Small, she praises a number of women who have led the WHFMS of the AME Zion Church, as well as women who have worked in the missionary field. Randolph affirms the women's pride in their history of missionary work; citing 1 Sam. 7:12 in which Samuel erected a stone and named it Ebenezer ("stone of help") to commemorate a victory over the Philistines, Randolph states, "Let us at this hour, with Samuel, raise our 'Ebenezer.'"

The primary theme of her address is that each person's attitude and outlook will determine the future of the missionary society. She states that "the Optimist is right and the Pessimist is right. . . . All depends upon how we take God." She stresses that "if we are going to succeed . . . our souls must have windows; we must look away from self and self effort to God and his promises that cannot fail." If we look at our own and others' human shortcomings pessimistically, then our work will indeed suffer as we become increasingly discouraged; if we look to God to give us strength to do God's work, however, our future will be full of possibilities.

She urges missionaries not to get caught up in looking at petty problems but to look at the work that needs to be done. She reminds her audience: "Jesus taught his disciples, his first missionaries, to lift up their eyes and look on the fields all ready to harvest—never mind about the Samaritan woman with whom you saw me talking or where I got the food from that ye know not of—lift up your eyes and look and you will see throngs of Samaritans coming this way seeking truth."

Here, Randolph refers to the fourth chapter of the Gospel of John, in which Jesus, to the chagrin of his disciples, speaks to a Samaritan woman. While the disciples concern themselves with petty issues—worrying about Jesus' speaking to a Samaritan woman and about finding Jesus something to eat—the Samaritan woman gathers a crowd of Samaritans to hear Jesus speak. Ultimately, many Samaritans become believers as a result of the woman's testimony. By citing this biblical reference, Randolph echoes a prevalent argument of preaching women—that it is a waste to expend energy on petty concerns about women's preaching, when all of God's people are needed to bring in "the harvest."

Randolph concludes by stating that the missionary society must be careful in choosing its outlook for the future. She challenges her audience by asking them "through which window are we looking—through the window of petty bickerings—of mis-understandings of foolish jealousy—or through the window of simple faith in God who said, 'Go, I'll be unto you wisdom, ask, I'll supply all of your needs and lo, I am with you always to the end of the world'"?

"LEANING THE WRONG WAY." In "Leaning the Wrong Way," Randolph discusses a number of issues. The central issue is morality. Subthemes include race and antimaterialism.

In this sermon, Randolph provides a social critique of white America and explicates the holiness doctrine of inner purification. She states that while there "are some people in the world who should be good because of their legacy," it is often those who have inherited good fortune who end up becoming "mixed up with sin and wickedness." The white race is a prime example of people's misusing their good fortune; Randolph asserts that "the white race with a legacy of thousands of years of wealth, culture and refinement behind them should be much better than they are." The white race, she suggests, is like Abraham's son Lot. Even though he had good blood, being the son of Abraham, he chose the "easy way to wealth, easy way to luxury" by living in Sodom. Easy luxury eventually destroyed Lot's beloved Sodom, and Randolph asserts that this is what "has Killed America[.] Easy money, Easy luxury, Easy living."

Randolph warns her audience not to follow in the footsteps of Lot, or, more to the point, of white America, by seeking the easy way. When God told Abraham that he would destroy Sodom because of its corruption, Abraham convinced him to spare the city if he could find but ten righteous people. As Randolph suggests, Abraham believed that surely his son would have been a good influence. Because Lot sought the easy way, however, not only did he fail in saving anyone from Sodom, but he lost everything he had; when God discovered that there were not even ten righteous people in Sodom, he destroyed the city.

The only way to be saved, Randolph reminds her audience, is through the painful struggle of casting out sins and living a pure and holy life in God. Critiquing those who would deny the holiness doctrine, Randolph states, "We have even found an easy way now . . . of getting saved." Quoting Mal. 3:3, Randolph reveals that God is like "a refiner and purifier of silver." While the process of refinement may be painful and difficult, one must, as Christ did, see "through the present cross the bliss of eternal gain." Inner purification is absolutely necessary for attaining eternal salvation, and thus it is only through love that God requires people to go through the difficult process of ridding themselves of sin. With this in mind, Randolph concludes her sermon by stating, "And his gold did not suffer a bit more heat, than was needed to make it pure."

_____o_____

In the text of her handwritten sermons, Randolph frequently wrote "Comment." This indicates that she digressed from the text to elaborate on a particular issue, to expand on the scriptures, or to provide contemporary examples of similar situations, events, or persons.

HOPE

Text: 1 Corinthians 13:13

Hope, says Dr. Pierson is the last thing in the world; when all else has gone out of life, hope is still left; and being left, all else becomes possible.[16]

In the 13th chap[ter] of 1st Cor[inthians] we find the three Christian graces, faith, hope, and charity, and the greatest of these is charity (or love). Yet we are taught in the same chapter that even charity, hopeth all things.

Paul says, "We are saved by hope, which hope we have as an anchor for the soul, both sure and steadfast."

As hopeful for the spiritual, we should also be hopeful for the temporal; for life while it reaches throughout all eternity, begins in this world; and if we would make this life what it should be, a foretaste of the heavenly, we must encourage a hopeful disposition; for with such a disposition the head and heart [are] set to work, and one is animated to do his or her utmost. And by continually pushing and assuring, a [seeming] impossibility is made to give way.

"Man would die but not hope sustain him," for when all else fails, hope still abideth; but we should only hope for things possible and probable, and add to hope action and industry, then concentrate every effort for the realization of our hopes.

It is folly, almost madness to become discouraged because things are not just as we would have them, or because our plans are often frustrated, for we must be defeated or disappointed often for our own good, many times what we consider a great evil at the time turns out in the future to be a great blessing in disguise. If we ever expect to accomplish anything in this life, we must possess a hopeful, persevering, energetic disposition; difficulty should only mean redoubled exertion; defeat more power, for when one starts thus, heights can be reached which at first seem unattainable.

History proves that every great man or woman in [the world] who has climbed the steep stairs of fame, and made a mark in the world was first inspired by hope, "auspicious hope." Though many of them were poor, they realized that life was action, life was duty, that God had given existence with full power and opportunity to improve it and be happy; or to despise the gift and be miserable. Life is a mission, or journey, and it is important that we do our utmost to make the journey a successful one.

We are in the world to make it better, to lift it to a higher level of enjoyment and progress, and there is a certain amount of responsibility resting upon each one from the least to the greatest.

Every man and every woman has his or her assignments in the duties and responsibilities of life and each should seek to find out just what his or her vocation is, then go to work with a will, resolute and unyielding, and in the fullness of time astounding results will be achieved. Be it remembered the Almighty God, in whose hand is all power, did not create the world in a single day, thus teaching man there is time for all things. Matters not how long the journey, step by step continued constantly will bring us to the end. Sir Isaac Newton who discovered the great law of gravitation, claims he owes all of his greatness to perseverance; and we are told that [Edward] Gibbon was nineteen years, writing his master piece, surely he must have been sustained by courage and hope. Then be the discouragements what they may, every one regardless of race, nationality, color, or condition, should aim high and hope to the end. We then as Afro-Americans, should forget our color and only remember that life is a great stage of action and we too must play our part. Success is gained only by perseverance, and since each of us is assigned a work, let us go about it diligently; we cannot all be geniuses, but we can each do something for the elevation and future progress of the race: for the day of small things is not to be despised. The Negro has a history which God intends shall never be blotted out though his Caucasian brother would try to rob him of it, and bring about a problem.

Let us cease to talk about problems, or wonder about opportunity but rather be ready for the opportunity when it comes.

The Negro with only thirty three (33) years behind him in spite of opposition and disadvantages has in numerous cases proven himself the equal of the Caucasians, still we are looked upon by some of that race as inferior and shiftless, therefore we cannot afford to stop and look back at the distance we have come, but remember we must reach the top of the mountain and it can only be reached by assiduous labor. It is not enough to reach it individually nor for a few to receive equal rights. We must have it as a race, but bear in mind we can only get what we can demand. The future development and progress of the Negro race is in the hands of the Negro, and if we want the condition of the race bettered, we must do something to make it better.

We must work unitedly, for united efforts bring great victories. We must not be contented simply to build churches, we must build race institutions of every kind and endeavor to support them independently. If there is one above another needed in these northern states it is a home of protection for girls. Believing that God helps those who help themselves, and being encouraged by hope; we are about to start a work that we believe to be one of the needs of the race, namely to establish in Jersey City, an Industrial Christian home for colored girls where the unfortunate Afro-American girl can start life anew; where the heart can be taught the pure love of God, the mind to think and the hand to work. Many a well desiring girl has gone further and further into vice and degradation in the hour of temptation, for the want of a single Christian friend. This is indeed a serious thought and should sink deep into the heart of every woman.

Are we looking forward to the next generation for a better condition of affairs? Then something must be done for the protection and elevation of our girls, for they are the future mothers, under their care will be reared the future men and women, who must fill the places of those who are now on the stage of action.

Every virtue in women has its influence on the world. One writer says, in speaking of women, "With all of our ministers, and churches, bibles, and sermons, man would be a prodigal without the restraint of women's virtues and the consecration of her religion."

A true woman is a blessing to the world, and in a quiet way peculiarly her own, accomplishes much good ofttimes unseen or noticed by the world; while a bad woman in a short time can cause an inconceivable amount of trouble or misery. Thus if the mother is unchaste, wicked, and degraded we can expect nothing more from the child for the general rule is, the character of the child is but the echo of the character of the parents.

The colored population of this state according to the last census taken seven (7) years ago is 48,352, and we do not know of a single rescue home for colored girls, in the state, though there are several for girls of other races.

Can we not support a single institution of this kind? "We will continue to hope." For we cannot, [and] must not stand and see our girls sink lower and lower into degradation, because there is no aid offered; no Christian home or shelter provided like other races. We must try and hold up our women, if we desire to see the race rise to a higher standard; for it is not the Negro's color but his condition that is the most detrimental; it is not a man or woman's color, but their merit, character and worth, and this has been proven by many of the race. Sisters, mothers and co-laborers in Christ, are we doing our whole duty, are we still holding our place in God's church, or are we growing careless, indifferent, and thoughtless, thinking only of self?

Remember the first commission was given to us.

Let us cease to find fault and [to] feel discouraged, for as a race we are (either blessed or cursed, which ever you are [of] a mind to term it) with a large number of critics or fault finders, and only a few who are willing to go into the hedges and highways into the attics and tenement houses, into the homes of the poor and the desolate, endeavoring to take a ray of sunshine; who can take a poor miserable, unfortunate, girl by the hand and call her sister, thus trying to lead her to a purer life. This is a real Christian's duty; and as followers of the blessed Christ we should think more of the poor unfortunate girl, struggling along amidst the temptations and allurements of life, feeling in her lowly hour, ["]no one cares for me,["] and knowing nothing of him who said,—"I came to seek and to save that which was lost"—she stumbles and falls by the wayside.

If we are doing this work to the best of our ability; regardless of the criticisms, we are doing the work that will tell in time and in eternity, and have found the key to true happiness, for true happiness exists in doing good for others, in self abnegation and self forgetfulness.

We hear much of worldly happiness but we see little, it is indeed of short duration, it promises much but gives little; there is not happiness in a selfish life, we promote our own happiness in the exact proportion we contribute to the comfort and happiness of others.

Let it be remembered, no man liveth to himself but each is his brother's keeper.

THE FRIENDS OF WICKEDNESS

TEXT: Mark 6:24; James 1:15

What shall I ask?
—Mark 6:24

We desire to point out to you the hideousness of sin—how one sin leads to another, and how important it is for every woman, especially every mother to know God.

Some great writer on speaking of Eve the mother of the human family said, "When she received the breath of life, the work of omnipotence was finished, nothing more remained to be done. Perfection was stamped on everything. 'All was good.' And then the morning stars sang together and all the sons of God shouted for Joy."

And thus the world loves to think of womankind as being good and tender and [perfectly] gentle. How we love to repeat the story of Miriam the prophetess from the time we saw her watching her infant brother Moses until we again find her on the other side of the [R]ed [S]ea leading the women of Israel.

How we admire Deborah the Judge who proved to the world woman's capacity for public affairs.

—COMMENT—

And then Ruth that noble woman who proved by her action how deeply and truly a woman can love the good and pure, and beautiful when she refused to be separated from [Naomia].

—COMMENT—

How we delight to repeat the story of the Queen of Sheba and that long and tedious journey she took seeking after *truth.*

—COMMENT—

And Queen Vashti that woman of independence who was more willing to throw aside all her imperial grandeur than to be controlled by a drunken haughty King.

With what pride and sacred devotion, we tell again and again of Esther and how she saved her people.

And we might go on to speak of Elizabeth the mother of John, or Hannah the mother of Samuel or Mary the mother of Jesus, of the faithful women who were with Jesus in life who did not forsake him in death, and who were first to behold Him after the resurrection, but with sorrow

we must change the [scene], as the subject of the text is the daughter of a
very wicked woman and we desire to learn from these two wicked characters—to shun sin in any and every form because sin leads to sin and the
end thereof is death.

Our text is "What shall I ask[?]" This question was asked a "mother"
by her daughter[,] a young girl. This mother was Herodias. And her
daughter Salome had pleased Herod Antipas greatly by dancing before
him and his friends—on a festive occasion on his birthday—and Herod
said to her, "Whatsoever thou shalt ask of me, I will give it thee, unto the
half of my Kingdom."

The mother's command to her child was, Ask for the head of John the
Baptist on a charger.

Let us notice in the first place who was John the Baptist. We find him
first in the arms of his Mother Elizabeth and when they had decided to
call him Zacharias after his father, we see old Zacharias taking his pen
and declaring his name is John. The scripture says he grew and waxed
strong in spirit and was in the deserts till the day of his showing unto
[Israel].

Isaiah speaks of him as the voice of one crying in the wilderness, prepare ye the way of the Lord, make his paths strait, while Malachi declares, "Behold I will send my messenger and he shall prepare the way
before me."

His birth was foretold by an Angel—it was foretold that he would be
filled with the Holy Ghost, that he would drink neither wine nor strong
drink, that his raiment would be of camel[']s hair and his food locusts and
wild honey.

See John standing on the banks of the [River] Jordan fearlessly pleading with men to repent—He is not attempting to smooth over men's sins,
but he is exposing unrighteousness and hypocrisy on every hand.

Hear him boldly speaking to the Roman Governor telling him it is not
lawful for thee to have thy brother's wife.

John [was] standing on dangerous ground daring to tell Herod and
Herodias of their sins and for this they cast him into prison.

—COMMENT—

Let us notice secondly how one sin leads to another. Herod and his wife
had a grudge against John and the [Word] says "And when he would
have put him to death, he feared the multitude because they counted him
as a prophet. Coward, this man who did not fear God yet feared the
people."

But at last the opportunity came as it always comes to those who desire
to plunge deeper and deeper into sin.

COMMENT ON HEROD'S BIRTHDAY
AND THE BANQUETING HALL—

What a part for a mother to play—think of the mother who first plants the seed of murder in the heart of her innocent child.

Let us bring the terrible lesson home to us.

In the first place Herodias was a godless mother and we hold that no woman without God is fit to become a mother or rear children.

2ndly when she was reproved by one who was willing to help her change her life she resented it, and became his bitter enemy.

In the 3rd place we find the fruits of a sinful life.

1st: Without God

2nd: Living in adultery

3rd: Bitter hatred taking possession of her being

4th: She is leading others down, down to hell

5th: Murder is determined and an innocent man is put to death

No wonder James tells us every man is tempted when he is drawn away of his own lust, and then when lust hath its reward, it bringeth forth sin and sin when it is finished bringeth forth death (James 1:15).

Thy word is power and life[;] it bids confusion cease. And changes envy, hatred, strife to love and joy and peace. Then let our hearts obey the gospel's glorious sound; And all its fruits from day to day—be in us and abound.

ANTIPATHY TO WOMEN PREACHERS

Text: Isaiah 62:11; Matthew 21:5;
John 12:15; Genesis 21:17, 26:24, 46:3;
Exodus 14:13; Micah 6:4

Isaiah had prophesied (62:11)[:] "Behold the Lord hath proclaimed unto the end of the world, say ye to the daughter of Zion, behold thy salvation cometh; behold his reward is with him and his work before him." Then away over in Matt. 21:5[,] "Tell ye the daughter of Zion Behold, thy King cometh unto thee meek, and sitting upon an ass, and a colt, the foal of an ass." And John 12:15[:] "Fear not, daughter of Zion, behold thy King cometh, sitting on an ass's colt." And to Hagar in the wilderness of Beersheba (Gen. 21:17)[:] "Fear not, Hagar, for God hath heard the voice of the lord where he is." We hear Him saying to Isaac and Beersheba[,] "Fear not, for I am with thee and will bless thee, and multiply thy seed for my servant Abraham's sake" (Gen. 26:24). To Jacob and the same Beersheba, "I am God, the God of thy father: Fear not to go down into Egypt for I will there make thee a great nation" (Gen. 46:3). To the children of Israel at the Red Sea (By the mouth of Moses)[:] "Fear ye not; stand still, and see the salvation of the Lord, which he will shew to you today."

(Exod. 14:13) To Moses on the eve of a deadly conflict with Og, King of Barsham[:] "Fear him not; for I have delivered him into thy hand, and all his people and his land; and thou shalt do to him as thou didst unto Sihon King of the Amorites."

(Isaiah) In Jeremiah, Ezekiel and Daniel we still find the fearnots. Hence we are not surprised that after the resurrection the first words spoken to the first preachers of the gospel are the words "Fear not ye." Fear not, women, because you are about a great work for I know that ye seek *Jesus,* who was crucified and I am not surprised for you ministered to Him during His life. In death you were not divided. You followed Him to the cross, notwithstanding the danger to which you were exposed and now you have come to weep at His tomb. But weep not. He is not here, for He is risen, as He said. But go quickly and take the glad news, preach the first gospel sermon, take the message to those who are to be the teachers of the whole human race. Go and find his disciples wherever they are. You have been faithful, you persevered for the truth and hence you are honored by God and are first commissioned.

But notwithstanding the fact that the first gospel message was delivered to the women, there always has been and still is great antipathy to women preachers. But God, with whom there is neither Jew nor Greek, bond nor free, male nor female, in His wonderful plan of salvation has called and chosen men and women according to His divine will as laborers together with Him for the salvation of the world.

It can be plainly seen from the very beginning that God destined that women should take an active part in the great drama of life and should indeed be man's helpmate. We see in the greatest event which makes up the history of Israel, woman is conspicuous and takes her part, for Miriam the prophetess is reckoned among the deliverers of Israel. We read from the Prophet—Micah 6:4 ". . . I sent before thee *Moses, Aaron,* and *Miriam.*"

Deborah the judge shows very plainly what is possible for a woman to do, especially a woman led of God and her work [withstands] forever the assertion of some that a woman if she be a wife and mother is only fit to look after her household. Deborah was a wife and mother in Israel yet her capacious soul embraced more than her own family. It reached thousands on the outside and we see her work, both in and *outside,* sweetly blended together. See her under the palm of Deborah between Ramah and Bethel in Mount Ephraim, and the children of Israel coming up to her for judgment. She was a great liberator. For 26 years her people were oppressed and enslaved.

IF I WERE WHITE

Text: Matthew 7:3–5; 1 John 4:20

In these strenuous war-torn days, when the entire Christian world is struggling to get its bearings as to the Church and its definite place in world adjustment, when men are in doubt, and thousands are already [losing] faith, not only in Christianity but even in God. If I were white I would speak in no uncertain language to my own people what I believe to be right, or in other words the truth as I see it respecting the American Negro. If I believed in Democracy as taught by Jesus I would preach and teach it, no difference who differed with me. If I really loved my country and believed that she, because of her high type of civilization, her superior resources, her wealth and culture, should lead the world into a just and durable peace—a peace that would bind all nations together so that wars should forever cease, then I would stress the fact that charity must begin at home. From my pulpit I would say as Jesus said in that wonderful sermon on the Mount, Matthew 7:3–5, "And why beholdest thou the mote that is in thy brother's eye, and considereth not the beam that is in thine own eye? Or how wilt thou say to thy brother, let me pull out the mote out of thine eye; and behold, a beam is in mine own eye? First, cast out the beam out of thine own eye and then thou shalt see clearly to cast out the mote out of thy brother's eye."

On Race Relations Sunday and during the entire Brotherhood Month, I would recommend as far as possible that Negro speakers of thought and education be invited to speak from white pulpits and [that] white ministers and other workers, who believe the Gospel they preach, [be invited] to speak from Negro pulpits. I would urge that Missionary Societies, Clubs, Young People[']s Groups, give some study to fourteen million black Americans in our own country, to their contributions to American culture, to their loyalty to the Country in every war. That when we sing, "The Old Flag has been in many a Fix, since Seventeen Seventy-Six, Yet She has never touched the Ground," I would tell that much is due to the loyalty of Negro men who with their White Brothers have willingly laid down their lives for their Country. For since 1776 when Crispus Attucks, a Negro, the first to die for freedom in the Revolutionary War, gave his all, up to this present day's struggle Negroes have proven themselves true and dependable.

If I were white and believed in God, in His Son Jesus Christ, and the Holy Bible, I would speak in no uncertain words against Race Prejudice, Hate, Oppression, and Injustice. I would prove my race superiority by my attitude towards minority races; towards oppressed people. I would remember that of one blood God made all nations of men to dwell upon the face of the earth[,] and further His Word says "If a man say, I love God, and hateth his brother, he is a liar: for he that loveth not his brother whom he hath seen, how can he love God whom he hath not seen?"

If I believed in skin superiority rather than fineness of personal character I would be much embarrassed in what happens in my own Country and many times in my own town when I looked at my white skin.

In the city of Summit, in which we are most interested, I would speak of the unjust housing problems [affecting] Negroes, the school problem, the movies, the hospital and certainly the Negro physician; the lack of Negro books in the library, the ignorance of Negro history because it[']s not taught in our schools. Whether my argument availed or not[,] I would be conscience free before him with whom I have to do. I slept, I dreamed, I seemed to climb a hard, ascending track, and just behind me labored one whose face was black. I pitied him, but hour by hour he gained upon my path. He stood beside me, stood upright, and then I turned in wrath. Go back, I cried[,] what right have you to stand beside me here? I paused, struck dumb with fear, For lo, the black man was not there, but Christ stood in his place. And Oh! the pain, the pain, the pain, that looked from that dear face.

CHRISTIAN PERFECTION

Text: Matthew 5:48; 1 Samuel 16:7;
Luke 6:26; 2 Timothy 3:12; Hebrews 1:7, 11:6;
Romans 1:20; Psalm 33:9; 1 Kings 8:27;
Acts 17:27–28

INTRODUCTORY REMARKS Our object for entering into this series of sermons is, for the strengthening of those who are hungering and thirsting after God and who long to come in closer touch with Him. Because of the large number of Christian men and women and also many ministers of the Gospel who do not believe in Holiness, we feel for our own salvation, the subject is worth considering. When we speak of perfection or being perfect, we do not mean "Angelic" but "Christian Perfection." We do not believe that men can be Angels, while clothed in the flesh, but we do believe there are lengths, and breadths, heights and depths to which we may attain that will bring us in such close proximity, such perfect conformity to His spiritual and moral image, that we will reflect, as it were, the very image of the Master; pressing upwards and onwards from one degree of moral and spiritual excellence to another. Jesus said, "Be ye therefore perfect, even as your father which is in heaven is perfect" (Matt. 5:48). Did He utter these words simply to be talking, knowing it would be impossible?

May the Holy Spirit lead us into truth and light. Some men of brilliant minds advocate the necessity of sin, or in other words they say, the same God that created good created evil and hence man is not responsible. We do not propose to try to discuss the above statement, as we feel the origins of evil is rather too weighty a subject for our small ability and furthermore, it is not our object.

Our object is to study the Christian graces as we find them laid down in the Bible and see what is requisite to a perfect life in Christ, or in other words what constitutes the perfect man in Christ. We fail to emphasize the "*in Christ,*" because this is where so many blunder and hence, get wrong and do more harm than good. They strive to be holy in the sight of man, which is impossible and this carries them into formality which is sin. For the Lord seeth not as man, for man looketh on the out-ward appearance, but God looketh on the heart (1 Sam. 16:7). And again the word of God says "Woe unto you, when all man shall speak well of you; for so did their fathers to the false prophets" (Luke 6:26).

We cannot be in harmony with the world, and in harmony with God at the same time. We cannot be at peace with the world and at peace with God at the same time. If we are pleasing God and going on to perfection we are displeasing the world and hence *must* suffer persecution.

Yea, and all that will live godly in Christ Jesus shall suffer persecution (2 Tim. 3:12). We believe the very first necessity towards a perfect life in Christ is the exercise of faith. Hence we shall consider the subject of faith first.

(Heb. 11:6) "But without faith it is impossible to please him: for he that cometh to God must believe that he is and that he is a rewarder of them that diligently seek him[.]"

THEME: "FAITH" Everything in life is accomplished by and through faith. For without faith or belief of some kind, no one would make a single effort in the world. The man or woman entering a business, investing perhaps all they possess in the world, certainly must have faith or belief of some kind in the business they are about to enter. They must believe that it is a profitable affair and if they manage it well, they will be rewarded with success, and thus perhaps double many times their investment. No sane person would enter into a contract or investment of any kind in which they had no faith: but nevertheless it is prerequisite that they exercise this faith, before they can realize the result.

This then plainly proves the words of the Apostle, "Faith is the substance of things hoped for, the evidence of things not seen." No man can find his way to God who does not believe in His existence.

If you felt deeply interested in the soul of an *atheist* or an *infidel* and you desired to change his persuasion of mind, the first thing necessary would be to prove to him in some way the existence of a God, of an eternal being and [that] that being [is] the cause and author of all creative beings. If you can succeed in this, you will then have placed him in the right way to find God. Hence the first step of faith is to believe that "God is."

The Apostle Paul declares [that] the existence and attributes of God[,] though unseen by the natural eye, are clearly revealed to the reason of men by the works of creation. "For the invisible things of him from the creation of the world are clearly seen, being understood by the things that are made, even his eternal power and Godhead: so that they are without excuse" (Rom. 1:20) for their willful ignorance and neglect of God.

—COMMENT—

The Psalmist viewing the heavens or firmament and beholding the sun, that most glorious heavenly body as he shed his rays of light and reemanating heat though no sound is heard and no word uttered, yet without these he sees the wonderful perfection of God and wisdom of his divine maker. The silent language of the night as the earth is shrouded over in darkness with nothing save the light of the moon, and the dazzling of the countless stars, tells the existence of a God; the brightness of the day, and the reviving heat of the noonday sun shows the harmonious revelation of God's perfection made by *His works* and *His word*. Thus [David] while praying for conformity to divine teaching (exclaimed) "The heavens declare the glory of God, and the firmament showeth his handiwork." (This then is the 1st step of faith.)

Believing then there is an eternal being, one without beginning or end-ing[,] the 2nd step of faith would be to seek to know of His power or omnipotence. The Scripture, which is the very best authority we can give, says His power is infinite, or in other words without circumscription. It proves to us that e'er worlds had beginnings and all we now behold of this great universe was yet unborn, uncreated, and non existent, that this great Being was, that He stepped out into space and by the word of His power heaven and earth rose out of *Chaos*. Who could doubt the power of such a Being[?]

—COMMENT—

Says David "He spake and it was done. He commanded and it stood fast. He stretcheth out the north over the empty place and hangeth the earth upon nothing. He bindeth up the waters in His thick clouds, and the cloud is not rent under them. He hath compassed the waters with bounds until the day and night come to an end. The pillars of heaven tremble and are astonished at His reproof" (Ps. 33:9).

And Isaiah says "Who hath measured the waters in the hollow of His hands and meted out the heavens with a span, and comprehended the dust of the earth in a measure, and weighed the mountains in scales, and the hills in a balance[?] All things as well as all creatures are in absolute sub-jection to His dominion. He maketh His angels spirits and His ministers a flame of fire" (Heb. 1:7). All nations before him are as nothing, and they are counted to him less than nothing and vanity, he spared not the angels that sinned, but cast them down to Hell, and delivered them unto chains of darkness to be reserved unto judgement and Job tells us these are parts of his ways, but how little a portion is heard of Him, the thunder of His power Who can understand?

He has always worked, He is working still, and the time is coming when all that are in the graves shall hear His voice and shall come forth. They that have done good unto the resurrection of life and they that have done evil unto the resurrection of damnation. Yea in that day the sun shall be darkened, and the moon shall not give her light, and the stars shall fall from heaven, and the powers of the heaven shall be shaken: and the wicked shall be turned away into everlasting punishment, but the righteous into life everlasting. (What a powerful God[!])

—COMMENT—

The 3rd step of faith is to believe in the omnipresence of God or existing everywhere at the same time. We learn in holy writ that his presence fills all space. *Ah:* if we could *realize* their *truth.*

—COMMENT—

(1 Kings 8:27) Behold, the heaven and heaven of heavens cannot contain Thee[.] Whither shall I go from Thy spirit or whither shall I flee from Thy presence? If I ascend up into heaven Thou art there: if I make my bed in hell behold Thou art there. If I take the wings of the morning, and dwell in the uttermost parts of the sea: even these shall Thy hand lead me, and Thy right hand shall hold me. Yea, the darkness hideth not from Thee: but the night shineth as the day, the darkness and the light are both alike to Thee. Yea we are at all times, and in all places in the presence of divinity. For in Him we live and move and have our being (Acts 17:27–28).

—COMMENT—

[Notations:] And must I be to judgement brought[?]

How careful then ought I to live. The 4th and last step of faith we shall speak of is belief in the omniscience of God or in other words His unbounded knowledge of the past, present, and the future that not the slightest thing shall escape His notice or remembrance. [Margin note: Job] We are told "Hell is naked before him, and destruction hath no covering, and divine eyeth. O Lord, thou hath searched me, and known me, thou knoweth my downsittings and mine uprising, thou understandeth my thoughts afar of: for there is not a word in my tongue but, lo, O lord thou knoweth it all together."

He realized that such knowledge was too wonderful for him, he could not attain unto it[,] but known unto God are all his works from the beginning of the world. Jesus in comforting his disciples said to them "Fear them not therefore, for there is nothing covered, that shall not be revealed: and hid that shall not be known. My Father and yours is even mindful of the sparrows, not one of them shall fall to the ground without his notice. Even the very hairs of your head are numbered. What knowledge it is indeed far beyond human comprehension and yet poor ignorant finite beings will dare to say what is possible and what is impossible." We are told that "all things are possible to him that believeth."

—COMMENT—

Faith saved the woman who had the issue of blood 12 years[.] Jesus said to her, be of good comfort. Thy faith hath made thee whole, "Go in peace."

Coming now directly to the language of the text, we find it is impossible without true faith. We have just been talking about "to please God." For he that cometh to God must not only believe that he is, but that he is a rewarder of them that diligently seek him. Or in other words "*constantly*," "*earnestly*[.]" We are quite willing to believe the existence and attributes of God, but when it comes to his dealing with us, his rewarding us, we immediately fall into doubt. We try to limit God's dealings with his children, forgetting that Jesus said to the man whose son had a dumb spirit, "If thou canst believe all things are possible Faith saved the man that was let down through the house top."

—COMMENT—

O that we could or would exercise a living faith in God. "A victorious faith."

—COMMENT—

O for a faith that will not shrink though pressed by every foe, that will not tremble on the brink of any earthly woe. That will not murmur nor complain beneath the chastening rod, but in the hour of grief or pain will lean upon its God.

A faith that shines more bright and clear when tempests rage without: that when in danger knows no fear[,] in darkness feel[s] no doubt. That bears unmoved the world[']s dread frown, nor heeds its scornful smile that seas of trouble cannot drown or satan's arts [beguile].

A faith that keeps the narrow way, till life's last hour is fled, and with a pure and heavenly ray illuminates a dying bed.

Lord give us such a faith as this and then what e'er may come we'll taste e'en here that hallowed bliss of an eternal home.

CONVERSION

Text: Luke 22:32; 2 Corinthians 5:17;
1 Peter 5:8; John 3:6, 8:33–41; Acts 3:19, 16:30

But I have prayed for thee, that thy faith fail not:
And when thou art converted,
strengthen thy brethren.

—Luke 22:32

Mr. Webster says Conversion means a changing or turning from one state to another. Hence a person who has been converted has undergone a change. Thus we might say to be converted is to be changed from one state to another.

In the verse preceding this text[,] Jesus[,] seeing the danger coming to Peter[,] forewarns him, or in other words puts him on his guard, and also gives him the blessed solace that *He* had prayed for him.

"Satan hath desired to have you that he might sift you as wheat[.] (That [s]ame Satan that deceived Judas[.]) But Knowing that your heart[,] your spirit is right though your flesh is weak[,] I have prayed for thee that thy faith fail not—I have prayed that though you fall you may not completely lose faith. And when the change comes because of your deep repentance, strengthen thy brethren."

Now there is a great difference between a believer and a thoroughly converted person.

Peter thought he was very strong—he said Lord, I am *ready* to go with thee both into prison and unto death. Sometimes I believe, my friends, it is easier to actually go to death or to prison than to stand up and face and contend with wicked men.

Now Peter really repented—and that is what conversion, or the change from a weak sinful life to a life in Christ Jesus will do.

[1st] The change is radical or entire[.] And Paul describes it thus in 2 Cor. 5:17[:] "Therefore if any man be in Christ[,] he is a new creature: old things are passed away[;] behold all things are become new."

This full change must obtain, being fixed up or patched over will not do—cannot last. Peter tell[s] us (1 Peter 5:8)[:] "Be vigilant, Be sober because your adversary the devil as a roaring Lion, walketh about, seeking whom he may devour: so we need [to] have Jesus pray for us—But I

have prayed for thee." No wonder Peter turned out such a strong character—with Jesus interceding for him.

—COMMENT—

2nd   The change is spiritual, or what is known as the second birth. It was
this that puzzled Nicodemus and he asked Jesus how could it be? Jesus
answered "Verily, verily I say unto thee Except a man be born again, he
cannot see the Kingdom of God."

(How can these things be?)

"Verily, verily I say unto thee Except a man be born of water and of the
spirit he cannot enter into the Kingdom of God. That which is born of the
flesh is flesh and that which is born of the spirit is spirit" (John 3:6).

3rd   This change or conversion is absolutely necessary because Jesus himself says "Except a man be born again, he cannot see the Kingdom of God."

Now we teach that the Kingdom of God is within you.

Then if your heart and mind are [filled] with the things of this world,
and all manner of sin, how can you see God[?] There has to come a radical change[,] a [thorough] house cleaning, in order that you might see God.

(Read John 8:33–41[.])

Of course today the scientists and advanced thinkers tell us it is a noble
character following the golden rule, being honest, and serving humanity
which are all very beautiful, but the Bible teaches it is doing and being all
of this through simple childlike faith in Jesus Christ and the power of his
shed blood.

4th   It is a special Command. ["]Repent ye therefore, and be converted
that your sins may be blotted out, when the times of refreshing shall come
from the presence of the Lord[,"] was the teaching of Peter (Acts 3:19).
When they marveled at the healing of the lame man—Peter hoped that all
they did to Christ was done through ignorance and now calls upon them
to repent.

Let us notice how this change is brought about (Acts 16:30)[.] When
the jailer who was astonished at the wonderful behaviour of Paul and
Silas asked, "Sirs what must I do to be saved?" [t]hey simply answered
"Believe in the Lord Jesus Christ and thou shalt be saved and thy house."

The new creature has changed his standing before God, he is no longer
a condemned criminal, doomed to death—but an heir to the Kingdom.

The new creature's motive and aim are high and lofty—whatever we
lose we will seek.

The new creature craves to know something of the word of God.

The general tenor of the man or woman who becomes a new creature is
changed, his walk[,] his conversation, his actions, his deportment[—]
everything shows a wonderful change.

WOMAN, THE BUILDER OF HER HOUSE

TEXT: Proverbs 9:13, 14:1, 31:31; Acts 20:32;
Ephesians 2:19–22; Psalms 127:1, 127:3, 128:3;
1 Kings 3:9, 3:28; Matthew 7:26

Every wise woman buildeth her house:
but the foolish plucketh it down with her hands.
—Prov. 14:1

The text speaks of two women, a wise woman, and a foolish woman and declares [that] the building, or in other words, the rise or fall of her house is her own work, or the work of her own hands.

We read a great deal in the scriptures about building, and we all know [that] to build a house, commonly speaking means to erect, to construct it; but our aim is to speak directly of the spiritual meaning or significance of the text.

However, let us just for a moment look at the natural, the temporal building; at our everyday life. Who can fully estimate the value of a wise prudent woman to her household? While she did not literally build the house, nor furnish it, yet she is the real homemaker. The house would not be complete without her. She alone has it in her power to make that house or home a paradise or to make it just the opposite[,] the most miserable place on earth. The actions and general deportment of the husband and father largely depend upon the wife and mother: her character and life will be to a great extent reflected in her children, though there are exceptions to the rule, yet the general rule is, the character of the child is but the ech[o] of the character of the parent, and especially the mother. Because the most critical period of the child's life is under her training and the early impressions are the most lasting and are apt to go with us through life, under the mother's influence is to be molded a character. She has the [responsibility for the] unfolding of human life, and the development of human souls. Hence all that tends upwards morally, spiritually and even intellectually, must to a very great extent come from the mother. No home should be without the family [altar], and no meal taken without God's blessing being asked. If the husband neglects this, his duty, then it falls to the wife.

—COMMENT—

For the building up of such a home is sure. Yes, where time is found to bow around the family altar to thank God for the many blessings of life;

to ask a blessing upon the meal whether simple or sumptuous, where the welfare of the husband and children are ever before the wife and mother[,] it can truly be said, "The heart of her husband doth safely trust in her, she will do him good, and not evil all the days of her life. Thus we see the relationship a wise woman sustains to her house, or the building up of her house even before she comes to a clear knowledge of God.

But we desire to emphasize the spiritual meaning of our text[,] wise woman "buildeth." Meaning 1st to strengthen, and increase in all the graces, *knowledge, faith,* [and] *love.*

—COMMENT—

As Paul said to the elders[,] "And now, brethren I commend you to God, and to the word of His grace, which is able to build you up, and to give you an inheritance among all of them which are sanctified" (Acts 20:32).

2nd "To cement and knit together spiritually. Now, therefore, ye are no more strangers and foreigners, but fellow citizens with the saints, and of the household of God; and are built upon the foundation of the Apostles and Prophets, Jesus Christ himself being the chief corner stone: in whom all the buildings fitly framed together groweth unto an holy temple in the Lord; in whom ye also are builded together for an habitation of God through the Spirit" (Eph. 2:19–22).

3rd To *reserve, bless,* and *prosper.* For the Word says, "Except the Lord build the house, they labour in vain that build it: except the Lord keep the city, the watchman waketh, but in vain" (Ps. 127:1).

4th It also signifies the blessedness of motherhood (Ps. 127:3).

"Lo children are an heritage of the Lord; and the fruit of the womb is his reward." Children are a blessing, though we do not regard them as such in this day in which we live. "Thy God's promise to the man who serves him and lives in his fear. Thy wife shall be as a fruitful vine by the sides of thine house: thy children like olive plants round about thy table" (Ps. 128:3).

Let us notice first, what is meant by a wise woman. We find it is possible to be great, to be learned and yet not be wise. Job says, great men are not always wise.

What then is true wisdom[?] True wisdom is the gift of God and comes from above. And the word says, Behold the fear of the Lord that is the beginning of wisdom; and to depart from evil that is understanding. The knowledge or wisdom of the world teaches us what is to be done, and what is not to be done. But true wisdom enables us to do things justly and fitly. It was this wisdom that Solomon craved.

—COMMENT—

There is scarcely a woman in the world, but knows what it takes to constitute a true home.

—COMMENT—

Give therefore thy servant an understanding heart to judge thy people that I may discern between good and bad: for who is able to judge this thy so great a people (1 Kings 3:9)?

And after he had judged so wisely between the dead and living child, the word says, "and all Israel heard of the judgment which the King had judged. And they feared the King: for they saw that the wisdom of God was in him to do judgment."

Our hearts should be established with grace, and not carried about with divers and strange doctrines for the word declares "Through wisdom is an house builded; and by understanding, it is established."

2ndly   But the foolish plucketh it down with her hands. Naturally speaking or according to the literal meaning when we say a person is foolish we generally mean an idiot or weak minded person[,] but dear friends[,] the scriptures characterizes the sinner and sin with fools and foolishness. David declared, "My wounds stink and are corrupt because of my foolishness, my sins."

The word says a foolish woman is clamorous, she is simple and knoweth nothing (Prov. 9:13). She lacks understanding.

Job said to his wife when she had so far forgotten the goodness of God to say to him, ["]curse God and die. Thou speaketh as one of the foolish women speaketh.["] What? Shall we receive good at the hand of God, and shall we not receive evil?

—COMMENT—

A foolish woman destroys her own house because she thinks more of the pleasures of the world, than of her business, her duty. She neglects the everlasting interest of her immortal soul, for the follies of this life. The wise woman's eyes are in her head, but the fool walketh in darkness. The heart of fools is in the house of mirth, says the scripture.

Jesus said, "Every one that heareth these sayings of mine, and doeth them not, shall be likened unto a foolish man, which built his house upon the sand" (Matt. 7:26).

In conclusion Dear Sisters, let us be wise unto salvation that at the end of life it may be said of us, strength and honour are her clothing; and she shall rejoice in time to come, she openeth her mouth with wisdom; and in her tongue is the law of kindness. She looketh well to the ways of her household, and eateth not the bread of idleness. Her children arise up and call her blessed; her husband also, and he praiseth her. Many daughters have done virtuously, but thou excelleth them all. Favour is deceitful, and beauty is vain, but a woman that feareth the Lord, she shall be praised. Give her of the fruit of her hands; and let her own works praise her in the gates [Prov. 31:31].

LOOKING BACKWARD AND FORWARD

Text: 1 Samuel 7:12; Proverbs 4:25, 23:7;
Romans 1:28; Matthew 28:19–20;
Mark 9:23; Isaiah 11:9

This memorable afternoon we are using two portions of scripture—one from the 1st. Book of Samuel, 7th. Chapter verse 12, "Hitherto hath the Lord helped us," and the other are the words of a wise man found in Proverbs 4th. Chapter verse 25, "Let thine eyes look right on and let thine eye lids look straight before thee." Hence, we are taking both, a backward and a forward look, as we rejoice in the leading of a mighty God.

When we say Hitherto—it means we are looking back on the distance we have come. For more than sixty (60) years God has led us.

When Samuel said Hitherto hath the Lord led us—he was looking back twenty (20) [years]—the length of time the ark of the Lord was kept in Kirjathgearim—he was thanking God for deliverance from the hands of the Philistines.

Some of us, this afternoon, are looking back not only 20 years, but 40, 50 and even 60. As one of our former General Presidents, the Rev. Mary J. Small, now in her 93rd year—looking all the way of our missionary life and are constrained to say—"Hitherto hath the Lord helped us."

This afternoon you, my dear co-workers, are looking back, back to your many prayers, your many dreams, many perished hopes, many disappointments, as well as your many joys. You have crossed your 60th. milestone—surely you can say, "Hitherto hath the Lord helped us."

But when we say "hitherto" and look back, we also look forward and then we say, "He who hath helped us 'hitherto' will help us all the journey through."

Hitherto—means we are not yet to the end, but thus far we have come. There are yet a few more trials, a few more joys, more of real work, old age, sickness, death—It[']s all over then?—No, a thousand times No—not to the believers in Jesus. When we are through looking backwards and forward in this life, we begin looking forward to a new life.

There is the awakening in Jesus' likeness, thrones, harps, songs, white robes, the great company of saints, of missionaries, the glory of God, the fullness of Eternity. Let us at this hour, with Samuel, raise our "Ebeneezer."

As we begin to retrospect, to think of the early days of our Zion—we recall not only James Varick and the early leaders, but the late Bishop

James Walker Hood as he swept through the old North State organizing churches—here and there—doing just what Jesus said—beginning at Jerusalem, and this made it possible that in the fullness of time the women became inspired to do a greater foreign work. Then we think of the work of our first General President—Mary J. Jones—and her co-workers. Then our new "set up" that began during the leadership of Mrs. Katie P. Hood—under the untiring efforts and far seeing vision of the late Annie W. Blackwell, Mary E. Washington, Anna L. Anderson and Daisy V. Johnson. They have gone from labor to reward.

When we think of our work in Africa—can we ever forget Andrew Cartwright and his wife, our first foreign missionaries, or the lamented Bishop J. B. Small—with his dying request, "Don't let my African work fail," or the late Alexander Walters, J. W. Hood, and others who have crossed the mystic streams and gone on ahead of us—With Bishop J. W. Brown so recently gone. But all I have said is now history, blessed history, sacred history.—We are now at a new beginning.

And now we come to the second part of our text, and to my mind the most important, "Let thine eyes look right on and let thine eye lids look straight before thee" (Prov. 4:25).

We are now in the midst of a great turmoil, a world at war, a troubled war torn world.—Men are living in doubt, they are saying—"Where is God?" "Why does he not reveal himself?" Let me say to you beloved, "God moves in a mysterious way, his wonders to perform—he plants his footsteps in the sea and rides upon the storm."

The sins of a disobedient rebellious, ungrateful world [have] caused God, as it were, to hide his face—or as the Apostle Paul wrote to the Romans (1:28), "And just as they did not think it fit to retain knowledge of God, so God left them with the minds of reprobates to do unseemly things with hearts filled with all sorts of dishonesty, mischief, greed, and malice; full of envy and bloodthirstiness, quarrelsome, crafty, spiteful, secret backbiters, open slanderers, hateful to God, insolent, haughty, ostentatious; inventors of mischief, disobedient, destitute of sense, faithless without affection and without pity." In short, though knowing well the sentence which God pronounces against such deeds as deserving of death, they not only do them, but applaud others who practice them.

We must look hopefully into the future, believing God that he will be with us to the end. Hear Jesus the Son of God as he instructs the first missionaries (Matt. 28:19–20), "Go ye therefore and teach all nations baptizing them in the name of the Father and of the Son and of the Holy Ghost—teaching them to observe all things what-so-ever I have commanded you and, lo, I am with you always even unto the end of the world."

In these words of Jesus to those early missionaries there was first (1) assurance, "All power is given unto me."

—COMMENT—

Second—(2) A great command, "Go ye therefore, and teach all nations."

—COMMENT—

"Teach them to observe *all things* what-so-ever I have commanded you."

—COMMENT—

Third—(3) A great promise, "Lo, I am with you always, even unto the end of the world."

A Poet reminds us, "Not many lives, but only one have we, *one only one*, How sacred should that life ever be,—That narrow sham—day after day filled up with blessed toil—Hour after hour—still bringing in new spoil." And so, to Bishops, Foreign Missionaries, Secretaries, Pastors, Laymen and Missionary Women Workers—the 60th. Chapter is closed. Whatever our joys and sorrows have been, whatever our failures or successes—the 60th. Chapter is closed; and today we enter upon a new beginning, a beginning full of hope, pregnant with possibilities and opportunities because we still have—God. So we are stressing the words—*"Looking Straight Before Thee."*

Oh! how much there is concealed in a look, there is the look of contempt, of indifference, of pity, of sympathy. I fancy it must have been the look of greatest sympathy that Jesus gave Peter after that dreadful denial for he went out and wept bitterly.

But there is also the mind's eye. In the material world our happiness and joys, our burdens and sorrows, our successes and failures all depend upon the way we look at things through the eye of the mind. Solomon said (Prov. 23:7), "For as he thinketh in his heart so is he," and Jesus himself says in Mark 9:23, "All things are possible to him that believeth." (This was when they brought the boy to Jesus whom the disciples could not heal.)

Thus the Optimist is right and the Pessimist is right. Each acts from his own view point, his own determination, his own belief.

All depends upon how we take God—. Do we take God seriously? Do we really believe the Bible we study?

We are all familiar with the story of Daniel.—Well, the average person after that decree would have fainted. Daniel had to fight with jealousy[,] the most cruel thing in all the world;—it is cruel as the grave—it will stoop to anything. But he did not only keep the window of his room open towards Jerusalem the Holy City, but he kept the window of soul, his mind[,] open towards God—and prayed and he conquered by the way he was able to look at things.

Now if we are going to succeed in this great missionary endeavor[,] building schools, and churches in our African fields, then our souls must have windows; we must look away from self and self effort to God and his promises that cannot fail.

So many lives are like rooms without windows, they have no soul look, no spiritual look, no great ideas or ideals,—all they see are material things—what they eat and drink and wear, and the things they want. There is nothing grand and noble that does not look beyond self and self gratification, or as one has said, "They are lives without ideas, without vistas, devoid of poetic vision, no windows out upon ethical, moral or altruistic ends." Our souls must have windows, open windows so that we may have [the] long view.—You know,—we are told when the eyes are tired, not to fix them on things near, but to look far away—there is less strain. So when the heart and soul are tired with the strains and stress of life, with hardships and ingratitude, many times from those we serve, we must look beyond it all to the hills from whence cometh our help, look by faith until we see God, and there will come a peace and quietness that the world cannot give, neither take away.

The people to be pitied are not the poor, the crippled or the blind, but the people who cannot see the beautiful, the honest, the earnest—they only see the fault finders[,] the critics, people who are indifferent to the cause.

We as missionaries, must learn to look to the hills, see the wonderful changes for a better world—see our work as we would have it, dream dreams and see visions of our work as we would have it, not as we would not have it.

When the Prophet Isaiah opened his window, he saw the extent of the Kingdom, "They shall not hurt nor destroy in all my holy mountains: for the earth shall be full of the knowledge of the Lord as the Waters cover the sea—" (Isa. 11:9).

When God was using Elisha, the Prophet, to save Israel from the King of Syria, and Elisha['s] servant, through physical eyes—saw that great host that encompassed the city[,] he cried, "Alas my Master, how shall we do?" But Elisha said, "Fear not, for they that be with us are more than they that be against us."

And Elisha asked God to open the young man's eyes *and he saw.* "Behold the mountain was full of horses and chariots of fire round about Elisha."

—COMMENT—

Jesus taught his disciples, his first missionaries, to lift up their eyes and look on the fields all ready to harvest—never mind about the Samaritan woman with whom you saw me talking or where I got the food from that

ye know not of—lift up your eyes and look and you will see throngs of
Samaritans coming this way seeking truth. Jesus wanted to destroy their
narrowness and awaken in them their duty to help make the world Christian and this Jesus is saying to me and to you—use your eyes lift them up
don't go through the world forever looking down and in, if you do you
will become self centered and narrow, you never will see the beauty of life
and service.—Like the Turtle—you will believe, "There is no ocean big-
ger than my well."

Look and see Africa with its teeming millions, see India, China, see the
isles of the sea, see the Virgin Islands and South America—they are all
waiting.

I read a story of two windows—one on the south and one on the east.
From the south window the writer saw a neglected weather beaten house
with its faded shades and flimsy curtains, a desolate picture that house
presented. My! what a little paint, a little fixing would do to that house, it
would transform it, but there it stood a sad fixture.—The writer closed
his eyes—, but presently opened them and looked out of the [e]ast
[w]indow—AH! he saw a pretty lawn, a rustic bower supporting a grape
vine, a row of majestic brick bungalows, a wonderful bed of flowers.—
My! what a difference, and he could see either by just the turning of his
head.

One depressed—the other inspired—. One showed shiftlessness, hopelessness, despondency—the other joy, peace, prosperity and beauty. How
much better to look out of the [e]ast window than the South.—

In this great missionary venture, this new beginning—if God permits
Bishop C. C. Alleyne's[17] return to the field—through which window are
we looking—through the window of petty bickerings—of misunder-
standings of foolish jealousy—or through the window of simple faith in
God who said, "Go, I'll be unto you wisdom, ask, I'll supply all of your
needs and lo, I am with you always to the end of the world." "Let thine
eyes look right on, and let thine eyelids look straight before thee."

Sometimes it is not bad to look back over the journey we have come—
in order that we might guard against old mistakes, that we might correct
old blunders. Sometimes it is well to look down just long enough to humble ourselves under the mighty arm of God that he might exalt us in due
season—and it is a real God given gift if we are able to look over and forgive an injury—forget an injustice.—

Let me emphasize in closing—"Look Ahead." It means something to
be constantly looking and working for eternity—surrounded as we are by
the things of time and sense. *But thank God—the things that are seen are
temporal, but the things that are not seen are eternal.*—

Perhaps we have not accomplished all we hoped for in the past 60 years; perhaps we have met with hardships and disappointments and perhaps ingratitude; some of us perhaps have had heartaches, have shed tears, but O, the joy of looking ahead to know that God himself is keeping watch. That we are not laboring for earthly rewards, for our reward is on high.

Let us then, dear co-workers, renew our vows, place our hand in his, and be ever mindful of the heritage we shall leave to those who will celebrate the next 60 years.—*This is our only chance.*

The bread that bringeth strength I want to give,
The water pure that bids the thirsty live;
I want to help the fainting day by day—
I'm sure I shall not pass again this way.—

I want to give the oil of joy for tears,—
The faith to conquer crowding doubts and fears,
Beauty for ashes may I give always,
I'm sure I shall not pass again this way.—

I want to give good measure running o'er,
And into angry hearts I want to pour—
The answer soft that turneth wrath away—
I'm sure I shall not pass again this way.—

"Let your eyes look straight ahead—gaze right in front of you to God."

LEANING THE WRONG WAY

TEXT: Genesis 19:1, 19:9; Malachi 3:3

And Lot sat in the gate of Sodom.
—Gen. 19:1

It is a sad sight to see good men and women leaning the wrong way.

They say a tree falls the way it leans and so with men. The way they lean, they generally go.

A good writer has said, "We never can understand any man until we know his Legacy."

What did he draw out of the store house of the past? Wealth or poverty? A great intellectual background or illiteracy[?]

What were his environments? [Were they] of a fine Christian nature or of common coarse ungodly surroundings? We must know if we are to judge accurately.

There are some people in the world who should be good because of their legacy. While there are others who have an awful battle to fight.

I hold [that] the white race with a legacy of thousands of years of wealth, culture and refinement behind them should be much better than they are. While there are other groups with nothing behind them but ignorance and poverty [who] must fight a hard battle for God and righteousness.

It is sad to see Lot here holding office in Sodom. He was wellborn, good blood flowed through his veins. At one time he and Abraham[,] the father of the faithful, lived together in "Ur of the Chaldees."

Then they traveled together, to the Land of promise. O the many days[,] weeks & months. Lot was journeying with this great spiritual man Abraham.

Is this not true in our day. Men and women who have been splendidly environed, with every opportunity to become strong characters[,] are often in the old place, mixed up with sin and wickedness.

Well, when the time came for Lot and Abraham to part[,] he [Lot] selected what he thought was easy. Easy way to wealth, easy way to luxury—

Now, that is the very thing that has Killed America[.] Easy money, Easy luxury, Easy living.

We have even found an easy way now of getting in the church, or rather of getting saved.

And so many, otherwise splendid people are wasting their life looking for the easy way.

Now what happened to Lot? Why[,] he [lost] out (Gen. 19:9). Lost his high standing as a Christian and lost the respect of the wicked city he was serving as judge.

So the very thing he was seeking after [all that] he [had] lost. Lost his influence and lost his wealth, and his family.

When Abraham asked God to save the city for ten righteous [persons,] he felt sure there would be at least ten righteous persons. *Is not Lot there?* Surely his influence has been for good.

But we cannot mingle with sinner people and save them. His influence was gone. In the next place he lost the wealth he tried to gain.

Think of the rich men in America who leaned the wrong way and lost their wealth.

And friends that's the way it is, you will lose in the end. The wages of sin is death, and sin kills in every way.

We lean the wrong way

1st   By associating with the wrong people

2nd   By being ashamed of the right

3rd   By not knowing the Bible

4th   By craving for things beyond our means

O, if we would only stand erect and be tested, I mean stand the test.

Mal. 3:3 says, "He shall sit as a refiner and purifier of silver."

God our Father who seeks to perfect His saints in Holiness, knows the value of the refiner's fire.

He sat by a fire of seven-fold heat, as he watched by the precious ore. And closer he bent with a searching gaze as he heated it more and more. He knew he had ore that could stand the test, and wanted the finest gold, to mould as a crown for the King to wear, set with gems with a price untold. So he laid our gold in the burning fire. Tho' we fain would have said to him "Nay." And he watched the cross that we had not seen, and it melted and passed away. And the gold grew brighter and yet more bright. But our eyes were so dim with tears, we saw but the fire—not the master[']s hand, and questioned with anxious fears.

Yet our gold shone out with a richer glow. As it mirrored a form above, that bent o'er the fire, tho' unseen by us, with a look of ineffable love. Can we think that it pleases his loving heart to cause us a moment[']s pain? Ah, no! but he saw through the present cross the bliss of eternal gain. So he waited there with a watchful eye, with a love that is strong and sure[.] And his gold did not suffer a bit more heat, than was needed to make it pure.

6

MARY G. EVANS

MARY G. EVANS WAS BORN in Washington, D.C., on January 13, 1891. Orphaned at the age of ten, she was adopted by the Reverend and Mrs. J. J. Evans, who resided in Louisville, Kentucky. Mr. Evans was a Methodist minister who pastored churches in different cities during Mary's adolescence, which meant that she was educated in public schools in Indiana; Louisville and Bowling Green, Kentucky; and Chicago.[1]

She received the call to preach at the age of twelve, preaching her first sermon in 1903. Dubbed the "girl preacher," she was highly praised for her sermonic discourses. At fourteen, she received her local preacher's license at the AME District Quarterly Conference meeting in Bethel AME Church in Chicago. She labored as a licensed preacher for one year, before entering the Indiana AME Conference under Bishop C. T. Shaffer.

Feeling strongly that ministers had an obligation to be educated, she entered Payne Theological Seminary at Wilberforce University to pursue a thorough theological course. She washed dishes and performed other menial tasks in return for her tuition, room, and board. When it became known that the "girl preacher" was struggling to acquire an education to prepare herself for public service, the Indiana State Federation of Colored Women's Clubs and the Indiana AME Conference raised funds to support her.[2] In 1911, Evans received a bachelor of divinity degree from the seminary.

Evans then entered into an active ministry. During the early 1920s, she studied theology at Union Theological Seminary and Columbia University. In 1924, she became the first woman to receive a doctor of divinity degree from Wilberforce, and the first woman to serve on the institution's board of trustees. By 1943, she had earned M.S. degrees in psychology and sociology from Columbia and had done postgraduate work at the University of Chicago and Butler University.[3]

Mary G. Evans

Source: *Center for African American History and Culture, Temple University.*

As an evangelist, Evans preached primarily in the South and Midwest. Described as an eloquent speaker with "a manner of delivery peculiar to herself," she attracted large crowds wherever she spoke. In 1913, the Indiana AME Conference sent her to Zurich, Switzerland, as a delegate to the world's Sunday School convention. She was one of two African Americans chosen to attend the meeting. After the convention, she studied in the Holy Land. There, she visited the River Jordan and was baptized in the river, very close to the spot in which Jesus was baptized.[4] She also traveled to Asia and North Africa.

By 1914, Evans had established a reputation as a leading evangelist. That fall, she conducted a series of revivals at Quinn Chapel AME Church. According to one observer, "Miss Evans preached the gospel. She did not take up the time finding fault with ministers and churches. Not that they are faultless, but it was her mission to preach to everybody, not to pick out certain classes to criticize." By 1922, similar to many urban evangelists of the time, Evans was delivering "fire and brimstone" sermons that focused on the sinfulness of Christians, including some ministers.[5]

A strikingly attractive young woman, Evans was highlighted in the *Chicago Defender* as she donned the popular "bobbed hair" style of the 1920s. In November 1922, she was the subject of great comment, preaching nightly revivals at the Institutional Church in Chicago for two weeks. She told listeners that their lives were filthy, the male clergy was immoral, and that the modern Church was ungodly in its practices of gambling and profiteering.[6] Described as a powerful preacher, Evans became one of a few African Americans women to pastor a church during the 1920s.

Between 1924 and 1966, she successfully pastored several churches, including the St. John AME Church in Indianapolis and the Cosmopolitan Community Church in Chicago, which had a membership of eight hundred in 1966. Practicing a gospel of faith and "rigid discipline" under her ministry, the Cosmopolitan Church financed a community center and a home for senior citizens and provided free education and medical and recreational facilities to persons of all faiths. Although Evans received no salary, by 1954 the church presented her with a "love offering" of $10,000 a year, more perhaps than any black minister in Chicago.[7]

Evans served as pastor of the Cosmopolitan Community Church for thirty-five years. A staunch supporter of the National Association for the Advancement of Colored People, it was widely known that when one joined the church, one also joined the NAACP. During her tenure, Evans's congregation contributed thousands of members to the organization.[8]

Evans challenged her congregation to live a life of love, faith, and good works. Although she urged those who could to tithe, she believed that there were many ways to give and that gifts of service were as significant as monetary contributions. Evans did not believe in church-sponsored entertainments for fundraising. She succeeded in implementing a program of tithing and general offerings that made the church financially sound and ensured the financing of many of its social welfare and community programs.[9]

At her death in 1966, Evans was remembered for her excellence as a spiritual leader, administrator, and disciplinarian. Eulogizing Evans, the *Chicago Defender* said, "The Cosmopolitan Community Church was built by a woman of strong beliefs—one whose faith in what each man could do to life and inspire the lives of others was frequently voiced by the minister when she quoted the Bible verse: 'Bring ye all the tithes into the storehouse that there may be meat in mine home.'"[10]

Evans's Sermon

In "The Wages of Sin Is Death," Evans's holiness doctrine is evident in her conviction that God's followers must seek Christian perfection and lead others to be perfect in Christ. She is certain that if she is truly to follow God, she must convict people of their sins at any cost. As she states, "I have to answer to God and not to you."

Convinced that true Christians must strive to be perfect, Evans tells her audience that if they participate in any kind of sin, no matter how harmless it may seem, they are "sinners just as bad as any in the world and you've got to answer for it." Churches, which should aid people in attaining inner purification, are worse than the corrupt "trusts of Wall street" if they participate in sins such as profiteering. Furthermore, Church members who lead unclean lives, for example by participating in adultery, make the Church unclean.

Whereas most other preaching women who emphasize Christian perfection focus on purification, Evans emphasizes her audience's filthy state of sin. Evans's underlying message, however, is the same as that of many other preaching women—that one must cast out sin and seek perfection to live a truly Christian life.

THE WAGES OF SIN IS DEATH

I am going to preach the truth if I have to walk out of Chicago. You may not like it, but I don't care whether you do or not. I have to answer to God and not to you.

Gambling, is an awful sin. Staking money, betting on a chance, the winner taking all, is a sin. Gambling and the gambler are bad. Yes, yes, they are bad. And you women in the church, you so-called Christians, scorn the gambler. He is not fit to come into your homes, you say. You pull your skirts aside and turn up your nose at him.

But in your homes you have your private, select card parties. You don't dare play for cold cash money outright—oh no, you won't do that, but you put the money in the cost of a dainty prize and say 'winner gets it, the winner gets it.' You are gambling and in the sight of God you are gamblers and sinners just as bad as any in the world and you've got to answer for it.

But gambling does not stop in your homes; you carry it on in the churches. In your church bazaar you put up prizes and sell chances. The winner gets it. The trusts of Wall [S]treet have nothing on the churches in profiteering. At your church festivals, you smug sisters dip up just as little ice cream as you can—[a] mere spoonful—and sell it for twenty-five cents. It's for the church, you say. Nothing but gambling and profiteering, and it's a sin.

You live double lives, you church hypocrites. You men with two living wives and you women with two living husbands! A man with a wife and a woman friend on the side—a woman with a husband and a man friend on the side. Your lives are filthy, you live in adultery, but you are in the church and because you are in it[,] it is unclean. But you church members are not by yourselves: your male preachers are just as immoral, just as filthy as you.

7

ELLA EUGENE WHITFIELD

ELLA EUGENE WHITFIELD, the daughter of Emmanuel and Ella Eugene Jones and the wife of the Reverend B. W. Whitfield, was born in Tolberton, Georgia, and reared in Texas. She graduated from Guadalupe College in Seguin, Texas, where she studied theology. After graduating, she became matron at the college, a position akin to dean of women, which brought her great recognition. Although she excelled in this post, she felt that God had other plans for her. Thus, she resigned to become a field-worker in Joanna Moore's Bible Band, a society for the daily study of the Bible. As a field-worker, she traveled extensively, organizing and lecturing for other societies. Her work in the Bible Band attracted national attention, and she was offered a position as missionary for the Woman's Convention Auxiliary National Baptist Convention and was later promoted to field secretary.[1]

Whitfield was one of the most active leaders in the Woman's Convention and among the most revered of the Baptist women. In her capacity as field secretary to the Woman's Convention, she gained national visibility traveling and speaking extensively in the United States, Cuba, and Canada, and raising funds. For years Whitfield was a key factor in the campaign to raise funds for the National Training School for Women and Girls, an institution founded by the Woman's Convention. Whitfield Hall on the school's campus was named after her, in honor of her dedicated service and success in fundraising and attracting supporters for the National Training School.[2]

Whitfield was highly successful in her work with the Woman's Convention. In 1911, she reportedly "delivered 491 addresses; visited 823 homes, 312 churches, and collected over $2,009." When evaluating Whitfield's success, Samuel W. Bacote, a renowned Baptist minister and the compiler of *Who's Who Among the Colored Baptists of the United States*, called her "a woman of untiring zeal and commanding appearance. She can hold an audience indefinitely, by the intensity of her earnestness and the clearness and appropriateness of her well-chosen words. The utility of her subjects and the excellence of her delivery have rendered her extremely popular as a public speaker." In 1920, in paying tribute to Whitfield's work, the Woman's Convention stated: "She is a post graduate in Race Psychology; she knows the race; she knows how to work with us and for us; she has handled more impossible problems and situations than any other Negro woman in the country."[3]

Whitfield's Sermons

Whitfield delivered "Salvation Is a Discovery Found in Jesus Christ" and "Making a Home a Safe Place for All That Enter Its Doors" in April 1926 at the Zion and Salem Baptist Churches in Jersey City, New Jersey. She presented the first sermon at a meeting organized by the Woman's Auxiliary and the second most likely as part of a Woman's Day program. Taken together, the two sermons argue that individual and race advancement are possible if one develops a closer relationship with God and the Church. Such advancement is also possible if one develops the home and leads a prudent, moral life by living in Christ and fighting "the good fight of faith." In both sermons, Whitfield gives very practical advice about how to live in Christ. She specifically targets issues related to early black migrants' urban problems.

Whitfield's sermons suggest the impact of her experience as matron at Guadalupe College and the tremendous influence that the philosophy of Nannie Helen Burroughs had on her. Burroughs, the corresponding secretary for the Woman's Convention, as well as Whitfield's supervisor, referred to the National Training School as the "school of the three B's," emphasizing the importance of the Bible, bath, and broom as tools for race advancement.[4] Whitfield's sermons also reflect the philosophy of the Woman's Auxiliary, which stressed what Evelyn Higginbotham calls the "Politics of Respectability." She states:

> For the Baptist women, respectability assumed a political dimension and may be likened to the variant of politics. . . . [In] the discourse sense, . . . something is "political" if it is contested across a range of different discursive arenas and among a range of different publics. While adherence to respectability enabled black women to counter racist images and structures, their discursive contestation was directed solely at white Americans; the black Baptist women condemned what they perceived to be negative practices and attitudes among their own

people. Their assimilationist leanings led to their insistence upon blacks' conformity to the dominant society's norms of manners and morals. Thus the discourse of respectability disclosed class and status differentiation.[5]

"SALVATION IS A DISCOVERY FOUND IN JESUS CHRIST." In "Salvation Is a Discovery Found in Jesus Christ," Whitfield admonishes her audience to read the fifth chapter of Galatians, in which the apostle Paul (5:16) asserts that Christ's followers must "walk in the Spirit," so that they will not succumb to their sinful nature. In order to overcome sin, Whitfield tells her audience, "Search your souls, for the things, that are hindering your progress morally, physically and industrially." Echoing the apostle Paul in his letter ("Ye did run well; who did hinder you that ye should not obey the truth?" [Gal. 5:7]), Whitfield asks her audience, "What has happened to you? . . . what has tangled you?" By reading 2 Cor. 12:9 to her audience ("And he said unto me, My grace is sufficient for thee: for my strength is made perfect in weakness."), she proclaims that no matter what entangles them or what weaknesses they have, Christ will enable them to overcome all adversity.

Suggesting, as Florence Spearing Randolph did, that the home is the woman's responsibility and the work world is the man's responsibility, Whitfield gives practical advice to women and men about how to overcome adversity in their respective spheres. Women should make sure that their children and husbands are clean and properly dressed, that their children study, and that their husbands and sons do not drink moonshine. Men should avoid "smutty" talk at work, and strive to be gentlemen, even when working at menial jobs. She challenges her audience to carry her advice to people who are not at church, for they are the ones that need it the most.

Whitfield strongly emphasizes the importance of education for individual and race advancement. She repeatedly admonishes parents to ensure that their children are well educated. She speaks directly to young people, challenging them to give up foolish pleasures that do not benefit them educationally and that threaten their health—such as "not dressing properly" (perhaps referring to the new, revealing fashions of the 1920s)—in order to strive for a better future. She also tells the older members of the congregation to improve their knowledge and skills so that the younger generation, whom they have "worked hard to educate," will not look down on them. The overarching message of the sermon, therefore, stresses that the entire congregation must never stop striving to improve their minds and bodies.

She concludes by stating that in addition to helping themselves, all must strive to uplift the whole community. She suggests that the congregation should imitate the lives of biblical figures who worked to save others. Reflecting the feminist strategy of many other preaching women, Whitfield deliberately highlights female biblical characters who were generally neglected by male preachers. In addition to stating that the apostle Paul "fought the battle" to save people, she also states that "Dorcas fought the battle to relieve suffering. Lydia fought the battle to help save [sinners]." Revealing that women as well as men have been called to do God's work, Whitfield asserts, "Many of our Fathers and Mothers help[ed] fight the battle."

"MAKING A HOME A SAFE PLACE FOR ALL THAT ENTER ITS DOORS." Addressing a primarily female congregation, Whitfield revisits the issue of homemaking, which she addressed in "Salvation Is a Discovery Found in Jesus Christ." While focusing primarily on the home in "Making a Home a Safe Place for All That Enter Its Doors," Whitfield addresses the same practical issues for individual and race advancement as she did in "Salvation Is a Discovery Found in Jesus Christ." She asserts that, through faith in God, all Christians must be modest, work hard, live within their means, educate themselves, guard their health, and help others. In order to make a home a "safe place," women must emphasize these issues so that they and their families may "advance to greater things."

Evoking the holiness doctrine tenet that all may be completely transformed through Christ, Whitfield argues that righteous living is within each person's grasp, no matter how one is living in the present. She urges her audience, "Make a start to get right with God. Make up your mind to turn around and get on the right road." She stresses that it is important not to gossip about people's past once they have decided to begin a new life in Christ and have decided to "try to do right." She states, "Loosen them and let them come. There is room—plenty of good room—for all." Everyone in the community, she stresses once again in this sermon, should support each other in working to improve the social and spiritual conditions for all.

SALVATION IS A DISCOVERY FOUND IN JESUS CHRIST

TEXT: Galatians 5:2; 2 Corinthians 11:13–33, 12:9

More men and women ought to go to Sunday School and learn of God, and there would not be so much grief and distress in the world. Salvation is a discovery found in Jesus Christ. What did we come out here for this afternoon? To hear about the wonderful accomplishments of wonderful people[?] Saved people and saved homes[?] Jesus said, "I did not come to call the righteous, but sinners to repentance."

Prayer is put out of some homes. The fight is on to put prayer in every home.

Do not put up a bluff fight, fight the good fight of faith.

If you want to win, hold fast to God.

Read Galatians Fifth Chapter.

Burdened souls, stop and consider. Strive to see light. What do you want to do? Where do you want to go?

Search your souls, for the things, that are hindering your progress morally, physically and industrially. The people thought once that you were going to be one of the great men and great women. What has happened to you? Others have gone on, and have not allowed things to tangle them and they are making high marks. I ask what has tangled you? Search your soul and write yourself a letter; mark the things that have tangled you[,] be willing and God will help you overcome.

Read 2nd Corinthians, 12th chapter, 9th verse. Sometimes our tongues get us tangled, the condition of our homes gets us tangled. Children not eating and sleeping right will get them tangled. Children ought to go to bed at night and not go out so much. They will be quick thinkers and live longer. Children ought not to go to school dirty and [with] no fasteners on their clothes, just pinned up. Other children in the same block clean up, button up and hook up.

Mothers, you ought not to go out so much at night, stay home and see after your children and see that they prepare their lessons. The school teachers cannot learn them, they must learn themselves. Put fasteners on your children's clothes.

I know you go out to work every day, but take the time you have and *succeed*. The Lord will provide. Wake up, there is danger on the line. Much is being done to destroy homes and happiness. What is meant by the words, Wake up? Study, prepare for service, so you can serve. Put prayer in your homes and bible reading.

Try to get along with people. Avoid difficulties. Get your husbands and sons not to drink moonshine. Bathe up and clean up on their work and they will receive more respect. Have pride in the home. The home is the foundation of every life. Do not have foolishness in the home, it will weaken the mind. Keep company with those who say nice things about people. Some never say anything good about anybody. Men that talk smutty on their work, are undesirables. The smutty talking men on their work, hinders good men from getting work. Work is God's gift to men; and the working place ought to be honored, on the garbage wagon; in the ditch, or any other place. Be a clean man, though you are a common laborer, you can be a gentleman.

The people that need this good advice are not here. Will you carry the word to them that they are asked to *clean up their tongues?*

Orderly people—You are the ones that are fighting the world's battle for noble things, rich or poor. You are the ones.

Our attitude would be different if we only knew them.

If we only knew the trouble we are making by carelessly talking about people, we would guard our tongues. Are you talking carelessly about people because you, want to hinder their progress? Are you jealous and envious?

Study and think and you will not have time to talk carelessly about people. Your knowledge of business principles and methods will gradually broaden and then you can step forward into a higher job.

Look ahead—Plan—Prepare yourself with all the business knowledge that you can get and success will follow. Get ready for tomorrow. Know how to do things in a systematic manner. It will save time in your homes. I beg the young people, stop doing foolish things. Stop wasting your lives by not dressing properly, to protect your health. Stop wasting your time— stop wasting your money—dressing extravagantly. Stop going to places not elevating. Use your spare time in reading and thinking how to improve yourself for greater things by reading about great men and women. Find their paths and walk therein.

Do not be content with a half-way preparation. Continue to prepare for nobler things. Study to show yourself a workman that need not be ashamed. It is important that you make up your mind—what are you going to do?

Not only prepare your children for their life's work, but keep yourselves fit. Go to night schools, learn all you can, get all the training you can. Strengthen yourselves; train willpower; memory, concentration, observation and reasoning. The young that you have worked hard to educate and train will look down upon your hairs when they become grey with scorn if you are not [trained].

If you are *fit*—stand on the platform of success, and press your claim, that you be given a chance.

Salvation is a discovery found in Jesus Christ.

The first thing to do is to give yourselves to the Lord—the Will Of God.

There is no friend like Jesus. He is All in All, in the midst of our success, faults, and failures. If you have been blessed with this world's goods, carry your bank book in your pocket—do not carry it [in] your hearts—it will fail you. Carry the people that are wandering and going astray, in your hearts. Encourage those that are pressing forward to fight on they will win the battle someday. Do not be turned around. If you are a worker for God, put on the uniform. Love, Hope and Charity. Do not be a deceitful worker, read 2nd Corinthians, 11th Chapter, 13th Verse, 33rd inclusive. If you only knew the burden that some people are bearing, your hearts would go out for them.

If you only knew the suffering of some you would be willing to help.

If we only knew the happiness we can give to others by a kind word, by a dollar, by bread, by a little clothing, we would be glad to help.

If we only knew the good that some people have done, we would stop talking discouragingly about them. Come out on God's battle field, with your home and life saving crew. Help save the people that are on the downward road. Paul fought the battle to have [them] saved. Dorcas fought the battle to relieve suffering. Lydia fought the battle to help save [sinners]. Many of our Fathers and Mothers help[ed] fight the battle and were praying fathers and mothers. We are living on their prayers today.

When we have done our best and the people withhold sunshine from us and try to push us back into the darkness of the night, we commit ourselves to your hands, Lord Jesus. Thou hast never lost a battle. Stand by[.] Let us pray.

Song: "Let Jesus Lead Us All The Way."

MAKING A HOME A SAFE PLACE
FOR ALL THAT ENTER ITS DOORS

You know all I am going to talk about. I am not trying to tell you any-thing you do not know. What I beg you all to do, is to individualize what I am going to say. Specialize it. Take it to yourself. Do not generalize, leave off Mrs. Jones' name, put [yours] there. I want to talk about making a home a safe place for all that enter its doors.

If you could live your life over what would you do? What would your home be? What would your children be? Could your children have had better features?

Have vision, foresight, courage, patience, look ahead, plan; advance to greater things.

Wait on the Lord. No good things [will be] withheld from them that walk uprightly.

Help fight the battle for Modesty. Take a stand for the right. Stand on your own feet. Do not be [led] around. Make your dresses that you wear, when you go out, a little longer. Do not get discouraged because your vision of soul does not come quickly. Work on.

If you are willing to pay the price, God will give you the desire of your heart some day. I beg you in Jesus' name, help the people that are droop-ing in darkness to see their opportunity to rise and come to higher grounds. Work out every opportunity for good. Profit by others['] mis-takes. The question is being asked every day, if you had your life to live over, what then? Make a start to get right with God. Make up your mind to turn around and get on the right road, before it is too late. When peo-ple try to do right, you good folks talk about what they once did. Loosen them and let them come. There is room—plenty of good room—for all.

My dear women: God is calling for you. Answer to the Roll Call. Let none say I can not do. The world is drooping in darkness. The Master is calling for you.

Young People: While you are young, try to overcome the little things that will hinder your progress in life. You have done well, but there are greater heights you can reach. You may be poor in money and colors, but be rich in knowledge. Stop going through the winter with low necks and short sleeves and low shoes and not much clothing on. A life is more to you than style. A style is what is used most. Start a style for the safety of your health. Learn the principles of health, eat right and sleep right. Stop wasting time; it will never come back to you again. Stop wasting your money, working in finery; have working clothes. Learn the principles of success. Make up your mind not to be a failure. It is not how much you work for, but it [is] how much you save.

A girl when she gets married, ought to be willing to live within her husband's means. She ought not expect luxuries, furs and jewelry, clothes sent to a laundry and sometimes an automobile.

Fathers and mothers ought to teach their children to live within their means.

Patch and darn and make old clothes over. Stay away from the places that only the rich can go to. It is alright to have pleasure of things that you can afford, and which is elevating. Fight the battle with economy and some day you will have a nice home and other things that will make you happy when you need it most.

For All: The pathway of life. Keep your eyes upon Jesus. Let Him lead you. Do not think because you are young and doing well that you can get along without Him. You have done well! You have fought great battles; and many have conquered. Fight on, the good fight of faith.

Let's pray.

8

RUTH R. DENNIS

RUTH R. DENNIS WAS BORN in Worcester, Massachusetts. She graduated from the New Haven, Connecticut High School, studied theology at Wilberforce University, and did special work in theology and classical literature at Columbia University. Her work as an AME evangelist and missionary worker began in 1917. From 1925 to 1927, she hosted a weekly program for the radio station WGBS (Gimbels Brothers Department Store), in which she discussed biblical subjects for twenty minutes. By 1927, she was a licensed evangelist in the New York AME Annual Conference and was connected with the Bethel AME Church in New York City. Of the sixteen ministers listed in the 1927 *Who's Who of Harlem*, Dennis was the only woman.[1]

Dennis's Sermons

"WHAT ARE WE GOING TO DO WITH THE CHILDREN?" In "What Are We Going to Do with the Children?" Dennis criticizes parents who fail to provide religious instruction for their children. Dennis declares that children living in the 1920s are exposed to numerous dangerous influences. She concludes that without religion, they succumb to the viciousness around them.

Dennis emphasizes that it is particularly important for race advancement to ensure that black children are reared properly. She suggests that because Christian living is the only true way for a people to prosper, African Americans, who face a uniquely heavy burden of economic and social oppression, most urgently need to live in Christ. She states, "The Negro especially can little afford to be careless or reluctant in the training of children in divine things," for God is the "only hope for a race or nation." Dennis asserts that, no matter what the circumstances, children's religious instruction must be a priority, for children will determine the future of their race.

Dennis acknowledges that, while economic and social oppression makes Christian instruction all the more important, those very economic circumstances can make it most difficult to devote time to instructing children in Christian living. She does not, however, excuse parents from their responsibilities on this count. She states that "a very general and dangerous indifference to the spiritual improvement . . . of . . . children" has contributed to an "economic and domestic arrangement when scarcely an hour in the week is devoted to religious instruction." She asserts that parents train their children in certain behaviors—and therefore must be devoting some time to instructing their children—but that parents focus on the wrong things in their instruction. She views it as problematic that children can "understand dancing and having beaus" while they are "kept in ignorance of religion."

Since proper child rearing is quite urgent, Dennis argues that it cannot be accomplished with lax methods. She urges her audience to forgo the "modern, humane way as it is called" to "reason with [children] on the impropriety of certain actions" and to follow instead King Solomon's advice in Prov. 23:15: "'Foolishness is bound up in the heart of the child; but the rod of correction shall drive it from him.'" Every measure, including "brutal floggings," must be employed to instill Christian virtue in children.

Dennis's overarching message is that religious education is essential for children so that they learn not only to "follow the path which leads to Heaven" but also to be "useful as members of society." In order to rear future leaders of the race who will be ethical and hardworking, African American parents must ensure that all aspects of their children's lives are consistent with "the Christian principle." This is parents' "sacred charge and duty," "which is owed not only to the children, but to themselves, to society, to Christianity and to God."

"THOUSANDS LOSING FAITH IN THE CHURCH." In "Thousands Losing Faith in the Church," Dennis maintains that most churchgoers harbor a distorted view of the purpose of attending church—namely, to hear a sermon. For some, the rise of radio ministries eliminated the need for church attendance. She posits that public worship is both an individual and social responsibility and should not be construed primarily as a time to hear the minister preach.

In this sermon, she reveals her conviction that all Christians must be actively engaged in church work, rather than laypeople's assuming that church work consists of "solos by professionals." Dennis critiques the way in which "modern folk regard the church as a Sunday club, the pulpit as an ecclesiastical lecture platform." While Dennis herself maintained a career in radio preaching, she asserts that listening to sermons on the radio exacerbates the problem of laypersons' living a passive Christian life.

Dennis argues that laypeople's disproportionally focusing on preachers rather than on their own life in Christ has caused preachers to cater to congregational tastes rather than to the word of God. Turning the preacher into a "pulpit idol" has created a breed of ministers who do "not presume to be either a leader of public opinion on religious themes or a fearless and faithful exponent of the divine law and gospel," but who please the crowds with their "eloquent" words. Preachers no longer play their proper role of condemning people for their sins. Dennis makes her point by referring to Acts 24:25 ("And as he reasoned of righteousness, temperance, and judgment to come, Felix trembled"). She states, "There was a time when as Paul preached, Felix trembled, but now Felix sits in the front pew, Paul trembles as he preaches." Whereas Paul was not afraid of preaching the truth even to Felix, the governor before whom Paul was tried, those who have taken up the preaching work of the apostle Paul fear those laypeople who sit in judgment of them.

In addition to chastising preachers for buckling under the pressure of contemporary congregations' expectations, Dennis suggests that congregations who reject pastors who preach unpopular messages are like Herod and Herodius, who had John the Baptist executed for denouncing their sins. She states, "In the days of John the Baptist, if a preacher preached the whole unsoftened truth and applied religion to practical life, they cut off his head. In these days they cut off his salary." Dennis asserts that unless the Church overcomes this problem, and refocuses all Church members' energies on working "toward the one end of lifting Jesus to the hundreds of thousands of struggling and dying people," the Church will fade into "oblivion." Evoking the holiness doctrine in her conclusion, Dennis states that the Church must cast out its corruption, for "Christ said that He would not dwell in an unclean temple and He meant it." Whether or not the organized Church survives, however, Dennis maintains that "the *truth will live on.*"

WHAT ARE WE GOING TO DO
WITH THE CHILDREN?

"What are we going to do with the children?" is the question puzzling the world today. I shall not attempt to answer it, but perhaps the subject itself will suggest a solution. One need not be a pessimist when after reflection over conditions of individuals, families or society at large, he finds the matter of the children of great magnitude and universal concern.

Notwithstanding all that has been said about youth being better today than yesteryear, it cannot be denied and should not be concealed that there prevails a very general and dangerous indifference to the spiritual improvement and eternal welfare of the children. This fact is obvious from the economic and domestic arrangement when scarcely an hour in the week is devoted to religious instruction; the family altar is almost an unheard of thing, while with everything pertaining to the "world" they are reared and tended with the greatest care. Children are considered by twentieth century parents too young to pray and receive religious instruction. "They don't understand what they are doing" is the excuse given for delinquency in religious activities. But they are not too young to understand dancing and having beaus—"that is cute." And everywhere may be seen babies in the cradle who can't talk (shame on parents of the race who encourage and teach their babies) but who can shake that thing and mess around. Children never seem too young to understand and sing the most vulgar suggestive songs that should be prohibited.

Christ said, "suffer little children to come unto me, forbid them not." He said it to parents of all ages and inattention to that command is criminal and parents who fail to obey must consider themselves responsible for dire results which are inevitable.

If children are kept in ignorance of religion, nothing that is good can be expected from them. They can neither live with comfort to themselves, nor with advantage to others; they cannot at least be so useful as members of society; and they cannot at all follow the path which leads to Heaven. How shall they believe in doctrines of which they never heard? How shall they perform duties, when they have had no training and ofttimes no example? How shall they feel and act with propriety if they know not the rules by which their minds and conduct ought to be regulated[?]

Were it not for the marvelous carelessness of many in this respect and of many from whom we should look for better things[,] these questions would not be necessary. It is obvious that something is lacking when we note how the majority of children spend their time. Of course, children must play—no one is denying that, but it is also just as necessary for them to employ time in the house of God in exercises of serious thinking.

Everyone knows that the average child is profane and vicious and it must be ascribed to the criminal inattention which it meets from its parents, who seem to think it a duty to allow it to speak and live as it pleases. The truth hurts, but it is a disgrace to the church by parents at the deplorable ignorance which children manifest when they come to ask religious privileges and when, by previous tuition, they should have been ready to embrace them. It is not shocking—the licentious, indulgences and atrocious crimes which they afterwards plunge with so little reluctance and remorse which may be so easily traced to the idle and evil habits of early life? The Negro especially can little afford to be careless or reluctant in the training of children in divine things. He should be foremost in engaging in that all important duty and that duty should be performed with enthusiasm and zeal and away with cold indifference with which it is frequently performed when performed at all.

Some excuse themselves in failing to encourage and teach children in things religious by pleading that they are not qualified. Children know more than they do—they cannot answer their questions. That is a lame excuse for anyone. "The way is so plain that a man though a fool need not err." How many children read the Bible daily, attend Sunday School regularly, prepare the lesson before they go? The only hope for a race or nation is in God. Children, the future of that race or nation, should be trained in the practice of religion and accustomed to the exercises of piety and virtue. Christ has said, "If you know these things happy are ye if ye do them." "Train up children in the way they should go and when they become old they will not depart from it."

Adults should set a pious, holy example before children. Keep the children as much as possible from bad company. The proper kind and degree of discipline should be exercised on children. Brutal floggings have long since been banished as degrading but any wise person will acknowledge the practical wisdom of Solomon who says on the subject: "Foolishness is bound up in the heart of the child; but the rod of correction shall drive it from him."

Those who argue against this mode seem always to forget that one great object to be gained in the attention paid to children, is to prevent them from acquiring evil habits and that any delay in the pursuit of this object is fatal to its accomplishment. You may reason with them on the impropriety of certain actions, you may employ the [winning] acts of persuasion, you may remonstrate, exhort, and entreat. You may bribe, promise, soothe, reprove, but [if] all the while you are persevering in this modern, humane way as it is called, the vicious actions from which the child should be guarded are repeated, they grow into fixed and firm habits, then what becomes of reasoning and entreaties[?] At length recourse is taken to the discipline which should have been used at the beginning.

What parent would refuse a child amusement? But the parent who is careful to regulate the amusement of the child fails when it comes to the more important duty of placing the amusement under the control of the Christian principle. "Do nothing that you would not want to be saying when Jesus comes; be nowhere you would not want to be when Jesus comes" is a principle which will hold good in [children's] lives at all times.

Every parent has the sacred charge and duty of bringing up children in the nurture and admonition of the Lord, a duty which is owed not only to the children, but to themselves, to society, to Christianity and to God.

THOUSANDS LOSING FAITH IN THE CHURCH

There has been so much discussion about the church that perhaps the subject has become a bit tiresome, but since spiritual truth is the most important element in our lives, it is only natural that a great deal must be said about it.

It is a simple fact, easily verified[,] that the general run of non–church goers and indeed a large proportion of regular church attendants regard an invitation to church as a request to "hear our preacher," or "to hear my sermon.["] The thought of public worship as both an individual and social duty as implied in the call to the house of God does not seem to be present to the average mind and conscience of today.

This is because the Sabbath meeting has come to mean the Sunday preaching—chiefly this and nothing more. Modern folk regard the church as a Sunday club, the pulpit as an ecclesiastical lecture platform, so they naturally reason that since such is the case[,] they are justified in attending church at home by tuning in on the radio and hearing sermons from the most learned divines, and solos by professionals.

May I not stay at home and "listen in" to a delightful service, asks the average non–church goer. Entirely with profit, if this matter of sermon hearing is all there is to your Sunday-go-to-meeting religion. And it seems, according to statistics, that men and women by the hundreds of thousands are losing faith in the church. It does not seem to meet their needs. Sermonizing seems to be the chief if not the only use for which the church exists. The more eloquent the preacher[,] the more popular he and his church become.

As a rule[,] the popular pulpit idol of the day is the man who does not presume to be either a leader of public opinion on religious themes or a fearless and faithful exponent of the divine law and gospel. The preacher of today who does not preach the "whole counsel of God," must acknowledge his part in being responsible for many of the shocking and debased misdemeanors perpetrated by so-called Christians. It is almost an acknowledged fact that the vilest persons of the community are the most "religious," according to present day standards of religion.

There was a time when as Paul preached, Felix trembled, but now Felix sits in the front pew, Paul trembles as he preaches. In the days of John the Baptist, if a preacher preached the whole unsoftened truth and applied religion to practical life, they cut off his head. In these days they cut off his salary.

Unless the church forgets creeds and the preacher popularity and works toward the one end of lifting Jesus to the hundreds of thousands of struggling and dying people who need to realize just one thing—that Jesus came to save them, and will save them now—unless the church works to fulfill that mission[,] she will die just as surely as God lives.

The church as organized today will die but the *truth will live on.* Christ said that He would not dwell in an unclean temple and He meant it. Different forms of organized churches have flourished and become corrupt and then passed into oblivion, but the truth still lived, so it shall happen again unless the church checks her downward course and "enquires for the old paths and walks therein." Genuine Christianity eliminated from the pulpit will be quickly followed by its disappearance from the pew.

The following seems to describe perfectly conditions as they are in the church today:

> Thus speaketh Christ our Lord
> Ye call me Master and obey me not;
> Ye call me Light and see me not;
>   Ye call me Way and walk not;
> Ye call me Life and desire me not;
> Ye call me Wise and follow me not;
> Ye call me Faith and love me not;
> Ye call me Rich and ask me not;
>   Ye call me Eternal and seek me not;
> Ye call me gracious and trust me not;
> Ye call me Noble and serve me not;
> Ye call me Mighty and honor me not;
> Ye call me just and fear me not;
> If I condemn you, *blame me not.*

9

MRS. RAIFF

LITTLE IS KNOWN ABOUT the Reverend Mrs. Raiff's background. It is likely that she was an AME evangelist.

In December 1927, Raiff delivered "Get the Right Ticket" at Payne Memorial Methodist Episcopal Church in Baltimore. In this sermon, she tells the congregation that the churches are full of persons who are "not right," and that in order to be saved, they must be born again. They should also "beware of bogus tickets for their trip to the Promised Land."[1] She employs a number of metaphorical strategies to convey the importance of conversion and sanctification for salvation.

First, Raiff uses the metaphor of a house mortgage for explaining the importance of living a life of Christian perfection. Conversion is like the deposit for "obtaining a mansion in Heaven." Living righteously throughout one's life is like maintaining "the payments" on one's eternal salvation. Conversion is not enough to obtain salvation, Raiff asserts, just like the first deposit on a house does not give one full ownership rights; it is only through regular "payments" of "good deeds" that "our ownership" of salvation "can never be [undermined]."

Raiff then turns to the metaphor of a ticket to explain the importance of authentic conversion. People will not be "accepted for passage" into heaven unless they have a "true ticket," one "stamped by [Jesus]." While people may believe they will be saved by investing in "other tickets," it is only through an authentic life in Jesus that one will have the "right ticket" for salvation.

Raiff reveals how people may invest in the wrong "ticket" when she states that many people "believe the giving of money and the assumption of a sanctified air while in [the] confines of the church, will assure their getting a place in Heaven." She declares that, rather than through outward appearances, it is only through true inner conversion and purification—only when the "heart" is "touched"—that Christians may "be considered on the right road."

Finally, Raiff evokes modern medical advances in cardiology as a metaphor for explaining that Christians must rely on Christ rather than on their own strengths to be truly saved. Just as "a person with a leaky heart needs a strong stimulant to sustain life," Raiff asserts, "so do those who are sin-sick at heart need the spiritual stimulation from above to help them along the way."

Raiff thus reveals a holiness doctrine similar to that of many other black preaching women. Her theology centers on the inner transformation of Christians through conversion and sanctification, and the importance of divine strength rather than human effort for living a life in Christ.

GET THE RIGHT TICKET

God ceased calling His followers "servants," and called them friends because He wanted them to feel [a] more intimate relationship with Him. That is why it is very necessary for us to get in close communion with God.

To insure our obtaining a mansion in Heaven after death, the preacher declared that we must pay our deposit on it while on earth. That deposit, she explained, consists in our being born again at the cross of Jesus. But even after we have paid this deposit, we must keep up the payments by our good deeds. Many of us pay the first deposit and then forget that there are other payments due before the mansion can be called ours. Once we have paid our deposit and kept up our payments, our ownership can never be underminded.

There're a lot of folks planning on going to Heaven, but some of them are going to be disappointed because they have bought the wrong tickets. The true ticket must be stamped by [Jesus], the Captain of the Good Ship Zion. We may even pay a higher price for other tickets, but only the true ticket will be accepted for passage.

We need to unshackle ourselves from the bondage of worldly encumbrances. Many churches today are full of people who believe the giving of money and the assumption of a sanctified air while in [the] confines of the church, will assure their getting a place in Heaven. The heart of these people must be touched, before they can be considered on the right road.

Sinners must unburden themselves of their sins and take up the cross. Just as a person with a leaky heart needs a strong stimulant to sustain life, so do those who are sin-sick at heart need the spiritual stimulation from above to help them along the way.

10

ROSA A. HORN

ROSA A. HORN WAS BORN ON December 2, 1880, in Sumter, South Carolina. She was the granddaughter of Ellen Hamilton, a slave who purchased not only her freedom but also that of her husband. Rosa was one of ten children born to Sarah Baker and her husband. Believing fervently that culture was a necessity, Sarah Baker sent all her children to a private school in Sumter.

Before becoming a preacher, Rosa was a dressmaker in Augusta, Georgia, where she lived for eight years with her husband, William Artimus, and her two children, Jessie and William Jr. In Augusta, she joined the Methodist Church. Impressed by the members of the Fire Baptized Pentecostal Church, however, she joined that church and became an evangelist. Following her husband's death during the early years of the Great Migration, she moved to Illinois and then to Indiana. There, Sister Woodworth Etter, a white minister, ordained her into the Pentecostal Church. She married William Horn and moved with him to Evanston, Illinois. In 1926, Horn settled in Brooklyn, New York.[1]

That same year, she established the Pentecostal Faith Church in Harlem. By 1934, the church was located in five cities. Dubbed Mother Horn by devotees, she was described as having a powerful presence, being an extremely effective speaker, and possessing great charisma.

By 1934, Horn was one of several women celebrated as Pentecostal, Holiness, or Spirituals preachers. Her ministry, like that of Elder Lucy Smith (Chicago), Bishop Ida Robinson (Philadelphia), Father Divine (Philadelphia), and Elder Michaux (New York), attracted a large following among southern migrants and working-class Blacks who crowded into the urban ghettos.[2] Unlike some of the other Pentecostal, Holiness, and Spiritualist preachers, however, Horn was educated and cultured.

Rosa A. Horn

Source: *Center for African American History and Culture, Temple University.*

Horn and Ida Robinson are among the women who conducted prayer ministries. In *The Prayer Tradition of Black People,* Harold Carter asserts that African American women "who lead in some form of prayer ministry across America seem to owe some of their calling to the inherited role of the African priestess. This is especially true where women, using the title of 'Mother,' minister to persons in the general areas of healing and family advice, and the normal problems of life." As Horn rose to power as the "Pray for Me Priestess," her church grew and her fame spread.[3]

Prayer has always been a powerful and respected force in the African American community. The black prayer tradition may be traced from slavery to the present. Carter observed that "Black people were sustained with prayer meetings in the midst of their slave experience. From camp to camp, log cabin to log cabin, brush arbor to brush arbor, prayer meetings were hours of communal expression far deeper than the White masters realized. In these gatherings prayer related the believers to the Ground of their being. Songs of the spirit burst forth, speaking to the basic needs of life. The freedom of open participation fostered a sense of personhood in community. Here life became meaningful and vital."[4]

The slave prayer meetings Carter described lived on in many Baptist and Methodist churches organized in the South after the Civil War. As African Americans migrated to the urban North, they tended to hold house-to-house prayer meetings that served many purposes, not the least of which were to help socialize newcomers and to forge bonds of fellowship. Thus the southern black tradition of prayer was transplanted to the urban North. Many migrants could be found in the churches established by Horn, Smith, and Robinson. Reflecting the traditional patterns of worship deeply ingrained in southern black folk culture, these women developed powerful prayer ministries.[5]

Prayer services were usually held weekly, at night, in Baptist, Pentecostal, Holiness, and other churches. The format of the meetings included song, prayer, and testimony. Individuals openly participated in these usually unstructured meetings, leading songs, praying, and testifying as they saw fit. In some cases, the minister would conclude the service with a Bible lesson or fervent praying. The length of the service depended on the participants: some prayer meetings lasted for hours, extending well into the night. In the case of Elder Smith and Rosa Horn, prayer accompanied healing.[6]

In 1933, at the invitation of the radio station WHN, Horn began a radio ministry, which brought her great recognition. WHN's publicity campaign made Horn's show compete with that of the well-known and controversial evangelist Elder Michaux. The radio station then sued

Father Divine for using illegal methods to intimidate Horn and run her Pentecostal Faith Church out of Harlem. Together, the competition and the lawsuit quadrupled the radio station's audience.[7]

Through WHN's publicity stunts, Mother Horn became famous. Beginning with a radio outlet through a single station, by 1936 the Pentecostal Faith Church was broadcast on numerous stations along the eastern seaboard. It was the first church in Upper Manhattan to be wired for radio broadcasting and to put on two programs a week. The church became a magnet for famous visitors, those who were curious, and the ill and lame who sought healing.[8]

Mother Horn's career as a radio preacher spanned thirty years. Her crusading efforts led her to have open confrontations with the owners and managers of cabarets, dance halls, pool rooms, and other places she defined as dens of iniquity. In 1959, after unsuccessful attempts to close down a New York cabaret, she moved to Baltimore. She died there on May 11, 1976.[9]

Horn's Sermons

Three sermons with distinctly different themes are presented here: "Was a Woman Called to Preach? Yes!"; "Is Jesus God the Father or Is He the Son of God?"; and "What Is Holiness? A Complete Life in Christ."

"WAS A WOMAN CALLED TO PREACH? YES!" Bishop Rosa Horn preached "Was a Woman Called to Preach? Yes!" at WBNX, a black radio station in New York City, during the late 1930s. The sermon addresses the biblical authority for women's preaching. Like Julia Foote in *A Brand Plucked from the Fire* (1879), Florence Spearing Randolph in "Antipathy to Women Preachers" (ca. 1930), Quinceila Whitlow in "The Woman in the Ministry of Jesus Christ" (1940), and Pauli Murray in "Women Seeking Admission to Holy Orders" (1974), Horn uses biblical text to argue for women's right to preach.

Horn begins "Was a Woman Called to Preach?" with the same biblical prophecy that Foote uses in "A 'Threshing' Sermon": "In the last days, I will pour out of my Spirit upon all flesh, and your sons and your daughters shall prophesy" (Joel 2:28; Acts 2:17). Horn explains that when God said that both men and women would prophesy, God meant that they would both preach. Drawing from 2 Tim. 3:16, Horn illuminates that prophesying and preaching are the same thing, for prophecy is good for "doctrine, (preaching) for correction, (preaching) for reproof, (preaching) for instruction, (preaching) in righteousness." Having revealed that "to prophesy" and "to preach" are used synonymously in Scripture, Horn asserts that the Bible clearly states that it was in God's plan for women to preach.

Horn asserts, as Foote did, that Joel's prophecy has indeed come true, for now women are preaching. Since Joel stated that women would prophesy in the last days, Horn suggests to her audience that they are witnessing the approach of the last days, and are thus living in a time when it is more urgent than ever for all of God's people to "gather in the harvest." Horn asserts that it is a waste of time to try keeping women out of the pulpit; she admonishes men not to expend energy to "fight the women," but instead to "use every moment of your life and all the breath that God gives you for the saving of precious souls." Horn further argues that it is a waste of time to fight the women because men cannot stop biblical prophecy—such as Jeremiah's words, "A woman shall encompass a man"—from coming true. No matter how much men protest, God will have women preach, for God needs them.

Undercutting the common argument that women were unfit to preach because of their female frailties, Horn argues that no human being, male or female, should rely on their own strength to do God's work. She refers her audience to Ps. 147:10: "He taketh not pleasure in the legs of a man." However, anyone who is filled with God's spirit—man, woman, or child—is amply fortified for the perils of religious leadership. Since it is "not by power nor by might, but by [God's] Spirit" (Zech. 4:6) that people are able to do God's work, it is not "the man, the woman, the boy or the girl, but the Spirit of God walking in that clean, sanctified, pure heart" that legitimizes an individual as a religious leader. Once again we see how the holiness doctrine supported preaching women's conviction that they were indeed called to preach, for, according to their doctrine, sanctification is the only requirement needed to be a preacher. When it comes to preaching, gender is irrelevant.

Horn refers to a vast array of biblical women to support her argument that God uses women to save others. She points out that it was women who received the first message from Jesus when he returned from the grave. Because the men did not listen to the women's message that Jesus had risen from the dead, Jesus' own disciples did not recognize him when they saw him. Repeatedly, Horn argues that biblical women were not only equal to men in leading godly lives but often outshone men in doing God's work.

Turning her attention to the Old Testament, Horn cites Judges, chapters 4 and 5, revealing that a woman, Deborah, was a judge, or ruler, in Israel, and that a man, Barak, was her assistant. Furthermore, one of Deborah's female contemporaries, Jael, killed "the Captain of the Canaanite Army." Thus, through using a woman, "God gave Deborah and Barak victory over their enemies and Israel had rest for forty years." Horn also highlights a woman prophet-preacher in 2 Kings 22:14–20 who gave the king of Judah a message from God. Horn even uses the milk cows of 1 Sam. 6:7–15 to reveal that the female has often outshone the male in biblical history. Horn states that when it came to the all-important task of bringing back the Lord's ark from its Philistine captivity, the Israelites chose two "female cows" to pull their treasure home, rather than the customary oxen.

When examining the New Testament, Horn reveals how Paul, the "Chief Apostle," sent Phoebe to a church and to be a "woman assist[ant] pastor." Horn emphasizes Paul's instructions that Phoebe was called to be "a servant in Christ, not a cook." Paul also affirmed Priscilla's ministry, telling Christians to receive her, "not to cook or scrub, but in the Lord." Furthermore, Acts 21:9 reveals that Philip "had four daughters which did prophesy." Thus, Horn asserts, both the Old and New Testaments make it amply clear that God uses and blesses women in positions of leadership.

"IS JESUS GOD THE FATHER OR IS HE THE SON OF GOD?" In the polemical sermon "Is Jesus God the Father or Is He the Son of God?" Horn denounces Bishop Garfield Thomas Haywood and the members of the Pentecostal Assemblies of the World, who argued that Jesus is God the Father.[10] Extensively citing biblical verses that refer to Jesus as "the Son," Horn forcefully argues that "Jesus the Son" and "God the Father" are two separate entities. A significant piece of her argument is her assertion that it is only through Jesus that one may be purified of sins. If humans stood before God without Jesus' intercession, they would have no hope of being forgiven for their iniquities. Only through Jesus' dying for humans' sins can people be forgiven and saved. "No man can walk with God except the carnal mind has been taken away," Horn declares, and only Jesus, God's son, can transform the carnal mind into a righteous reflection of the divine.

Criticizing churches that give their members rote phrases to repeat in order to be saved, Horn argues that genuine salvation comes only through truly repenting of one's sins so that Jesus will have mercy on them. Revealing the importance of Jesus the Son in the holiness doctrine—stressing that it is only through Jesus the Son that repentant souls may be brought before God the Father—Horn emphasizes that those who would seek inner purification can only "keep yourselves in the love of God" by "looking for the mercy of our Lord Jesus Christ unto eternal life."

"WHAT IS HOLINESS? A COMPLETE LIFE IN CHRIST." Horn's "What Is Holiness? A Complete Life in Christ" has many similarities with both

Foote's and Randolph's sermons entitled "Christian Perfection." While Horn emphasizes the importance of conversion and sanctification, just as Foote, Randolph, and other Methodist preaching women did, Horn's Pentecostal bent is evident in her particular emphasis on the Holy Ghost—an emphasis that distinguishes her holiness theology from that of Foote, Randolph, and other black preaching women who remained within Methodist denominations. While many of the black preaching women in this anthology see sanctification as the quintessence of Christian salvation, Horn suggests that sanctification is merely a preliminary stage of salvation that prepares the Christian to receive the Holy Ghost. According to Horn, God's "plans of salvation are not completed in your life, until you do receive" the Holy Ghost. Thus, Horn preaches that Christians must go through three distinct stages of salvation: conversion, sanctification, and baptism in the Holy Ghost.

In the first half of her sermon, Horn uses much of the same imagery and language as Foote and Randolph to argue for the importance of conversion and sanctification. When one is converted, one is "born again" into the family of God. After conversion, one must be "washed, and made clean" like a baby who has just been born: this is the cleansing process in sanctification. Horn expounds extensively on the importance of sanctification. Just as a newborn baby is literally covered with birthing residue, so are humans' souls covered with iniquity, even after they have been converted to Christianity. Thus, Christians must not "run away in a converted state," but must "wait for the purging process" of the casting out of sins to attain inner purification, or sanctification, for God will not "use anyone until they are clean, every whit." Like many Holiness preachers of her day, Horn declares that inner purification must be combined with righteous living, which requires one to reject such pleasures as playing cards, dancing, and smoking tobacco.

Having established the importance of sanctification, Horn devotes the second half of her sermon to the importance of baptism in the Holy Spirit. She states that once Jesus sanctified his disciples, he "commanded them, that they should wait for the promise of the Father, which is the Holy Ghost" (Acts 1:1–5). Even though sanctification is crucial, because "the Holy Ghost is not for sinners," Horn critiques those who focus solely on the importance of sanctification; she does this by asserting that sanctified Christians should "tarry for the Holy Ghost" as Jesus' first disciples did. They will know that they have received the Holy Ghost when they speak in tongues, as the early Christians did on the day of Pentecost. It is only through this process—conversion, sanctification, and baptism in the Holy Spirit—that Christians may attain the "joy unspeakable" of salvation.

WAS A WOMAN CALLED TO PREACH? YES!

Text: Acts 2:17–18; 2 Timothy 3:16;
Jeremiah 31:22; 2 Kings 22:14–20; Romans 16;
Psalms 147:10; Acts 8:38–40, 21:9;
1 Samuel 6:7–15

God said, "In the last days, I will pour out of my Spirit upon all flesh, and your sons and your daughters shall prophesy (preach)," etc. (Acts 2:17–18). Prophecy covers the past, present, and future tense, unfolding the blessed Word of God, and is profitable for doctrine, (preaching) for correction, (preaching) for reproof, (preaching) for instruction, (preaching) in righteousness" (2 Tim. 3:16).

Did not God tell Ezekiel to prophesy (preach) to the dry bones in the valley? And the dry bones came together and received life. Go, ye women and prophesy (preach) to the dry bones, that they may hear God's Word and live. Time is almost out and millions and billions of souls are being lost.

Men, don't take time to fight the women. You need to use every moment of your life and all the breath that God gives you for the saving of precious souls.

Note that when God said your sons and your daughters shall prophesy (preach)[,] that meant man and woman. You can't hinder the woman anyhow, for the prophecy of Jeremiah 31:22, 606 B.C., is now being fulfilled, which saith, "For the Lord hath created a new thing in the earth, A woman shall encompass a man." That's the Word! Are they not doing it? They are filling the pulpits and not only filling the pulpits, but bringing in precious sheaves for the Master, for He is coming soon.

Did not the Lord say that He would pour out His spirit upon all flesh in the last days? Yes, the last days, saith God, the last days. When you see the women preaching in the pulpit, preaching in the house, preaching in the streets, preaching everywhere, these are some of the signs of the last days, the last days saith God; healing the sick, raising the dead, casting out devils, speaking in other tongues, living holy without spot or blemish; these are some of the signs of the last days. Yea, the Lord Jesus will soon descend with a host of angels on clouds of bright glory, to catch away His waiting Bride. Are you ready to meet Him and [bring] your sheaves with you? If not, get ready, stay ready, be ready when Jesus comes.

To whom did Jesus give the first message? Did He not say to the Marys at the tomb, "Go and tell Peter and my disciples to meet me in Galilee?"

Instead of obeying the Word of God given to them by the women, those disciples were standing around talking and Jesus, passing by two of the men, asked them "what conversation have ye among yourselves and are sad?" Not knowing it was Jesus who spake with them; they didn't believe He was risen, as the women told them; they answered Jesus, "Are you just new in Jerusalem and have not heard how they crucified Jesus of Nazareth?" Jesus said, "Oh thou fools and slow of heart to believe," etc. Previously, Thomas[,] one of those men[,] said, "Except I can see the nail-prints in His hands and thrust my finger into His side, I will not believe."

Surely the Lord has called the women, under the Law and under Grace and he uses them whenever he needs them.

Was it not 1336 years B.C. that we find Deborah, a woman judge, a ruler in Israel[?] The first three judges were Othniel, Ehud, and Shamgar. Deborah and Barak were the fourth and fifth judges. Barak was Deborah's assistant. At the time to go to battle, Barak said, "I will not go except thou go with me," and Deborah said, "I will go but the honor will be given to a woman this day." When Sisera, the Captain of the Canaanite Army, fled, he was slain by Jael, another woman in Israel, and so God gave Deborah and Barak victory over their enemies and Israel had rest for forty years.

Did not Hilkiah the priest and Ahikam, and Achbor, and Shaphan, and Asahiah go unto Huldah the prophetess (a woman preacher) who dwelt in the college of Jerusalem to inquire of her what thus saith the Lord? She said, "Thus saith the Lord, I will bring evil upon this place, as I have said," etc., "but concerning the King of Judah which sent you to inquire of the Lord, say ye to him; because thine heart was tender and thou hast humbled thyself, etc., I will bring thee to thy fathers in peace" (2 Kings 22:14–20). Another message from God to a man by the mouth of a woman; 624 years B.C. and 684 years before Paul's letter to the church concerning [Phoebe] (Rom. 16).

Paul said, "I commend unto you [Phoebe] our sister, a servant of the church which is at [Cenchraea]: That ye receive her in the Lord as becometh saints, and that ye assist her in whatsoever business she hath need of you: for she hath been a succourer of many, and of myself also." She took his place, in other words; a woman assist[ant] pastor. Paul said a servant in Christ, not a cook.

Oh, yes, God bless the bravery of the woman, I say too, help her, obey her. Paul, the Chief Apostle said obey her, assist her. Woman messenger, above all the obstacles and hindrances; run, carry the glad message to whosoever will receive it. Why, God has even said that a little child shall lead them. Many times I've seen little boys and girls of all ages, preaching the unadulterated Word of God, another sign of His soon coming.

Did not the Lord say, "I will write my law in the fleshly table of their hearts and stamp it in their minds?" Again He saith, "I shall be in them and I shall walk in them and I shall talk in them." Not the spirit of you, oh man, whoever thou art. In Psalms 147:10, God said, "He taketh not pleasure in the legs of a man." Again the Lord saith, "Not by power nor by might, but by my Spirit and if any have not the Spirit of God, he is none of His." Not the man, the woman, the boy or the girl, but the Spirit of God walking in that clean, sanctified, pure heart, without spot or wrinkle; bringing victory and honor and glory unto His Holy Name. Oh, hallelujah! Glory to God!

What about the church in the house of Priscilla and Aquila, man and wife preaching God's Word[?] Paul said also to receive them in the Lord; not to cook or scrub, but in the Lord.

What about Philip, the evangelist, the man who was caught away by the Spirit of God out of the eyesight of the eunuch and the next time he was seen was at Azotus (Acts 8:38–40)[?] He walked closer to God than we have been able to yet, but keep on striving. This Philip had four daughters which did prophesy (Acts 21:9). Prophesying is preaching as I told you before. Come on Ezekiel and help me now.

Here is a beautiful type of God using the women in the ministry.

When Israel was in great distress because the ark of the Lord had been captured by the Philistines, who was it that brought back the ark after it had been in the country of the Philistines for seven months? They didn't tie oxen to the cart which was the custom then as is today, but in 1 Samuel 6:7–15, we read how the men tied two milk kine to the cart and shut up their calves at home. Nobody said, why are you hitching up those female cows instead of male oxen? They were in great distress and only those pure, clean female cows could answer the purpose.

And they laid the ark of the Lord upon the cart, and the kine took the straight way to the Bethshemesh, and went along the highway, lowing as they went, and turned not aside to the right hand or to the left. Take note, those women cows didn't turn to the right hand nor to the left, but they led those five lords of Philistines the straight way. No man directed the kine where to go, but those five men watched and followed the ark. No one was driving them, but God led those female milking cows and they brought the ark of the Lord back home, into a wheat field. The reapers of the wheat harvest looked up and saw the ark and rejoiced.

The kine stood with the ark right by a great stone in the field. There those Philistine lords made restitution to the Israelites. The stone is a type of our blessed Saviour; yes that great stone that was hewn out of a mountain, tearing down the kingdoms of this world, the Rock Christ Jesus, oh Hallelujah!

Take note, women preachers, the kine stood the ark by the great stone and they also left their little ones willingly; shouldering the ark. The five men watched the kine as they went the straight way[,] by the way, and followed them. Glory! Preach the Word.

Let me say to the women whom God has called.

Go Carry the Word to one and all!
And God will give you a great reward[.]
Cry aloud, don't take down,
The day will soon be gone,
God will bless you on that glorious morn,
For all the golden sheaves you've won.

IS JESUS GOD THE FATHER

OR IS HE THE SON OF GOD?

TEXT: Matthew 1:21, 28:19; Hebrews 5:5;
1 John 2:22, 5:5; 1 Timothy 2:5; John 1:34,
14:23–24, 28; Luke 8:28; Ephesians 5:11;
2 Corinthians 11:13–15; Acts 2:38; Exodus
3:13–15; Proverbs 30:4; 2 Timothy 2:15;
Judges 17; Revelation 4:2–3, 5:1–13

And she shall bring forth a Son,
(Yes, He is the Son) and thou shalt call His name Jesus,
for He shall save His people from their sins.

—Matt. 1:21

The children of God are warned against apostates, who deny the deity of Christ and say that Jesus is God, the Father. Jesus is not the Father; Jesus is the Son of the Father. (Heb. 5:5) God said to Jesus, "Thou art my Son, this day have I begotten Thee." (1 John 2:22) "Who is a liar but he that denieth that Jesus is the Christ? He is antichrist, that denieth the Father and the Son." Jesus is the Son of God. I believe the Bible, don't you?

The Word teaches that there is a Father in Heaven and a Son. (1 Tim. 2:5) "For there is one God and one mediator between God and men, the man Christ Jesus." That makes Jesus an Intercessor, interceding to the Father for us. Thank God, He is our intercessor and not the Father, but the Son. All right, Glory to God! Amen.

Away with [any skeptic] who says Jesus is God. His head is stopped up and needs to be blasted with the Power of the Holy Ghost; not a ghost, but Heaven's Holy Ghost. The words of John the Baptist (John 1:34), "And I saw, and bear record that this is the Son of God." Amen.

When Jesus rebuked the devils out of the man (Luke 8:28), the devil cried out, "What have I to do with thee, Jesus, thou Son of God most high? I beseech thee, torment me not." The devils confessed that Jesus is the Son of God. Would you let the Devil be better than you, who say that Jesus is God the Father? Jesus is not God the Father, but the Son, as He said. Praise the Lord! (John 14:28) Jesus said, "My Father is greater than I," and why do you contradict Jesus, by saying Jesus is the Father? Jesus is not God the Father, but He is the Son, as He said. (John 14:23) Jesus answered and said unto him, "If a man love me, he will keep my words and my Father will love him and we will come unto him and make our abode with him." "My Father and I," (plural) said Jesus, "will take up our (plural) abode with him." Is Jesus not speaking of His Father here? Thou child of the Devil, trying to confuse the Word of God. (John 14:24) "He that loveth me not keepeth not my sayings: and the word which ye hear is not mine, but the Father's which sent me[.]" The scripture shows that you don't love Jesus. Jesus said if you don't love Him, you wouldn't keep His sayings.

You not only fail to love him, but try to make Him a liar, but you can't do it; thank God. The Word is too plain. Jesus said His Father sent Him and you say Jesus Himself is the Father. I believe Jesus. God said, "Let every man's word be a lie and My word the truth." I believe the Word of God, not you.

Let me warn you, dear children of God, who have been standing up for the truth. May God help you to stand firmly on the Apostles' Doctrine and "Have no fellowship with the unfruitful works of darkness, but rather reprove them" (Eph. 5:11). (2 Cor. 11:13–15) "For such are false apostles of Christ. And no marvel for Satan himself is transformed into an angel of light. Therefore it is no great thing if his ministers also be transformed as the ministers of righteousness; whose end shall be according to their works."

(1 John 5:5) "Who is he that overcometh the world, but he that believeth that Jesus is the Son of God?" And the 7th verse says, "For there are three that bear record in Heaven, the Father, the Word and the Holy Ghost." Beloved, don't deny the Father and the Son, for 1 John 2:22 tells us, "He is an antichrist that denieth the Father and the Son."

Now to any innocent reader of this tract, who does not understand the doctrine of Jesus; if you are going to be baptized, you are privileged to ask how they baptize, for these [skeptics] baptize in the name of Jesus only, which is not scriptural. Jesus said in Matthew 28:19, "Go ye, therefore, and teach all nations, baptizing them in the name of the Father and of the Son, and of the Holy Ghost."

Peter on the Day of Pentecost, told the Jews and all who had not received Jesus, as they had only been baptized unto John's baptism (Acts 2:38) to be baptized in the name of the Lord Jesus; not to deny the Father, whom they had already accepted, but to believe in Jesus, also. If it is right to baptize in the name of Jesus only, in whose name did John baptize?

Beloved, be careful to watch your salvation. When you sin that puts you out from under the Blood of Jesus and you are susceptible to take on any spirit of delusion. God's Word says, "Because of the hardness of your heart, I will send strong delusion upon you, and you will rather believe a lie than the truth."

When Elder [Haywood] was turned out of the Pentecostal Church at Indianapolis, Indiana for his hardness and misbehavior, that is when he went into this terrible delusion, saying that God's name is Jesus, made himself a bishop and began to spread it before he died. Mark my words, his followers will say to you, "If God is Jesus' Father, what is His name?" They will answer for you, "His name is Jesus." Such delusion is absurd.

There is only one place under the lids of the Bible where God told His name to anyone and that was Moses. When the Lord sent Moses to deliver the children of Israel from Egypt's bondage, Moses said unto God, "Behold when I come unto the children of Israel and shall say unto them, the God of your fathers hath sent me unto you; and they shall say unto me, what is His name, what shall I say unto them?" And God said unto Moses, "Thou shalt say unto the children of Israel, I *am* hath sent me unto you. This is my Name forever, and this is my Memorial, unto all generations" (Exod. 3:13–15).

Let no man beguile you of your reward, intruding into things that ye know not of vainly puffed up by your fleshly minds. Is this thing essential to salvation? No, but saving souls is.

In Proverbs 30:4, we read, "Who hath ascended up into heaven, or descended? Who hath bound the waters in a garment? Who hath established all the ends of the earth? What is His name, and what is His Son's name, if thou canst tell?" These questions are not hid from the people of God.

Let us be careful how we divide the Word of God. Paul said to Timothy, "Study to show thyself approved unto God, a workman that needeth not to be ashamed, rightly dividing the Word of Truth" (2 Tim. 2:15); and there is a way that seemeth right unto man but the end thereof is the way of death. "Search the scriptures," Jesus said, "For in them ye think ye have eternal life and [there] are they which testify of me."

One of the things that is causing much trouble in the church of God today, is hurrying the seekers through. I've seen them telling the seekers something to say real fast, such as glory, save me, save me, or hallelujah; (many times they don't even say hallelujah but lu, lu, lu) instead of teaching them to repent of their sins. Hence, the unsaved are being fellowshipped into the church as saved. There we have much trouble. No man can walk with God except the carnal mind has been taken away, for the carnal mind is not subject to the Will of God, neither indeed can be. The only remedy is to wait at the altar until the work is done. You won't need anyone to tell you. "Let the sinner forsake his ways," saith the Lord, "and the unrighteous man his thoughts and let them return unto the Lord and He will have mercy upon them, and to our God, for He will abundantly pardon." Godly sorrow worketh repentance and out of your mouth confession is made unto salvation.

Ah, beloved, if you would see Jesus, tarry before God, in humble heartfelt contrition, pouring out your soul. There, the tears of joy will begin to flow. One taste of God calls for another. You will know when the work is done and you won't have any more trouble with [your] old self, but you will have joy unspeakable and full of glory.

(Judges, beginning at the 17th verse) "But, beloved, remember ye the words which were spoken before of the apostles of our Lord Jesus Christ; how that they told you there should be mockers in the last time, who should walk after their own ungodly lusts. These be they who separate themselves, sensual, having not the Spirit. But ye, beloved building up yourselves on your most holy faith, praying in the Holy Ghost, keep yourselves in the love of God, looking for the mercy of our Lord Jesus Christ unto eternal life. And of some have compassion, making a difference; and others have with fear, pulling them out of the fire; hating even the garment spotted by the flesh."

Here is another beautiful picture of the Father and the Son. In Revelation 4:2–3, John the Revelator said, "And immediately I was in the spirit; and behold, a throne was set in heaven, and one sat on the throne. And He that sat was to look upon a jasper and a sardine stone: and there was a rainbow round about the throne, in sight like unto an emerald."

> (Rev. 5:1–13) And I saw in the right hand of Him that sat on the throne, (God the Father) a book written within and on the back, sealed with seven seals. And I saw a strong angel proclaiming with a loud voice, "who is worthy to open the book, and to loose the seals thereof?" And no man in heaven, nor in earth, neither under the earth, was able to open the book, neither to look thereon. And I wept much, because no man was found worthy to open and to read the book, neither to look thereon. And one of the elders saith unto me, "Weep not: behold, the Lion of the tribe of Judah, the Root of David, (Jesus) hath prevailed to open the book, and to loose the seals thereof." And I beheld, and lo, in the midst of the throne and of the four beasts, and in the midst of the elders, stood a Lamb as it had been slain, having seven horns and seven eyes, which are the seven Spirits of God sent forth into all the earth. And He (Jesus) came and took the book out of the right hand of Him (God the Father) that sat upon the throne.

And who is this sitting upon the throne? God, the Father. Who is this who took the book out of the right hand of Him that sat upon the throne? Jesus, for He is the only Lion of the tribe of Judah, the Son of the living God.

"And when He had taken the book, the four beasts and the four and twenty elders fell down before the Lamb, having every one of them harps, and golden vials full of odors, which are the prayers of the saints." (Oh, thank God, the prayers of the righteous availeth much.)

> And they sung a new song, saying, Thou art worthy to take the book, and to open the seals thereof: for Thou wast slain, (Jesus) and hast redeemed us to God (God the Father) by Thy blood out of every kindred, and tongue, and people, and nation: And hast made us unto our God kings and priests: and we shall reign on the earth. And I beheld, and I heard the voice of many angels round about the throne and the beasts and the elders: and the number of them was ten thousand times ten thousand, and thousands of thousands; saying with a loud voice, Worthy is the Lamb that was slain (Jesus) to receive power, and riches, and wisdom, and strength, and honor, and glory, and blessing. And every creature which is in heaven, and on the earth, and under the earth, and such as are in the sea and all that are in them, heard I saying, blessing, and honor, and glory, and power, be unto Him that sitteth upon the throne, (God the Father) and unto the Lamb (Jesus the Son) forever and ever.

Amen.

WHAT IS HOLINESS? A COMPLETE LIFE IN CHRIST

TEXT: 1 Corinthians 6:19–20, 15:22; Isaiah 1:18,
9:16–17, 55:7, 56:10; Psalms 10, 19:7, 51:5, 10;
Acts 1:1–5, 2:4, 3:7, 19, 10:44–47, 19;
Hebrews 9:13–14; 1 John 1:8, 9; John 3:3–8,
14:16–17, 17:17; Romans 6:12; 2 Timothy 2:21;
1 Thessalonians 4:3–7, 5:22; Luke 24:49

SANCTIFICATION Sanctification is a clean life, a vessel set apart for the Master's use (1 Cor. 6:19–20).

"What! know ye not that your body is the temple of the Holy Ghost, which is in you, which ye have of God and ye are not your own? For ye are bought with a price, therefore, glorify God in your body, and in your spirit, which are God's."

If we are born in sin, and shaped in iniquity—yes, we are—for as in Adam all men die, so in Christ we live. (Isa. 55:7) "Let the sinner forsake his way, and the unrighteous man his thoughts and let him return unto the Lord, and He will have mercy upon him; and to our God, for He will abundantly pardon." Again, He said, "If any man would come after Him, he must first believe that He is, and that He is a Rewarder of them that diligently seek Him," therefore, we must be converted; for Jesus died that we might live through His death. (Ps. 19:7) "The Law of the Lord is perfect, converting the soul, the testimony of the Lord is sure, making wise the simple." (Acts 3:19) "Repent ye, therefore and be converted that your sins may be blotted out when the times of refreshing shall come from the presence of the Lord."

Now, then, when you have been made to believe the Word of God, and God, for Christ's sake forgives you of your sins, don't run away in a converted state, but wait for the purging process; wait for an instantaneous second work of grace. (Heb. 9:13–14) "For if the blood of bulls and of goats, and the ashes of an heifer, sprinkling the unclean, sanctifieth to the purifying of the flesh: How much more shall the blood of Christ, who through the eternal spirit, offered Himself without spot to God, purge your conscience from dead works to serve the living God?"

Some will say, "I have no sins, I've always been good." Does not 1 John 1:8, say, "If we say we have no sin, we deceive ourselves, and the truth is not in us?" Here is deliverance—(1 John 1:9) "If we confess our sins, He (God) is faithful and just to forgive us our sins and to cleanse us from all unrighteousness (iniquities)." Some people argue this question, by saying, "If they join some church, pay their debts, treat their neighbors right," that makes them a Christian. An unconverted, unclean person, trying to serve God, not having been led right in doctrinal points climbing up some other way, they become ignorant of the righteousness of God. The shepherds are to blame, as said the prophet (Isa. 56:10), "His watchmen are blind: they are all ignorant, they are all dumb dogs, they cannot bark, sleeping, lying down, loving to slumber. Yea, they are greedy dogs which can never have enough and they all look to their own way, everyone for his gain, from his quarter."

Again He said (Isa. 1:18), "come, now, let us reason together, saith the Lord, though your sins be as scarlet, they shall be white as snow; though they be red like crimson, they shall be as wool." (Ps. 51:5) "Behold, I was shapen in iniquity; and in sin, did my mother conceive me." This is true. (1 Cor. 15:22) "For as in Adam all die, even so in Christ shall all be made alive."

Did not Jesus say to the good Pharisee, who kept the moral law, blameless (John 3:3–8), "Verily, verily, I say unto thee, ye must be born again. Nicodemus said unto Him, how can a man be born when he is old? Can he enter the second time into his mother's womb and be born? Jesus answered, "Verily, verily I say unto thee, except a man be born of the water, and of the Spirit, he cannot enter into the Kingdom of God: that which is born of the flesh is flesh; that which is born of the Spirit is Spirit. Marvel not that I said unto thee, ye must be born again. The wind bloweth where it listeth, and thou hearest the sound thereof, but canst not tell whence it cometh, and whither it goeth; so is every one that is born of the Spirit."

Take for instance, when the vessel is made or bought for us, is it not washed, cleansed or sterilized, before using; or would anyone use an unclean plate, or any unwashed vessel? No, not by any means, neither can the Lord use anyone until they are clean, every whit. (Rom. 6:12) "What shall we say, then, shall we continue in sin, that grace may abound? God forbid. How shall we that are dead to sin, live any longer therein?" Beloved, don't be foolish, or deceived with vain words of man's wisdom, but seek the mind of Christ, that we might know how to please our God. Didn't God forgive David for his sins? After that, wasn't he found faithful, even until death He prayed to God (David's prayer) (Ps. 51:10), "Create in me a clean heart, oh, God, and renew a right spirit within me—then shall I teach transgressors thy ways, and sinners shall be converted unto Thee." Praise God for His Word, and He says, "If my Word be hid to any at all, it is hid to them that are lost." Don't be lost, but seek the Lord, with your whole heart. Seek and you shall find, ask, and it shall be given, knock, and the door shall be opened unto you.

Some will say, "I have been converted and I am a member of the church and I received all, when I was converted." When a baby is born, is that all? No there is something else. The baby is born; then, the baby is washed, and made clean. When we are converted, is that washed, and made clean—when we are born again, is that all? No, to be converted is the same thing as [being] born again, which makes one a member of the holy family; in other words, we have been brought into relationship with God. Shall we stop there, in a converted state, just born? No, but there is a purging, cleansing process; circumcision of the heart, which is sanctification.

Now then, we are born again, washed and circumcised—converted, cleansed, sanctified. After we have been converted we must be sanctified and set apart from the world of sin; card-playing, dancing for the devil, telling lies, joking, hatred, malice, strife, heresy, busy-bodies always meddling in other men's matters, trouble-makers, truce-breakers, false accusers, respect of person, swearing, jealousy, backbiting your neighbors, and all other uncleanness, as mentioned—tobacco is also an unclean habit. (2 Tim. 2:21) "If a man will therefore purge himself from these things, he shall be a vessel unto honor sanctified, and meat for the Master's use." (1 Thess. 5:22) "Abstain from all appearance of evil, and the very God of Peace will sanctify you wholly, and I pray God your whole Spirit and soul anybody be preserved, blameless, unto the coming of our Lord Jesus Christ. Faithful is He that calleth you, who also will do it. I charge you that this epistle be read unto all the holy brethren.

(1 Thess. 4:3–7) "This is the will of God, even your sanctification, that ye should abstain from fornication, and that every one of you should know how to possess his vessel in sanctification and honor:—For God hath not called us unto uncleanness, but unto Holiness." Jesus also prayed to God, for his disciples, when he was getting ready to leave them (John 17:17), that the Lord would not sanctify them on their death-beds, as said the unwise leaders, but that He would sanctify them, in this present world and keep them sanctified. Don't listen to the untruthful leaders, as said Isaiah 9:16–17, "The leaders of this people do cause them to err, and do make hypocrites of them." Consequently they never live the life, because they have not the keeping-power, and neither are some of them sanctified, but are kept back by false leaders, etc., but hear what thus saith the Lord, through Jesus Christ. Jesus not only sanctified them, but commanded them, that they should wait for the promise of the Father, which is the Holy Ghost (Acts 1:1–5).

Again, He said in Luke 24:49, to His disciples, when he was getting ready to leave them, "Behold, I send the promise of my Father upon you, but tarry ye in the city of Jerusalem, until ye be endued with power from on high." Did they obey Him? They gladly returned to Jerusalem, with great joy, after He went up, and were continually in the temple, daily, blessing and praising God, until the Holy Ghost came, which He promised to send in His name. Positive proof of receiving the Holy Ghost, which Jesus sent, according to His promise, while they tarried. (Acts 2:4) "And when the day of Pentecost was fully come, they were all with one accord, in one place; and suddenly there came a sound from heaven, as of a rushing mighty wind—and it filled all the house, where they were sitting; and there appeared unto them cloven tongues, like as of fire, and it sat upon each of them; and they were all filled with the Holy Ghost, and began to speak with other tongues, as the Spirit gave them utterance."

Another clear proof that the Holy Ghost is not for sinners, but for those who are saved, already. (Acts 10:44–47) Cornelius, a devout, clean man, one who feared God, with all his household, with whom the angels spake, and told him to send for Peter. Cornelius was a converted, clean sanctified man, and the Lord talked with him. If his life was clean, and he had to be taught of Peter; what was it then?—nothing but the baptism of the Holy Ghost, for the scripture says, (44th verse) "While Peter yet spake these words, the Holy Ghost fell on all which heard the Word." (How do we know they received the Holy Ghost[?]) [The] 47th verse says, "For they heard them; speak with tongues, and magnify God." The Bible evidence of the Holy Ghost coming in, is that they speak with tongues.

(John 14:16–17) "And I will pray the Father, and He shall give you another Comforter, that He may abide with you forever; even the Spirit of truth, whom the world cannot receive because it seeth Him not, neither knoweth Him, but ye know Him, for He dwelleth with you, and shall be in you." Is that conversion? Were not the disciples converted before they went up on the Mount of Transfiguration, and saw the Glory of God? Or is the baptism of the Holy Ghost sanctification? Were they not sanctified (John 17:17) before Jesus was even crucified? Were not those disciples sanctified in Acts 19, when Paul reminded them of John telling them, when he baptized them, that they should receive the baptism of the Holy Ghost, afterwards? What is the baptism unto repentance, but conversion? Nothing else but being born again, of the water and of the Spirit. Does not circumcision after birth, typify Sanctification? Can you circumcise a baby before it is born? Circumcision is nothing else than sanctification—taking away the foreskin of the heart.

What saith Jude, the servant of Jesus Christ, and brother of James, to them that are sanctified by God the Father and preserved in Jesus Christ, and called, Mercy unto you, and peace and love be multiplied, Was he not talking to a sanctified people?—did he not say, "To them that are sanctified by God the Father?" If conversion and sanctification are all that a person needs, why did he say in the 3rd verse, "Beloved when I gave all diligence to write unto you and exhort you that ye should earnestly contend for the faith which was once delivered unto the saints." If he is writing to a sanctified people, what is he exhorting them to tarry for? Is he not telling them to tarry for the Holy Ghost? Did he not also warn them that they would be destroyed like the children of Israel were, because of unbelief, if they failed to earnestly contend, which is to tarry and wait? And is not this scripture in harmony with Acts 1, where Jesus commanded His disciples to tarry in Jerusalem, for the power, which is the Holy Ghost? The plans of salvation are not completed in your life, until you do receive it.

Sanctification is not the baptism of the Holy Ghost. You must be cleansed, first, by a cleansing, purging process, which is sanctification. Does not the scripture say, "The Holy Ghost will not come into an unclean temple?" Then you must be sanctified, first. Some continue to argue, saying they don't have to speak with tongues, when they receive the Holy Ghost. I say too, we don't have to, and can't do anything; but when the Holy Ghost comes in, He will speak as the Spirit gives utterance, not you. Just obey the Word, and tarry until He comes, then you will have joy unspeakable, and full of Glory.

IDA B. ROBINSON

IDA B. ROBINSON WAS BORN on August 3, 1891, in Hazelhurst, Georgia. When Ida was young, her family moved to Pensacola, Florida, where she resided until 1917. In 1908, she affiliated with the Church of God. This experience made a profound impression on her, and presented an opportunity for her to enter the ministry. Two years later, she married Oliver Robinson. Hoping to improve their economic status and obtain jobs, in 1917 the Robinsons migrated to Philadelphia, where she affiliated with the United Holy Church of America. Beginning her career as a street evangelist, Ida Robinson was ordained an elder and, in 1919, was appointed pastor of Mount Olive Church, a small mission.[1]

Ida Robinson's forcefulness as a holiness preacher and her concern that women receive full clergy rights led to the 1924 founding of a denomination, the Mount Sinai Holy Church of America, Inc. Beginning with the mother church in Philadelphia, Mount Sinai rapidly expanded as churches in other states affiliated. Robinson was elected bishop, and in 1925, Mount Sinai held its first national convocation. From this inauspicious beginning, Mount Sinai became one of the largest Pentecostal organizations, later expanding to Cuba and British Guiana (now Guyana), South America. Mount Sinai was of particular importance among holiness organizations in the extent and degree to which women participated. As bishop, Robinson ordained women throughout the United States. Although there were male preachers and officers, the predominance of the church's elders, ministers, and administrators were women.[2]

Though little is known about her formal education, Robinson's sermons, speeches, and writings indicate a high level of intelligence. Bishop Robinson was a student of the Bible, a powerful, forceful, and charismatic preacher whose impact on her time and on black religion was singular. Although Ida Robinson has not received adequate recognition and is still

Ida B. Robinson

Source: *Center for African American History and Culture, Temple University.*

virtually unknown to scholars and the general public, she is well known to Pentecostal Holiness advocates, and her legacy survives through the denomination she founded and the church she established in Philadelphia. She died on April 20, 1946, in Winter Haven, Florida.[3]

Robinson's Sermons

Robinson delivered "Who Shall Be Able to Stand?" and "Can These Bones Live?" on May 6, 1934, at the Mount Sinai Holy Church of America in Philadelphia, at the morning and evening services, respectively. In both sermons, Robinson elaborates most extensively on her holiness theology and stresses the importance of purifying God's Church through the sanctification of all Christians.

She delivered "The Economic Persecution" in 1935. This sermon speaks about pressing social issues and raises questions of morality. One of the most crucial issues, lynching, was widely discussed in the black community. As a response to the efforts of the NAACP to secure passage of a federal law against lynching, several bills were introduced in Congress between 1919 and 1935. The Costigan-Wagner Bill of 1935 sparked debates that inspired Robinson's sermon.[4]

"WHO SHALL BE ABLE TO STAND?" Robinson bases the message of "Who Shall Be Able to Stand?" on Mal. 3:2: "But who can endure the day of his coming? Who can stand when he appears?" Robinson asserts that only those who are "born again, regenerated by the spirit and kept by the power of Almighty God . . . shall be able to stand." In "this sin-polluted age," only those who have been born of the Spirit and transformed through sanctification will be saved.

Robinson cites John the Baptist as an example of a true follower of God. Suggesting that John the Baptist was sent to prepare people to "stand" before God, she quotes Mal. 3:1: "Behold, I send my messenger that he shall prepare the way before Me." She indicates that those who listen to the "real unadulterated gospel" from preachers such as John the Baptist will be able to stand on Judgment Day.

While John the Baptist represents true preachers who point the way to the Lord, Robinson warns her audience to avoid "false prophets and seductive, lustful doctrines." She suggests that false prophets are distinguished from true preachers by whether they are able to overcome sin in their own lives. Only the sanctified Christian can preach the pure, unadulterated gospel.

"CAN THESE BONES LIVE?" In "Can These Bones Live?" Robinson asserts that sin is rampant in society because preachers fail to embrace the holiness doctrine and to condemn many sins. Robinson argues that sin is inherent in "modern" gambling, such as playing and writing numbers, as well as in fornication and adultery.

Robinson compares the Church to the dry bones in the thirty-seventh chapter of Ezekiel. Just as the dry bones, symbolizing the hopelessness of exiled Israel, were resuscitated by the Lord's breath, so the contemporary Church must overcome its hopeless sinfulness. As in "Who Shall Be Able to Stand?" Robinson chastises the Church, which she defines as the body of believers, for its pollution and its attachment to false doctrines. Robinson states that if church leaders kept "our bodies as a fit vessel for the dwelling of the Holy Spirit," and denounced the sins of church members uncompromisingly, "there would be fewer people on the downward road of destruction."

Robinson declares that in order to be saved, people must overcome "all unrighteousness." The "dry bones" of the Church can only live again by being transformed and purified in Christ.

"THE ECONOMIC PERSECUTION." In "The Economic Persecution," Robinson urges her audience to take a firm stand against contemporary "enemies of Jesus Christ," including southern white Christians who persecute Blacks, and Christians who are influenced by "so-called liberalism, modernism, and various other kinds of isms . . . which tend to minimize God's word." She parallels false Christians' persecution of true Christians with the persecution of the early Christians by "ferocious pagans." She cites lynching, segregation, and discrimination to question the nature of the Christianity to which white southerners professed to adhere. She denounces the rank hypocrisy inherent in those who profess to love God, whom they have never seen, while hating their black brothers and sisters, whom they see every day.

In the first half of her sermon, Robinson describes the economic and political context that led to the persecution of the early Christians, and states that "at present the same conditions [prevail] in substance." Threatened by the presence of Christians, the pagan priests orchestrated a severe repression of Christianity, for fear that they would lose the "influence they had hereto maintained over the people's minds and properties." Alluding to the vicious methods Whites employed to maintain political and economic control in the South, Robinson asserts that, just as the early Christians were "persecuted indescribably" by power-hungry pagans, "our people in certain southern states, are killed, their bodies dismembered and thrown to vultures" by "modern pagans."

Robinson furthers the parallel between early Christians and southern Blacks by stating that just as Constantine saved the early Christians by convincing the Persian emperor in a letter to stop the persecution of Christians, so Blacks need a "Constantine of our day (if there be one)" to send "a letter to the modern pagans in the [polluted] southland in the form of 'Anti-lynch' legislation that is now pending in Congress." Robinson urges her audience to have courage, for just as early Christians overcame their persecution through changes in legislation, so will Blacks be able to "overcome, right here in this present world, the persecutions we [are] made to suffer, by our unjust brethren."

Robinson illuminates the irony of "modern pagans" who profess to be Christians, even though they "trample under feet the laws of Christianity and utterly ignore the words of the sacred 'Book' they pretend to love so dearly." Quoting 1 John 4:20, as Florence Randolph does in "If I Were White," Robinson emphasizes that those who persecute Blacks cannot be Christians, for "'if a man says he loves God and hateth his brother, he is a liar.'" Challenging those who argue that Blacks are not included in "the brotherhood" of "mankind," Robinson refers to Eph. 4:5–6 ("One Lord, one faith, one baptism, One God and Father of all"), stating that "if God is the Father of all, the relationship that [exists] between Gentile and Jew, as well as Ethiopians, is [inseparable]." Here, Robinson alludes to the Ethiopian in Acts 8:26–39, whom Philip baptized. In making this reference, she asserts that the Bible affirms those of African blood as part of God's kingdom.

In the second half of her sermon, Robinson outlines the tenets of a genuine Christian theology. She states that through "liberalism" and "modernism," many ministers are "engaged at this very time in battling against the policies of our Lord Jesus." She illustrates this with statistics showing that over half of all ministers "don't believe in the devil or hell." Convinced of the reality of evil within humanity, and of the spiritual source of that evil (the devil) and the consequence of that evil (hell), Robinson denounces those who would undermine this theology of evil.

Having asserted the reality of the devil and hell, Robinson stresses the importance of sanctification, the process by which Jesus will "cleanse us from all unrighteousness," so that we may be saved. Humans urgently need to be sanctified, for life is fleeting and Christ's return is imminent. Robinson illuminates this point with the metaphor of a shadow. Quoting Shakespeare ("Life is but a walking shadow") and Job ("Our days on earth are as a shadow"), Robinson points out that life is as transitory as a quickly vanishing shadow. Shifting her use of the metaphor, Robinson states that shadows have often been used to "measure the time of day." The present, Robinson asserts, is the time of Christ's imminent return. She states: "I appeal to you who have clocks, watches, charts, maps, and various other scientific [materials] acquainting you with the knowledge on this world[.] But oh ye children of light can't you look out and see the shadow of our Lord Jesus and how His arrival is inevitable?"

Since Christ will return soon, it is of utmost importance that Christians tend to the iniquities in the world and in their own souls. Those who see the coming of the Lord "know it is time to pray."

"AND A LITTLE CHILD SHALL LEAD THEM." In "And a Little Child Shall Lead Them," Robinson chastises her audience for not concentrating on the sermon while at church. As a model for the adults to imitate, she tells the story of Bobby Wallace, a three-year-old boy in Brooklyn who told his mother to heed a lesson they had heard in church. The boy, Robinson suggests, listened more carefully to the preacher than the adults. Quoting Isa. 11:6 ("And a little child shall lead them") and Jesus' admonishment that God's followers must receive the Kingdom of Heaven "as a little child," Robinson asserts that Bobby's words exemplify this biblical focus on children's leadership.

Revisiting the theme of church purification in this sermon, as she did in "Who Shall Be Able to Stand?" and "Can These Bones Live?" Robinson declares that those who do not give "proper attention" to the preacher's words will bring down the church. If one does not focus on the theology lessons offered at the pulpit, one will never learn the "doctrine of the church," and thus will not be able to defend that doctrine. Enemies who wish to criticize the church, Robinson warns, will "hold high this stupid and slothful servant," which will reflect badly even on those church members "who are striving for higher spiritual attainments." Robinson concludes by suggesting that her audience follow the example of the little child who listened to the preacher.

WHO SHALL BE ABLE TO STAND?

TEXT: Malachi 3:2; Psalms 107–117

For Jesus is coming back for a church without spot or blemish. This church is not a building or structure, nor a holy edifice, but the souls of those who have been walking uprightly before Him. Tell me who, then, shall be able to stand? Who can stand in this sin-polluted age? Only he who has been born again, regenerated by the spirit and kept by the power of Almighty God. He, it is, that shall be able to stand. Within my heart the proposition is fixed and settled to be the servant God is calling for, regardless to the cost. In the dawning of the rapture morning, when the bridegroom in midair shall appear, who shall be able to stand? God has promised if we keep our minds on Him he would keep us in perfect peace. Let us humble ourselves and pray and God will destroy sin that we in the great day of judgment receive a righteous reward.

"Behold, I send my messenger that he shall prepare the way before Me. Who shall be able to stand? Everyone denying himself picking up his cross to follow me."

In John's exhortation to the priests and Levites that came up from Jerusalem, inquiring if he be Christ, John was not a hypocrite like we find hiding in the churches today, denying the real unadulterated gospel. John the Baptist denied not the coming of our Lord, but readily confessed "I am not the Christ. Yea! not the light. I am the voice of one crying in the wilderness; make straight the way of the Lord." Unlike the false prophets of these evil days, declaring themselves to be Christ, others, God the creator of all things, even so the Heaven and the earth. Yet they cannot master the depression which is harboring within their own doors. (Ps. 107–117) The Christ whom I serve has not yet come, but until his coming has promised to work together for the good of all things for those who love him.

Beware of anti-Christs, false prophets and seductive, lustful doctrines. Who shall be able to stand? Those who are swift witnesses against sin. All unrighteousness is sin. Who shall be able to stand? Who shall pass through the pearly gates of that beautiful city whose ruler and builder is God?

CAN THESE BONES LIVE?

TEXT: Ezekiel 37:3–4

"Oh! ye dry bones, hear ye the word of the Lord." By the resurrection of dry bones, the dead hope of Israel is revived. Let me exhort you, one and all, the calamity of the churches today is simply because they are polluted with sin, so much so until pride and false doctrine has separated the people from the good old pathway as recorded by Isaiah: "A way shall be there, and it shall be called the Highway of Holiness."

We, the leaders or pastors, should be the true fruit of the vine, being first partakers of the fruit ourselves. But it is we who allow our earthly tabernacle to decay, that is why Israel is liken unto dry bones. Since Jehovah, our God, is coming for a ready church, let us keep our bodies as a fit vessel for the dwelling of the Holy Spirit. For it abides in no other temple except that which is clean.

Referring to the churches of this day, let us picture the church as a tree, birds of all descriptions have lodged in its branches, from the pulpit to the door. "O! ye dry bones, hear ye the word of the Lord." Hypocrites on every hand, preaching and testifying: "I'm on my way to Heaven with a shout of victory in my soul." Answer me just one question and I will prove to you that you're on your way to hell in a cramp. Victory means to conquer. Have you conquered sin? All unrighteousness is sin. Can you make the straight gate, playing and writing numbers? You are playing to win or lose—high class gambling in a modern way. Fornicating, having a good wife, but you must have your sweetheart, too. Adultery. Two and three living wives. Whoremongers. Cannot be satisfied with one wife, trying to flirt with every woman or man you meet. Liars, preaching the word of God, diluting it to fit your own lives. Such that has been dilapidated with sin. O! you know I am preaching the truth and you might as well say, Amen! because I have opened my mouth unto the Lord and I will not compromise with the world if I don't have a friend.

If, we, the preachers and leaders, and supposed shepherds of His people, were more firmly in our undertakings, there would be fewer people on the downward road of destruction. We are the lights of the gospel, yet thousands of souls are racing into hell daily as thoughtless horses into battle, because those preaching the word have become very careless. Oh, ye dry bones, hear ye the word of the Lord. These things you call no harm have many innocent souls blindfolded. Oh, my people, Jesus is coming.

Are you ready to meet Him? No sin can enter the city. Can these bones live again? Providing you are regenerated and become reconciled with God, claiming a part in this same Christ.

Jesus said: "I am the bread of life. All who partake of this bread shall live and thrive by the spirit of the true and living God. Behold, I come quickly, My reward with Me, to pay every man according to his works. For every man's work shall be brought into judgment." Oh, ye dry bones, hear ye the word of the Lord.

THE ECONOMIC PERSECUTION

TEXT: 1 John 4:20; Acts 2:4

In the early days of Christianity, under the old order of things, everyone who openly called on the name of the Lord Jesus was persecuted indescribably. Many of them died calling on the name of the Lord to the very end.

During the dark days of early civilization[,] the gospel having spread itself into Persia, the pagan priests who worshipped the sun were greatly alarmed, and dreaded the loss of that influence they had hereto maintained over the people's minds and properties. Hence they thought it expedient to complain to the emperor that the Christians were enemies to the state, and held a treasonable correspondence with the Romans, the great enemies of Persia.

Well, the Persian emperor Sapores, being naturally an enemy of Jesus and Christianity, easily believed the lie told on the Christians by the wicked officers, and gave orders to persecute them throughout his empire. Due to this mandate many persons eminent in the church and state fell martyrs at the hands of the ferocious pagans whose scheme to humiliate the Christians went over in a big way, but God always finds a way to deliver His saints out of the hands of their enemies. It was through Constantine the great, [that] God worked during a consecration period of the saints. God heard the [fervent] and effectual prayers of the church and gave it favor in the eyes of Constantine the Great. For days after, the Christians prayed for the Emperor's conversion.

One day at high noon, God showed the great Constantine a sign in heaven[;] a flaming cross appeared in the element with the legend, (by this we conquer), which resulted in his confession of Jesus Christ. Meantime, a great persecution of the saints had begun as a result of the false report made by the Persian officers to Sapores, the Persian Emperor[.] Constantine the Great, now saved and a witness of Jesus Christ, and a powerful friend of the church[,] sent a letter to Sapores protesting the treatment of the Christians, [by the] wicked subordinates. In his letter he told just how God had prospered him and blessed all of his undertakings because of this friendship with Jesus and fellowship with His saints. At the reception of this letter the persecution was ordered ceased and the gospel was spread throughout the domain of Persia.

At present the same conditions [prevail] in substance. Our people in certain southern states, are killed, their bodies dismembered and thrown to vultures. This, of course, is a common occurrence, and, unfortunately, [occurs] where "Christianity" is more prevalent than any other part of our Union. For in this section of the country laws are made to uphold "Christianity" in their states, and to prevent any teachings in their institutions of learning that [tend] to distort, minimize or otherwise change the principle of the doctrine of Christianity as taught in the Bible.

We hereby decree as it is written in their laws condemning modernism or any other doctrine hostile to the teachings of Jesus "that if anyone is found guilty of teaching doctrine contrary to Christianity in any [state-] supported schools or schools, such as elementary, high, university, college, seminary, academy or any other institution[,] shall be punished to the extent of the law, mentioning the extent to which the law provides. But these same people, in these same sections will toss their own laws to the four winds and trample under feet the laws of Christianity and utterly ignore the words of the sacred "Book" they pretend to love so dearly, and esteem so highly which says: "If a man says he loves God and hateth his brother, he is a liar: for he that loveth not his brother whom he has seen, how can he love God whom he has not seen" (1 John 4:20).

Someone has questioned the brotherhood of all mankind. Well! let us appeal to the wisdom and justice of the sacred "book" as regards Christianity. There is but "One Lord one faith and one baptism" so that, if God is the Father of all, the relationship that [exists] between Gentile and Jew, as well as Ethiopians, is [inseparable] and unquestionably established[.] So let us saints, pray that the Constantine of our day (if there be one) sends a letter to the modern pagans in the [polluted] southland in the form of "Anti-lynch" legislation that is now pending in Congress. We can overcome and we will overcome, and we will overcome, right here in this present world, the persecutions we [are] made to suffer, by our unjust brethren. It is written that "Ethiopians shall stretch their hands in righteousness to God" and by the help of God and the agencies He has so gloriously provided, we shall overcome.

It is easy to understand why the God[s] of this world are working so feverishly to overthrow the kingdom and one doctrine that will not interfere with their disgraceful acts. At present many of the so-called preachers who are parading under ministerial banners with the loyal forces of righteousness are in reality enemies of Jesus Christ. For example, a recent survey was made by a very dependable organization with a wide reputation for its accuracy in sounding out public opinion[.] [This organization] just completed its work in quizzing ministers. They ask "Do you believe in the existence of hell and the devil?" To this question 54 percent of the ministers that were asked answered No. In other words 54 ministers out of every 100 don't believe in the devil or hell.

Many of them are engaged at this very time in battling against the policies of our Lord Jesus through channels of so-called liberalism, modernism, and various other kinds of *isms* and *cisms* which tend to minimize God's word. But we who are children of the light, cannot be swerved by any of this present-day ministerial gossip.

We believe that Jesus died and rose again. We believe that if we acknowledge His death according to the Bible we have access to the father through this acknowledgement. We believe if we confess our sins He will forgive us of the same and by, through, and with His blood, cleanse us from all unrighteousness, which is sanctification of course. We believe that if we pray to the Father He will send us another comforter which is the Holy Ghost according to Acts 2:4.

Shakespeare—

Life is but a walking shadow[.]
Shadows are as changeable and [fidgety] as a little child.
A shadow being made by the sun, follows its movements and is in
    constant variation until at last it quietly vanishes and disappears.

In this the life of man is frequently compared to a shadow. The always philosophical Job says "Our days on earth are as a shadow." Possibly he was also thinking of time. Long before man had sense enough to make a clock or watch he used his shadow to measure the time of day. The Mohammedan stands up against the sun and by the length of his shadow in the sand determines that the hour of prayer is come. Weary workmen did not watch the clock but their shadow.

Now I appeal to you who have clocks, watches, charts, maps, and various other scientific [materials] acquainting you with the knowledge of this world[.] But oh ye children of light can't you look out and see the shadow of our Lord Jesus and how His arrival is inevitable? We may look out and see wars developing in all parts of our land. Unrest and confusion are found everywhere. This truly indicates the shadow of our Lord and we know it is time to pray.

AND A LITTLE CHILD SHALL LEAD THEM

TEXT: Isaiah 11:6

The prophet Isaiah, in picturing the peaceful reign of our Lord Jesus, pictured the big bad wolf dwelling with the lamb, and the leopard shall lie down with the kid, and calf, and the young lion and the fatling together, "And a little child shall lead them."

One of the strangest things occurred just recently which fulfills to the letter the significance of the above, and moreover, the King Himself, as indicated in the above prophesy said, while demonstrating the principles of the kingdom, "If ye receive not the Kingdom of Heaven as a little child, ye shall in nowise enter therein." The words of the Prophet as well as those of our Lord Jesus were eventuated in the life of little Bobby Wallace, the three [year] old son of Brother and Sister Wallace of St. Marks [Church in] Brooklyn.

It was during the course of preparing a meal that Bro[ther] Wallace suggested that a choice vegetable be used to complete the menu, while Sister Wallace wanted another. With all the subtlety of feminine oratory ingeniously devised, she lost, and Bro[ther] Wallace contended for his [greens]. But my friends, before she conceded the debate to the proud winner, which was probably the only one, she made a last attempt to hold on. Said she, "Well s——ht, let's play like we are having both." At that point the little 3 year old son Bobby who had been listening in on the conversation, chirped in. "Mamma" said Bobby, "[y]ou know do Mamma Nambert say w'en she p'each you mus' not play." Well sir! this is one of the gems of childhood leadership.

This little boy is one of our most faithful scholars in the Primary Department of our Sunday School. Apparently he is unobservant, but the above is a clear indication of his interest in what his pastor was saying. This is an example, or at least should be, for every adult who is not giving the proper attention to those who are responsible for his spiritual development.

There are those, who by reason of their obstinacy, hinder the progress of those who are striving for higher spiritual attainments which are promised to those who walk uprightly and hew to the Biblical line. Those who sit about carelessly in the church, paying attention to the least, while discarding the greatest, do more to depreciate the church than help it. If when the minister is preaching the things of the spirit, this person who has had a "good time" as it is called in the praise and testimonial services, so that he is too "full" to give attention to what is said by the preacher, I say to you, Children of Mt. Sinai, that person is better home than in the church. In the first place, the above person is not versed in the doctrine of the church. Second, the above person cannot defend the church's doctrine because he does not know it. Third, the enemy of Christ and the church will hold high this stupid and slothful servant as a target of criticism which will, of course, reflect upon the church[,] bringing discredit to its membership. A little child shall lead you.

12

ROSA EDWARDS

VERY LITTLE IS KNOWN about Elder Rosa Edwards's life. She delivered "Ministers Are Examples" in 1935 as the assistant pastor at Bethel Holy Church in Harlem, New York. In the sermon, she pays tribute to Ida Robinson, a pastor and the bishop of Mount Sinai Holy Church of America. Edwards's sermon asserts that ministers must follow their own teachings, that they are examples to those who follow them. For Edwards, there is no better example of a godly preacher than Robinson.

Edwards parallels Robinson with the apostle Paul, who, like Robinson, "knew all about the life of a real holiness preacher," including the persecution, poverty, and other obstacles to doing God's work. Because of the suffering he endured to bring the gospel to others, Paul was ideally suited to guide other preachers in their ministries; likewise, Robinson serves as "a real example,—pattern—model" for God's followers. Edwards praises Robinson for "birthing" Mount Sinai Holy Church, and urges the ministers of this church to "be real pillars in Mount Sinai and keep the arms of our noble Bishop uplifted and God will do wonders in our midst through her."

In order to make Mount Sinai a "Model Church," Edwards challenges ministers to "put into practice every teaching of the Doctrine of Mount Sinai." For instance, Edwards stresses the church's emphasis on "Divine Healing," saying that if ministers are to be examples, they should "never be tempted to take medicine" when they are sick. Edwards's explication of Mount Sinai's doctrines reveals how the holiness theology of black preaching women involved in Holiness and Pentecostal movements differed from that of preaching women who remained in mainline denominations. While many mainline black preaching women stressed the importance of inner transformation through sanctification, black Holiness and Pentecostal preaching women often emphasized that sanctification be followed by signs of the Holy Ghost's presence, such as speaking in tongues or healing.

MINISTERS ARE EXAMPLES

TEXT: 1 Timothy 4:12; Matthew 5:44;
1 Thessalonians 5:15

Be thou an example of the believers.
—1 Tim. 4:12

Of all the ministers in the Bible (after Christ) we have none greater than the Apostle Paul, who is here, exhorting the young man Timothy "to be an example of the believers." Paul knew all about the life of a real holiness preacher; he knew what it was to be hungry—he knew what it meant to have real friends and bitter foes; and to suffer persecutions. None of the other Apostles seemed more able to instruct ministers [than] Paul, for he seemed to have suffered most for the Gospel's sake.

But praise God we have a living epistle right in our midst—a real example,—pattern—model—copy—a wonderful illustration of "an example of the believers" in the person of our Most Worthy Bishop, Ida Robinson. We do praise and thank God for such a wonderful Bishop and Pastor—also for the standard of Mount Sinai that was [birthed] through her. If *all* the ministers would follow Bishop as she follows Christ, and be doers of His word as she is—put into practice every teaching of the Doctrine of Mount Sinai, which is in the word of God: we will have a Model Church.

When we preach and teach on "Divine Healing" let us never be tempted to take medicine when we are sick. When we teach to "pay tithes," let us never be a robber of God, but pay our tithes in *full.* I am afraid that is why so many ministers are suffering today—saying God knows their heart and they need it—yes and you *know* the Word of God: and He is never slack concerning His promises. When we teach "love without [dissimulation]" let us not be [hypocrites] and murder each other with our tongue, and put stumbling blocks and [hindrances] in each [other's] way. When we teach "Christ like love" (Matt. 5:44)[,] "See that none render evil for evil unto any man, but ever follow that which is good both among yourselves, and to all men" (1 Thess. 5:15).

Then let us as real ministers of Christ, be loyal and cheerfully obey the Doctrine and keep the Standard of Mount Sinai high. Then we shall see the weaker members advance more. For it is a fact, we can never push others up higher than we are ourselves. So let us put our shoulders to the wheel and be real doers as well as teachers of His Word—always praying the Lord to increase our faith. Let us be real pillars in Mount Sinai and keep the arms of our noble Bishop uplifted and God will do wonders in our midst through her.

Let us ever live [like] real children of the Day so when Jesus comes or sends we will be ready.

Pray for me that I will make a real minister of God, and ever practice what I preach—I thank God for He truly did snatch me just in time from the brink of hell, converting my soul—sanctified me Holy—sealed me with the Holy Ghost—speaking in other tongues as the Spirit of God [gives] utterance. I am looking for His coming again whether asleep or awake—so that I might reign with Him throughout eternity.

13

QUINCEILA WHITLOW

QUINCEILA WHITLOW WAS BORN in Mercer, Tennessee. A graduate of the Chicago School of Nursing, she worked for several years as a nurse before accepting the call to the ministry. Very little is known about her life or her career as an evangelist. In 1940, however, the editor of the CME *Christian Index* described her as "an Evangelist of high standing," whose "lectures are splendid and far-reaching. Those who hear her can never forget." At that date she resided in Tulsa, Oklahoma.[1]

Whitlow's Sermon

In "The Woman in the Ministry of Jesus Christ," Whitlow affirms women's right to be ministers of the gospel, and speaks about women's changing status in the Church. Whitlow's sermon reflects the rhetoric of campaigns to recruit women into the workplace during World War II. Declaring that there is a "growing spirit of equality" in the country as "new fields of labor" open to women, Whitlow asserts that the Church, like the workplace, needs "eager and alert woman, talented and accomplished woman, skilled and artistic woman."

Whitlow credits Christianity for this increasing sense of equality, for "no one has done so much for womanhood as Jesus." Citing the apostle Paul's words in Gal. 3:28 ("There is neither male nor female: for ye are all one in Christ Jesus"), Whitlow declares that Jesus' dying to save all people from their sins reveals that in Christ there is "'neither male nor female['] but He is the Saviour of all." Mirroring the arguments of many black preaching women before her, Whitlow asserts that gender is irrelevant when it comes to doing God's work; conversion and sanctification, not gender, truly qualify someone for the ministry.

Whitlow uses another common argument in support of preaching women when she asserts that Christian women are desperately needed in the battle to save lost souls, for "modern denial continues to rain blasphemous blows upon our Saviour." Since all God's people are called to do God's work, and all God's people are needed to do God's work, woman must "stand fast in her calling" despite all opposition. Whitlow prays that God will "save the woman of the Gospel from the brazen rejection of the narrow minded critic."

Having established the legitimacy of women preachers, Whitlow warns preaching women against practices that would discredit their work in the pulpit. She especially targets women who work as Spiritualist mediums and who do "fortune telling in God's church."[2] Whitlow indicates the prevalence of women Spiritualists in some sectors of the Holiness movement when she declares that fortune-telling has become so popular that "90 per cent of our ministers are practicing it and more of the women than men." Whitlow argues that these fraudulent practices have diverted the Church's attention away from the all-important issue of salvation; thus, fortune-telling is being performed at the "cost of righteousness." She asserts that it is better to be unpopular and to work to "stamp out witchcraft in our churches" than to "please men at the cost of their souls." She states that even if one is rejected in this world for doing God's work, one will be blessed in the "next world" for being true to Christ.

THE WOMAN IN THE
MINISTRY OF JESUS CHRIST

We need in our churches today eager and alert woman, talented and accomplished woman, skilled and artistic woman, but far more than that we need Christian woman, who with trusting faith and undaunted hope, will behold the Saviour despised and rejected of men, a man of sorrow and acquainted with grief. And in His lowliness, His bleeding agony, confess Him as their Lord and Saviour, who has redeemed them, lost and condemned creatures, purchased and won them from the power of the devil, not with gold or silver, but with His innocent suffering and death that they might be His own.

No one has done so much for womanhood as Jesus. When His words proclaimed that in Him there is, "neither male nor female["] but He is the Saviour of all that blessed truth became the Christian constitution for womanhood.

The position which woman occupies today under the elevating influence of Christianity and the growing spirit of equality is a matter of rejoicing among the best and most thoughtful minds in all classes. The new fields of labor that are opening to her, the widening spheres of influence which she is entering and filling with highest credit to herself and with greatest benefit to mankind. This cannot but awaken gratitude and hope in the heart of womanhood.

Can you not see why womanhood has found a powerful appeal in the Gospel of Jesus Christ[?] May God save the woman of the Gospel from the brazen rejection of the narrow minded critic.

Let the woman stand fast in her calling. We cannot sit idly by while modern denial continues to rain blasphemous blows upon our Saviour. We must plead His cause and stand up for His truth. We must be prepared to stand alone to uphold the glorious truth of the Gospel.

I say let the message of the cross be your theme, avoid the things that do not belong in the pulpit. Let the self respecting woman minister lay aside law-defying [fraudulence] such as [Spiritualist mediums and] fortune telling in God's church[;] let them flee this false doctrine as they would [flee] from one East Indian cobra, or a hissing rattler.

I am praying to God that the ministers of our churches will help to stamp out this false doctrine that is being practiced in our churches today. Let us learn that all good comes from God and money cannot buy luck.

The good that is in store for us is without price. Seek the Kingdom of God and all these things shall be added unto you.

We can all agree. I feel sure that speaking against fortune telling in our churches is not a popular and pleasing subject of public discussion. It has become such a favor in the church that 90 per cent of our ministers are practicing it and more of the women than men. I pray to God that ministers will stop telling fortunes and giving hands for luck and preach the Gospel of Christ, the one story that will lead people to the light and out of darkness. I have found some ministers using the Gospel as a cloak to get into our churches, not for the love of the church, but for money. I wish to God the Presiding Elders would stop licensing women and men to preach that carry on such foolishness in God's churches. Let us be firm on this issue. Let us stamp out witchcraft in our churches. We have held our peace too long at the cost of righteousness. Let us tell dying men and women about God and His power mighty to save them from sin. Tell the blessed story of the Christ and the cross. My sister and brother in the ministry, preach that cross, teach that cross, live that cross, exalt that cross. The world will think little of you but are we to please men at the cost of their souls? The world may not remember your self-denial but some solemn hour when human souls approach the threshold of the next world[,] their faith will bless you for your loyalty. I charge thee, therefore before God and our Lord Jesus Christ, the Judge of the living and the dead, preach the Word, live the Word.

14

F. E. REDWINE

VERY LITTLE IS KNOWN of Mrs. F. E. Redwine's life or ministry. A CME evangelist, she delivered "What Woman Is" on Woman's Day at Runnel's Chapel in Flint, Texas, on May 2, 1948. The text for the sermon was Gen. 2:21–25.[1]

After making some introductory remarks in "What Woman Is," Redwine outlines the issues she plans to discuss in her sermon. Although she states that she will discuss women and the school and women as evangelists, the text of the sermon that has survived does not directly address these issues; rather, it falls under the subheadings "Woman, a Helpmeet," "Woman's Influence," "Woman, Queen of the Home," and "Woman in the Church." She does address women's role as teachers of their children in "Woman, Queen of the Home." Redwine also refers, in the final section, to women evangelists. The sermon's overarching message is that women are indispensable to the well-being of the family, the Church, and civilization at large.

The first issue Redwine discusses is woman's creation. Referring to the second chapter of Genesis, Redwine retells the creation story in which God took one of Adam's ribs to make Eve. Redwine repeats Adam's words—"She shall be called woman, because she was taken out of man. She is flesh of my flesh and bone of my bone" (Gen. 2:23). Redwine declares that if contemporary men took these words to heart, there would be less wife beating. Historically, domestic abuse has rarely been addressed publicly in the African American community.

In "Woman, a Helpmeet," Redwine then expounds on Gen. 2:18 ("And the Lord God said, It is not good that the man should be alone; I will make him an helpmeet for him"). After describing various ways in which biblical women helped men, Redwine affirms modern-day women's efforts to be helpmeets and stresses the need for women to work with men

F. E. Redwine

Source: *Center for African American History and Culture, Temple University.*

to support the family and run the home. Redwine suggests that women's work is invaluable to men's well-being in an economically precarious world. This issue was of critical importance to the African American community at every juncture, because of the difficulties black men have faced in finding gainful employment and the large percentage of black women who have served as heads of the household.

In "Woman's Influence" and "Woman, Queen of the Home," Redwine asserts that women are not only indispensable helpmeets to men in tangible ways, but that women's moral influence has a profound effect on the world. Redwine argues that through choosing good or evil, women have the power either to destroy or to save civilization. While Eve's enticing Adam to eat the forbidden fruit "ruined the race," the "influence of Mary, the mother of our Lord," helped bring the Savior to the human race that Eve ruined. Redwine asserts that present-day women should use their influence as "queens" of the home for the good of humankind, for women are "fashioned to refine, soothe[,] lift[,] and irradiate home, society[,] and the world." One of the most important ways women can use their moral influence well is to rear their children to follow the path to salvation.

Finally, in "Woman in the Church," Redwine asserts that women are indispensable to the well-being of the Church. Through rearing their children as Christians and through their evangelistic work, women have contributed greatly to "the numerical and spiritual as well as financial strength of the Church." Thus, Redwine argues, if women were not involved, "the church doors would be closed." Redwine concludes by encouraging women involved in missionary work to stand strong despite the struggle and suffering they encounter, for they will have their reward in the life to come.

WHAT WOMAN IS

TEXT: Genesis 2:21–25, 24:13; Ruth 2:3–8;
John 4–7; Matthew 24:41; Proverbs 31:13–31

Before entering whole heartedly into the subject[,] I feel that I need to pay tribute to the members of Runnel's Chapel, because of the effort you have exhibited in remodeling your church so as to put it in A Class rural [condition]; with your electric lights, up to date—walls, ceiling, lovely spacious shaded lawn, and recreation grounds. I have never received an invitation that I have appreciated more than I do yours. It affords me inexpressible joy to worship with you to-day.

WHAT WOMAN IS We shall attempt to discuss this subject under the following captions:
1. Why so named?—
(a). Woman's creation, Woman a [helpmeet], Woman's influence, a creature from God. Woman in the church and school, Woman as an Evangelist.
(b). Genesis—2nd chapter—Tells us that the Lord God (after God had created Adam) He saw that it was not good for man to be alone and the Lord, God, caused Adam to fall into a deep sleep and He took one of his ribs out, closed up the flesh, and made woman. When he brought woman unto Adam; Adam said, "She shall be called woman, because she was taken out of man. She is flesh of my flesh and bone of my bone." The woman is flesh and bone of her husband. When men in this day realize this fact more seriously, I venture to say that there will be less flesh bruised, fewer bones battered and fewer applications for divorces. It would show non-evidence of self-love for a man to be guilty of such conduct.

WOMAN, A HELPMEET Woman has been a [helpmeet] to man all down through the ages, in whatever pursuit of life—he has been engaged.
Women went to harvest fields and gleaned with their husbands. You will find that Ruth (2:3–8); John (4:7); Gen. (24:13)—say "They brought the water from the well[."] Matt. (24:41)—says "Woman ground the grain for daily use," prepared meals, spun wool and made the clothing, took care of her household affairs and taught the children religious truths. (Prov. 31:13–31) The modern day [helpmeet] to man—teaches with him or

teaches to help him while he does some other job –(if he can find one)—
She rarely ever makes the clothes, but she buys them instead. She is good
at helping to provide in every way for well-cooked meals and knows how
to serve. In every avenue of life—from lowly homes to mansions, from the
humblest job to the highest class job—woman as a [helpmeet] to man is
indispensable.

WOMAN'S INFLUENCE   Woman's nobility—it has been said, consists in
the exercise of her Christian influence. Woman's influence for evil has
beclouded civilization in a great measure. It will take the prayers of the
Christian woman to dispel the clouds. Just think a little while about Eve—
and the influence that she had upon Adam—her husband. Eve's one picking of fruit and influencing her husband to eat of it ruined the race.

I think it was Dr. Talmadge, who said, "The frail arm of woman can
strike a blow which will resound through all eternity, down among the
dungeons or up among the throngs."[2] An evil woman drove a spike
through Sisera's, the warrior's[,] head. Esther overcame Royalty and
Abigail halted a host because of her beauty. There was one Corduay who
stuck a dagger in the man's head, who killed her lover. Evil influences
bring misery and woe. The influence of Mary, the mother of our Lord,
will indeed be worthy of Christian emulation. Lois, a woman of noted
Christian influence[,] spent much time in training her grandson, Timothy.
Mother Eve's evil conduct brought sin and shame.

WOMAN, QUEEN OF THE HOME   Woman is the queen of the home,
being spoken of with respect and accorded honor. Her law or command
is respected. Her knowledge or judgment on a subject relating to home
affairs is entitled to be accepted. A noted theologian in speaking of
woman as queen of the home said, "Queen Isabella fled from the Spanish
Throne pursued by the Nation's anathema; but she who is queen in a
home will never lose her throne for earth [itself] will be the annexation of
heavenly principalities." To get the grandest mental picture of a queen—
let us not reflect upon any historical queen, but on that plain, kind
hearted, loving woman, who sat facing your father at the table, at meal-
time, or walked with him, shoulder to shoulder, down the path of life,
regardless to life's upheavals and depressions, but always together. That
is the queen. Dr. T. DeWitt Talmadge defines woman as a creature direct
from God, a sacred, delicate gift, with affections so great that nothing
short of the infinite God can tell their bounds; fashioned to refine,
soothe[,] lift[,] and irradiate home, society[,] and the world.

Missionary women, of this and adjoining communities—*you are the queens of your homes*. The husband and the children, look to you to solace and sweeten their lives. It is woman's pleasure as well as her responsibility to correct the waywardness of her children, train and direct as to education and good or bad effects of social circles, ever impressing upon their minds always: It's not the gale but the set of the sail that leads on to the goal of their future desires. Influence of the *queen of the home* is the mightiest and most lasting influence.

In calculating the various forces, which decide the destiny of all nations, we find that the mightiest influence comes from the home where the wife cheers up despondency, fatigue, and sorrow by her own sympathy, and as a mother, trains her children for heaven starting their little feet on their way to the Celestial City—Early—*not too late*. Timothy was reared under God's guidance of his mother and grandmother who were queens in their homes.

WOMAN IN THE CHURCH   I very much fear the pastor would resign and the church doors would be closed, if there were no women in it. Woman's work, her prayers, her collection of influence in shaping the lives of children while they're young—Woman has been granted recognition in the Evangelistic work of the church and her profound interest as it was in Paul's time of preaching, has added much interest in the numerical and spiritual as well as financial strength of the Church.

Missionary sisters: There is promise to the *faithful servants* who hold out to the end. Heaven for the aching and broken hearts, and Heaven for anguished bitter frames. Some of us will never enjoy rest on this earth—it will be toil, suffering and struggling all the way onward and upward in the effort of building God's Kingdom. Though seeming hard the task, our reward is sure. God has a crown for us; He's making it now and whenever we weep a tear while doing His good will, He puts a star in that crown[;] whenever we have a pang of the body or soul, He puts stars in our crown. When all manner of evil is spoken of us for His name sake He puts another star. Our Father will declare the crown finished and demand of an angel—to let us up to wear the crown and prepare for the heavenly banquet prepared for us.

15

PAULI MURRAY

PAULI MURRAY, AN EDUCATOR, attorney, and Episcopal priest, was born in Baltimore on November 20, 1910, the fourth of six children born to William Henry and Agnes Georgianna Fitzgerald Murray. Her grandfather, Robert Fitzgerald, was born free in Delaware. During the Civil War, he was a soldier in the Union Army. After the war, he settled in North Carolina, where he established schools for newly freed slaves. Her mother was a nurse, one of the first graduates of Hampton Institute, and her father was a secondary school principal.[1]

According to her own testimony, Murray was an "unabashed feminist" and an outspoken advocate of women's rights. Her encounters with racism and sexism convinced her of the need to fight discrimination in every form. She wrote the amendment that provided for inclusion of women in Title VII of the Civil Rights Act of 1964, prohibiting discrimination in employment. She wrote the brief for *White* v. *Crook*, which dismantled state laws denying women the right to serve on juries. She pioneered the struggle to have women admitted to law schools. With Betty Friedan, she founded the National Organization for Women.[2]

A lifelong activist, she was jailed in the early 1940s for her civil rights work in the South. In 1944, she sued Harvard University's law school for refusing to admit her on the basis of gender. Instead of Harvard, she attended the Howard University Law School in the 1940s, where she developed the strategy for employing nonviolent civil action that was widely used in the South during the 1960s civil rights movement. Murray uncovered the Washington, D.C., nineteenth-century city ordinance prohibiting discrimination in public accommodations, which Mary Church Terrell used in a 1953 Supreme Court case to challenge the legality of segregation in the District of Columbia. Murray criticized black leaders

Pauli Murray

Source: *The Schlesinger Library, Radcliffe College.*

during the famous 1963 March on Washington for their "token recognition" of black women's contributions.[3]

Murray pursued several careers in law and education. The recipient of three law degrees, she was the only female attorney hired during the late 1950s by the prestigious New York firm of Paul, Weiss, Rifkin, Wharton, and Garrison. As an educator, she served in 1967 as vice president of Benedict College in Columbia, South Carolina, and from 1968 to 1973 as Distinguished Professor of Law and Politics at Brandeis University. She wrote several books, including *States' Laws on Race and Color,* published in 1951; and two autobiographies—*Proud Shoes: The Story of An American Family* and *Song in a Weary Throat: An American Pilgrimage.*[4]

After a distinguished career as a lawyer, educator, and activist, on January 8, 1977, at the age of sixty-seven, Pauli Murray was ordained an Episcopal priest at the National Cathedral in Washington, D.C. She was the first black female, and the second African American, to be ordained a priest in the Protestant Episcopal Church. For several years, she served as priest of the Episcopal Church of the Atonement in Washington, D.C. In 1982, she was forced to retire. Episcopal Church law required that priests retire at age seventy-two. They could continue to function as priests, but only in temporary positions. Unable to secure a permanent appointment, she served as priest of a "floating parish" for the hospitalized and homebound in Alexandria, Virginia, and as priest of the Church of the Holy Nativity in Baltimore. Even though age limited her service, she optimistically reminded her supporters that "Jesus Christ our Lord had a ministry of only three years."[5]

During the 1970s, Murray was much in demand as a minister and lecturer. She delivered some of her most powerful sermons during that time. She spoke and preached in black and white churches of all denominations. She was much revered by churchwomen, who frequently invited her to deliver Woman's Day sermons.

Pauli Murray died of cancer in Pittsburgh, Pennsylvania, on July 8, 1985.

Murray's Sermons

Eight of Murray's sermons have been selected for inclusion in this collection, including "Male and Female He Created Them," "Women Seeking Admission to Holy Orders—As Crucifers Carrying the Cross," "Mary Has Chosen the Best Part," "The Holy Spirit," "The Gift of the Holy Spirit," "The Dilemma of the Minority Christian," "Salvation and Liberation," and "Can These Bones Live Again?"

"MALE AND FEMALE HE CREATED THEM." Murray preached "Male and Female He Created Them" on May 21, 1978, at Lincoln Temple, United Church of Christ, in Washington, D.C. She stresses that *man,* as used in Genesis, means male and female. The historical distortion of the text validates the oppression of women in the Church and society. Murray argues that, in fact, this text is the genesis of the theological subordination of women; the text provides the basis for the arguments against changing women's status and role and for opposition to women in the priesthood.

Murray asserts that because all humanity, male and female, was modeled after God, sexism directly opposes God's plan for creation. By suppressing the feminine in biblical interpretation, the Church and society have created a "dangerous imbalance" in God's creation. Asserting that sexism is the root of human oppression, Murray states that patriarchy "has served as a model for other forms of human exploitation and alienation."

Drawing on the thought of Mary Daly, Erik Erikson, Patricia Martin Doyle, and others, Murray asserts that "feminine" traits should be valued not only in society but also in the image of God. Arguing that there is an intimate "connection between naming and power," Murray states that if women are to reclaim their rightful power, they must challenge the patriarchal Church's naming of women as subordinate beings. They should focus on the female imagery of God in the Bible and other religious writings to affirm that women were created in God's image, just as men were. Countering the Church's sexist misinterpretation of Creation, Murray juxtaposes the Genesis story with twentieth-century poet James Weldon Johnson's poem "The Creation," which refers to God the Creator as "a mammy bending over her baby."

Murray also moves beyond imaging humanity and God with a male-female dichotomy. She extensively references the work of Phyllis Trible, who argues that the first being created was "androgynous," which reflected the wholeness of God's being, "containing the potentiality of both sexes."[6] Murray asserts that both men and women must be set free from the "rigid roles dominated by a male-oriented hierarchy" in order "to be wholly human," as they were originally created to be.

The sermon's overarching message is that women must reclaim the aspects of the Christian tradition that affirm their full humanity in order to overcome their theological and historical subordination. Only when women are emancipated will social imbalances be overcome, allowing everyone to live fully in God's divine image. When this happens, Murray concludes, churches will no longer set aside only one day of the year to focus on women, but "every [church] service will be Women's Day, Men's Day and Children's Day in which all participate in worship according to our individual gifts."

"WOMEN SEEKING ADMISSION TO HOLY ORDERS—AS CRUCIFERS CARRYING THE CROSS." As a candidate for holy orders in the Episcopal Church, Pauli Murray delivered her "Inaugural" sermon, "Women Seeking Admission to Holy Orders—As Crucifers Carrying the Cross," on March 3, 1974, the first Sunday in Lent. She addresses the issue of gender discrimination in the Episcopal Church, which she and other women confronted as they sought admission to holy orders.

Responding to those who question why women seek to change the male dominance in the Episcopal Church, Murray states that in "periods of human crisis, God has called forth prophets who will not be silenced, who will not be coopted by the established hierarchies whether they be clerical or secular." Murray parallels the moral decay of the contemporary United States with the moral crises of ancient Israel, and asserts that women preachers are like the prophets of Israel who denounce the corruption inherent in society. Murray argues that God calls messengers from "the ranks of the dispossessed," for they are the people most in touch with the human suffering that results from injustice. Thus, Murray challenges, it is no wonder that God has called women to the ministry.

In a manner similar to that of her predecessors, Murray responds to the argument that women are not suited for the ministry because they are by nature too weak spiritually, morally, and mentally; Murray asserts that no human being, male or female, can rely on his or her own strength to do God's work. Only by relying on God's power are we able to serve God. Murray declares that all ministers, male and female alike, are "like the prophet Isaiah and the other prophets of the Old Testament" in that "we are compelled to believe that sinful, rebellious, broken as we are, God is using us as instruments of his will."

It is futile to oppose women ministers, Murray suggests, for those whom God calls must do God's work, no matter what the obstacles. Murray says that "we have no choice in the matter." Since the "United States of 1974 is frighteningly like the people of Israel with their divided kingdoms in the 8th and 7th centuries B.C.," women are called to do God's work with the same urgency and purpose that Isaiah and other Old Testament prophets were called. Murray states that only an extreme "moral and social crisis," such as that in which the United States finds itself, "could impel [women ministers] to face the incredible barriers which have existed for thousands of years, to endure the ridicule and even violence of their detractors, and the continual heartache of rejection which blocks their path and makes their burden almost intolerable."

Only a genuine call from God, Murray argues, would give women the courage and will to travel such a path. Those who would reject women ministers contribute to the moral crisis of the day that these women have been called to battle. Thus, Murray presents a brilliantly constructed challenge in this sermon to those who would oppose admitting women into holy orders.

"MARY HAS CHOSEN THE BEST PART." "Mary Has Chosen the Best Part" was delivered July 14, 1977, on the seventh Sunday after Pentecost. Murray chose Mary as the subject of the sermon to emphasize that a woman can reject the gender conventions of her day, and yet receive Jesus' blessings. Murray compares Mary to female divinity students, who also reject gender-defined roles that would exclude them from the ministry.

Murray begins the sermon with the story of Mary and Martha of Bethany, found in the Gospel of Luke, in order to open her discussion of women's roles in society. Murray states that Luke's gospel often addressed issues of concern to women, as is evident in his recounting of the story of Mary and Martha. Murray suggests that she is following Luke's example by focusing on women in this sermon.

Murray first provides the conventional analysis of the Mary and Martha story, and then approaches the story with a feminist hermeneutic. Martha, as she is typically scripted in sermons on this story, represents those who are "concerned with material things," while Mary represents those who are concerned with spiritual matters. Martha, laboring to provide Jesus with food while Mary sits and listens to Jesus, must be reminded that spiritual food is more important than bodily food. Approaching the story from this angle, Murray warns her audience not to get caught up as Martha did in the material world; we should not become "too involved in the competitive rat race" in the constant pursuit of "more *things*." It is important to follow Mary's example so that we never lose focus of "the ultimate meaning of our lives."

Turning to her feminist hermeneutic, Murray suggests that there is "another level of meaning in the story of Mary and Martha," besides the usual focus on material or spiritual matters. As Murray argues, the story also reveals that Jesus affirms women who break out of traditional gender roles in the pursuit of "knowledge of God." While Martha was intent on fulfilling her prescribed role as a woman, Jesus not only allowed Mary "the privilege of sitting at his feet as if she were a young male divinity student," but also encouraged Martha to put away her prescribed tasks and follow Mary's example.

Murray reveals that the very next passage after this story in Luke is the Lord's Prayer, which entreats that God's "will be done, on *earth* as in heaven." Murray suggests that this juxtaposition of the story of Martha and Mary and the Lord's Prayer reveals that "the central purpose" of all

of God's followers, women as well as men, is to work toward "the end
that God's will *is* done on earth." Jesus called Martha and Mary, like his
other disciples, to leave behind their mundane work to bring salvation to
earth in the form of a more just, moral society.

Having given this analysis of the Martha and Mary story, Murray holds
up Alice Paul and Eleanor Roosevelt, two modern women who followed
Jesus' call to do God's work here on earth. Alice Paul lived from 1885 to
1977, dying the weekend before Murray's sermon. Paul had an activist
career that "bridged the two movements for women's rights in the United
States," enabling her to participate in both the suffragist movement and
the women's liberation movement of the 1960s and 1970s. Using her
intelligence and political savvy throughout her life to work for gender justice, Alice Paul contributed to human rights at a similar level to Eleanor
Roosevelt, her "great contemporary" in Murray's words. Murray asserts
that while these women functioned in different arenas, they both were
true to "the Christian tradition" by making "a lasting impact upon the
world in which they lived by their unswerving devotion to the cause of
human rights." Breaking out of traditional roles ascribed to women in
order to do God's will here on earth, Alice Paul and Eleanor Roosevelt,
like Mary, have "chosen the best part." Murray encourages her audience
to follow the example of these exceptional women, obeying God rather
than social conventions.

"THE HOLY SPIRIT" AND "THE GIFT OF THE HOLY SPIRIT." In the tradition of
the pioneering black women preachers, Pauli Murray believed in holiness.
Two of the sermons presented here emphasize this theme. "The Holy
Spirit," delivered at Calvary Protestant Episcopal Church in Washington,
D.C., on May 22, 1977, interprets the meaning of the Holy Spirit. Murray
emphasizes that for believers, the Holy Spirit is seen in God's eternal presence, serving in many capacities as teacher, comforter, guide, and sustainer.
She states, "When the Spirit dwells in us, we are able to let go [of] our own
self-centeredness and yield ourselves up to the workings of the love of God,
knowing that we shall be safe." In the second holiness sermon, "The Gift
of the Holy Spirit," delivered at Trinity Episcopal Church in Washington,
D.C., on May 29, 1977, Murray defines the Holy Spirit's gift as a transformative force in our lives. The transformation is not instantaneous, but is a
continuous process that requires "struggle and sacrifice." Murray emphasizes that the Spirit "works through humanity individually and socially."

While many black preaching women of the nineteenth and early twentieth centuries treated inner purification, or sanctification, as a prerequisite to attaining salvation in the life to come, Murray's holiness doctrine

focuses on the importance of living in Christ in order to attain salvation in the present world. While Murray does acknowledge the importance of the afterlife, stating that death "calls into question all our human values and would make our earthly existence seem futile if we did not have this hope through our faith in Christ of the new life after death," the overarching theme of her holiness sermons, as in all of her sermons, is that living in Christ improves life in the here and now, both individually and socially.

In "The Holy Spirit," Murray states that the Holy Spirit makes it possible for humans to live in connection to God. Jesus, before his ascension to heaven, promised his disciples that the Holy Spirit would take his place as "their Counselor and helper, teacher and guide." Just as Jesus was God in the flesh walking among humanity, so is the Holy Spirit "God's presence . . . with us at all times and in all places . . . working in and through every moment of history in the affairs of mankind." If we live in connection to God through the Holy Spirit, God will guide us, giving us "serenity in the midst of conflict, trouble, or confusion."

While "things fall into place" when one lives in communion with God, sin, in the form of personal and social turmoil, causes alienation from God. Because of God's gift of free will, humans often choose to rely on their own strengths and live "in ignorance of and estrangement from God." For that reason, social problems abound. It is only through "God's grace and forgiveness" that "we are healed of our sinfulness, the estrangement is overcome and we are restored to community with God." Sanctification, therefore, makes possible the joyful communion between God and God's people, here on earth.

In "The Gift of the Holy Spirit," Murray more explicitly reveals the political and social significance of her holiness theology. Retelling the story of the Pentecost in the Book of Acts, in which the apostles were filled with the Holy Spirit, Murray interprets the apostle's ability to speak in tongues as the ability to transcend "barriers of language and nationality so that many people from different countries living in Jerusalem were able to understand what they were saying." Thus, Murray infuses the meaning of the Baptism of the Holy Spirit with a political and social significance. Just as the Baptism of the Holy Spirit enabled the apostles to transcend social and political differences of their day, so must contemporary people receive the Holy Spirit to overcome present-day social and political divisions.

Having interpreted the Holy Spirit's significance in this way, Murray parallels the 1963 speech that Martin Luther King Jr., made at the Lincoln Memorial with the "Spirit-filled utterance" of the apostles on the day of Pentecost. Although people of different "colors, ages and religions" gatheied to hear King preach on that day, he spoke in a language that all could understand. He called for all people to overcome their divisions so that "'the glory of the Lord shall be revealed, and all flesh shall see it together.'" Murray suggests that the Holy Spirit inspired him to do this.

Murray asserts in this sermon, as she did in "The Holy Spirit," that the world's social ills result from people's willful separation from God. Only through living in communion with God through the Holy Spirit can people live righteously and work for a more righteous world. Throughout both of these holiness sermons, Murray asserts that living in Christ through the Holy Spirit has profound sociopolitical implications, for "it is only when we are one in Christ that we can rise above those things which separate us from one another—differences of race, sex, age, class, economic or social position—and share that supreme gift of communion."

"THE DILEMMA OF THE MINORITY CHRISTIAN." In "The Dilemma of the Minority Christian," delivered on May 19, 1974—Woman's Day—at the St. James Presbyterian Church in New York City, Murray argues that as a minority, African Americans are the objects of "contempt, injustice and oppression," which literally forces them to arm themselves and fight for recognition and respect in a society that would deny them their very humanity and personhood. This militant position is not in keeping with the Christian belief that "self-pride is a stumbling block to salvation." The dilemma is whether to submit passively to injustice, or to resist. Murray admits that she does not have a solution to the problem.

Murray begins the sermon by reflecting on the fifty-third chapter of Isaiah, in which the prophet describes the "Suffering Servant" on whom God will lay "the iniquity of us all." Stating that Isaiah's words "found their most perfect expression in the life and work of . . . Jesus Christ," who suffered rejection and death in order to fulfill God's will, Murray argues that Jesus' life provides a challenging—and problematic—model for minority Christians. Since Jesus did not rebel against the torture inflicted upon him, Murray questions whether minority Christians are called to follow Jesus' example in this way.

In her 1979 sermon "Salvation and Liberation," Murray argues that it is not God's will for Christians to be like the humble, suffering servant when injustices are inflicted upon them. In this 1974 sermon, however, Murray is not convinced that minority Christians should be exempt from suffering servanthood when faced with injustices. Instead, Murray suggests that minority Christians draw strength from God to face the world's injustices humbly and peacefully, as Jesus did. Since Jesus offered the Jews salvation from sin, rather than political liberation, Murray suggests that "salvation does not mean that we will avoid suffering, shame, humiliation, or defeat. It does mean that we are not alone—that God's love . . . is always with us."

Murray does not discount the gravity of the oppression that minorities face; in fact, the very gravity of this oppression makes Murray encourage her audience to look beyond the social problems they face. While it is important to "carry on our struggles for social justice and human dignity," Christians must realize that America's social ills may be too great to overcome. Comparing the United States with ancient Israel, as she does in many of her sermons, Murray refers to William Stringfellow's perspective: "Stringfellow sees the death of a nation [the United States] as the great Old Testament prophets—Amos, Hosea, Micah, Isaiah, and Jeremiah—saw the destruction of the people of Israel."[7] Stringfellow asserts that there is no hope for the United States, and Murray declares that if Stringfellow is right, then Christians must not focus all their energies on overcoming social injustices. They must realize that through Christ, they can transcend their "racial or social status." Murray suggests that Christians are "called to a higher purpose than a social ethic." This higher purpose, she asserts, is the "call to righteousness, to repentance and salvation"—the salvation that transcends worldly evil. Salvation in the here and now, she explains, is "living without fear, living with serenity in confidence that we are the objects of God's unfailing love," no matter what the social circumstances.

"SALVATION AND LIBERATION." Murray delivered "Salvation and Liberation" on April 1, 1979, at the Unitarian Society of Germantown in Philadelphia. The sermon discusses the relationship between salvation and liberation and explores the liberationist theology philosophies of the time, particularly as they relate to African Americans and women.

In 1978, the *Anglican Theological Review* published Murray's article "Black Theology and Feminist Theology: A Comparative View."[8] In that article, she critiqued and summarized an ongoing debate among Christian theologians about various oppressed peoples' liberation movements. The debate, which began in the 1960s, generated a significant body of literature, variously called "theology of liberation," "theology of hope," "theology of revolution," or "political theology." Murray argued that their common theme was "the relation between Christian theology and social action." Although most of the writing emanated from Europe and Latin America, black theology and feminist theology in the United States emerged from the black liberation and women's liberation movements. "Salvation and Liberation," delivered over a year after the publication of her article, states her conclusions.

"Salvation and Liberation" reveals that, by 1979, Murray's theology had significantly shifted since her 1974 sermon, "The Dilemma of the Minority Christian." In "The Dilemma of the Minority Christian," Murray struggled to reconcile her commitment to Christian humility with her commitment to social justice. In "Salvation and Liberation," inspired by the new proliferation of liberation theologies, Murray argues that Christian theology and practice need to be revamped so as not to encourage people to accept suffering humbly. Instead, Christianity should encourage people to work actively to overcome social conditions that cause suffering. Thus, in "Salvation and Liberation," Murray resolves the "dilemma" of minority Christians through the theology of liberation, which reinterprets the Christian tradition in ways that completely affirm minorities in their struggle against oppression.

Throughout "Salvation and Liberation," Murray examines how liberation theologies reenvision Christianity's role. One of the central tenets of liberation theology, as reflected in the sermon's title, is that salvation is concerned not only with the afterlife but also with liberating the oppressed in this world; salvation and liberation, therefore, are synonymous concepts in liberation theology. Murray states that in liberation theology, "there is a decided shift from an other-worldly to a this-worldly emphasis." The central question of Christianity, as it is understood in liberation theology, is no longer concerned with how individuals will gain immortality but with how Christianity will "give strength and hope to those who struggle against the 'Powers and Principalities'—the institutionalized evils and injustices which destroy the humanity of whole peoples and which are virtually immune to individual morality."

Power is a central issue in liberation theology. The unequal relationship between the powerful and the powerless in the world is at the root of much of the world's problems. Sin is defined no longer merely in terms of individuals' transgressions, therefore, but more in terms of "corporate or social evil" that perpetuates the system of domination and oppression. Salvation from sin is not an "escape" into an otherworldly "heaven," but is instead "the power and the possibility of transforming the world, restoring creation and seeking to overcome suffering." Thus, when the Church commits to liberation, it ceases to be a place people go to attain an otherworldly salvation, but instead becomes an institution that serves the oppressed in their struggle for liberation.

Attaining this salvation is, not surprisingly, much more complex than the conversion and sanctification process of an otherworldly theology. Given the complexities of social ills, liberation theologies must use a variety of approaches in addressing the problem of salvation from evil. Liberation theologies, therefore, do not provide "overall systems of dogma," but address the particular issues of specific contexts. Black liberation theology, Latin American liberation theology, feminist liberation theology, and other liberation theologies respond to the particular needs of those groups as they struggle to overcome particular forms of oppression.

Liberation theologians stress that "our perceptions of God are shaped by the culture in which we live and by historical experience"; therefore, traditional Christian theology, as it has been predominantly constructed by white males, reflects the historical experience of those white males, and excludes the experience of Blacks and women. Thus, liberation theologies reenvision God and Christian doctrine in ways that are liberating to Blacks, women, and other groups of oppressed peoples. For example, feminist liberation theology challenges the "images of an exclusively male God as Father, King, Lord and Master," which have supported "a patriarchal world-view in which subordination of women has been the model for the oppression of other groups." Likewise, black theologies have challenged the "traditional Christian doctrines which stress obedience, meekness, humility and suffering servanthood," arguing that those doctrines wrongly "invoke divine approval for patterns of dominance and submission in human relationships," as the disempowered are urged to accept their powerlessness humbly. Since both black theology and feminist theology seek to "reclaim a people from humiliation" that centuries of oppression have caused, anger and pride become virtues in these liberation theologies, and "love of self . . . is not seen as selfishness but as self-respect."

In this sermon, Murray clearly asserts that the Christian faith is "highly political." From this perspective, therefore, conversion to Christianity entails a commitment to social change. It is only through such commitment that the Church will maintain any relevance in the modern world.

"CAN THESE BONES LIVE AGAIN?" Murray delivered "Can These Bones Live Again?" at the St. Ambrose Episcopal Church in Raleigh, North Carolina, on March 12, 1978, which was Woman's Day. Murray imports a traditional African American sermonic theme—Ezekiel's dry bones.

Using Ezek. 37:1–7, Murray compares African Americans' twentieth-century migration from the South to the North with the forced exile of Ezekiel and other Hebrew leaders from Babylon. She emphasizes that although they were not captured and taken away, Blacks were "driven out by the intolerable conditions which they faced."

Enlarging her comparison beyond the two exiles, Murray asserts that "we Negroes/blacks of the South have long seen the parallel between our own enslavement in the United States and [the stories of the Israelites in] the Old Testament." Like the Israelites, who missed their homeland,

African Americans have longed for their roots ever since they were forcibly brought to the Americas and harsh conditions in southern states forced them to migrate to the North.

Many feel like strangers throughout the United States, according to Murray. Just as Israelites were strangers in Babylon, Blacks have "painfully discovered that the Babylon of the spirit is everywhere in the United States." Murray states that exiled Blacks, especially those "scattered about in the crumbling urban areas" of the North, are like the "dry bones" in Ezekiel.

Referencing the work of William Stringfellow, as she did in "The Dilemma of the Minority Christian," as well as the works of other black scholars, poets, politicians, and ministers, Murray illuminates the devastating effects of the African American exile in the United States, as well as how Blacks have courageously struggled to survive in exile.

Despite the problems that exile has caused, there is hope for these "dry bones," Murray asserts. While in "The Dilemma of the Minority Christian," Murray appears to accept Stringfellow's assertion that there is little hope for overcoming social problems in the United States, in "Can These Bones Live Again?" Murray declares that she is more optimistic than Stringfellow. She states that while she acknowledges the "potential gloom and doom" in Stringfellow's prophecy, her life experiences have made her more inclined "to follow in the footsteps of Ezekiel." Ezekiel promised that dry bones would live again, and prophesied "the eventual restoration of the exiles to their homeland"; likewise, Murray is convinced that Blacks and other oppressed groups will overcome their outcast status. Murray concludes her sermon by suggesting that "out of these dry bones, the outcasts of the earth—even women—shall arise and the House of Israel shall be reborn."

MALE AND FEMALE HE CREATED THEM

TEXT: Genesis 1:27–31

So God created man in his own image. In his image he created him; male and female he created them. And God blessed them, and God said to them, "Be fruitful and multiply, and fill the earth and subdue it; and have dominion over the fish of the sea and over the birds of the air and over every living thing that moves upon the earth. . . . And God saw everything that he had made, and behold, it was very good."

—Gen. 1:27–31

Here in the poetry of ancient Hebrew literature, we have the glorious story of creation . . . ending with the creation of Man. Let us also hear this story in the words of James Weldon Johnson, one of our own twentieth-century poets in his poem "The Creation" (A Negro Sermon from *God's Trombones*):

Then God walked around,
And God looked around
On all that He had made. . .
He looked on His world
With all its living things,
And God said: "I'm lonely still."
Then God sat down—
On the side of a hill where He could think;
By a deep, wide river He sat down;
With His head in His hands,
God thought and thought,
Till He thought: "I'll make me a man!"
Up from the bed of the river
God scooped the clay;
And by the bank of the river
He kneeled Him down;
And there the Great God Almighty,
Who lit the sun and fixed it in the sky,
Who flung the stars to the most far corner of the night,
Who rounded the earth in the middle of His hand;

This Great God,
Like a mammy bending over her baby,
Kneeled down in the dust
Toiling over a lump of clay
Till he shaped it in His own image;
Then into it He blew the breath of life,
And man became a living soul.
Amen. Amen.

In the very beginning of Holy Scripture is expressed the most liberating idea known to humanity—Man is made in the image of God, and Man here means male *and* female. *They,* not *he,* are to have dominion over the earth. This theme is repeated in Gen. 5: "When God created man, he made him in the likeness of God. Male and female he created them, and he blessed them and named them Man when they were created."

Despite the clarity of this language that male and female both share the reflection of their Creator at the creaturely level and both share equally in the dominion over the earth, what has in fact happened is that sexism— the dominance of a patriarchal male-oriented society—is the oldest and most stubborn form of human oppression and has served as a model for other forms of human exploitation and alienation.

Nowhere is this more apparent than in the language, symbolisms and structures of organized religion. As Casey Miller and Kate Swift have pointed out in their perceptive study, *Women and Language:*

> Since the major Western religions all originate in patriarchal societies and continue to defend a patriarchal world view, the metaphors used to express their insights are by tradition and habit overwhelmingly male-oriented. As apologists of these religions have insisted for tens of centuries, the symbolization of a male God must not be taken to mean that God really *is* male. In fact, it must be understood that God has no sex at all. But inevitably, when words like father and king are used to evoke the image of a personal God, at some level of consciousness it is a male image that takes hold. And since the same symbols are used of male human beings—from whom, out of the need for analogy, the images of God have been drawn—female human beings become less Godlike, less perfect, different, "the other."[9]

We are indebted to contemporary women scholars and theologians for a critical reexamination of the Biblical myths which lie at the foundation of the [Judeo]-Christian tradition, and who call attention to their misinterpretation over thousands of years. Miller and Swift continue their analysis:

"From antiquity, people have recognized the connection between *naming* and *power* [*Roots;* Kunta Kinte].[10] The master-subject relationship, which corrupts the master and degrades the subject, is foreshadowed in one of the biblical creation myths when the primal male assumes the right to name his equal, the primal female. The notion that *the sexes were created equal and at the same time* is not widely accepted."[11] Here they are referring to the second and older version of the Creation story found in Gen. 2:4 and following; the myth of Adam and Eve. In the second chapter of Genesis "God formed man of the dust of the ground" and later made woman out of one of his ribs. In this version, the man said:

> This at last is bone of my bones
> and flesh of my flesh,
> she shall be called Woman,
> because she was taken out of Man.

> —Gen. 2:23

From this kind of Biblical anthropology comes the notion [that] Man is the head of woman, the confusion of the generic term *man* with the specific term *male* and the biblical justification for the dominance of males over females. Dr. Phyllis Trible, associate professor at Andover Newton Theological School, has examined this story in the original Hebrew and finds that much of its meaning has been distorted in the English translation. She points out that the "man" formed out of the dust of the ground is *'adham,* a generic term in ancient Hebrew which means, not male, but humankind.[12]

This original being was sexually undifferentiated, having the potentiality of both sexes. The term used to describe such a being is *androgynous*— "being both male and female." The King James Version continues, "And the Lord God said, It is not good that the man should be alone; I will make him an *help meet* for him.["] The Revised Standard Version uses the term: "a fit helper." The New English Bible, uses the word "partner."[13]

Until God performs surgery upon the sleeping *'adham,* this androgynous creature containing the potentiality of both sexes is given the power to name the animals and assert authority over them, but they are not *'adham's* equals. Professor Trible notes that it is only *after* the rib surgery that the generic term *'adham* is now accompanied by two additional terms: the Hebrew words specifying the human male, *'ish*, and the human female, *'ishshah*. "*'Adham*, whose flesh and bones have now been sexu ally identified as female and male, speaks of the two sexes in the third person. 'She shall be called woman' (*'ishshah*), because she was *differentiated from* man (*'ish*) provides a valid alternative for the Hebrew term usually rendered 'taken out of.'"[14]

Thus, according to Trible, "She shall be called woman" is not an act of naming. Only later, after God has already judged the couple but has not yet expelled them from the Garden of Eden, does the man, "invoking the same formula used in naming the animals and asserting supremacy over them, 'called his wife's name Eve.' Trible concludes, 'The naming itself faults the man for corrupting a relationship of mutuality and equality,' and then God evicts the primal couple from Eden."[15]

Following up on Professor Trible's analysis, Miller and Swift observe: "The recorder of that early human effort to understand the nature and meaning of existence speaks across the millenniums of patriarchy. The story is far different from the male-oriented interpretation of creation that has embedded itself in our conscious understanding and our less conscious use of language. In English the once truly generic word *man* has come to mean *male,* so that males are seen as representing the species in a way females are not. Humanity, divided against itself, become the norm and the deviation, the namer and the named."[16]

Here we have the genesis of the theological subordination of women, the arguments against the change of the status and role of women, the opposition to women in the priesthood, particularly in the liturgical communions of the Christian Church and the Orthodox Hebrew faith. Recently, I met a conductor on the Metroliner [train] between Washington and New York. He saw my clerical collar and we got to talking. It turned out that he was an Episcopalian who has left the Church and says he is going to become an Orthodox Hebrew, his reason being that not in his lifetime will *that* particular faith admit women to an ordained ministry.

As patriarchy has distorted the role and function of women (and men), so it has distorted our perceptions of God. And, as one feminist theologian has pointed out [Phyllis Bird], "the Old Testament is a man's 'book' . . . a collection of writings by males from a society dominated by males. These writings portray a man's world. They speak of events and activities engaged in primarily or exclusively by males (war, cult and government) and of a jealously singular God, who is described and addressed in terms normally used for males."[17]

And while we say in theory that God has no sex—in fact, the images of God handed down to us from our Christian tradition are almost exclusively male: "God the Father," for example. It is here that James Weldon Johnson's poetry on the Creation has a special significance for women. The image:

> This Great God[,]
> Like a mammy bending over her baby,
> Kneeled [down] in the dust
> Toiling over a lump of clay.

The female imagery of the Divine Being has been ignored or suppressed, so much so that a brilliant theologian from the Roman Catholic tradition like my friend and colleague, Mary Daly, has felt impelled to call herself a post-Christian and to write a book called *Beyond God the Father*.[18] But the female imagery is there—in the [Wisdom] literature, in Jesus of Nazareth brooding over Jerusalem like a Mother Hen, in the 11th century English bishop, theologian and monk St. Anselm of Canterbury who refers to Jesus as "Our Mother" in his prayers, and sees Christ, according to Eleanor McLaughlin, "as our caring mother who comforts, gentles, revives, consoles."[19] Divine motherhood is also depicted by the 14th century mystic and anchoress, Dame Julian of Norwich, England, who experienced God in a feminine way and also referred to Christ as our Mother. She wrote:

> The human mother will suckle her child with her own milk, but our beloved Mother, Jesus, feeds us with himself, and, with the most tender courtesy, does it by means of the Blessed Sacrament. . . . The human mother may put her child tenderly to her breast, but our tender Mother Jesus simply leads us into his blessed breast through his open side, and there gives us a glimpse of the Godhead and heavenly joy— the inner certainty of eternal bliss.[20]

If I have come down hard on patriarchal religion, it is because both men and women are imprisoned in rigid roles dominated by a male-oriented hierarchy. All one has to do is to look at CBS television news each night, or listen to Agronsky's panel, to see *who* dominates the world and *in what terms*—males depicting and analyzing wars and terrorism and cynical politics, all instigated and carried out by other males for the most part.[21] The world society is in dangerous imbalance, and the cultural patterns developed by males, as Erik Erikson and others point out[,] "have about reached their limit of value, utility and rationality, unless society is considerably modified by feminine input. . . ."[22] This framework even—or perhaps, especially—infects the perception of God, so that "the Ultimate is invoked to substantiate a destructively masculine world," says theologian Patricia Martin Doyle. With Erikson, she agrees that "Such a gigantic one-sidedness, . . . has brought us to our current appalling situation in which the traditional feminine values of realism in householding, responsibility in upbringing, resourcefulness in keeping and making the peace, devotion to healing, creativity in fostering life, hitherto ignored, must find a new emphasis and input into our cultural life."[23] When this happens, and we are free to be wholly human, there will be no need for special Women's Day services in the Christian Church. Every service will be Women's Day, Men's Day and Children's Day in which all participate in worship according to our individual gifts to the glory of God, our Father and Mother, who created us in the Divine image. *Amen.*

WOMEN SEEKING ADMISSION TO HOLY ORDERS— AS CRUCIFERS CARRYING THE CROSS

TEXT: Isaiah 61:1–4

1. *The Spirit of the Lord God is upon me; because the Lord hath anointed me to preach good tidings unto the meek; he hath sent me to bind up the broken-hearted, to proclaim liberty to the captives, and the opening of the prison to them that are bound;*

2. *To proclaim the acceptable year of the Lord, and the day of vengeance of our God; to comfort all that mourn;*

3. *To appoint unto them that mourn in Zion, to give unto them beauty for ashes, the oil of joy for mourning, the garment of praise for the spirit of heaviness; that they might be called trees of righteousness, the planting of the Lord, that he might be glorified[;]*

4. *And they shall build the old wastes, they shall raise up the former desolations and they shall repair the waste cities, the desolation of many generations.*

—Isa. 61:1–4

I have selected this passage for our reflections because it seems to describe more eloquently than anything I can say to you this morning where I am and where many women of our Church are who are seeking admission to Holy Orders as their vocation. Six months ago, you sent me forth as a member of your congregation with your blessings and prayers to begin my training for the Sacred Ministry. This is my first opportunity to return to my home parish church and give an account of myself. I must confess I am torn between the joy of being back in my sponsoring parish and the nervousness of any first year seminarian called upon to proclaim the Word of God from the pulpit.

One of the first lessons we learn at Seminary is a profound sense of our own unworthiness and the awesomeness of the task we have set for ourselves in tension with a commitment which will not permit us to escape the pain, the doubts, the fears that assail every confessed Christian in moments of personal crisis.

Secondly, we learn that every Christian baptized into our Church is admitted to membership in the royal priesthood of Christ and has a min istry, whether one is male or female, old or young, white or black, lay member or clergy. Those of us who feel a special call to seek Holy Orders do so, not because we are better Christians or more able than our brothers and sisters, but because something has happened to us and there has taken place a radical shift of God's moving from the periphery to the very center of our lives. We dare to answer this call because, in a very real sense, we have no choice in the matter. God has spoken to us through an event or through a series of events which point us in one direction— toward full time service of God. Like the prophet Isaiah and the other prophets of the Old Testament, we are compelled to believe that sinful, rebellious, broken as we are, God is using us as instruments of his will— not ours—to love and serve him and our fellow human beings to the greater glory of God our Creator and Redeemer.

This decision makes us vulnerable to hurt, to heartache, to sorrow and suffering—for our very striving to be open to God's will intensifies our sensitivity to the tragedies of the human condition and we soon learn that without the love of God we are all lost, rudderless, without direction—an aircraft out of control and without a pilot. We have made the choice to reject our human drive to be self-sufficient and self-dependent and to follow the example of Jesus Christ in utter dependence upon God and radical obedience to God's will, not our own. Each day as we try to follow this example, we are chastened and humbled by our own shortcomings, our own self-willed disobedience and sinfulness and excessive self-centeredness in which state of being we hurt others and fail to live up to our commitments. Each day we are made more acutely conscious of how difficult it is to be a Christian, even in a small intimate community of committed Christians headed by twenty-three or more ordained priests.

Our failures, our weaknesses would overwhelm us were it not for the fact that each day we gain a growing sense of God's infinitely tender love and mercy and the gifts of grace bestowed upon us impel us to sing out spontaneously in hymns of joy, thanksgiving, and praise.

Because I am a woman, I must speak of this *call* through the experience of a woman—my own experiences and those of other women seminarians who have shared their hopes and dreams and tears of heartbreak with me.

Why is it that at this particular moment in the history of our church and of other faiths women are beginning to rise up and seek the ordained priesthood with such determined insistence? Is it a product of the Women's Liberation movement as others suggest? Cannot women be content to serve as members of the royal priesthood of Christ as they have served from the beginning of the Church? Why do they clamor to be admitted to all levels of the clergy—the Diaconate, the Priesthood, the Episcopacy? Why, in the face of the devastating rejection at the Louisville General Convention of last October, 1973—a rejection which Bishop Paul Moore of New York has called the violation of the very core of their personhood— [have they] only increased their determination to enter the higher levels of the clergy? And why must their *call* no longer be denied?

As I have pondered these questions since I left you last August and searched for answers, I find myself reflecting upon human history and looking at comparable periods in the long pilgrimage of humankind toward God, our Creator, Redeemer and Savior from death and nothingness.

The God of the Christian faith and the God of the Prophets of Israel moves, acts, and speaks in history through events and through individuals. Throughout all human history—today as well as 2500 years or more ago—our God is active in the affairs of humankind to bring us to redemption, salvation, and reconciliation with Him, the source of our being. We were created in His image and are the objects of an ineffable love which passes or transcends all human understanding. But we were also created with the freedom of will—the choice to love God and obey him or *not* to love God. Being human, finite, and therefore imperfect, *each of us, all of us,* from the dawn of human history, cannot resist the temptation to try to be God ourselves, to set our wills, our goals, our selfish interests above the will of God.

The more our cunning brains invent and the more dominion we achieve over the world we live in, the more our tendency is to rely upon ourselves, and even to shift the blame for our own sins and shortcomings upon God. How often have we heard skeptics say, "How could a loving God let such terrible things happen in the world?" In our drive for possessions, for dominion over nature, for power, status and prestige, we too often forget that our relation to the earth is that of stewardship—not ownership; that our destiny is not limited to our finite life; that we continually stand in God's judgement, and that we can escape the terrible consequences of our many failings only through God's grace; that we are engaged in a pilgrimage toward a higher and better life—toward union with God—and that this life we now live is a stage of our preparation for this higher destiny.

This radical departure from our Godward destiny has been particularly evident in certain periods of human history and has produced crises which have destroyed whole nations and peoples. The United States of 1974 is frighteningly like the people of Israel with their divided kingdoms in the

8th and 7th centuries B.C. In both periods of history we see certain common features: a comparatively advanced civilization[,] militarized dominion over weaker peoples, governmental intrigues, political assassinations, exploitations of the poor by the rich, neglect of the weak and defenseless, dishonesty and deceit in the marketplace, bribery and corruption of public officials and of the administration of justice, the drive for affluent living, carousing, and lavishment in food and drink, the jockeying for supremacy by the international great powers—and above all, the apostasy of the chosen people—the falling away from God. In the 8th Century B.C., the people gave lip service to Yahweh and took for granted that as the *elect*, God's chosen people, they would be saved. In the United States of the late 20th Century, we have relied upon our military strength, our bountiful natural resources, our "America First" mentality and our historical ethos of "Manifest Destiny."

And we are now in a deep and pervasive national crisis not unlike the crisis the 8th Century prophets and their successors foresaw in their own era. In such periods of human crisis, God has called forth prophets who will not be silenced, who will not be coopted by the established hierarchies whether they be clerical or secular. The role of these prophets is to call the people to repentance, to a return to the God of salvation. Their message is two-fold. They speak of the awful judgment of God's anger and the infinite tenderness and mercy of God's love. They proclaim that the gloom which attends the devastation will be followed by salvation and joy and the rebuilding on the part of those who remain faithful to God.

I believe that today God has chosen his messengers to warn of God's judgment upon a sinful and rebellious people and simultaneously to bring a gospel of hope and joy to those who will listen and have faith. I believe that God is choosing these messengers from the ranks of the dispossessed, the oppressed, and from those who have listened to his Word and are open to feel deeply the sorrow of the human condition. And I believe that many women of all ages are answering that call because they have suffered and endured and are particularly vulnerable to human sorrow and need.

Nothing less than the urgency of their mission, born of the depths of our moral and social crisis, could impel them to face the incredible barriers which have existed for thousands of years, to endure the ridicule and even violence of their detractors, and the continual heartache of rejection which blocks their path and makes their burden almost intolerable. I believe that these women are in truth the Suffering Servants of Christ, "despised and rejected," women of sorrows and acquainted with grief. They are answering to a higher authority than that of the political structures of our Church, and in the fullness of time God will sweep away those barriers and free the Church to carry forward its mission of renewal as a living force and God's witness in our society.

As I have already said, the remarkable quality of the Old Testament prophets is their dual message of judgment and salvation. It is this hope of reconciliation with God and our sisters and brothers which is the Christian joy—an ebullient, loving, giving and forgiving joyousness which we experience in our beloved associate rectors, Al Kershaw and Jack Greeley. (I hope you will forgive my irreverence when I tell you that I call Al Kershaw an outsized Pixie and Jack Greeley the Jolly Green Giant!) We see it in those great spirits like the late Eleanor Roosevelt, and others who have endured many agonies of loss, or privation or even oppression, but who, sustained by an abiding faith that they are children of God and the objects of his love, grow through their trials and radiate a spirit of loving kindness to everyone.

I sense this joy in the women of our Church who, supported by their own faith and by the open and sincere concern of many of their brother clergy, realize that tears sown in this night of temporary despair will bring joy in the morning. As I have watched my sisters in Seminary serving as acolytes at the altar, as crucifers carrying the cross, as lay readers and intercessors, as senior seminarians leading the morning prayer and evensong, as they carry on their ministries to one another, to their male brethren, to the sick and the dying, I am brought back to the words of Isaiah and the prophecy which will be fulfilled when the Church recognizes their full humanity:

1. "The Spirit of the Lord God is upon me; because the Lord hath anointed me to preach good tidings unto the meek; he hath sent me to bind up the broken-hearted, to proclaim liberty to the captives, and the opening of the prison to them that are bound. . . .

3. ". . . to give unto them beauty for ashes, the oil of joy for mourning, the garment of praise for the spirit of heaviness. . . .

4. "And they shall build the old wastes, they shall raise up the former desolations, and they shall repair the waste cities, the desolations of many generations."

Let us pray.

MARY HAS CHOSEN THE BEST PART

TEXT: Luke 10:42b

The part that Mary has chosen is best;
and it shall not be taken away from her.
—Luke 10:42b

Our Gospel reading today is also the Gospel text for July 29, set aside in the Church Calendar as a day of special devotion for Mary and Martha of Bethany. This little story of Mary and Martha is found only in Luke. One New Testament scholar has noted that we find many more stories that include women in Luke than in Matthew and Mark. Luke appears to be addressing his gospel to a setting in which there were a substantial number of women present, either as students of the primitive catechism or potential converts to the early missionary churches. Quite often he puts together the parables in "pairs"—for example, he couples the parable of the man and the lost sheep with that of the woman and the lost coin. Just before the passage we read today, Luke records the parable of the Good Samaritan which is directed toward men; the Mary and Martha story is directed toward woman. And so, we will talk about women today.

Luke gives us an intimate glimpse of two women who were disciples of Jesus of Nazareth. Martha, the mistress of the house, seems to be a fuss-budget who wants to make elaborate preparations for their guest. She is "distracted with much serving." She is concerned with material things, and in her anxiety to make Jesus welcome, she takes on too much. She bustles about, tiring herself out, and getting more and more frustrated because she is missing all the joy of Jesus' conversation. She becomes irritated because her sister Mary is not lending a hand.

For Mary, however, it is more important to give her undivided attention to the Lord and listen to his words than to overwhelm him with food and entertainment. Jesus, who has been watching this little human drama, perhaps in fond amusement, is probably not at all surprised when Martha complains to him about Mary's behavior. He gently chides her, "Martha, Martha, you are fretting and fussing about so many things; but *one* thing is necessary."

What was the purpose of Jesus' visit if it were not fellowship and communion? Martha's failing was not one of intent. She loved the Lord and wanted to serve him, but she was so entangled in her own plans and preparations that her encounter with the Lord became an onerous duty instead of an occasion for joy.

Martha's dilemma is, of course, our own today. All too often we are caught up in the frantic search for security, for material comforts, for worldly success, for new experiences and more and more *things*; in fact we may become so enslaved to the tyranny of possessions that we lose the ultimate meaning of our lives. One is reminded of those lines from [Wordsworth]:

> The world is too much with us; late and soon[,]
> Getting and spending[,] we lay waste our [powers].[24]

When we are younger, we may be too involved in the competitive rat race to consider this possibility. When we become older and acutely aware of eternity, we are more apt to reflect upon our past and wonder what we have done with our lives that has any significance beyond our own struggle for existence.

Perhaps it is here that we can see another level of meaning in the story of Mary and Martha. Martha followed traditional custom in conformity with the position of women in her time. Women in the Jewish culture were not permitted to study the Torah or to engage in theological conversation with a Rabbi. In [society] they were invisible; a husband was not even to speak to his wife in public. In this perspective, we can see Mary as an unusual woman, one who was unwilling to accept the role defined for her and was drawn to Jesus of Nazareth because he treated her as a *person* with an intellect and a quest for knowledge of God. Jesus recognized her thirst and encouraged it. He permitted her the privilege of sitting at his feet as if she were a young male divinity student, and he defended her decision. "The part that Mary has chosen is best; and it shall not be taken from her."

We do not know how Mary translated this experience into action; we are permitted to see only her impulse to enlarge her vision beyond the ordinary—in her case, an intense concentration upon the Word of God. But we do know what Jesus expected of all disciples and all Christians. In the very next passage of Luke, he teaches his disciples to pray "Thy kingdom come," and according to one witness, "Thy will be done, on *earth* as in heaven."

The central purpose of our existence, then, is that God's will be done on earth. Salvation is not some otherworldly experience; it is a process which begins here and now. I do not believe that we can hope for individual salvation without reference to the world in which we live. I believe that the heart of the Gospel message in the two Great Commandments means that Christians are called upon by God to transform the world, to work for a more just and humane society; that God's purposes for creation are working themselves out in human history to the end that God's will *is* done on earth.

None of us can escape the deeper implications of a society which breeds the kind of lawlessness and looting which happened in New York City last week on the night the lights went out. Without for one moment defending the looters, we have to ask ourselves, "What does it mean to live in a world in which one's appetite is constantly whetted for *things* through advertising, and yet one lives in a crowded ghetto where unemployment among black and Hispanic teenagers soars from 40 percent to 80 percent, in some areas, where people are hungry and angry, and where they live without hope, without goals?"

Obviously, no simplistic diagnosis can explain this human tragedy, but I think it may be a symptom of the moral disintegration within a society which neglects the deep-seated causes of poverty and powerlessness within its own population in its preoccupation with world power relationships. For example, the United States since 1945 has stockpiled enough nuclear weapons to *have a potential kill-power of 12 times the present world population.* What does this say for our moral values? What does it say about the millions of people in this country who call themselves Christians?

To say that the Christian mission is to transform the world is frightening to most of us. We feel that the problems of our time are too complex, that we are only one person, and that we, individually, can make very little impact upon society. Jesus, himself, was aware of this human frailty when he said to his disciples, "O Ye of little faith!" Yet all around us are examples of individuals who felt themselves called to a mission and who helped to change the face of society.

It seems appropriate here to point to the life of Alice Paul, founder of the National Woman's Party, who died last Saturday, July 9, at the age of 92. Her life, spanning almost a century, bridged the two movements for women's rights in the United States. Born of Quaker parents, she was educated to become a social worker. At the age of 22, after two years of settlement house work in New York, she went to England to study social work, and while there met the leaders of the British women's suffrage movement, and began her life long advocacy of women's rights.

When she returned to this country around 1912, she joined the suffrage movement, which had reached an all time low, and infused it with new energy. She made her headquarters in Washington and for the next eight years led marches, demonstrations and parades with banners and costumes. In 1917 Dr. Paul, who had earned her Ph.D., and several of her followers were jailed for their activities, and went on a hunger strike, which lasted three weeks and as a result of which she was force-fed. Such harsh treatment of these imprisoned women aroused angry public response and brought about national recognition of the suffrage issue. In 1920, as you know, the Nineteenth Amendment to the Constitution was adopted and women had the vote after 72 years of continuous agitation.

Alice Paul quickly realized that the struggle for equality was not over, and in 1923 she wrote and had introduced into Congress the first Equal Rights Amendment ever proposed for women. For 49 years Dr. Paul and her valiant little band of women in the National Woman's Party introduced the Equal Rights Amendment into every session of Congress until its final passage in 1972. She lived to see 35 states ratify the amendment and only three more are required to make it become part of the Constitution.[25]

Alice Paul possessed a singlemindedness bordering on fanaticism, but only such singleness of purpose and total dedication could have kept this issue alive during the intervening years. She was well equipped to supply the leadership and vision necessary for this task. Ten years after earning her Ph.D. at the University of Pennsylvania, she took a law degree, and by 1928 had earned both a Master's and a Doctorate in Law at American University. She had the courage to outface the criticism and ridicule heaped upon her and the dwindling membership of her organization as the members of the suffrage movement passed off the scene. She held to her course until ERA caught the imagination of a new generation of young feminists in the late 1960s and blossomed into a national movement. Miss Paul remained in Washington until Congress passed ERA, and then continued active work on behalf of the various states' campaigns in Connecticut until about three years ago when she became incapacitated by ill health.

Here, then, was a life pervaded by a sense of purpose and wholly dedicated to the fulfillment of her mission. We are reminded of another great contemporary of Alice Paul—Mrs. Eleanor Roosevelt. Miss Paul was one year younger than Mrs. Roosevelt and her life continued for 15 years after Mrs. Roosevelt's death. And while their lifestyles were different and they operated in different arenas, each of these two women in her own way, standing in the Christian tradition, made a lasting impact upon the world in which they lived by their unswerving devotion to the cause of human rights. Of Alice Paul, as of Eleanor Roosevelt, I think it can be said: "She has chosen the best part; and it shall not be taken away from her." What have *we* chosen? *Amen.*

THE HOLY SPIRIT

Text: John 14:26, 15:26; Psalms 139:7–10

*When the Comforter is come, whom I will send to you from
the Father, even the Spirit of Truth, which proceedeth from the
Father, he will testify of me; and you shall also bear witness,
because you have been with me from the beginning.*

—John 15:26

On this Sunday after Ascension Day, we also celebrate the 76th Anniversary of Calvary Protestant Episcopal Church. An anniversary is a joyous occasion in which we look back to our beginnings and give thanks for the blessings which have brought us thus far, and we recommit ourselves to God as disciples of his Son Jesus, the Christ, to carry on the mission and outreach of this church. We recall that first meeting of nine people held in a private home on Florida Avenue in 1902, and of the faith which enabled this tiny Christian mission to grow into a robust parish.

In reading the history of this church, I learned that it took its name from Calvary Church in New York City. This tradition has a special meaning for me because Calvary in New York was the church in which Mrs. Eleanor Roosevelt was christened as an infant back in 1884 or 1885. It is also the church I attended when I was in New York and it was there in 1973 that I first talked with my friend the Rector, the Rev. Tom Pike, about the possibility of entering the ordained ministry.

Our Gospel text this morning takes us back to the very beginnings of the Christian community to which we belong. Jesus is in the Upper Room sharing his last meal with his closest disciples before his arrest and crucifixion. His earthly mission is drawing to a close, and he knows that he must rely upon these few disciples, weak and fearful though they may be, to carry on the work he has begun. The atmosphere is not one of joyous celebration, but one of heavy-heartedness. Jesus knows that very soon he will be separated from his disciples and they will be scattered in confusion, shattered by grief and overwhelmed with fear. Patiently, in the few minutes they have left together, he tries to summarize his teachings, to comfort them and give them courage and hope so they will be able to withstand the tribulations, the persecutions which lie ahead. He must make them understand that they will not be alone; that the Holy Spirit will be with them and remain with them always. The word *Comforter* is a translation from the Greek work *Paraclete,* which also means *Counselor, Advocate,* or *Helper.* Jesus also refers to it as the Holy Spirit.

During his earthly ministry, *Jesus* has been with his disciples as their Counselor and helper, teacher and guide. Now that he will no longer be with them in the flesh, the Holy Spirit will come in his place. At one point he tells them, "The Paraclete, the Holy Spirit, whom the Father will send in my name, will instruct you in everything, and remind you of all that I told you" (John 14:26). The Spirit is the bequest of the glorified Christ to all who believe in him.

In our church life, we tend to emphasize the gift of the Holy Spirit on very special sacramental occasions—at Baptism, or at confirmation, or at an Ordination. But we must remember that the Spirit of God's presence is with us at all times and in all places, in every possible situation—at home, in school, at work, in politics, in social life, in the marketplace, in joy, in the depths of sorrow, sin, sickness and despair—the ever present companion, friend and helper, the Eternal One working in and through every moment of history in the affairs of mankind.

Whether we are consciously aware of it or not, God is with us every moment of our lives in everything we do. I think sometimes we shrink from the idea of the nearness of God because we think of it as such a fearful and awesome thing. But God is not alien or distant from us; his Spirit is as close as the touch of a loved one's hand. Remember the Psalmist in the 139th Psalm:

> Whither can I go then from your Spirit?
> Where can I flee from your presence?
> If I climb up to heaven you are there,
> If I make the grave my bed, you are there also,
> If I take the wings of the morning
>   and dwell in the uttermost parts of the sea,
> Even there your hand will lead me,
>   and your right hand will hold me fast.

I, personally, am not a good flyer and when I am in a plane I have to remind myself that God is there just as much as when I am on the [ground] driving my own car. When we feel alone and desolate, it is not *God* who has shut us out but *we* who have tried to shut out God. When we are open to the presence of the Holy Spirit, we feel a certain serenity in the midst of conflict, trouble, or confusion. God's power works in us and through us, to guide us in our critical decisions, to comfort us when we are bereaved, to strengthen us when we are overcome with fear and apprehension. As one Christian writer has said, "There is a wonderful, loved, protected feeling that embraces one who realizes that God is always near."

To dwell in the Holy Spirit is to dwell in Christ. The Spirit replaces the visible presence of Jesus, and the Church is the Spirit-filled community bound to one another in Christ. In our communion we share the supreme gift of the Spirit expressed in the benediction, "The grace of our Lord Jesus Christ, and the love of God, and the fellowship of the Holy Spirit, be with us all evermore."

When we speak of the "fellowship of the Holy Spirit," we are speaking of God's faithfulness in all situations. The Psalmist says, "Even though I walk in the valley of the shadow of death, I fear no evil, for thou art with me, thy rod and thy staff, they comfort me." Any one of us who has stood by the bedside of a beloved relative or friend who is dying understands the meaning of this verse. We also speak of God's responsiveness—and it is this responsiveness which is the foundation of our faith in prayer. Prayer is our attempt to bring our whole being before God—our thankfulness, our needs, our hopes, our fears—in the expectation that God will respond to our needs. So often we find that when we rest our lives and our plans in God, things work out for us better than any plans we can make for ourselves—things fall into place.

We also believe that God understands us better than we understand ourselves. God understands our needs, and sometimes, in retrospect, we realize that something we have greatly desired has been withheld from us in God's wisdom for our own best interest.

The "fellowship of the Holy Spirit" also speaks to us of the forgiveness of God. Mankind was created for community with God. We are linked to the eternal in the midst of transitory existence. Yet in our wilfulness, all too often we live in ignorance of and estrangement from God. When we become aware of our estrangement we are conscious of sin. And when we are separated from God, we are also separated from our fellow human beings. It is the alienation from God which brings about enmities and conflicts between human beings. Through God's grace and forgiveness we are healed of our sinfulness, the estrangement is overcome and we are restored to community with God.

Jesus said, "Love one another even as I have loved you," and this is the standard for the Christian community. Through faith in the Risen Christ and in his message of love and his sacrifice, we are bound together in Christ in at-one-ment with God and at-one-ment with one another.

Above all, it is the assurance of being united with Jesus and his life which overcomes death. Mankind has never been able to come to terms with death; it calls into question all our human values and would make our earthly existence seem futile if we did not have this hope through our faith in Christ of the new life after death. We do not know what life after death will be like, but in faith we can say with the devout theologian who spent his life studying the Holy Scripture, and when he was nearing death was asked about the life beyond; he replied, "I do not know; I know only that I shall be safe."

The Holy Spirit, then, as Jesus promised his disciples, is God's eternal presence with us always, coming to us as he came to us in Jesus of [Nazareth]; loving us, sustaining us, guiding us, forgiving us, never letting us go, transforming our lives, and leading us toward the consummation of God's ultimate plan for all his creation. When the Spirit dwells in us, we are able to let go [of] our own self-centeredness and yield ourselves up to the workings of the love of God, knowing that we shall be safe. *Let us pray.*

Almighty and everlasting God, behold us your children gathered once again to give praise and thanks for this holy house dedicated to your service. Mercifully grant, that recalling our own dedication as living temples of your Holy Spirit, we may be enabled to govern our souls and bodies according to your commandment, and to the glory of your holy name; through Jesus Christ our Lord. *Amen.*

THE GIFT OF THE HOLY SPIRIT

Text: John 14:16–17

*And I will pray to the Father, and he will give you another
Counselor, to be with you forever, even the Spirit of truth, whom
the world cannot receive, because it neither sees him nor knows
him; you know him, for he dwells with you, and will be in you.*

—John 14:16–17

This was the promise Jesus gave his disciples during this farewell meal
with them in the Upper Room before he went out to meet his death by
crucifixion. And, according to the Book of Acts, this promise was fulfilled
on the Day of Pentecost, the "fiftieth day" after Passover, commemorated
in Jewish tradition as the day on which the Law of Moses was given. In
Christian tradition, Pentecost, (or Whitsunday) is the day on which the
Apostles received the gift of the Holy Spirit, and has become the climax
of the Easter season.

Acts gives us a dramatic account of this event. The Apostles had come
together in Jerusalem to observe Pentecost, when suddenly the Holy Spirit
filled the heaven with [a] sound like the rush of a mighty wind, and the
Apostles were so filled with it that they seemed to be on fire. They could
not contain themselves and each broke into ecstatic utterance praising the
mighty works of God. Their enthusiasm communicated itself to the people in the vicinity, and a great multitude assembled to find out what had
caused all the excitement. The Apostles' speech transcended barriers of
language and nationality so that many people from different countries living in Jerusalem were able to understand what they were saying. We learn
that after Peter stood up and preached that day, 3000 souls were baptized
into the Christian faith, and devoted themselves to the apostles' teaching
and fellowship, to the breaking of bread and prayers.

As in the Apostles' time, the Holy Spirit comes to us in moments when
we least expect it—it may be a great Church festival when thousands of
people are united in prayer and hymns of praise, or it may even manifest
itself in a political event. In retrospect, I think the Holy Spirit was very
much in evidence on that day in August 1963 when 240,000 people of all
colors, ages and religions came together in Washington for a common
ennobling purpose, marched to the Lincoln Memorial and heard the late
Dr. Martin Luther King, Jr., among others, burst into what was essentially

a Spirit-filled utterance—"I have a Dream that one day every valley shall be exalted, every hill and mountain shall be made low, the rough places will be made plain and the crooked places will be made straight, and the glory of the Lord shall be revealed, and all flesh shall see it together."

We pray for the gift of the Holy Spirit on very special sacramental occasions in our Church life—at Baptism, at Confirmation, and during an Ordination. We may consciously *feel* the Spirit in such deeply devotional moments. We need to remind ourselves, however, that the Holy Spirit is God's abiding presence with us at all times and in all places, in every possible situation—at home, at work, in school, in the marketplace, in social life, in politics, in joy, in the depth of sorrow, sin, sickness and despair—the ever faithful companion, friend and Counselor, the Eternal One working in and through every moment of history in the affairs of mankind.

I think sometimes we shrink from the thought of this ever present Spirit because our awareness of being in God's presence at all times is a fearful and awesome thing. We *are* afraid when we contemplate the Holy, the fear which a priest or a lay minister experiences standing at the altar or attempting to preach the Word of God. Our realization of how small we are and how infinitely great is the Creator and Preserver of our universe inspires our awe. Our consciousness of how far we fall short of our true selves, and that God's judgment is upon us every moment of our lives makes us afraid.

But God is not alien or distant from us, and his Spirit is as close as the touch of a loved one's hand. We were created for community with God, and we are linked with the eternal in the midst of our transitory life. We become alienated from God when we forget our link to eternity and elevate the things of this world to supreme importance. When, however, we rest ourselves in God and are open to the Holy Spirit, we feel a certain serenity in the midst of all the conflict and confusion of life. God's power is working in us and through us, to guide us in our critical decisions, to strengthen us when we are disheartened, to comfort us when we are bereaved. In the words of a Christian writer, "There is a wonderful, loved, protected feeling that embraces one who realizes that God is always near."

Yet it would be wrong to think that the Holy Spirit comes to us merely to give us comfort or ease. The work of the Holy Spirit is to transform our lives and to conform us to Christ, to perfect us. We are told in the Outline of Faith of our Proposed Book of Common Prayer that "We recognize the presence of the Holy Spirit when we confess Jesus Christ as Lord and are brought into harmony with God, with ourselves, with our neighbors, and with all creation."

This transformation is an ongoing process requiring struggle and sacrifice—struggle against our own wilful impulses, sacrifice of our own selfish desires, slowly and often painfully learning obedience to God's will. It involves a discipline made possible only by the Holy Spirit, pressing upon us to bring our disordered lives into an integrated pattern of spiritual harmony.

The Holy Spirit works through humanity individually and socially. In a little book, *The Faith of the Church,* we are told that the Spirit brings men and women together for great purposes, "drives the people of the earth into closer community with one another . . . insists that the order of human society be conformed more closely to the will of God, and shatters our complacent self-interest until we are prepared to cooperate toward that end."

We may often doubt that this is the case when we read the daily headlines or listen to the news media of all the violence, hunger, poverty, crime, corruption, disorder and injustice in the world. In moments of spiritual crisis we ask ourselves, "If God is all-good and all-powerful, what about the evil in the world? How can God's Holy Spirit be at work if these terrible things happen?"

This question has probably come to each of us at some time or other in our lives. It is at the heart of our Christian faith.

But our faith teaches us that God has created us with the freedom to do evil as well as good. God is a loving God who does not coerce his creatures to do his will, but seeks through love to draw them to himself. Evil is the fruit of sin, and sin means separation from God, from ourselves, and from our fellow human beings. We become separated from God when we forget the true source of our strength, intelligence or well being and feel ourselves self-sufficient, or on the other hand, when we become so pre-occupied with our own concerns that we are consumed with self-pity when things go wrong and feel ourselves alone and desolate.

Faith teaches us that God has not abandoned us to evil and suffering, that his Spirit is with us continually in our pain and brokenness, reconciling us and the world to himself. We believe that God came to us in Jesus of Nazareth, humans as we are human, yet so possessed by God that we can only say, "This is God with us as man." God in Jesus Christ met us where we are, and suffered all that man can suffer in defeat and death. It was Christ's victory over the Cross and the grave which gives us the hope that with God-in-Christ we, too, may conquer sin and death. This is the meaning of the words, "God so loved the world that he gave his only-begotten Son, to the end that all who believe in him shall not perish, but have everlasting life."

It was the disciples' conviction that they had seen the Risen Lord which set their hearts on fire and drove them to proclaim the Good News with such passion that thousands of people felt the overpowering experience of being in touch with the Living Christ.

On this belief stands the Christian Church, "the Body of Christ," "the blessed company of all faithful people," the place where we come together in community to worship and to receive the strengthening gift of the Holy Spirit, so that we may be empowered to witness God's redeeming love in Christ in all that we do. As baptized Christians, whether lay or ordained, we are all ministers of the Church, and have the same fundamental ministry—to represent Christ and his Church, to bear witness to him wherever we may be, and according to the gifts given to us, to carry on Christ's work of reconciliation in the world.

The Holy Spirit replaces the visible presence of Jesus, and the Church is the Spirit-filled community in which we are bound to one another in Christ. For it is only when we are one in Christ that we can rise above those things which separate us from one another—differences of race, sex, age, class, economic or social position—and share that supreme gift of communion expressed in the benediction, "The grace of our Lord Jesus Christ, the love of God, and the fellowship of the Holy Spirit be with us all evermore." *Amen.*

THE DILEMMA OF THE MINORITY CHRISTIAN

Text: Isaiah 53:3–6

He was despised and rejected by men,
a man of sorrows, and acquainted with grief;
and as one from whom men hide their faces,
he was despised, and we esteemed him not.

Surely he has borne our griefs
and carried our sorrows;
yet we supposed him stricken,
smitten by God, and afflicted.

But he was wounded for our transgressions,
he was bruised for our iniquities;
upon him was the chastisement that made us whole,
and with his stripes we are healed.

All we like sheep have gone astray,
we have turned every one to his own way;
and the Lord has laid on him the iniquity of us all.

—Isa. 53:3–6

The Word of God comes to us and fastens upon our minds and hearts in many strange, wonderful and unforeseen ways. The beginning lines of the passage just read first came to me, not through reading the Bible but through music—a song written by an unknown Hebrew prophet living in exile in Babylon some twenty-four hundred years ago, caught up in the music of the 18th century German-born composer, George Friedrich Handel, who wrote the *Messiah,* and brought to us through the voice of our own mid-twentieth century American artist, Marian Anderson.

I used to play the record, *Great Songs of Faith,* whenever I felt downcast and in despair, for immediately after the song *He Was Despised and Rejected,* Marian Anderson sang that consoling aria from Mendelssohn's *Elijah:*

O rest in the Lord; wait patiently for Him,
and He shall give thee thy heart's desires.
Commit thy way unto Him, and trust in Him,
and fret not thyself because of evil doers.

To continue the song from *Isaiah*—

> Tortured, he endured it submissively,
> and opened not his mouth;
> like sheep that is led to the slaughter,
> like a lamb before its shearers,
> he was dumb and opened not his mouth.

Here, then, in poetry, in music, in the gift of the human voice, we encounter the Suffering Servant, the Servant of the Lord. Behind this song was the longing of the people of Israel for a savior, a redeemer, who would deliver them from their enemies and restore them to their status as a nation. They looked for a Messiah, a royal king, a powerful political leader, who would restore the throne of David and vindicate them as God's chosen people, God's elect before all nations.

But the poet-prophet who wrote the Servant Songs had something else in mind. He knew that what was needed before restoration could take place was *conversion*; someone who could call the people back from their sins, someone who could intervene on their behalf, and bring about atonement for their alienation from God.

The savior he envisioned was not a royal, kingly, powerful leader, but a man loathed and shunned by the community, and looked upon with contempt. We are told earlier in the song:

> He had no form or comeliness
> that should have made us give heed to him;
> there was no beauty that should have made us desire him;
> His appearance was so marred, beyond human semblance,
> and his form beyond that of the sons of men.

Yet, this was the man chosen by God for a special task—to lead the people of Israel to true penitence and godliness, and thus make possible true restoration and bring back to Jerusalem those who were scattered in exile. A man who was burdened by suffering—not for his own sins—but for the sins of others. A man who must endure disease, misery, and pain in order to accomplish his mission—the salvation of others. He is subjected to opposition, ridicule, many blows, ill-treatment and humiliation. For his suffering, healing and forgiveness are brought to others.

How is he able to endure his miserable lot? He knows that he has been chosen by God for his task. He tells us:

God formed me from the womb to be his servant. . .
the Lord Yahweh says—
Therefore I will make you a light to the nations,
that my salvation may reach to the ends of the earth. . .

The Servant is discouraged with his mission, but God tells him it is greater than the mere redemption of the people of Israel—it is for the salvation of all peoples of the world.

Some five hundred years after these Servant Songs were written, they found their most perfect expression in the life and work of another prophet and teacher, Jesus Christ. He was in conflict with the Jews because he saw his mission, not as the powerful political Messiah who would restore the Kingdom of David, but as the self-giving Suffering Servant of the Lord, obedient to God even unto death.

For me, as perhaps it is for many thoughtful Christians, this is one of the most difficult passages in the Holy Scripture—difficult because it is the model which Jesus Christ chose for his own life, the standard he has set for us to attempt to meet if we profess to be Christians—and therefore I must take it with the utmost seriousness. The Suffering Servant says of himself:

But I was not rebellious,
I turned not backward,
I gave my back to the smiters,
my cheeks to those who pulled out the beard,
I hid not my face from shame and spitting.

But I *am* rebellious; I *am* impatient. I do not want to suffer for others; I do not want to suffer silently. When someone is unjust to me, I want to scream and yell and tell them off. I do not want to be despised and rejected. I do not want to be humiliated. When things get too tough, I want to run and hide.

The Servant of the Lord answers—

But the Lord Yahweh helps me,
therefore I shall not be put to shame.
Therefore I set my face like a flint,
and know that I shall not be made ashamed.
He that vindicates me is near; who will contend with me?

Here, then, is the challenge and the promise of the Christian message—but am I willing to accept it?

Am I willing to relinquish my self-interest, my self-centeredness, my dependence upon my own resources or upon others, and surrender my entire will, my entire life to God? Am I willing to trust in God absolutely and without any reservations? Am I prepared to acknowledge that all I am and all I have belongs to my Creator, that I am not here for my own purposes, my own glory, but for the purposes and glory of God? Am I ready to confess that the only way to salvation and redemption is utter surrender to God's will?

And if I cannot do this, am I prepared to face God's judgment? What does salvation mean to me, anyhow? Too often we have thought of salvation as something to be hoped for when we die—an insurance against the consequences of death and judgment. But salvation is *here* and *now* we are beginning to learn. Eternal life is *here* and *now,* as Jesus Christ taught us when he said, "The Kingdom of God is at hand."

Put in its simplest terms, salvation is feeling safe, living without fear, living with serenity in confidence that we are the objects of God's unfailing love, and that we will always be safe whatever happens, in life or in death, if we have a complete and childlike trust in God's love and tender mercy.

This is the great leap of faith which does not come easy, which deserts us continually, and which we achieve only by the greatest pain and effort—every day a trial, every breath a prayer. Salvation does not mean that we will avoid suffering, shame, humiliation, or defeat. It does mean that we are not alone—that God's love which was poured out for us in Jesus Christ is always with us, to strengthen and save us in every situation, if we have trust in his love.

To be a Christian, to follow Jesus Christ, means to be self-giving, pouring out love upon others even when they are unlovely and unlovable. And this is the hardest part of our faith. We were not made to live alone. We were made to live in community. And it is in community that we come in conflict with others. It is easy to respond to those who love and cherish us. It is much harder to see Jesus Christ in those who dislike us, who even hate and despise us, or who try to hurt us. It is difficult to be gentle with those who are unkind, who say and do harmful things about us and to us. Yet, the hard truth is that this is the only way. For when we respond with resentment and retaliation, the greatest damage is not what we do to others but what we do to ourselves—by cutting ourselves off from God's love, by alienating ourselves from a sense of community, and winding up feeling lost and alone.

For those of us who have been born into a group which has been the object of contempt, injustice and oppression, the figure of the Suffering Servant, the example of Jesus Christ, presents us with a most difficult dilemma. On the one hand we strive for self-respect and pride in ourselves and our achievements against those who would deny our humanity and our personhood. On the other hand we are told that self-pride is a stumbling block to salvation. Are we expected to endure injustice submissively? To give our backs to the smiters? Not to be rebellious when all around us we see evil and injustice?

I would be dishonest if I told you that I have answers to these questions. I wrestle with them daily. For in them lies the ultimate test of our faith in God—a faith that God is in control of the universe and of our own destiny; that God moves in history; that God is continually working to reconcile humankind to Himself and His love; that whatever we suffer is a part of God's ultimate plan; that we are in fact God's Suffering Servants in the salvation history of the world.

Somehow, I feel that we have a destiny which is beyond our struggle for civil rights and human rights, or social justice, and that our consciousness of this destiny must permeate all that we do *here* and *now*, in *this time* and *this place*, and in *this country*.

In the words of a great prophet of our own time, the late Dr. Martin Luther King, who, when faced with the massive violence of the segregation system, told his followers:

> Our most fruitful course is to stand firm, move forward nonviolently, accept disappointments, and cling to hope. Our determined refusal not to be stopped will eventually open the door to fulfillment. By recognizing the necessity of suffering in a righteous cause, we may achieve our humanity's stature. To guard ourselves from bitterness, we need the vision to see in this generation's ordeals the opportunity to transfigure both ourselves and American society.

Critics of Dr. King charged him with not dealing squarely with the issue of *immoral power* in collision with *powerless morality*, but in retrospect it becomes crystal clear to us that Jesus Christ uttered an incontestable truth when he said, "Those who take to the sword shall be slain by the sword." And one wonders if Dr. King did not glimpse the true problem when he said, "The struggle is not between black and white, but between good and evil."

And since Dr. King's death, another prophet has arisen to tell us that "the apparent chaos, the deadly atmosphere which pervades America"—

of which racism, sexism, or the accumulated social injustices and corruptions are symptoms—"is a condition which the Bible designates as the Fall." In his provocative book, *An Ethic for Christians and Other Aliens in a Strange Land*, William Stringfellow writes:

> The nation *is* fallen. America is a demonic principality, or a complex or constellation or conglomeration of principalities and powers in which death furnishes the meaning, in which death is the reigning idol, enshrined in multifarious forms and guises, enslaving human beings, exacting human sacrifices, capturing and captivating Presidents as well as intimidating and dehumanizing ordinary citizens.[26]

Stringfellow sees the death of a nation as the great Old Testament prophets—Amos, Hosea, Micah, Isaiah, and Jeremiah—saw the destruction of the people of Israel. He asks, "Is there no promise for America? Is there no American hope? The categorical answer is *no.*" He goes on, "The answer for those who are Christians is *no,* and therefore, the answer which Christians commend to other human beings is *no.*"[27]

If Stringfellow is right—and we cannot afford to take lightly his prophecy of doom, for we too have seen the signs of moral corruption and decay—then we are aliens as Christians in a profound sense which transcends our racial or social status. Although in our daily lives we must continue to carry on our struggles for social justice and human dignity, for honesty and integrity, we as Christians find ourselves called to a higher purpose than a social ethic—a call which we can no longer evade—a call to righteousness, to repentance and salvation. Jesus Christ has shown us the way—a faith which transcends death and gives us hope.

And if we make the effort to enter upon this path, we can say with the Suffering Servant of the Lord:

> But the Lord Yahweh helps me,
> therefore I shall not be put to shame.

And we can join that magnificent chorus in Handel's *Messiah,* singing

> But Thou didst not leave his soul in hell; nor didst
> Thou suffer Thy Holy One to see corruption.

SALVATION AND LIBERATION

There is today a fermentation at work in Christian theology which may well signal a rebirth of religious consciousness and a reintegration of faith at new levels of understanding. This fermentation has important implications for religious communities growing out of the Judeo-Christian tradition, despite their divergences in doctrine and symbolism, for they share a common search for salvation from the forces of alienation and violence in today's world. As a framework for our reflections on this new development, let me read the opening paragraphs of the Foreword to Letty M. Russell's *Human Liberation in [a] Feminist Perspective,* which focuses on our theme. Elizabeth Moltmann-Wendel and Jurgen Moltmann, authors of the Foreword, have this to say:

> Just as the call for salvation from transitoriness to attain immortality could be heard in every corner of the ancient world, today a cry for liberation is shouted by the oppressed, the humiliated, and the offended in this inhuman world. In those early days the Christian Church heard this call for salvation. People experienced saving power in Christ, in the proclamation of the gospel and in the Sacraments. With comprehensive integrity Christian theologians gave an account of the gospel message of salvation.
>
> Will the Christian Church hear the cry of liberation this time and suffer with those who suffer? Will men and women experience the compelling force of God's liberation "on earth as it is in heaven . . ."? Will Christian theologians be able, this time, to account for "the hope that is in them"?
>
> This seems to be the decisive question now, not only for Christians—so often of little faith—but also for humanity as a whole—which seems to have lost its sense of direction.[28]

Dr. Rollo May, a well known psychotherapist, approaches the same problem from a different perspective. Concerned with the sources of violence, he writes in his book *Power and Innocence*:

> We live at the end of an era. The age that began with the Renaissance, born out of the twilight of the Middle Ages, is now at a close; . . . and there are as yet only dim harbingers, only partly conscious, of what the new age will be. . . . In the present gap between ages, power is

disengaged from its hereditary lines, confused, and "up for grabs." Those who have occupied the numbing position of subordinate groups—the Blacks and Chicanos, women, students, mental patients, convicts—are springing to life, announcing their existence, and presenting their demands. Power becomes a new and urgent issue not only for those groups, but for every individual in our culture who is trying to get his bearings and find his place in the turbulence. Powerlessness in such periods—often called by its alternate names, alienation and helplessness—becomes very painful.[29]

"Violence," says Dr. May, "is a symptom. The disease is variously called powerlessness, insignificance, injustice—in short, a conviction that I am less than human and I am homeless in the world. . . . To strike the disease at its core requires that we deal with the impotence. Ideally, we must find ways of sharing and distributing power so that every person, in whatever realm of our bureaucratic society, can feel that he too counts, that he too makes a difference to his fellows and is not cast out on the dunghill of indifference as a nonperson."[30]

These two statements describe the contemporary world situation which challenges Christianity as a viable faith. Since the late 1960s, in response to the human liberation movements of oppressed peoples around the world, Catholic and Protestant theologians in Europe, Latin America and the United States have been evolving what is variously called theology of liberation, political theology, theology of hope and theology of revolution. Black theology and feminist theology, arising out of the parallel struggles of blacks and women, are native to the United States.

The central question for all of these theologies of liberation is: What does the Christian faith have to say that will give strength and hope to those who struggle against the "Powers and Principalities"—the institutionalized evils and injustices which destroy the humanity of whole peoples and which are virtually immune to individual morality? Some writers[,] convinced that the Christian Church is too deeply implicated in supporting the *status quo* to be a force for liberation, have gone beyond Christianity and seek new religious symbols. Most, however, have remained within the Christian tradition, while developing new concepts and challenging the content of orthodox doctrines at crucial points. Dr. Rosemary Ruether, perhaps, gives the best description of this theological undertaking when she says it

will focus on the question of human liberation primarily from the situation of the "oppressor-oppressed" relationship, as this applies to Christian anti-Semitism, racism, sexism, and colonialism. It will ask

questions of the resources of the Christian tradition to provide symbols for the liberation of peoples whom the very culture created in the
name of Christianity has helped to oppress. It will be looking to what
transformations need to take place to transform Christianity from a
Constantinian to a prophetic religion; from the ideology of the oppressor to a gospel of liberation for the oppressed, and through the
oppressed, for the oppressor as well.[31]

I can touch only briefly upon some of the common perspectives of this
new development, but think they may find resonance in your own religious experience.

Liberation theologies are not overall systems of dogma. They grow out
of specific contexts. As Letty Russell says, they "try to express the gospel
[of salvation] in the light of the experience of oppression out of which
they are written, whether that be racial or sexual, social or economic, psy-
chological or physical."[32] In their efforts to illuminate the human situation, they undertake social and historical analysis and draw upon many
disciplines instead of one particular theological tradition. They develop
through a method called *praxis,* continuous action concurrent with reflection, and to this extent they are experimental and open-ended. They are
concerned with the relation of faith to social change and are oriented
toward the transformation of the world in history, the "shared efforts [of
men and women] to abolish the current unjust situation and to build a
different society, freer and more human," as Gustavo Gutierrez, the Latin
American theologian puts it;[33] or in Ruether's words "an overthrowing of
this false world which has been created out of man's self-alienation, and
a restoration of the world to its proper destiny as the 'place where God's
will is done on earth, as it is in heaven.'"[34] This restoration refers to the
physical environment as well as social organization.

There is a decided shift from an other-worldly to a this-worldly emphasis. Some of these theologians envision, ultimately, a new human being in
history. Ruether speaks of "a movement of the whole globe toward a new
unity" throughout the spread of "a revolutionary momentum, in the form
of a demand for the improvement of life. . . . Development toward a new
planetary humanity goes hand in hand with the revolt of every oppressed
group, in demands for national, class, racial, and sexual integrity and
identity."[35] Along with this emphasis is the effort to reexamine and rein-
terpret the Christian faith so that it has relevance for people committed
to the search for liberation in today's society.

The new society envisioned is one in which diversity is valued, and is
so structured as to encourage each individual to develop to the fullness of
his or her own potential. Dr. Major J. Jones, writing on black theology,

says "we move, as if we were indeed under some power of the future, toward some larger context wherein every person, race, or ethnic group shall take comfort in the fact of separateness or difference. . . . There will be pluralism in ideologies, interests, aims and aspirations, and personhood, and no one will for any purpose be denied opportunity to achieve or be excluded from community."[36]

Feminist writer Sheila D. Collins speaks of a "wholeness of vision" which "does not imply an eradication of differences between the sexes" but which "may lead to a multiplication of differences. . . . Only through an affirmation and celebration of our differences can we come to an understanding of the ties that bind the whole creation together. A holistic ethic [in a pluralistic world] affirms singleness within community, diversity within unity, the validity of *both and* rather than *either or.*"[37]

This vision of a new humanity in history, it seems to me, reflects a broadening of the common ground shared by humanists and those who accept the divinity of Jesus Christ. Although Dr. Charles P. Price, professor of theology at Virginia Theological Seminary and an Episcopal priest, was not speaking in the context of liberation theology, he came close to reconciling these divergent beliefs when he wrote:

"Divinity is the depth-dimension of human being. Every person is potentially open to it. Man, after all, was made to be in the image of God. In the case of Jesus, this potentiality was actualized. Far from losing his humanity or in fact, far from having his humanity qualified in any way, Jesus of Nazareth, the Son of God, in his living, dying and resurrection was a revelation of what human being essentially is. His work is for us and can be appropriated by us. He is 'the firstborn of many brethren.'"[38]

Liberation theologians maintain that our perceptions of God are shaped by the culture in which we live and by historical experience. Theologies change as cultural experience changes. A major critique of traditional Christian theology by blacks and women is that, historically, theologians have been white and male and that the historical experiences of blacks and women have been excluded. To this extent these groups find some traditional doctrines and interpretations inadequate for their self-understanding.

For example, consider the impact of traditional Christian doctrines which stress obedience, meekness, humility and suffering servanthood. Many oppressed people are turned off by these doctrines, seen to be expressions of their own powerlessness and used to invoke divine approval for patterns of dominance and submission in human relationships, as in the experience of blacks during slavery. "Servanthood," as Letty Russell points out, "presents problems for women and other oppressed groups who have been condemned to play a servant role not of their own choosing. For these groups humanization is experienced, not so much through service, as through bonding together in supportive communities that can provide new identity and hope." Russell finds that even when the Biblical image is clarified to indicate that the true meaning of servanthood is not inferiority or subordination but "the privilege of God's gracious choice" of one to act as "an instrument of divine help to someone else's need," the debasing connotation of this term is not dispelled for women and other groups struggling against roles of subordination in church and society. Black theology sees that much of its task is to reclaim a people from humiliation and therefore it is less concerned with "such unrelated subjects as humility before men and guilt before God."[39]

Traditional Christian spirituality looks upon anger and pride as negative qualities, but as Ruether asserts, they are crucial "virtues" in the salvation of the oppressed community. In this context, anger "is felt as the power to revolt against and judge a system of oppression to which one was formerly a powerless . . . victim. Pride is experienced as the recovery of that authentic humanity and good created nature 'upon which God looked in the beginning and, behold, it was very good.'"[40] Stress is placed upon the second half of the commandment to love one's neighbor *as one's self*. Only as we love ourselves are we prepared to love our neighbor. Love of self, here, is not seen as selfishness but as self-respect.

More radical feminist theologians like Sheila D. Collins challenge Christianity, as practiced by the official Church, as a "death-loving rather than a life-affirming religion, as attested to by its heavy emphasis on the crucifixion and the atonement rather than on Jesus' life and ministry and the concrete, time-realized hope and courage he gave to those with whom he came in contact."[41]

A second important perspective of liberation theologies is that of salvation as a social and historical event. Salvation is interpreted as a deliverance from sin and from political and social oppression. Russell speaks of the "broadening of the understanding of individual salvation in the afterlife to include the beginnings of salvation in the lives of men and women in society. . . . Emphasis is placed upon the longed-for eternal life as a quality of existence in the *here and now*." Salvation is stressed, not as an escape into "heaven" but rather "the power and the possibility of transforming the world, restoring creation and seeking to overcome suffering."[42] Gutierrez, a Roman Catholic, speaks of the growth of the Kingdom of God as "a process which occurs historically *in* liberation, insofar as liberation means a greater fulfillment of man. . . . Without liberating historical events, there would be no growth of the Kingdom."[43]

Sin also acquires a different meaning in this perspective, and is seen to include corporate or social evil as well as individual transgression. This view attempts to correct tendencies within the traditional Church to concentrate upon sin as an individual, private, or merely interior reality necessitating a "spiritual" redemption while ignoring the presence of sin in institutional structures which alienate and oppress people and prevent their communion with God and with one another. Rosemary Ruether charges that the concentration on individualistic repentance and "private confession" has, in effect, "involved people in a process of kneeling down to examine a speck of dirt on the floor while remaining oblivious to the monsters which are towering over their backs" and which cannot be overcome individually.[44] Dr. J. Deotis Roberts of Howard University['s] School of Religion argues that while we should not abandon the quest for strengthening the inner spiritual life, the Christian faith today must be understood in a highly political context and that the only gospel suitable for the new consciousness "is one that opts for radical and massive change in oppressive attitudes and structures of power."[45]

This analysis confronts us with our own participation in collective evil and our responsibility to change the social structures which bring it about. From Gutierrez's perspective, conversion to Christ means commitment to one's neighbor and to "participate in the struggle for the liberation of those oppressed by others."[46] Dr. Martin Luther King, Jr., explaining how he came to embrace nonviolent boycotts and demonstrations in the struggle against racial segregation, said that he became convinced that to accept passively an evil system was as immoral as active perpetuation of it, "thereby making the oppressed as evil as the oppressor," and that in order to be true to one's conscience and to God, a righteous person has no alternative but to refuse to cooperate with an evil system.[47]

The process of liberation is said to begin with an awareness of restrictions, alienations and limitations, and moves on to affirm liberation from these restrictions and toward a vision of [wholeness] and unity. Heightened consciousness impels action because we are no longer willing to accept the old order of things. Self-affirmation involves throwing off old stereotypes of one's self imposed by the dominant culture and achieving self-esteem through self-definition. A major concern of black theology has been to redefine the term "black" and to transform it into a symbol of "new self-understanding of persons in black skin who are equal in nature and grace with all humans."[48]

Self-definition for women involves recognition that the chief source of their limitations has been the Judeo-Christian tradition and the culture to which it has given rise. As Ruether and others point out, religion is the single most important factor in shaping and enforcing the image and role of women in society, and has reflected sexual domination and subjugation in both its doctrines and practices as a social institution. Witness the present revolt of women in Iran who fear that fundamentalist Islamic elements will rob them of their social gains and reduce them to second-class citizens.

The most devastating critique of the Judeo-Christian faith has come from feminist theologians who point to its images of an exclusively male God as Father, King, Lord and Master, and assert that it has projected a patriarchal world-view in which subordination of women has been the model for the oppression of other groups. As Ruether sees it: "Traditional theological images of God as father have been the sanctification of sexism and hierarchicalism precisely by defining this relationship of God as father to humanity in a domination-subordination model and by allowing ruling-class males to identify themselves with the divine fatherhood in such a way as to establish themselves in the same kind of hierarchical relationship to women and lower classes."[49] This challenges Biblical religion at its root and forecasts attempts to correct the content of Judeo-Christian symbolism and imagery which, if the Church were to take it seriously, as one feminist theologian suggests, it might find itself turned completely inside out.

Finally, theology of liberation also calls for a redefinition of the task of the Church in the world. It asserts that salvation is not limited to the action of the Church but is a reality which occurs in history. Therefore, the Church must cease looking upon itself as the exclusive place of salvation and orient itself to a new and radical service to the people. As a sacramental community and a sign of the liberation of humanity and history, the Church in its concrete existence should be a place of liberation which reflects in its own structure a witness to the salvation whose fulfillment it announces. True renewal of the Church must be on the basis of an effective awareness of the world and a commitment to it. According to Gutierrez, "the Church must be the visible sign of the presence of the Lord within the aspiration for liberation and the struggle for a more human and just society. Only in this way will the message of love which the Church bears be made credible and efficacious."[50]

In short, liberation theology, born in world crisis and developing in the turmoil of transition, may prove to be a catalytic force for changes in the Christian tradition as profound as those of the Protestant Reformation of the 16th century. It has accepted the challenge to redirect the Christian faith so that the Church in fact[,] as well as in proclamation[,] becomes a witnessing community to the new age.

CAN THESE BONES LIVE AGAIN?

TEXT: Ezekiel 37:1–7

Today is Passion Sunday on which the Christian world begins its commemoration of Passiontide, that two-week period in the life of Jesus of Nazareth which marked his final journey to Jerusalem, this triumphant entry, his increasing encounters with his enemies, the Last Supper with his closest friends and disciples, his agony in the Garden of Gethsemane, his betrayal by Judas, his arrest and abandonment by those on whom he had depended, Peter's denial, his trial and conviction before Pilate, his crucifixion—the shameful death reserved for the worst of criminals—all this culminating in the resurrection of Christ the Lord on Easter morn.

The Old Testament lesson for today is a prophetic pointer toward this Christ event which changed the course of human history. It is taken from the book of the prophet Ezek. 37:1–7, which begins:

> The hand of the Lord came upon me, and he carried me out by his spirit and put me down in a valley full of bones . . . they covered the valley, countless numbers of them and they were very dry. . . [.] He said to me, "Man, can these bones live again?" I answered, ["]Only thou knowest that, Lord God." He said to me, "Prophesy over these bones and say to them, 'O dry bones, hear the word of the Lord. This is the word of the Lord God to these bones: I will put breath in you, and you shall live.'"

I am one of those who has trouble with the Holy Scripture unless I can relate it to my own life and experience. It is the Word of God through human lips. When I visited North Carolina a year ago in a deeply moving ceremony at the Chapel of the Cross in Chapel Hill, I was instructed by the sermon of its rector, the Rev. Peter Lee, who said, "You remind us vividly by your presence that the Christian faith is radically specific, grounded in history, related to real people, to flesh and blood, to the grandeur and degradation of human life as it is."

Whenever I read this passage in Ezekiel and reflect upon its impact upon my own life, the image comes to me of a little child in Durham, North Carolina, tugging at the hand of her aging grandmother, saying, "Come on in the house, Gran-ma, and I'll read to you in the Psalms. I'll

even try to read a little about Ezekiel in the valley of the dry bones. . . ."
The recorded story of this child continues:

> I had touched on Grandmother's . . . favorite Bible selection(s). And
> she treasured that ragged old Bible Miss Mary Smith of Chapel Hill
> had given her more than any other article in the house. She said she
> got it when she was a little girl and was confirmed at the Chapel of
> the Cross. It was over one hundred years old. It was the one book
> Grandmother tried to read herself, peering through her glasses and
> spelling out the Psalms a word at [a] time. I had learned to read some
> of the Psalms by now and every Sunday evening I would read to
> Grandmother some of her favorite passages. She seemed so proud of
> having me read to her from the big Bible that I loved it as much as
> she did. I liked the huge print and the way the verses were divided on
> the pages. I liked the sound of the words rolling off my tongue and I
> would let my voice rise and fall like a wailing wind, just as I had
> heard Rev. Small chant the Morning Lesson at St. Titus on Sundays.
> Grandmother had utmost respect for the Holy Word.

Why Ezekiel? We who live in a technocratic age are prone to overlook
both our prophets and the prophetic incidents in our lives. Little did that
child know then that some sixty years later—when she was as old as her
Grandmother was at that time—she would be called upon to interpret
those "dry bones," so vivid in her Grandmother's prophetic vision, as a
priest in Christ's Holy Catholic Church.

Ezekiel was a Hebrew prophet who lived at the time of Jeremiah. He
was first and last a priest and poet. We are told that when Jerusalem was
captured by Babylonian forces in 597 B.C., he nevertheless had a vision
of hope, of rebirth, and the eventual restoration of the exiles to their
homeland. (Commentary: Keith W. Carley.)[51]

The persistent strength of the human desire for roots is seen in the continuing Middle East crisis today, some 2500 years after those early dis-
persals of the people of the Kingdoms of Israel and Judah. What the loss
of a sense of belonging meant to the Hebrew people of the Old Testament
is embodied in the 137th Psalm (King James version):

> By the waters of Babylon, there we sat down,
> Yea, we wept, when we remembered Zion.
> We hanged our harps upon the willows in the midst thereof
> For they that carried us away captive required of us a song;

> . . . How shall we sing the Lord's song in a strange land?
> If I forget thee, O Jerusalem, let my right hand forget
>   her cunning . . . let my tongue cleave to the roof of my mouth . . .

In our own immediate past history, there has been a symbolic reenact-
ment of the Exile of Israel. At the end of slavery in 1865, the North American South was the homeland of 90 percent of the people of color in the
United States. As one of our poets cried out during World War II:

> We have no other dream, no land but this:
> With slow deliberate hands these years
> Have set her image on our brows.
> We are her seed; have borne a fruit
> Native and pure as unblemished cotton.

For more than a century now a process of dispersal has been taking place,
until today about half or more of our people live outside the South—their
ancestors not captured and taken away, but driven out by the intolerable
conditions which they faced. Many of these migrants continued to look
backward toward their roots, and their children have painfully discovered
that the Babylon of the spirit is everywhere in the United States. This has
been the prophetic message of our fellow Episcopalian, William Stringfellow, who is also an attorney and who is a kind of modern Jeremiah. Like
the Psalmist from Jerusalem, a political refugee from the American South
wrote in 1959 during the most intense period of the struggle to desegre-
gate the public schools:

> We were the vanquished, the self-exiled;
> Renounced our inheritance, land of our fathers:
> We were the wanderers; journeyed to cities,
> Searching and seeking, seeking and searching;
> Plunged into entrails of ghettoes,
> Submerged in garbage of slumlands;
> Toiled by day, learned by night,
> Won degrees from great universities—
> Found them worthless souvenirs of effort
> Yellowing in a drawer or battered suitcase,
> Valued less than leavings of cigarettes
> Scooped from gutters and hoarded in cans!
> Flotsam in tenements, watchers at knotholes,

Barred from the contest; rusting from disuse;
Condemned to idleness; frozen to bottom rung;
Battling cockroaches in cheap rooming houses;
Passed over in hiring halls—*"They don't hire colored!"*
"No job available—you're overqualified!"
We pawned our clothes, class pins and watches;
Tried to buy jobs as skilled laborers. No go!
We, too, have known ultimate surrender,
Hauled down our tattered pride, made the long march—
The last cent was borrowed, nothing left to pawn,
The hominy grits gave out, the cigarette butts were gone.
The rent was overdue, the salt-and-water
No longer eased our hunger pains.
We have gone, not without shame,
Sneaking like thieves in the night, concealing our hurt,
To the office of Emergency Home Relief!
Waited our turn to nibble at Public Assistance!
Stripped down until we were naked,
Our secrets exposed; our private embarrassments
All written down in a public record—
Exchanged our pride for a Case Number—
The city's poor, society's backwash,
Painfully learning the rules of the destitute.

This image of Negro migrants in cities of the North during the Depression years of the 1930s has changed very little for all too many. The third generation of these exiles constitute the "dry bones" still scattered about in the crumbling urban areas. We take considerable pride in the fact that one of our own modern Joans of Arc—Secretary of Housing and Urban Affairs Patricia Roberts Harris—who just happens to be an Episcopalian—is leading an historic campaign against entrenched economic interests to see to it that "these dry bones live." When her fellow Episcopalian, Senator William Proxmire, was giving Pat Harris a hard time during her confirmation hearings a year or more ago, I suggested to somebody in the White House that both of them were in need of some good Baptist "born again" prayers. As I read the political barometer today, I wonder if the White House may not be in need of some of our good Episcopalian prayers, decorous though they may be. We may operate on the principle of the separation of Church and State, but all we have to do is to look at the White House today to see that the Gospel and politics are all mixed up together!

We Negroes/blacks of the South have long seen the parallel between our own enslavement in the United States and [the stories of the Israelites in] the Old Testament. Alex Haley's *Roots,* Margaret Walker's *Jubilee,* and my *Proud Shoes*—published in reverse order, in 1956, 1966, and 1976, respectively—in various ways have told the stories of Abraham and Hagar, and Ishmael, the outcast, of the bondage of the people of Israel in Egypt, the Exodus, and the wandering in the Wilderness.[52] Martin Luther King, Jr.[,] glimpsed the Promised Land, and I think he may have been dreaming of a reborn South. Writers like Richard Wright, Ann Petry, James Baldwin, Toni Morrison, and poets like Langston Hughes, Gwendolyn [Brooks], Countee Cullen have documented the Exile years. Robert Hayden and I have attempted epic poetry telling the story from the slave-ships in Africa to modern times. And if you will forgive the self reference, I would like to share with you what the younger generation of prophets think of us in our sixties. Several weeks ago I received a letter from a young black woman seminarian studying at Colgate-Rochester Divinity School. She had been a pre-med student in college who finally chose theology instead of medicine. She wrote:

> Before coming to Seminary learning of your ordination further inspired my own decision. I've long wanted to meet you—though you may find it amusing that in grade and high school, when reading your poetry, I assumed that like Hughes, Cullen, Dunbar and others, you too had long since passed away. . . .

Although her letter sent me into hysterics of laughter, it scared me into thinking I might "pass away" before I complete my mission in life—whatever that mission may be.

But there is another side to the story of the Exile. We must remember that not all of the people of Israel and Judah were deported to Babylonia. The Babylonian captors took the Jewish leaders—priests, prophets, skilled artisans, and so on. Those who were left behind in ransacked Jerusalem and the land of Palestine had to endure a half century or more of military and political domination until a new leadership was developed and some of the Exiles returned. They carried on life and inched ahead despite the suffering—both physical and spiritual—of being outcasts in the land of their roots.

Even in exile, however, Ezekiel saw the power of God's divine grace to raise up a "new and holy Israel" which would be reborn out of the "dry bones of an old battlefield." Unconsciously influenced by his vivid imagery of those dry bones and informed by the New Testament story of the Resurrection and the Christian hope of rebirth and renewal, our twentieth century exile from the American South addressing the embattled school children in 1959, declared:

> Gentle warriors, we salute you. . .
> We, the wounded and dead of former campaigns. . .
> The nameless millions, native and migrant,
> We are legion and we support you. . .
> From restless graves in swamps and bayous. . .
> We hear your marching feet and rise,
> Silently we walk beside you!
>
> *We have returned from a place beyond hope;*
> *We have returned from wastelands of despair;*
> *We have come to reclaim our heritage;*
> *We have come to redeem our honor!*

And so, while I acknowledge the potential gloom and doom in my brother William Stringfellow's prophecy—his justifiable embarrassment at being an Episcopalian as he wrote in a recent issue of *The Witness,* our forward-looking church magazine which is leading the struggle for social justice—nevertheless my own life experiences lead me to follow in the footsteps of Ezekiel. For the Christ event has intervened between the Exile and today. And the Christ event confirmed Ezekiel's vision. Symbolically, I am a returning exile to the American South after an absence of more than fifty years. I am the fourth generation of a family who migrated here and cast its lot with the Southern people during Reconstruction. Many of my generation fled the South in the 1920s, 1930s and 1940s. What does it say to you that a member of the fifth generation is now resettling in Atlanta, Georgia, and is representative of a modern trend?

Just before I left North Carolina in 1927 to live permanently in the North—I was a teenager—17 at the time—my Aunt Pauline, who Durhamites may remember as Mrs. Pauline Fitzgerald Dame, my mother by adoption, brought me here to Raleigh to visit Bishop Henry B. Delany, who had confirmed me at St. Titus when I was nine years old and who was then on his death-bed. At the end of our visit we had prayers and Bishop Delany blessed me and said, "You are a child of destiny." For the next fifty years I pondered this prophecy of a holy man. Did he see then what I could not see—that God was calling me, even a woman, against the weight of every traditional theological argument and a two thousand year tradition, to be a priest in Christ's Holy Catholic Church and to say to you today that out of these dry bones, the outcasts of the earth—even women—shall arise and the House of Israel shall be reborn? *Let us pray.*

> Almighty God, giver of all good things,
> We thank you for the faith we have inherited in all its rich variety.
> Help us, O Lord, to finish the good work here begun.
> Strengthen our efforts to blot out ignorance and prejudice,
>   to abolish poverty and crime.
> Hasten the day when men and women, black, red, white and
>   yellow, will stand as equals and brothers and sisters before one
>   another as they now stand in your sight.
> And hasten the day when all people, everywhere, with many voices
>   in one united chorus, will glorify your holy Name,
> Through Jesus of Nazareth, the Crucified, the Risen Lord.
> *Amen.*

EPILOGUE:
FORGING AHEAD
TOWARD EQUALITY

IN THEIR DAY, African American preaching women served as pioneers and role models. Through their lives and work, they touched many people, black and white, male and female, and traversed many religious traditions. Belief in the Holy Spirit and the pursuit of ordination were powerful themes in the majority of their lives.

Although ordination was desirable, lacking ordination provided no barrier to women committed to pursuing careers in the ministry. What women fought for was full recognition and the privileges granted a minister, which ordination provided.

Throughout U.S. history, black women have chosen many paths to the pulpit. Some have been ordained by white and black denominations. Some received a local preacher's license. Many functioned as exhorters and evangelists. Some founded independent churches and denominations, in which they served as pastors and bishops. Some used missionary societies to launch careers as preachers.

Whatever path they chose to advance in the polity, they felt a strong sense of mission and possessed an enormous confidence in themselves and in their God. Regardless of their denominational affiliation or the time in which they lived, the majority of preaching women emphasized that God empowered them to preach the gospel. Thus, we see women as disparate and distant in time and denominational philosophy as Jarena Lee, Julia Foote, Florence Randolph, Rosa Horn, Ida Robinson, and Pauli Murray articulating similar views and quoting related biblical text to declare women's rights to preach and to determine their destiny. Many of their sermons are literary treatises that expound the doctrine of equal rights for women and reconcile their roles in the Church and in society.

One of the most significant changes to occur in the early twentieth century was the movement of some black women out of the Baptist and Methodist denominations into Pentecostal, Holiness, and Spiritualist churches. The adamant refusal of some of the major black denominations to ordain women clergy, as well as rank sexism, encouraged many black women to establish independent churches. Independent churches often began in private homes and apartments and later advanced to storefronts and church buildings. Many of these churches exist today. In the 1920s and 1930s, Lucy Smith established the All Nations Pentecostal Church in Chicago, Rosa Horn organized the Pentecostal Faith Church in Harlem, and Ida Robinson founded a denomination, the Mount Sinai Holy Church of America, Inc. Through the power of their preaching and radio ministries, these women were able to attract substantial followings and build large churches.

Contrary to popular myth, which tends to portray the early Pentecostal clergywomen as ignorant, emotional preachers with little substance who preyed on the backward Southern black peasantry that poured into the cities, the sermons and the ministries of Horn and Robinson demonstrate that these women were well versed in the Bible and extremely perceptive of the needs of the people they served. Moreover, their sermons indicate an intellectual depth akin to the best in the preaching profession, irrespective of gender or race.

Smith, Horn, and Robinson were spiritual mothers to many other Pentecostal women who founded their own churches.[1] Today, the independent tradition is seen in the example of Audrey Bronson, founder of the Sanctuary Church of God in Philadelphia; Johnnie Coleman of the Christ Universal Temple in Chicago; and Barbara King of the Hillside International Truth Center in Atlanta. Like Smith, Horn, and Robinson, they have succeeded in attracting thousands of members to their congregations.

As the number of female evangelists and ministers grew and as missionary women began to preach, women preachers were no longer a novelty by the 1940s and 1950s. In the mainline denominations such as the AME, AME Zion, and CME Church, they were acceptable as long as they remained in subordinate positions. Although the AME Zion Church could boast of hundreds of ordained women ministers, by 1940, few of these women were appointed to pastor churches of any size and significance, and many continued to pursue careers as evangelists. After the 1948 legislation sanctioning the ordination of AME women as local deacons, it became clear that they, like their AME Zion counterparts, would either serve small missions or continue as evangelists. The same pattern prevailed in the CME Church after the 1960 granting of full ordination rights for women. Although some progress has been made, today we see more black women stuck in the position of assistant or associate minister with little opportunity for advancement.

Interestingly enough, black women clergy such as Pauli Murray, Leontine Kelly, and Barbara Harris have achieved the highest recognition in the predominantly white denominations, and after official restrictions against ordination were eliminated, they have found more fertile fields for pastoring churches in the Presbyterian, Episcopalian, and Methodist Episcopal denominations. In 1977, Pauli Murray was ordained an Episcopal priest at the National Cathedral in Washington, D.C., becoming the first African American female ordained to the priesthood in the two-hundred-year history of the Protestant Episcopal Church.[2] In 1984, Leontine Kelly became the first black woman bishop in any major U.S. denomination and the second woman to be chosen bishop in the United Methodist Church. In September 1988, the Episcopal Church elected Barbara Clementine Harris a suffragan bishop of the Massachusetts diocese, making her the second black woman bishop in the United States. In February 1989, she became the Right Reverend Barbara Clementine Harris. Her elevation to the episcopate distinguished her as the first female bishop in more than four hundred years of tradition in the Anglican Communion. On this historic occasion, Harris became a symbol for the 2.5 million–member Protestant Episcopal Church and for Anglicans throughout the world.[3]

Although new opportunities have developed for black women to preach and to be ordained, there is still opposition in most denominations. The ordination and advancement of women to higher levels in the Church polity has not meant denominational acceptance or approval of women clergy.

Reflecting on the potential power of churchwomen, Peter Paris has stated that "while approximately seventy percent of the membership of the black churches is women, it is generally assumed that a large percentage of these have negative attitudes about clergywomen." He appropriately concludes that "one should not expect any great differences between them with respect to the predominant traditions, customs and values governing their lives."[4] Given their numbers, black churchwomen could effectively eliminate sexism and gender discrimination in the Church. There is significant evidence that black Christian women have consistently raised their voices—in the pulpit and in the pew—against these forms of discrimination. Many have felt more threatened by racism than by sexism, however, and have chosen to devote their energies almost exclusively to eradicating racism. Black churchwomen continue to be divided over which is of greater importance—racism or sexism.[4]

Table 1 indicates the increasing number of clergywomen, both black and white, for the years reported in the U.S. census. From 1870 to 1900,

Table 1. Clergywomen in the United States, by Race, 1870–1990.

Year	Total	White	Black
1870	67	—	—
1880	165	—	—
1890	1,143	1,094	49
1900	3,373	3,207	164
1910	685	614	68
1920	1,787	1,559	228
1930	3,276	2,772	494
...			
1960	4,367	3,859	508
1970	6,237	5,638	500
1980	16,434	15,085	965
1990	32,511	30,205	2,306

Note: *Figures for 1870–1900 are for all religious workers; clergywomen were not counted separately until 1910. Figures for 1940 and 1950 are unavailable.*
Source: *U.S. Bureau of the Census.*

the census made no distinction between clergy and religious workers. The 1910 census was the first to define and report separate figures for these two occupations. The first breakdown by race appeared in 1890.[5]

In 1951, the National Council of Churches conducted its own survey. It reported a total of 131 black ordained clergywomen, 70 of whom were church pastors. Seven others were Baptist and were not pastoring churches. Unfortunately, the report listed only three of the historically black denominations—the National Baptist Convention U.S.A., the AME Church, and the AME Zion Church. Although the report cited a number of white denominations that included black members, there were no figures for black female clergy.[6]

It is difficult to determine census accuracy, and undercounting is always a possibility. Recent statistics indicate that women, both black and white, have been entering and graduating from the major Protestant seminaries in greater numbers. According to the Association of Theological Schools, the accrediting agency for graduate theological education, the number of black women seminarians almost doubled between 1989 and 1994. In 1994, more than 1,000 black women pursued ministry degrees, compared with 662 in 1989 and 92 in 1972. With a degree in hand, many have gone forth to an uncertain future, confronting new challenges. In 1996, fewer than 5 percent were pastoring black churches.

In Baptist, Presbyterian, and many other churches in which congregations hire the pastor, women do not fare well. Traditionally, black women
have pastored more Methodist churches in which bishops appoint ministers to churches. Recent studies show that tradition and prejudice still
operate to shut women out of the pulpit. Many clergymen still use biblical references to assert the inferiority of women and to reinforce traditional role expectations. The most often quoted biblical source is the
apostle Paul, who wrote that "Women should be silent in the churches"
(1 Cor. 14:34) and "I do not permit a woman to teach or have authority
over a man" (1 Tim. 2:12).[7]

In spite of all the opposition, African American women continue to
forge ahead, preaching and teaching, determined to pursue a ministry
ordained by God himself.

NOTES

RISING ABOVE ADVERSITY: THE STRUGGLE TO PREACH

1. See Evelyn Brooks Higginbotham, *Righteous Discontent*. Higginbotham
states: "Research on women preachers, while of great value, does not capture the more representative role of the majority of women church members. Left obscured is the interrelation between the rising black churches
in the late nineteenth and early twentieth centuries and the indefatigable
efforts of black women's organizations. Left unheard are women's voices
within the public discourse of racial and gender self determination. In short,
the focus on the ministry fails to capture adequately the gender dimension
of the church's racial mission" (p. 3).

   This statement does not consider the impact of early black women
preachers on the women in the pews. Between 1880 and 1920, the period
Higginbotham studied, preacher women traveled extensively, speaking to
thousands of women who came out to support their ministries and to
hear their powerful messages, the subtext of which was often female
empowerment. Moreover, the female preachers' impact on the laywomen
who led the NACW and other organizations is unmistakable. To make that
connection, however, one must understand the interdependent relationship
among the laywomen, the religious denomination, and the preaching
women.

2. Many prominent NACW leaders were well-known community activists,
and—with few exceptions—were leaders in their respective denominations.
Eliza Gardner, an outspoken AME Zion feminist activist in Boston, argued
forcefully for female advancement in her denomination and was a prominent NACW organizer. Mary McLeod Bethune, a member of the Methodist
Episcopal denomination, a founder of the Bethune Cookman College,
the eighth NACW president, and the founder and first president of the
National Council of Negro Women, wrote and spoke extensively about the
treatment of women and African Americans. Frances Ellen Watkins Harper,
Katherine Davis Tillman, Hallie Quinn Brown, and Mary Handy, all prominent AME women, wrote and spoke about sexism in the Church and in
society, and argued for political equality for women in these arenas. Maria

Lawton, a leading Presbyterian woman and political activist, was a key figure in organizing black women in early antilynching campaigns.

Baptist women leaders included: Fannie Barrier Williams, a founder of the NACW; Nannie Helen Burroughs, the founder of the Washington, D.C.–based National Training School for Girls; and S. Willie Layten, an officer in the Philadelphia Association for the Protection of Girls. Burroughs and Layton organized and served for more than fifty years as the key officers of the Woman's Convention Auxiliary to the National Baptist Convention. They were also NACW leaders.

For biographical details on these women, see Jessie Carney Smith (ed.), *Notable Black American Women*; Darlene Clark Hine, Elsa Barkley Brown, and Rosalyn Terborg-Penn (eds.), *Black Women in America*.

3. Jarena Lee, Zilpha Elaw, Rebecca Cox Jackson, Amanda Berry Smith, Sojourner Truth, Julia Foote, Mary Small, and Florence Spearing Randolph are excellent examples of well-known nineteenth-century preaching women who challenged the black male clergy on such issues. For the spiritual autobiographies of Lee, Elaw, Foote, Jackson, and Smith, see William L. Andrews (ed.), *Sisters of the Spirit*; Jean McMahon Humez, *Gifts of Power*; Amanda Berry Smith, *An Autobiography*. For more about other Christian feminist activists, see Bettye Collier-Thomas, "Minister and Feminist Reformer," in Judith Weisenfeld and Richard Newman (eds.), *This Far by Faith*, pp. 177–188; Glenda Elizabeth Gilmore, "Pettey, Sarah E. C. Dudley (1869–1906)," in Hine, Brown, and Terborg-Penn, *Black Women*, vol. 2, p. 918. For information about Katherine Davis Tillman, see Lawson A. Scruggs, *Women of Distinction*, p. 203. For more on Alice Felts, see her "Timely Reminder."

4. Andrews, *Sisters of the Spirit*, p. 4; Nellie Y. McKay, "Nineteenth-Century Black Women's Spiritual Autobiographies," in Personal Narratives Group (ed.), *Interpreting Women's Lives*, pp. 141–142, 152.

5. For an excellent discussion of these six tenets, see Nancy Hardesty, Lucille Sider Dayton, and Donald W. Dayton, "Women in the Holiness Movement," pp. 241–249.

6. Joseph M. Murphy, *Working the Spirit*, p. ix. Also see chap. 6, "The Black Church in the United States," which shows how the Spirit manifests itself in African American religious tradition.

7. Andrews, *Sisters of the Spirit*, p. 164.

8. C. Eric Lincoln and Lawrence H. Mamiya, *The Black Church in the African American Experience*, p. 78. For a list of where and when the camp

meetings were held, see Charles Edwin Jones, *Perfectionist Persuasion,* pp. 184–187; Vinson Synan, *The Holiness-Pentecostal Movement in the United States,* pp. 35–36.

9. Jones, *Perfectionist Persuasion,* pp. 16–22; Melvin Easterday Dieter, "Revivalism and Holiness," pp. 112–117, 119, 130; Synan, *Holiness-Pentecostal Movement,* pp. 16–24.

10. Julia A. J. Foote, "Christian Perfection."

11. A. B. Smith, *Autobiography,* pp. 179, 184–185, 206–211, 223.

12. Jarena Lee, "The Life and Religious Experience of Jarena Lee, A Coloured Lady," in Andrews, *Sisters of the Spirit,* pp. 25–48.

13. U.S. Bureau of the Census, *Negro Population in the United States, 1790–1915.* In 1890, the census reported a total of 2,673,977 members of black denominations. Of that number, 1,403,559, or 52 percent, were Baptist; 1,190,860, or 45 percent, were Methodist; 29,561, or 1 percent, were Presbyterian; and 14,517, or 0.5 percent, were Catholic. Remaining denominations cited were Protestant Episcopal, Reformed Episcopal, Church of God in North America, General Eldership of the Congregationalists, Disciples of Christians, and Lutheran Bodies; Lincoln and Mamiya, *Black Church,* pp. 27, 28, 63.

14. Hardesty, Dayton, and Dayton, "Women in the Holiness Movement," pp. 227–229.

15. Ibid.

16. Ibid., p. 232.

17. Black Methodists differed in their beliefs about how one experienced sanctification and how it was manifested in one's behavior. For examples of their views, see the following *Christian Recorder* articles: H. Davis, "Sanctification,"; Jabez P. Campbell, "On Gradual and Immediate Sanctification"; and H. A. Grant, "Sermon: On Sanctification." See also Julia A. J. Foote, "How to Obtain Sanctification," in Andrews, *Sisters of the Spirit,* pp. 233–234.

18. To see how black Methodists represented the holiness doctrine in their nineteenth-century writing, see the *Christian Recorder* from 1854 to 1880, and the *Star of Zion* from 1885 to 1900. We lack such sources for the years prior to 1854, so it is difficult to document this discussion in the black religious press. For particularly good discussions of sanctification, see Andrews, *Sisters of the Spirit,* pp. 192–193, 208.

19. Campbell, "On Gradual and Immediate Sanctification."

20. A. B. Smith, *Autobiography,* pp. 138, 141, 142. In New York, Smith attended a number of holiness meetings, including those held by the noted white holiness advocate Phoebe Palmer. Smith also attended meetings of white Free Methodists and those sponsored by African Americans such as Mrs. Clark, an AME woman who held well-attended weekly holiness meetings at her house.

21. Ibid., p. 146.

22. Ibid.; Andrews, *Sisters of the Spirit,* pp. 200–201, 202, 204–205. For a discussion of nineteenth-century AME women, see Jualynne Elizabeth Dodson, "Nineteenth-Century A.M.E. Preaching Women"; also see sermons by Foote, Randolph, Horn, Robinson, and Murray.

23. For a brief historical overview of white women preachers, see David Albert Farmer and Edwina Hunter (eds.), *And Blessed Is She,* pp. 3–14. For biographical details on Elizabeth, see "Elizabeth," in Bert James Lowenberg and Ruth Bogin, *Black Women in Nineteenth-Century American Life,* pp. 127–134; Lincoln and Mamiya, *Black Church,* p. 279; Zilpha Elaw, "Memoirs of the Life, Religious Experience, Ministerial Travels and Labours of Mrs. Zilpha Elaw, an American Female of Colour," in Andrews, *Sisters of the Spirit,* pp. 59–60.

24. Farmer and Hunter, *And Blessed Is She,* pp. 8, 9.

25. Ibid., pp. 10–11; Ruth Tucker and Walter Liefield, *Daughters of the Church,* p. 279.

26. For discussion of women's roles as exhorters and evangelists, see Dodson, "Women's Collective Power," pp. 105, 108, 124.

27. Ibid., p. 113.

28. Ibid., p. 114.

29. Ibid., pp. 113–115.

30. For information regarding the African American oral and written discourse on suffrage, see Rosalyn Terborg-Penn, "Afro-Americans in the Struggle for Woman's Suffrage." For examples of the discourse on gender equality in the Church, see the following *Christian Recorder* articles: Alice S. Felts, "Women in the Church"; Rev. Theophilus Gould Steward, "Work for Women of the Church"; Rev. R. Seymour, "Ought Women to Be Admitted to Membership in the Legislative Bodies of the Church?"; "Taxation Without Representation." See also Mrs. Bishop C. C. Pettey, "Woman's Column: Some Prominent Elders in Zion."

31. "New York African Methodism"; Daniel A. Payne, *History of the African Methodist Episcopal Church,* pp. 237, 301; Dodson, "Nineteenth-Century Women," pp. 280–281.

32. William Jacob Walls, *The African Methodist Episcopal Zion Church*, p. 111.

33. Rev. C. R. Harris (comp.), *Daily Proceedings of the Seventeenth Quadren nial Session of the General Conference of the A.M.E. Zion Church of America*, pp. 111, 145.

34. Note that Julia Foote was ordained a deacon by Bishop James Walker Hood on May 13, 1895, and not on May 20, 1894, as originally indicated in Walls, *The African Methodist Episcopal Zion Church*, p. 111, and re- peated in all subsequent publications, most notably in Lincoln and Mamiya's monumental study, *The Black Church in the African American Experience*, p. 285. News of Foote's ordination in the New York Confer- ence reached the Philadelphia and Baltimore Conference, which convened on May 15, 1895, in York, Pennsylvania, at the AME Zion church pastored by Bishop John B. Small. Encouraged by the news of Foote's ordination, the conference nominated Mary Small for the same office. On May 20, 1895, Mary Small was ordained a deacon. Three years later, on May 23, 1898, she was ordained an elder. On Foote's ordination, see *Minutes of the New York Conference*, pp. 21, 31. For documentation of Small's ordination to deacon and elder, see W. J. Smith, "Philadelphia and Baltimore Conference"; "A Female Elder," *Star of Zion*, June 2, 1898; Pettey, "Woman's Column"; "Mrs. Mary Jane Small," *A.M.E. Zion Quarterly Review*, 1978, 90(3), 122.

35. Lincoln and Mamiya, *Black Church*, p. 285; David Henry Bradley Sr., *A History of the A.M.E. Zion Church*, vol. 2, p. 393.

36. For a discussion of the debate over Mary J. Small's ordination as an elder, see the following *Star of Zion* articles: "A Female Elder"; Rev. B. J. Bold- ing, "Woman Ordination"; Rev. S. A. Chambers, "Redhot Cannon Ball"; Bishop J. W. Hood, "Rev. Mrs. Small's Case"; Bishop John Bryan Small, "Mrs. Small's Case"; Rev. J. H. McMullen, "Bishop Small Errs"; Mrs. Rev. W. L. Moore, "Eyes of Jealousy"; Pettey, "Woman's Column."

37. Walls, *Church*, p. 111; Harris, *Daily Proceedings*, pp. 111, 145.

38. Pettey, "Woman's Column."

39. Rev. George C. Clement, "Some Things Pertinent"; Walls, *Church*, pp. 103–104; Lincoln and Mamiya, *Black Church*, p. 453 n. 36.

40. Jacquelyn Grant, "Black Theology and the Black Woman."

41. The relationship between the NACW and Christian feminist activists has not been explored. In the late nineteenth century, prominent churchwomen such as Eliza Gardner, Katherine Davis Tillman, and Hallie Quinn Brown used the NACW as a base for developing strategies to challenge and dis- mantle sexist structures in the community. As an organization of diverse local clubs, the NACW consisted of women from distinct religious traditions

and associations throughout the United States. Through its publications *Woman's Era* and *National Notes,* the NACW was able to indoctrinate its readers with subtle and sometimes not so subtle messages about ways to attack racism in the women's movement, as well as sexism in the black community. Much more research needs to be done on the clubs' activities and members, the state and city federations, and the clubs' relationship to religious leaders and institutions at both the local and national levels.

42. Stephen Ward Angell, "The Controversy over Women's Ministry in the African Methodist Episcopal Church During the 1880s," in Weisenfeld and Newman, *This Far by Faith,* pp. 94–109.

43. Lincoln and Mamiya, *Black Church,* p. 286.

44. Othal Hawthorne Lakey and Betty Beene Stephens, *God in My Mama's House,* p. 133; idem, *The History of the C.M.E. Church,* p. 406; Eula Wallace Harris and Maxie Harris Craig, *Christian Methodist Episcopal Church Through the Years; C.M.E. Quadrennial Address,* p. 48.

45. "A Sabbath in New Madrid"; "Colored Methodism's Pioneer Woman Preacher"; Rev. J. W. Roberts, "The Only Ordained Woman in the C.M.E. Church, Corrected."

46. *The Doctrines and Discipline of the Colored Methodist Episcopal Church, Revised 1950,* p. 67; *Journal of the Twenty-Sixth General Conference,* p. 60; *The Doctrines and Discipline of the Christian Methodist Episcopal Church, Revised 1986,* p. 90; "Rev. Virgie Ghant."

47. Lincoln and Mamiya, *Black Church,* pp. 286–287.

48. Ibid., pp. 76–77; Cheryl J. Sanders, *Saints in Exile,* pp. 4–5.

49. Lincoln and Mamiya, *Black Church,* pp. 76–77; Sanders, *Saints in Exile,* pp. 4–5; Pearl Williams-Jones, "A Minority Report," p. 40.

50. Williams-Jones, "Minority Report," p. 41; Lincoln and Mamiya, *Black Church,* pp. 288–289; Cheryl Townsend Gilkes, "'Together and in Harness,'" pp. 682, 684, 688–689; Jualynne E. Dodson and Cheryl Townsend Gilkes, "Something Within," p. 87.

51. Murphy, *Working the Spirit,* p. 157.

52. Hans A. Baer, *The Black Spiritual Movement,* pp. 9, 165, 168; Harold A. Carter, *The Prayer Tradition of Black People,* p. 78.

53. Murphy, *Working the Spirit,* pp. 13–17; Carter, *Prayer Tradition,* p. 79.

54. St. Clair Drake and Horace R. Clayton, *Black Metropolis: A Study of Negro Life,* p. 30.

55. For a historical overview of the black women's club movement during this period, see Dorothy Salem, *To Better Our World: Black Women in Orga-*

nized Reform, 1890–1920. For a discussion of the organizing efforts of southern black women during this era, see Cynthia Neverdon Morton, "Advancement of the Race Through African American Women's Organizations in the South, 1895–1925."

56. John Hope Franklin, *From Slavery to Freedom,* p. 266; Rosalyn Terborg-Penn, "African-American Women's Networks in the Anti-Lynching Crusade," pp. 148–161.

57. Fannie Barrier Williams, "The Intellectual Progress of the Colored Women of the United States," pp. 696–711.

58. E. Glenn Hinson, "The Church."

59. "Bishop Coffin Makes Chicago District Appointments," *Chicago Defender,* Oct. 4, 1919; "Methodists Hold Session at St. Paul," *Chicago Defender,* Sept. 24, 1927.

60. *Doctrines and Disciplines of the African Methodist Episcopal Church, 1900,* p. 175; AME *Journal of the Thirtieth Quadrennial Session, May 6–18, 1936,* p. 81; Lincoln and Mamiya, *Black Church,* p. 286.

61. Cheryl Townsend Gilkes, "Religion," in Hine, Brown, and Terborg-Penn, *Black Women,* vol. 2, p. 967; Lincoln and Mamiya, *Black Church,* pp. 287–288.

62. Joseph R. Washington Jr., *Black Sects and Cults,* pp. 65–67; Lincoln and Mamiya, *Black Church,* pp. 120–121.

63. "Women in Methodist Church Want Trustees," *Chicago Defender,* Jan. 17, 1925.

64. "Woman Pastor," *Baltimore Afro-American.*

65. For a list of African American women's achievements, see Jamie Hart and Elsa Barkley Brown, "Black Women in the United States," pp. 1309–1332; Evelyn Brooks Higginbotham, "Clubwomen and Electoral Politics in the 1920s," pp. 140–147; "Negro Preacher out for Assembly," undated typescript, Florence Spearing Randolph Collection, Center for African American History and Culture, Temple University, Philadelphia.

66. "Women Lose Fight to Become A.M.E. Elders," *Chicago Defender,* May 23, 1936; "Predicts Women Will Be Ordained at Next General Conference of AME Church to Be Held in 1944," *New York Age,* Mar. 15, 1944; "Thirteenth District Salutes Dr. Martha Jayne Keys," *Voice of Missions,* Sept. 1960, p. 11.

67. Lincoln and Mamiya, *Black Church,* pp. 285–286; "AME's Vote Women Right to Become Ordained Deacons," *Baltimore Afro-American,* May 22, 1948.

68. Farmer and Hunter, *And Blessed Is She*, pp. 13–14.

69. Ibid.

70. These societies included the Woman's Convention Auxiliary to the National Baptist Convention, the Woman's Home and Foreign Missionary Society (AME Zion), the Woman's Parent Mite Missionary Society, Woman's Home (AME), Foreign Missionary Society (AME), Woman's Home Missionary Society (Methodist Episcopal), and the Woman's Connectional Missionary Council (CME).

71. For discussions of the work of the denominational missionary societies, see Higginbotham, *Righteous Discontent*; Walls, *Church*, pp. 388–424; Richard R. Wright, *Encyclopaedia of the African Methodist Episcopal Church*, pp. 423–425; Ruth G. Garter and others, *To a Higher Glory*; Lakey and Stephens, *God in My Mama's House*, pp. 82–85, 89–94, 129–141.

CHAPTER ONE: WOMEN WHO PAVED THE WAY

1. Deborah Gray White, *Ar'nt I a Woman?* p. 131. In discussing the impact of slave women's leadership on the plantation, White refers to a slave woman named Sinda, a "self proclaimed prophetess" who preached that the end of the world was coming on a certain day. Sinda's pronouncement generated a work stoppage that effectively undermined the master's power. White's brief mention suggests that there were slave women whose spiritual gifts were recognized. There is, however, no substantive scholarship that discusses these women and the nature of their ministry.

2. In 1889, the Philadelphia Quakers issued a tract called "Elizabeth: A Colored Minister of the Gospel, Born in Slavery." Were it not for this publication, a short biographical sketch of Elizabeth's life based upon verbal testimony that she gave her Quaker benefactors at the age of ninety-seven, Elizabeth would most likely have remained obscure. For a reprinted excerpt of the tract, see Lowenberg and Bogin, *Black Women in American Life*, pp. 127–134; Lincoln and Mamiya, *Black Church*, p. 279.

3. Lowenberg and Bogin, *Black Women in American Life*, pp. 130, 131.

4. Ibid., p. 132. In 1808, two black Methodist religious groups were meeting in Baltimore: the Sharp Street Methodist Episcopal and Bethel Methodist Episcopal congregations. It is most probable that Elizabeth held the meeting in the Sharp Street Church. For information regarding this church, see Bettye Collier-Thomas, "History of the Sharp Street Memorial Methodist Episcopal Church," in *One Hundred Seventy-Fifth Anniversary*.

5. Lowenberg and Bogin, *Black Women in American Life*, pp. 133, 134.

6. Andrews, *Sisters of the Spirit*, p. 27.

7. Ibid., p. 28.

8. Ibid., pp. 28, 29.

9. Ibid., p. 36.

10. Ibid., pp. 27, 39–41.

11. Bettye Collier-Thomas, *Freedom and Community*, p. 51; Andrews, *Sisters of the Spirit*, pp. 36, 42–48.

12. Andrews, *Sisters of the Spirit*, pp. 25, 29.

13. Ibid., p. 36.

14. Ibid.; Dodson, "Nineteenth-Century Women," p. 278.

15. Dodson, "Women's Collective Power," p. 335.

16. Andrews, *Sisters of the Spirit*, p. 2.

17. Elaw, "Memoirs."

18. Andrews, *Sisters of the Spirit*, p. 3.

19. Ibid., pp. 53–61.

20. Ibid., pp. 61–65.

21. Ibid., pp. 67–73.

22. Ibid., pp. 78–82.

23. Ibid., pp. 90–138.

24. Jean McMahon Humez, "Jackson, Rebecca Cox," pp. 626–627; Humez, *Gifts of Power*.

25. Humez, "Jackson, Rebecca Cox," pp. 626–627.

26. A. B. Smith, *Autobiography*, p. 22.

27. Ibid., p. v.

28. Ibid., pp. 28, 31.

29. Ibid., pp. 42–49.

30. Ibid., pp. 57–62.

31. Ibid., p. 62.

32. Ibid., pp. 77–79. John Inskip was a prominent holiness preacher and a leading figure in the National Holiness Association. He was the editor of the *Guide to Holiness*, a periodical published by this organization. See John E. Searles, *The Life of John S. Inskip* (Boston: McDonald & Gill, 1885).

33. A. B. Smith, *Autobiography*, p. 80.

34. Ibid., pp. 132, 152.

35. Ibid., p. 157.

36. Ibid., pp. 158–163.

37. Ibid., pp. 200–201.

38. Ibid., p. 200.

39. Ibid., pp. 164–165; Hardesty, Dayton, and Dayton, "Women in the Holiness Movement," pp. 236–239.

40. A. B. Smith, *Autobiography,* pp. 174, 182–184.

41. Ibid., pp. 193–195. For Smith's experience with discrimination in Philadelphia, see pp. 197–198.

42. Ibid., p. 198.

43. Carlton Mabee and Susan Mabee Newhouse, *Sojourner Truth,* pp. 26, 27.

44. Ibid.

45. In a paper I delivered at a conference, I first suggested this analysis of Sojourner Truth's and Amanda Berry Smith's symbolic roles among white women activists. The conference was "Afro-American Women and the Vote: From Abolitionism to the Voting Rights Act." It was held at the University of Massachusetts in fall 1987. See Ann D. Gordon and others, *African American Women and the Vote,* pp. 56–57. The argument as relates to Sojourner Truth is extended and fully explored in Nell Irvin Painter, *Sojourner Truth.*

46. Mabee and Newhouse, *Sojourner Truth,* pp. 30–36.

47. Painter, *Sojourner Truth,* p. 74.

48. Mabee and Newhouse, *Sojourner Truth,* pp. 44, 45.

49. Bettye Collier-Thomas, *Black Women in America: Contributors to Our Heritage.*

50. Foote, *A Brand Plucked from the Fire,* p. 208.

CHAPTER TWO: JULIA A. J. FOOTE

1. Bettye Collier-Thomas, "Julia A. J. Foote (1823–1901)," pp. 227–228.

2. Ibid.; Andrews, *Sisters of the Spirit,* p. 4.

3. *Minutes of the New York Conference,* pp. 21, 31.

4. "Woman Preacher Dead"; Alexander Walters, *My Life and Work,* pp. 45–46.

5. In the sermon "Christian Perfection," Foote directly refers to "Western New York," which by definition is the Burned Over District. For a discussion of antebellum perfectionist movements in New York, see Whitney R. Cross, *The Burned-Over District: The Social and Intellectual History of*

Enthusiastic Religion in Western New York, 1800–1850; Andrews, *Sisters of the Spirit,* p. 4.

6. Foote, "Christian Perfection"; A. B. Smith, *Autobiography,* p. 193; Jones, *Perfectionist Persuasion,* pp. 2–6. Having attended some of Phoebe Palmer's meetings in New York, Amanda Berry Smith was exposed to the teachings of Christian perfection. Palmer, a white Methodist, was a major advocate of Christian perfection. There were basically two schools of thought on Christian perfection, one which embraced John Wesley's emphasis on the perfection of love as a process, and the other which stressed entire sanctification accompanied by immediate "external evidence of the internal work." According to Charles Edwin Jones, Palmer "likened entire sanctification to baptism, an inward cleansing followed by a circumspect life."

7. Andrews, *Sisters of the Spirit,* p. 232.

8. Synan, *Holiness-Pentecostal Movement,* p. 27. The Oneida Perfectionists, a utopian experiment, launched several innovations, the most controversial of which was the institution of "complex marriage." They sanctioned a type of "sanctified promiscuity," which the Oneida community regulated.

9. Painter, *Sojourner Truth,* pp. 48–51, 79–80; Mabee and Newhouse, *Sojourner Truth,* pp. 32–33.

10. Painter, *Sojourner Truth,* pp. 48–51, 79–80; Mabee and Newhouse, *Sojourner Truth,* pp. 32–33. The Burned Over District was the center of great controversy during the antebellum period. The religious forces that originated there influenced social movements throughout the United States. For a detailed study of this phenomenon, see Cross, *Burned-Over District.*

11. The Reverend Dr. Daniel Curry edited the *Christian Advocate,* which included discussions of John Wesley, slavery, and Christian perfection. For Curry's views on perfectionism, see Daniel Curry, *Perfect Love;* idem, *Fragments, Religious and Theological.*

CHAPTER THREE: HARRIET A. BAKER

1. John H. Acornley (ed.), *The Colored Lady Evangelist,* p. 46; also see Dodson, "Nineteenth-Century Women," pp. 341–342.

2. Acornley, *Colored Lady Evangelist,* pp. 31, 32.

3. Ibid., p. 32.

4. Ibid., p. 35.

5. Ibid., p. 36.

6. Ibid., p. 37.

7. Ibid., p. 38.

8. Ibid., pp. 39, 40.

9. Ibid., p. 41.

10. Ibid., p. 42.

11. Frank Whelan, "Black Evangelist's Allentown Work to Be Honored."

CHAPTER FOUR: MARY J. SMALL

1. Bishop C. C. Alleyne, "For God Took Her"; Bradley, *History of Church*, vol. 2, pp. 393–394.

2. Bishop John Bryan Small, a native of Barbados, was one of the most educated, erudite, and intellectual bishops in the AME Zion Church. He wrote four books, published numerous articles in newspapers and magazines, and was acclaimed "the most voluminous writer" of his church and of "any other Negro Church." Widely known for his eloquence, Small was a Latin and Greek scholar, as well. He perceived that his brilliance threatened many of the bishops and that, for this reason, he was passed over several times in his bid to become a bishop. For biographical details about Bishop Small, see Rev. B. F. Wheeler, D.D., "The Late Bishop J. B. Small, D.D."; Walls, *Church*, pp. 586–587.

3. Wheeler, "Late Bishop J. B. Small."

4. Walls, *Church*, pp. 586–587; Mrs. Carissa Betties, "Let Rev. Mrs. Small Alone"; "A Female Elder"; Chambers, "Redhot Cannon Ball"; Hood, "Rev. Mrs. Small's Case"; J. B. Small, "Mrs. Small's Case"; McMullen, "Bishop Small Errs."

5. Walls, *Church*, pp. 260, 404.

6. For a discussion of Sarah Pettey, see Glenda Elizabeth Gilmore, *Gender and Jim Crow*, p. 128.

7. Alleyne, "For God Took Her."

CHAPTER FIVE: FLORENCE SPEARING RANDOLPH

1. See Collier-Thomas, "Minister and Reformer," pp. 177–185.

2. Ibid.

3. Florence Spearing Randolph, "Florence Randolph Life and Work in Part," and "School Days," handwritten transcripts, Randolph Collection.

4. Florence Spearing Randolph, "My First Trip away from Home," "My Second Trip from Home," and "Marriage," handwritten transcripts, Randolph Collection.

5. Ibid.

6. Ibid.

7. Ibid.

8. Florence Spearing Randolph, "Home Mission Work," handwritten transcript, Randolph Collection.

9. Randolph, "Life and Work in Part."

10. Ibid.

11. Ibid.

12. Clement Richardson, *The National Cyclopedia of the Colored Race,* vol. 1, p. 215.

13. Florence Spearing Randolph, "The Rev. Mrs. Florence Randolph, Evangelist," typescript, n.d., Randolph Collection.

14. Richardson, *National Cyclopedia.*

15. "Rev. Mrs. Florence Randolph," *New York Age,* Aug. 31, 1905.

16. See the following works by Arthur T. Pierson: *An Unbeliever Convinced; The Bible and Spiritual Life; Woman as a Factor in the World's Evangelization; Many Infallible Proofs.*

17. Bishop Cameron Chesterfield Alleyne was the AME Zion Church's first resident bishop in Africa, serving from 1924 to 1928. For biographical details regarding Alleyne, see Walls, *Church,* pp. 240–242, 600–601. In 1943, there was a movement to have Alleyne reappointed to the denomination's African mission in Liberia.

CHAPTER SIX: MARY G. EVANS

1. "Great Work of an Evangelist," Baltimore *Afro-American.*

2. Ibid.

3. Ibid.; "Wilberforce University Honors Prominent Woman"; "Woman Pastor's Faith Is Her Guiding Light."

4. "Great Works of an Evangelist"; "Wilberforce University Honors Prominent Woman"; "Woman Pastor's Faith."

5. See "Quinn Chapel."

6. J. Blaine Poindexter, "Church 'Amens' Stop." In 1922, the year of Poindexter's article, many considered "bobbed hair" to indicate licentious behavior. By referring to Evans's hair, the reporter indirectly questioned her credibility as an advocate for morality. This reference to "bobbed hair" also challenges the general assumption that women who preached were neither feminine nor attractive, and suggests that Evans was not in this mold.

7. "Rev. Dr. Mary G. Evans Is Conducting Unusual Revival at St. Mark's"; "Woman Pastor"; "Woman Pastor's Faith"; "Lady Preachers," pp. 26–28.

8. "Rev. Mary Evans, Noted Church Leader, Is Dead," *Chicago Defender,* July 16, 1966.

9. "The History of Cosmopolitan Community Church, 1923–1993," souvenir program, pp. 3–4.

10. Ibid.

CHAPTER SEVEN: ELLA EUGENE WHITFIELD

1. Samuel W. Bacote, *Who's Who Among the Colored Baptists of the United States,* pp. 101–103.

2. "Mrs. E. E. Whitfield Stirs Members of Zion Baptist Church in Jersey City"; Higginbotham, *Righteous Discontent,* pp. 161, 220.

3. Bacote, *Who's Who,* p. 102; National Baptist Convention, *Journal of the Twentieth Annual Session,* p. 326.

4. Hine, Brown, and Terborg-Penn, *Black Women,* vol. 2, p. 204.

5. Higginbotham, *Righteous Discontent,* p. 187.

CHAPTER EIGHT: RUTH R. DENNIS

1. Ruth. R. Dennis, "Thousands Losing Faith in Church," reproduced in "'Thousands Losing Faith in Church,' Says Woman Evangelist"; idem, "What Are We Going to Do with the Children?" reproduced in "Babies 'Too Young to Pray' Can 'Shake That Thing,' Says Writer"; Floyd J. Calvin, "Heads of Big Churches All Southerners: Women Found in All Professions."

CHAPTER NINE: MRS. RAIFF

1. Mrs. Raiff, "Get the Right Ticket," reproduced in "Woman Preaches at Payne Memorial Church."

CHAPTER TEN: ROSA A. HORN

1. "In Loving Memory of the Late Bishop Emeritus Mother Rosa A. Horn," funeral program, May 15, 1976, Rosa Artimus Horn Collection, Center for African American History and Culture, Temple University, Philadelphia; "Rosa A. Horn, 96," *New York Post,* May 14, 1976; H. Norton Browne, "You Pray for Me."

2. For a discussion of Smith, Robinson, Divine, and Michaux, and for information about other Pentecostal, Holiness, and Spirituals leaders and
   movements during the 1920s and 1930s, see Miles Mark Fisher, "Organized Religion and the Cults," pp. 8–10, 29–30; Allan H. Spear, *Black
   Chicago*, p. 176; Herbert M. Smith, "Three Negro Preachers in Chicago,"
   pp. 17–19; Sherry Sherrod DuPree (ed.), *Biographical Dictionary of
   African-American, Holiness-Pentecostals, 1880–1990*; Jessie Carney Smith,
   "Lucy Smith (1875–1952)," pp. 601–603; Robert Weisbrot, *Father Divine
   and the Struggle for Racial Equality*; Carter, *Prayer Tradition*, pp. 71–72.

3. Browne, "You Pray for Me"; Carter, *Prayer Tradition*, pp. 78–79.

4. Carter, *Prayer Tradition*, p. 72.

5. Ibid., pp. 73–75.

6. Ibid., pp. 71–72.

7. H. Norton Browne, "Woman Evangelist Rival Is Radio's Answer to Elder
   Michaux."

8. "Radio Once Devil's Tool to Mother Horn."

9. "Mother Horn in Fight with Dance Hall Owner."

10. Garfield Thomas Haywood died in 1931. From 1909 to 1914, Elder
    Haywood presided over a mission in Indianapolis, Indiana. In 1914, he
    became the first presiding bishop of the Pentecostal Assemblies of the
    World. Members of this organization believed in "Jesus Only," a doctrine
    advocating that Christians be baptized or rebaptized in the name of "Jesus
    Only." In 1924, as the result of a racial schism in the Pentecostal Assem-
    blies of the World, many white members withdrew and formed the United
    Pentecostal Church (UPC). For information on the Pentecostal Assemblies
    of the World, see Sherry Sherrod DuPree (ed.), *African-American Holiness
    Pentecostal Movement*, p. 263. For a discussion of Haywood's role in the
    Trinitarian versus Unitarian controversy, see Robert Mapes Anderson,
    Vision of the Disinherited: The Making of American Pentecostalism,
    pp. 176–194. For biographical data about Bishop Haywood, see DuPree,
    Biographical Dictionary, pp. 119–120.

CHAPTER ELEVEN: IDA B. ROBINSON

1. Mount Sinai Holy Church of America, Inc., "Mount Sinai Training Institute," typescript, n.d., Ida Robinson Collection, Center for African American History and Culture, Temple University, Philadelphia.

2. Arthur Huff Fauset, *Black Gods of the Metropolis*, pp. 13–21; Minerva
   Bell, "Significant Female Religious Leaders and Factors Leading to Their

Success," pp. 48–53; Mount Sinai Holy Church of America, Inc., *Commemorative Journal of the Mount Sinai Holy Church of America, Inc.,* p. 10.

3. "Bishop Ida Bell Robinson Dies in Winter Haven, Fla."; Dean Harold Trulear, "Reshaping Black Pastoral Theology," pp. 17–31.

4. Franklin, *From Slavery to Freedom,* p. 352.

CHAPTER THIRTEEN: QUINCEILA WHITLOW

1. "Evangelist Available," p. 5.

2. Baer, *Black Spiritual Movement,* p. 4. Baer found that by 1980, African American Spirituals were rejecting the term "Spiritualist." It appears, however, to have been in widespread use before 1960, and is widely used in a number of scholarly studies about African American religion. For examples of this, see Zora Neale Hurston, "Hoodoo in America," pp. 317–417; Fauset, *Black Gods;* Benjamin E. Mays and Joseph William Nicholson, *The Negro's Church;* Washington, *Black Sects and Cults;* E. Franklin Frazier, *The Negro Church in America.*

CHAPTER FOURTEEN: F. E. REDWINE

1. "Guest Speaker at Flint, Texas," p. 5.

2. Higginbotham, *Righteous Discontent,* p. 139. T. Dewitt Talmadge, a white minister, was extremely popular among African Americans, especially women ministers. His syndicated column appeared in a number of black newspapers.

CHAPTER FIFTEEN: PAULI MURRAY

1. Pauli Murray, *Song in a Weary Throat,* pp. 2, 4–6. For biographical sketches of Murray, see Collier-Thomas, *Black Women in America;* Marsha C. Vick, "Pauli Murray (1910–1985)," pp. 783–788; Sylvia M. Jacobs, "Murray, Pauli (1910–1985)," pp. 825–826.

2. Murray, *Song in a Weary Throat,* pp. 238–244, 358, 363–364, 368.

3. Ibid., pp. 202–209, 229–231, 353.

4. Ibid., pp. 287, 310–314, 316, 373.

5. Ibid., pp. 426–435.

6. For works by Phyllis Trible, see *Two Women in a Man's World* and *God and the Rhetoric of Sexuality.*

7. William Stringfellow, *An Ethic for Christians and Other Aliens in a Strange Land.*

8. Pauli Murray, "Black Theology and Feminist Theology," in James H. Cone and Gayraud S. Wilmore (eds.), *Black Theology,* vol. 1, pp. 304–322.

9. Casey Miller and Kate Swift, *Words and Women* (New York: Anchor Books, 1976), pp. 71–72.

10. Murray's mention of Kunta Kinte, a central character in Alex Haley's *Roots,* is to illustrate the connection between naming and power. Kunta Kinte's master beat him until he agreed to take the name Toby, a name chosen by his master. The television presentation adapted from the book was the most watched series in history.

11. Miller and Swift, *Words and Women,* p. 16 (emphases and parenthetical notation added by Murray).

12. Murray cites Trible's "Depatriarchalization in Biblical Interpretation" as referenced in Miller and Swift, *Words and Women,* pp. 16–17.

13. Miller and Swift, *Words and Women,* pp. 16–17.

14. Ibid.

15. Ibid.

16. Ibid.

17. Phyllis Bird, "The Image of Woman in the Old Testament," typescript, Temple University, 1972. The brackets are Murray's.

18. Mary Daly, *Beyond God the Father.*

19. Saint Anselm, *Works*; Eleanor T. McLaughlin, *Interim Legacy.*

20. Julian of Norwich, *The Revelations of Divine Love of Julian of Norwich.*

21. "Agronsky's panel" refers to *Agronsky and Company,* a popular weekly news talk show produced in 1978, in which Murray delivered this sermon.

22. Erik Erikson, *Dimensions of a New Identity.*

23. Patricia Martin Doyle, "An Educator's Perspective on Language About God," in *Consultation on Language About God.*

24. William Wordsworth, "The World Is Too Much with Us." In her sermon, Murray attributed the poem to "Wadsworth" and made some errors when reproducing the verse. I have substituted the corrections in brackets.

25. No additional states ratified the ERA, so it ultimately never became part of the Constitution.

26. Stringfellow, *Ethic for Christians.*

27. Ibid.

28. Elizabeth Moltmann-Wendel and Jurgen Moltmann, foreword to Letty M. Russell, *Human Liberation in a Feminist Perspective.*

29. Rollo May, *Power and Innocence.*

30. Ibid.

31. For Ruether's views on liberation theology, see Rosemary Radford Ruether, *New Woman, New Earth;* idem, *Liberation Theology.*

32. Russell, *Human Liberation.* The brackets are Murray's.

33. Gustavo Gutierrez, *A Theology of Liberation,* p. ix. For his views on liberation theology, see this work and also his *Liberation and Change.*

34. Ruether, *Liberation Theology,* p. 9.

35. Ibid., p. 189.

36. For Jones's views on black theology, see Major J. Jones, *Christian Ethics for Black Theology;* idem, *Black Awareness.*

37. Sheila D. Collins, *A Different Heaven and Earth.* The brackets are Murray's.

38. Charles P. Price, *Ordination of Women in Theological Perspective.*

39. Russell, *Human Liberation.*

40. Ruether, *Liberation Theology,* p. 12.

41. Collins, *Different Heaven and Earth.*

42. Russell, *Human Liberation.*

43. Gutierrez, *Theology of Liberation,* p. 177.

44. Ruether, *Liberation Theology,* p. 8.

45. For J. Deotis Roberts's beliefs, see the following books of his: *A Black Political Theology; Black Churches and Family Empowerment; Opening Closed Doors.*

46. Gutierrez, *Theology of Liberation.*

47. Murray, "Black Theology and Feminist Theology," pp. 310–311. In this essay, Murray discusses the ethical implications of strategies for liberation, particularly the use of nonviolence as an alternative to violence as defined by Martin Luther King Jr. Her source for this discussion is Jones, *Christian Ethics,* p. 142.

48. Russell, *Human Liberation.*

49. Ruether, *New Woman, New Earth,* p. 65.

50. Gutierrez, *Theology of Liberation,* p. 262.

51. Murray cites Carley here because his book, *Ezekiel Among the Prophets,* provides an in-depth analysis of the prophet's historical context, message, and theological importance.

52. Haley, *Roots;* Margaret Walker, *Jubilee;* Pauli Murray, *Proud Shoes.*

EPILOGUE: FORGING AHEAD TOWARD EQUALITY

1. H. M. Smith, "Three Negro Preachers," pp. 7–19; DuPree, *African American Holiness Pentecostal Movement*; Fisher, "Organized Religion," pp. 9–10; Williams-Jones, "Minority Report," pp. 40–41; Trulear, "Reshaping Theology," pp. 17–31.

2. For biographical details on Murray, see Vick, "Murray," pp. 783–786; and Murray, *Song in a Weary Throat*.

3. For biographical details on Kelly and Harris, see De Witt C. Dykes Jr., "Leontine Kelly (1920–)," pp. 621–625; and Aleathia Dolores Nicholson, "Barbara Harris (1930–)," pp. 462–465.

4. Peter Paris, "From Womanist Thought to Womanist Action."

5. For a breakdown of clergy by gender and race in the United States, see the following U.S. Bureau of the Census publications: *Compendium of the Ninth Census, 1870*, table 65; *Compendium of the Tenth Census, 1880*, tab. 103; *Special Census Report on the Occupations of the Population of the United States at the Eleventh Census, 1890*, p. 11 (tab. 6, pp. 70–71, includes occupational listings by sex for 1870, 1880, and 1890); *Twelfth Census of the United States in 1900, Population*, vol. 2, tab. 37; *Thirteenth Census of the United States in 1910, Population*, vol. 4, tab. 6; *Fourteenth Census of the United States in 1920, Population*, vol. 4, tab. 4; *Fifteenth Census of the United States in 1930*, vol. 5, tab. 3; *Sixteenth Census of the United States in 1940*, vol. 3, tab. 62; *Seventeenth Census of the United States in 1950: Characteristics of the Population, U.S. Summary*, tab. 128; *Eighteenth Census of the United States in 1960: Occupational Characteristics*, tab. 3; *Nineteenth Census of the United States Population: Characteristics of the Population, U.S. Summary*, vol. 1, pt. 1, sec. 2, pp. 1–739; *1980 United States Census of Population: Occupation by Industry*, vol. 2: *Subject Reports* , pp. 1–177. Also see *Women in Gainful Occupations, 1870 to 1920*, pp. 182–183; *Negro Population in the United States, 1790–1915*, pp. 510, 526; *Negroes in the United States, 1920–1932*, tab. 27.

6. G. F. Ketcham, *Yearbook of American Churches*, pp. 239–243.

7. Lincoln and Mamiya, *Black Church*, pp. 289–301. This work includes an excellent discussion of data collected as part of a nationwide survey of black clergy and black churches in the seven major historically black denominations. The survey's purpose was to determine male clergy attitudes toward having female preachers and pastors. See also Tim Funk, "Black Women Are Heeding the Call"; Harriet Jackson Scarupa, "Women in Ministry," pp. 6–15.

SELECTED BIBLIOGRAPHY

MANUSCRIPT COLLECTIONS

Murray, Pauli. Pauli Murray Collection. Schlesinger Library, Radcliffe College, Cambridge, Mass.

Randolph, Florence Spearing. Florence Spearing Randolph Sermon Collection. Center for African American History and Culture, Temple University, Philadelphia, Pa.

Small, John B. *Journals,* Vol. 12. Carnegie Library, Livingstone College, Salisbury, N.C.

PRIMARY SOURCES:

BOOKS, PERIODICALS, AND GOVERNMENT DOCUMENTS

AME Journal of the Thirtieth Quadrennial Session, May 6–18, 1936. Philadelphia: AME Book Concern, 1936.

Acornley, John H. (ed.). *The Colored Lady Evangelist: Being the Life, Labors and Experiences, of Mrs. Harriet Baker.* Brooklyn, N.Y.: 1892.

Alleyne, C. C. "For God Took Her." *Star of Zion,* Oct. 4, 1945.

Betties, Carissa. "Let Rev. Mrs. Small Alone." *Star of Zion,* Dec. 22, 1898.

"Bishop Ida Bell Robinson Dies in Winter Haven, Fla." *Philadelphia Tribune,* Apr. 27, 1946.

Bolding, B. J. "Woman Ordination: Scripture Does Not Forbid It." *Star of Zion,* July 7, 1898.

Browne, H. Norton. "You Pray for Me." *New York Amsterdam News,* Oct. 13, 1934.

Browne, H. Norton. "Woman Evangelist Rival is Radio's Answer to Elder Michaux." *Baltimore Afro-American,* Oct. 20, 1934.

Calvin, Floyd J. "Heads of Big Churches All Southerners: Women Found in All Professions." *Pittsburgh Courier,* July 2, 1927.

Campbell, Jabez P. "On Gradual and Immediate Sanctification." *Christian Recorder,* Mar. 26, 1864.

Chambers, S. A. "Redhot Cannon Ball: No Authority in Scripture for the Ordination of Women." *Star of Zion,* June 16, 1898.

Clement, George C. "Some Things Pertinent: Episcopal Authority and Presiding Elders." *Star of Zion*, Feb. 9, 1898.

C.M.E. *Quadrennial Address of the Bishops of the Colored Methodist Episcopal Church to the Delegates of the Eighteenth General Conference Assembled in Hot Springs, Arkansas, May 1938.* Memphis, Tenn.: C.M.E. Publishing House, 1938.

"Colored Methodism's Pioneer Woman Preacher." *Christian Index*, Feb. 12, 1925.

Davis, H. "Sanctification." *Christian Recorder*, Apr. 4, 1855.

The Doctrines and Discipline of the African Methodist Episcopal Church, 1900. Philadelphia: AME Book Concern, 1900.

The Doctrines and Discipline of the Colored Methodist Episcopal Church, Revised 1950. Memphis, Tenn.: C.M.E. Publishing House, 1950.

The Doctrines and Discipline of the Colored Methodist Episcopal Church, Revised 1986. Memphis, Tenn.: C.M.E. Publishing House, 1986.

Elaw, Zilpha. *Memoirs of the Life and Religious Experience, Ministerial Travels and Labours of Mrs. Zilpha Elaw, an American Female of Colour; Together with Some Account of the Great Religious Revivals in America.* In William L. Andrews (ed.), *Sisters of the Spirit: Three Black Women's Autobiographies of the Nineteenth Century.* Bloomington: Indiana University Press, 1986. (Originally published 1846.)

Elizabeth. "Elizabeth: A Colored Minister of the Gospel, Born in Slavery." In Bert James Lowenberg and Ruth Bogin (eds.), *Black Women in Nineteenth-Century American Life.* University Park: Pennsylvania State University Press, 1976. (Originally published 1889.)

"Episcopal Dots: Woman Elders—Railroad Discrimination—Coleman Factory." *Star of Zion*, July 7, 1898.

"Evangelist Available." *Christian Index*, Dec. 19, 1940.

Felts, Alice. "Women in the Church." *Christian Recorder*, Feb. 18, 1886.

Felts, Alice. "A Timely Reminder." *Christian Recorder*, May 24, 1894.

"A Female Elder." *Star of Zion*, June 2, 1898.

Foote, Julia A. J. *A Brand Plucked from the Fire: An Autobiographical Sketch by Mrs. Julia A. J. Foote.* Cleveland, Ohio: Schneider, 1879.

Funk, Tim. "Black Women Are Heeding the Call to the Ministry." *Philadelphia Inquirer*, Aug. 11, 1996.

Grant, H. A. "Sermon: On Sanctification." *Christian Recorder*, Dec. 21, 1877.

"Great Work of an Evangelist." *Baltimore Afro-American Ledger*, July 4, 1914.

"Guest Speaker at Flint, Texas." *Messenger*, July 1948.

Harris, C. R. (comp.). *Daily Proceedings of the Seventeenth Quadrennial Session of the General Conference of the A.M.E. Zion Church in America: Held in New York City, May, 1884.* New York: A.M.E. Zion Book Concern, 1884.

Hood, James Walker. "Rev. Mrs. Small's Case." *Star of Zion*, June 9, 1898.

Humez, Jean McMahon. *Gifts of Power: The Writings of Rebecca Cox Jackson, Black Visionary, Shaker Eldress*. Amherst: University of Massachusetts Press, 1981.

Journal of the Twenty-Sixth General Conference and the Twenty-Fifth Quadrennial Session of the Christian Methodist Episcopal Church: Held with Trinity C.M.E. Church, May 4–15, 1966. Memphis, Tenn.: C.M.E. Publishing House, 1966.

"Lady Preachers." *Jet*, Feb. 18, 1954.

Lee, Jarena. *The Life and Religious Experience of Jarena Lee, A Coloured Lady, Giving an Account of Her Call to Preach the Gospel. Revised and Corrected from the Original Manuscript, Written by Herself*. In William L. Andrews (ed.), *Sisters of the Spirit: Three Black Women's Autobiographies of the Nineteenth Century*. Bloomington: Indiana University Press, 1986. (Originally published 1836.)

McMullen, J. H. "Bishop Small Errs: The General Conference Never Dreamed of Women Elders." *Star of Zion*, June 30, 1898.

Minutes of the New York Conference African Methodist Episcopal Zion Church, Seventy-Fourth Session: Held at A.M.E. Zion Church, Newburgh, N.Y., May 8th–13th, 1895. Salisbury, N.C.: Livingstone College Press, 1895.

Mitchell, Ella Pearson (ed.). *Those Preachin' Women: Sermons by Black Women Preachers*, Vol. 1. Valley Forge, Pa.: Judson Press, 1985.

Mitchell, Ella Pearson (ed.). *Those Preaching Women: More Sermons by Black Women Preachers*, Vol. 2. Valley Forge, Pa.: Judson Press, 1988.

Mitchell, Ella Pearson (ed.). *Women: To Preach or Not to Preach: Twenty-One Outstanding Preachers Say YES!* Valley Forge, Pa.: Judson Press, 1991.

Moore, W. L. "Eyes of Jealousy." *Star of Zion*, July 28, 1898.

"Mother Horn in Fight with Dance Hall Owner." *New York Age*, Dec. 12, 1959.

Mount Sinai Holy Church of America, Inc. *Commemorative Journal of the Mount Sinai Holy Church of America, Inc.: Celebrating Sixty-Five Years of "Serving God with What We Have."* Philadelphia, 1989.

"Mrs. E. E. Whitfield Stirs Members of Zion Baptist Church in Jersey City." *New York Age*, Apr. 17, 1926.

National Baptist Convention. *Journal of the Twentieth Annual Session of the Woman's Convention Auxiliary to the National Baptist Convention: Held with the Second Baptist Church, Indianapolis, Indiana, September 8–13, 1920*. Nashville, Tenn.: National Baptist Publishing Board, 1921.

"New York African Methodism." *Christian Recorder*, May 14, 1936.

Pettey, Mrs. Bishop C. C. "Woman's Column: Some Prominent Elders in Zion." *Star of Zion*, June 16, 1898.

"Quinn Chapel." *Chicago Defender*, Oct. 17, 24; Nov. 7, 21, 28; Dec. 5, 1914.

"Radio Once Devil's Tool to Mother Horn—Now It's Blessing." *Amsterdam News,* Oct. 31, 1936.

"Rev. Dr. Mary G. Evans Is Conducting Unusual Revival at St. Mark's." *New York Age,* July 31, 1926.

"Rev. Virgie Ghant." *Christian Index,* Apr. 15, 1992.

Roberts, J. W. "The Only Ordained Woman in the C.M.E. Church, Corrected." *Christian Index,* Nov. 4, 1943.

"A Sabbath in New Madrid." *Christian Index,* Aug. 28, 1897.

Seymour, R. "Ought Women to Be Admitted to Membership in the Legislative Bodies of the Church?" *Christian Recorder,* Nov. 6, 13, 20, 1890.

Small, John Bryan. "Mrs. Small's Case: Bishop Small Speaks." *Star of Zion,* June 16, 1898.

Smith, Amanda Berry. *An Autobiography: The Story of the Lord's Dealing with Mrs. Amanda Smith.* Chicago: Christian Witness, 1893.

Smith, W. J. "Philadelphia and Baltimore Conference." *Star of Zion,* June 6, 1895.

Smith, W. J. "Zion in Rochester." *Star of Zion,* June 18, 1896.

Smith, W. J. "Rev. J. B. Small, D.D., Scholar, Poet and Theologian." *Quarterly Review,* Oct. 1898, pp. 289–293.

Sparks, Lillia M. "Woman's Rights." *Latter Day Messenger,* 1934, 2(2), 3.

Steward, Theophilus Gould. "Work for Women of the Church." *Christian Recorder,* Mar. 20, 1890.

"Taxation Without Representation." *Christian Recorder,* Jan. 24, 1895.

U.S. Bureau of the Census. *A Compendium of the Ninth Census, 1870.* Washington, D.C.: Government Printing Office, 1872.

U.S. Bureau of the Census. *A Compendium of the Tenth Census, 1880.* Washington, D.C.: Government Printing Office, 1883.

U.S. Bureau of the Census. *Special Census Report on the Occupations of the Population of the United States at the Eleventh Census, 1890.* Washington, D.C.: Government Printing Office, 1896.

U.S. Bureau of the Census. *Twelfth Census of the United States in 1900, Population.* Vol. 2. Washington, D.C.: Government Printing Office, 1902.

U.S. Bureau of the Census. *Thirteenth Census of the United States in 1910, Population.* Vol. 4. Washington, D.C.: Government Printing Office, 1914.

U.S. Bureau of the Census. *Negro Population in the United States, 1790–1915.* Washington, D.C.: Government Printing Office, 1918.

U.S. Bureau of the Census. *Fourteenth Census of the United States in 1920, Population.* Vol. 4. Washington, D.C.: Government Printing Office, 1923.

U.S. Bureau of the Census. *Women in Gainful Occupations, 1870 to 1920.* Washington, D.C.: Government Printing Office, 1929.

U.S. Bureau of the Census. *Fifteenth Census of the United States in 1930.* Vol. 5. Washington, D.C.: Government Printing Office, 1933.

U.S. Bureau of the Census. *Negroes in the United States, 1920–1932*. Washington, D.C.: Government Printing Office, 1935.

U.S. Bureau of the Census. *Sixteenth Census of the United States in 1940*. Vol. 3. Washington, D.C.: Government Printing Office, 1943.

U.S. Bureau of the Census. *Seventeenth Census of the United States in 1950: Characteristics of the Population, U.S. Summary*. Washington, D.C.: Government Printing Office, 1953.

U.S. Bureau of the Census. *Eighteenth Census of the United States in 1960: Occupational Characteristics*. Washington, D.C.: Government Printing Office, 1963.

U.S. Bureau of the Census. *Nineteenth Census of the United States in 1970: Characteristics of the Population, U.S. Summary*. Washington, D.C.: Government Printing Office, 1973.

U.S. Bureau of the Census. *1980 United States Census of Population: Detailed Population Characteristics*. Washington, D.C.: Government Printing Office, 1984.

Walters, Alexander. *My Life and Work*. Grand Rapids, Mich.: Revell, 1917.

Watley, William D., and Johnson Cook, Suzan. *Preaching in Two Voices: Sermons on the Women in Jesus' Life*. Valley Forge, Pa.: Judson Press, 1992.

Weems, Renita. "Amen, Sister!" *Essence*, Sept. 1988.

Wheeler, B. F. "The Late Bishop J. B. Small, D.D." *A.M.E. Zion Quarterly Review*, 1905, 4(2), 34–38.

Whelan, Frank. "Black Evangelist's Allentown Work to Be Honored." *Morning Call*, May 3, 1990.

"Wilberforce University Honors Prominent Woman." *Washington Tribune*, July 19, 1924.

"Woman Pastor." *Baltimore Afro-American*, Oct. 24, 1924.

"Woman Pastor's Faith Is Her Guiding Light." *Chicago Defender*, July 31, 1943.

"Woman Preacher Dead." *Star of Zion*, Nov. 27, 1901.

SERMONS

Baker, Harriet A. "Behold the Man." In John H. Acornley (ed.), *The Colored Lady Evangelist: Being the Life, Labors and Experiences, of Mrs. Harriet Baker*. Brooklyn, N.Y.: 1892.

Baker, Harriet A. "Jesus Weeping over Jerusalem." In John H. Acornley (ed.), *The Colored Lady Evangelist: Being the Life, Labors and Experiences, of Mrs. Harriet Baker*. Brooklyn, N.Y.: 1892.

Dennis, Ruth R. "Thousands Losing Faith in Church." Reproduced in "'Thousands Losing Faith in Church,' Says Woman Evangelist." *Pittsburgh Courier*, June 25, 1927.

Dennis, Ruth R. "What Are We Going to Do with the Children?" Reproduced in "Babies 'Too Young to Pray' Can 'Shake That Thing,' Says Writer." *Pittsburgh Courier*, July 30, 1927.

Edwards, Rosa. "Ministers Are Examples." *Latter Day Messenger,* 1935, 10(5), 2–3.

Evans, Mary G. "The Wages of Sin Is Death." Reproduced in J. Blaine Poindexter, "Church 'Amens' Stop: Too Much Truth Is Told." *Chicago Defender,* Dec. 2, 1922.

Foote, Julia A. J. "A 'Threshing' Sermon." In *A Brand Plucked from the Fire: An Autobiographical Sketch by Mrs. Julia A. J. Foote.* Cleveland, Ohio: Schneider, 1879.

Foote, Julia A. J. "Christian Perfection." *Star of Zion,* June 28, 1894.

Horn, Rosa A. "Is Jesus God the Father or Is He the Son of God?" Sermon delivered on "Broadcast Sunday," WBNX, New York, n.d. Pentecostal Faith Church, New York.

Horn, Rosa A. "Was a Woman Called to Preach?" Sermon delivered on "Broadcast Sunday," WBNX, New York, n.d. Pentecostal Faith Church, New York.

Horn, Rosa A. "What Is Holiness? A Complete Life in Christ." Sermon possibly delivered on "Broadcast Sunday," WBNX, New York, n.d. Pentecostal Faith Church, New York.

Murray, Pauli. "Can These Bones Live Again?" A Woman's Day sermon delivered on Passion Sunday at St. Ambrose Episcopal Church, Raleigh, N.C., Mar. 18, 1978. Pauli Murray Collection, Schlesinger Library, Radcliffe College, Cambridge, Mass.

Murray, Pauli. "The Dilemma of the Minority Christian." Sermon delivered on Woman's Day at St. James Presbyterian Church, New York, May 19, 1974. Pauli Murray Collection, Schlesinger Library, Radcliffe College, Cambridge, Mass.

Murray, Pauli. "The Gift of the Holy Spirit." Sermon delivered on Pentecost (Whitsunday) at Trinity Episcopal Church, Washington, D.C., May 29, 1977. Pauli Murray Collection, Schlesinger Library, Radcliffe College, Cambridge, Mass.

Murray, Pauli. "The Holy Spirit." Sermon delivered on 76th Anniversary Sunday (Sunday after Ascension Day) at Calvary Protestant Episcopal Church, Washington, D.C., May 22, 1977. Pauli Murray Collection, Schlesinger Library, Radcliffe College, Cambridge, Mass.

Murray, Pauli. "Male and Female He Created Them." A Woman's Day sermon delivered on Trinity Sunday at Lincoln Temple, United Church of Christ, Washington, D.C., May 21, 1978. Pauli Murray Collection, Schlesinger Library, Radcliffe College, Cambridge, Mass.

Murray, Pauli. "Mary Has Chosen the Best Part." Sermon delivered on the seventh Sunday after Pentecost at Good Shepherd Episcopal Church, Silver Spring, Md., July 14, 1977. Pauli Murray Collection, Schlesinger Library, Radcliffe College, Cambridge, Mass.

Murray, Pauli. "Salvation and Liberation." Sermon delivered at the Unitarian Society of Germantown, Philadelphia, Pa., Apr. 1, 1979. Pauli Murray Collection, Schlesinger Library, Radcliffe College, Cambridge, Mass.

Murray, Pauli. "Women Seeking Admission to Holy Orders." An "Inaugural" sermon ("Pauli Murray, Candidate for Holy Orders") delivered on the first Sunday in Lent at Emmanuel Church, Boston, Mar. 3, 1974. Pauli Murray Collection, Schlesinger Library, Radcliffe College, Cambridge, Mass.

Raiff, Mrs. "Get the Right Ticket." Reproduced in "Woman Preaches at Payne Memorial Church." *Baltimore Afro-American,* Dec. 24, 1927.

Randolph, Florence Spearing. "Antipathy to Women Preachers." N.d. Florence Spearing Randolph Sermon Collection, Center for African American History and Culture, Temple University, Philadelphia, Pa.

Randolph, Florence Spearing. "Looking Backward and Forward." Sermon delivered on the Sixtieth Anniversary of the Women's Home and Foreign Missionary Society, 1943. Florence Spearing Randolph Sermon Collection. Center for African American History and Culture, Temple University, Philadelphia, Pa.

Randolph, Florence Spearing. "Hope." Sermon delivered in Jersey City, N.J., 1898 and 1945. Florence Spearing Randolph Sermon Collection, Center for African American History and Culture, Temple University, Philadelphia, Pa.

Randolph, Florence Spearing. "The Friends of Wickedness." Sermon delivered in Trenton, N.J., Mar. 21, 1909; Newburgh, N.Y., May 16, 1909; Branch of St. Marks A.M.E. Zion Church, New York, 1911; A.M.E. Zion Church, Brooklyn, N.Y., Jan. 29, 1911. Florence Spearing Randolph Sermon Collection, Center for African American History and Culture, Temple University, Philadelphia, Pa.

Randolph, Florence Spearing. "Woman, the Builder of Her House." Sermon delivered in Newburgh, N.Y., 1909, possibly on Woman's Day. Florence Spearing Randolph Sermon Collection, Center for African American History and Culture, Temple University, Philadelphia, Pa.

Randolph, Florence Spearing. "Christian Perfection." Sermon delivered at Wallace Chapel, Summit, N.J., Oct. 3, 1926. Florence Spearing Randolph Sermon Collection, Center for African American History and Culture, Temple University, Philadelphia, Pa.

Randolph, Florence Spearing. "Conversion." Sermon delivered at Wallace Chapel, Summit, N.J., 1931. Florence Spearing Randolph Sermon Collection, Center for African American History and Culture, Temple University, Philadelphia, Pa.

Randolph, Florence Spearing. "Salvation." Sermon delivered at Wallace Chapel, Summit, N.J., Feb. 10, 1933; Oct. 29, 1937; June 5, 1941. Florence Spearing Randolph Sermon Collection, Center for African American History and Culture, Temple University, Philadelphia, Pa.

Randolph, Florence Spearing. "Leaning the Wrong Way." Sermon delivered at Wallace Chapel, Summit, N.J., May 21, 1934. Florence Spearing Randolph Sermon Collection, Center for African American History and Culture, Temple University, Philadelphia, Pa.

Randolph, Florence Spearing. "If I Were White." Sermon delivered on Race Relations Sunday at Wallace Chapel, Summit, N.J., Feb. 14, 1941. Florence Spearing Randolph Sermon Collection, Center for African American History and Culture, Temple University, Philadelphia, Pa.

Redwine, F. E. "What Woman Is." *Messenger,* July 1948.

Robinson, Ida Bell. "Can These Bones Live?" *Latter Day Messenger,* 1934, 2(2), 6.

Robinson, Ida Bell. "Who Shall Be Able to Stand?" *Latter Day Messenger,* 1934, 2(2), 6.

Robinson, Ida Bell. "And a Little Child Shall Lead Them." *Latter Day Messenger,* 1935, *10*(5), 2.

Robinson, Ida Bell. "The Economic Persecution." *Latter Day Messenger,* 1935, *10*(5), 2–3.

Small, Mary Julia. "Zion's Mission Work." *Star of Zion,* Jan. 27, 1898.

Whitfield, Ella Eugene. "Making a Home a Safe Place for All That Enter Its Doors." Reprinted in "Sermon by Mrs. E. E. Whitfield to Women at Salem Baptist Church." *New York Age,* Apr. 17, 1926.

Whitfield, Ella Eugene. "Salvation Is a Discovery Found in Jesus Christ." Reproduced in "Mrs. E. E. Whitfield Stirs Members of Zion Baptist Church in Jersey City." *New York Age,* Apr. 17, 1926.

Whitlow, Quinceila. "The Woman in the Ministry of Jesus Christ." *Christian Index,* Aug. 8, 1940.

SECONDARY SOURCES

Anderson, Robert Mapes. *Vision of the Disinherited: The Making of American Pentecostalism.* New York: Oxford University Press, 1979.

Angell, Stephen Ward. "The Controversy over Women's Ministry in the African Methodist Episcopal Church During the 1880s: The Case of Sarah Ann Hughes." In Judith Weisenfeld and Richard Newman (eds.), *This Far by Faith: Readings in African-American Women's Religious Biography.* New York: Routledge, 1996.

Anselm, Saint, Archbishop of Canterbury. *Works.* 3 vols. Lewiston, N.Y.: Mellen Press, 1974.

Bacote, Samuel W. *Who's Who Among the Colored Baptists of the United States.* Kansas City, Mo.: Franklin Hudson, 1912.

Baer, Hans A. *The Black Spiritual Movement: A Religious Response to Racism.* Knoxville: University of Tennessee Press, 1984.

Bradley, David Henry, Sr. *A History of the A.M.E. Zion Church,* vol. 2: *1872–1968.* Nashville, Tenn.: Parthenon Press, 1970.

Cannon, Katie G. "Womanist Interpretation and Preaching in the Black Church." In Elizabeth Schüssler Fiorenza (ed.), *Searching the Scriptures,* Vol. 1: *A Feminist Introduction.* New York: Crossroad, 1993.

Carley, Keith W. *Ezekiel Among the Prophets: A Study of Ezekiel's Place in Prophetic Tradition.* London: SCM Press, 1975.

Carter, Harold A. *The Prayer Tradition of Black People.* Valley Forge, Pa.: Judson Press, 1976.

Chilcote, Paul W. *John Wesley and the Women Preachers of Early Methodism.* Metuchen, N.J.: Scarecrow Press, 1991.

Chilcote, Paul W. *She Offered Them Christ: The Legacy of Women Preachers in Early Methodism.* Nashville, Tenn.: Abingdon Press, 1993.

Collier-Thomas, Bettye. "History of the Sharp Street Memorial Methodist Episcopal Church, 1789–1920." In *One Hundred Seventy-Fifth Anniversary of Sharp Street Memorial United Methodist Church.* Baltimore: Sharp Street Memorial Church, 1977.

Collier-Thomas, Bettye. *Black Women in America: Contributors to Our Heritage.* Washington, D.C.: Bethune Museum and Archives, 1983.

Collier-Thomas, Bettye. *Freedom and Community: Nineteenth Century Black Pennsylvania.* Philadelphia: Center for African American History and Culture, Temple University, 1992.

Collier-Thomas, Bettye. "Florence Spearing Randolph (1866–1951)." In Jessie Carney Smith (ed.), *Notable Black American Women,* Vol. 2. Detroit: Gale Research, 1996.

Collier-Thomas, Bettye. "Julia A. J. Foote (1823–1901)." In Jessie Carney Smith (ed.), *Notable Black American Women,* Vol. 2. Detroit: Gale Research, 1996.

Collier-Thomas, Bettye. "Minister and Feminist Reformer: The Life of Florence Spearing Randolph." In Judith Weisenfeld and Richard Newman (eds.), *This Far by Faith: Readings in African-American Women's Religious Biography.* New York: Routledge, 1996.

Collins, Sheila D. *A Different Heaven and Earth.* Valley Forge, Pa.: Judson Press, 1974.

Cone, James H., and Wilmore, Gayraud S. (eds.). *Black Theology: A Documentary History,* Vol. 1: *1966–1979,* Vol. 2: *1980–1992.* Maryknoll, N.Y.: Orbis, 1993.

Cross, Whitney R. *The Burned-Over District: The Social and Intellectual History of Enthusiastic Religion in Western New York, 1800–1850.* New York: Harper and Row, 1965.

Curry, Daniel. *Perfect Love.* New York: Tibbals, 1878.

Curry, Daniel. *Fragments, Religious and Theological: A Collection of Independent Papers Relating to Various Points of Christian Life and Doctrine.* New York: Phillips and Hunt, 1880.

Daly, Mary. *Beyond God the Father: Toward a Philosophy of Women's Liberation*. Boston: Beacon Press, 1973.

Dayton, Donald W., and Dayton, Lucille Sider. "Women as Preachers: Evangelical Precedents." *Christianity Today*, May 23, 1975, pp. 4–7.

Dayton, Donald W., and Dayton, Lucille Sider. "'Your Daughters Shall Prophesy': Feminism in the Holiness Movement." *Methodist History*, 1975–1976, 14, 67–92.

Denham, Ann G. "The Power of Language in Preaching." In William D. Watley (ed.), *The Word and Words: Beyond Gender in Theological and Liturgical Language*. Princeton, N.J.: Women's Task Force, Worship Commission of the Consultation on Church Union, 1983.

Dodson, Jualynne Elizabeth. "Nineteenth-Century A.M.E. Preaching Women: Cutting Edge of Women's Inclusion in Church Polity." In Hilah F. Thomas and Rosemary Skinner Keller (eds.), *Women in New Worlds: Historical Perspectives on the Wesleyan Tradition*. Nashville, Tenn.: Abingdon Press, 1981.

Dodson, Jualynne Elizabeth, and Gilkes, Cheryl Townsend. "Something Within: Social Change and Collective Endurance in the Sacred World of Black Christian Women." In Rosemary Radford Ruether and Rosemary Skinner Keller (eds.), *Women and Religion in America*, Vol. 3: *1900–1968*. San Francisco: Harper and Row, 1986.

Doyle, Patricia Martin. "An Educator's Perspective on Language About God." In *Consultation on Language About God*. New York: United Presbyterian Church in the U.S.A., 1977.

Drake, St. Clair, and Cayton, Horace R. *Black Metropolis: A Study of Negro Life in a Northern City*. New York: Harcourt Brace, 1945.

DuPree, Sherry Sherrod (ed.). *Biographical Dictionary of African-American, Holiness-Pentecostals, 1880–1990*. Washington, D.C.: Middle Atlantic Regional Press, 1989.

DuPree, Sherry Sherrod (ed.). *African-American Holiness Pentecostal Movement: An Annotated Bibliography*. New York: Garland, 1996.

Dykes, De Witt C., Jr. "Leontine Kelly (1920–)." In Jessie Carney Smith (ed.), *Notable Black American Women*, Vol. 1. Detroit: Gale Research, 1992.

Earl, Riggins R. "The Black Church, Black Women and the Call." *Liturgy*, 1989, 7(4), 87–95.

Erikson, Erik. *Dimensions of a New Identity*. New York: Norton, 1974.

Farmer, David Albert, and Hunter, Edwina (eds.). *And Blessed Is She: Sermons by Women*. San Francisco: Harper San Francisco, 1990.

Fauset, Arthur Huff. *Black Gods of the Metropolis*. Philadelphia: University of Pennsylvania Press, 1944.

Fisher, Miles Mark. "Organized Religion and the Cults." *Crisis*, Jan. 1937, pp. 8–10, 29–30.

Franklin, John Hope. *From Slavery to Freedom: A History of Negro Americans* (5th ed.). New York: Knopf, 1980.

Frazier, E. Franklin. *The Negro Church in America.* New York: Schocken Books, 1974.

Garter, Ruth G., and others. *To a Higher Glory: The Growth and Development of Black Women Organized for Mission in the Methodist Church, 1940–1968.* New York: United Methodist Church, 1968.

Gilbert, O., and Titus, F. (eds.). *Narrative of Sojourner Truth.* Battle Creek, Mich.: 1878.

Gilkes, Cheryl Townsend. "Together and in Harness: Women's Traditions in the Sanctified Church." *Signs: Journal of Women in Culture and Society,* 1985, *10*(4), 678–699.

Gilkes, Cheryl Townsend. "Some Mother's Son and Some Father's Daughter: Gender and Biblical Language in Afro-Christian Worship Tradition." In *Shaping New Vision: Gender and Values in American Culture.* Harvard Women's Studies in Religion, Vol. 5. Ann Arbor: University of Michigan Research Press, 1987.

Gilmore, Glenda Elizabeth. "Pettey, Sarah E. C. Dudley (1869–1906)." In Darlene Clark Hine, Elsa Barkley Brown, and Rosalyn Terborg-Penn (eds.), *Black Women in America: An Historical Encyclopedia.* Vol. 2. Brooklyn, N.Y.: Carlson, 1993.

Gilmore, Glenda Elizabeth. *Gender and Jim Crow: Women and the Politics of White Supremacy in North Carolina, 1896–1920.* Chapel Hill: University of North Carolina Press, 1996.

Gordon, Ann D., and others. *African American Women and the Vote, 1837–1965.* Amherst: University of Massachusetts Press, 1997.

Grant, Jacquelyn. "Black Theology and the Black Woman." In James H. Cone and Gayraud S. Wilmore (eds.), *Black Theology: A Documentary History,* Vol. 1 (2nd ed., rev.). Maryknoll, N.Y.: Orbis, 1993.

Gutierrez, Gustavo. *Liberation and Change.* Atlanta: John Knox, 1977.

Gutierrez, Gustavo. *A Theology of Liberation: History, Politics and Salvation.* Maryknoll, N.Y.: Orbis, 1973.

Haley, Alex. *Roots.* New York: Doubleday, 1976.

Hardesty, Nancy, Dayton, Lucille Sider, and Dayton, Donald W. "Women in the Holiness Movement: Feminism in the Evangelical Tradition." In Rosemary Radford Ruether and Eleanor T. McLaughlin (eds.), *Women of Spirit: Female Leadership in the Jewish and Christian Traditions.* New York: Simon & Schuster, 1979.

Harris, Eula Wallace, and Craig, Maxie Harris. *Christian Methodist Episcopal Church Through the Years.* Memphis, Tenn.: C.M.E. Publishing House, 1965.

Hart, Jamie, and Brown, Elsa Barkley (comps.). "Black Women in the United States." In Darlene Clark Hine, Elsa Barkley Brown, and Rosalyn Terborg-Penn (eds.), *Black Women in America: An Historical Encyclopedia,* Vol. 2. Brooklyn, N.Y.: Carlson, 1993.

Higginbotham, Evelyn Brooks. *Righteous Discontent: The Woman's Movement in the Black Baptist Church, 1880–1920.* Cambridge, Mass.: Harvard University Press, 1993.

Higginbotham, Evelyn Brooks. "Clubwomen and Electoral Politics in the 1920s." In Ann D. Gordon and others, *African American Women and the Vote, 1837–1965.* Amherst: University of Massachusetts Press, 1997.

Hine, Darlene Clark, Brown, Elsa Barkley, and Terborg-Penn, Rosalyn (eds.). *Black Women in America: An Historical Encyclopedia.* 2 vols. Brooklyn, N.Y.: Carlson, 1993.

Hinson, E. Glenn. "The Church: Liberator or Oppressor of Women?" *Review and Expositor,* 1975, 72(1).

Humez, Jean McMahon. "Visionary Experience and Power: The Career of Rebecca Cox Jackson." In David Wills and Richard Newman (eds.), *Black Apostles at Home and Abroad: Afro-Americans and the Christian Mission from the Revolution to Reconstruction.* New York: G. K. Hall, 1982.

Humez, Jean McMahon. "'My Spirit Eye': Some Functions of Spiritual and Visionary Experience in the Lives of Five Black Women Preachers, 1810–1880." In Barbara Harris and Joann K. McNamara (eds.), *Women and the Structure of Society: Selected Research from the Fifth Berkshire Conference on the History of Women.* Durham, N.C.: Duke University Press, 1984.

Humez, Jean McMahon. "Jackson, Rebecca Cox." In Darlene Clark Hine, Elsa Barkley Brown, and Rosalyn Terborg-Penn (eds.), *Black Women in America: An Historical Encyclopedia.* Vol. 1. Brooklyn, N.Y.: Carlson, 1993.

Hurston, Zora Neale. "Hoodoo in America." *Journal of American Folklore,* 1931, *44,* 317–417.

Irwin, Joyce L. "Women as Preachers and Prophets." In Joyce L. Irwin (ed.), *Womanhood in Radical Protestantism, 1525–1675.* Lewiston, N.Y.: Mellen Press, 1979.

Jacobs, Sylvia M. "Murray, Pauli (1910–1985)." In Darlene Clark Hine, Elsa Barkley Brown, and Rosalyn Terborg-Penn (eds.), *Black Women in America: An Historical Encyclopedia,* Vol. 2. Brooklyn, N.Y.: Carlson, 1993.

Jones, Charles Edwin. *Perfectionist Persuasion: The Holiness Movement and American Methodism, 1867–1936.* Metuchen, N.J.: Scarecrow Press, 1974.

Jones, Major J. *Black Awareness: A Theology of Hope.* Nashville, Tenn.: Abingdon Press, 1971.

Jones, Major J. *Christian Ethics for Black Theology.* Nashville, Tenn.: Abingdon Press, 1974.

Julian of Norwich. *The Revelations of Divine Love of Julian of Norwich.* St. Meinrad, Ind.: Abbey Press, 1975.

Kelly, Leontine T. C. "Preaching in the Black Tradition." In Judith L. Weidman (ed.), *Women Ministers.* San Francisco: Harper and Row, 1985.

Ketcham, G. F. (ed.). *Yearbook of American Churches.* Nashville, Tenn.: National Council of the Churches of Christ in the U.S.A., 1951.

Lakey, Othal Hawthorne. *The History of the C.M.E. Church.* Memphis, Tenn.: C.M.E. Publishing House, 1985.

Lakey, Othal Hawthorne, and Stephens, Betty Beene. *God in My Mama's House: The Women's Movement in the C.M.E. Church.* Memphis, Tenn.: C.M.E. Publishing House, 1994.

Lawless, Elaine J. "Not So Different a Story After All: Pentecostal Women in the Pulpit." In *Women's Leadership in Marginal Religions: Explorations Outside the Mainstream.* Urbana: University of Illinois Press, 1993.

Lincoln, C. Eric, and Mamiya, Lawrence H. *The Black Church in the African American Experience.* Durham, N.C.: Duke University Press, 1990.

Logan, Rayford W., and Winston, Michael R. (eds.). *Dictionary of American Negro Biography.* New York: Norton, 1980.

Lowenberg, Bert James, and Bogin, Ruth (eds.). *Black Women in Nineteenth-Century American Life.* University Park: Pennsylvania State University Press, 1976.

Mabee, Carlton, and Newhouse, Susan Mabee. *Sojourner Truth: Slave, Prophet, Legend.* New York: New York University Press, 1995.

May, Rollo. *Power and Innocence: A Search for the Sources of Violence.* New York: Norton, 1972.

Mays, Benjamin E., and Nicholson, Joseph William. *The Negro's Church.* New York: Institute of Social and Religious Research, 1933.

McAfee, L. D. *History of the Woman's Missionary Society: In the Colored Methodist Episcopal Church.* Phenix City, Ala: Phenix City Herald, 1945.

McFadden, Margaret. "The Ironies of Pentecost: Phoebe Palmer, World Evangelism, and Female Networks." *Methodist History,* 1992–1993, *31,* 63–75.

McKay, Nellie Y. "Nineteenth-Century Black Women's Spiritual Autobiographies: Religious Faith and Self-Empowerment." In Personal Narratives Group (eds.), *Interpreting Women's Lives: Feminist Theory and Personal Narratives.* Bloomington: Indiana University Press, 1989.

McLaughlin, Eleanor T. *Interim Legacy: A Collection of Poems.* New York: Carlton Press, 1972.

Morton, Cynthia Neverdon. "Advancement of the Race Through African American Women's Organizations in the South, 1895–1925." In Ann D. Gordon and others, *African American Women and the Vote, 1837–1965.* Amherst: University of Massachusetts Press, 1997.

Murphy, Joseph M. *Working the Spirit: Ceremonies of the African Diaspora.* Boston: Beacon Press, 1994.

Murray, Pauli. *Proud Shoes: The Story of an American Family.* New York: Harper and Row, 1956.

Murray, Pauli. *Song in a Weary Throat: An American Pilgrimage.* New York: Harper and Row, 1987.

Murray, Pauli. "Black Theology and Feminist Theology: A Comparative View." In James H. Cone and Gayraud S. Wilmore (eds.), *Black Theology: A Documentary History,* Vol. 1: *1966–1979.* Maryknoll, N.Y.: Orbis Books, 1993.

Nicholson, Aleathia Dolores. "Barbara Harris (1930–)." In Jessie Carney Smith (ed.), *Notable Black American Women,* Vol. 1. Detroit: Gale Research, 1992.

Noren, Carol M. *The Woman in the Pulpit.* Nashville, Tenn.: Abingdon Press, 1991.

Norwood, Frederick A. "Expanding Horizons: Women in the Methodist Movement." In *Triumph over Silence: Women in Protestant History.* Vol. 15. Westport, Conn.: Greenwood Press, 1985.

Overton, Betty J. "Black Women Preachers: A Literary Overview." *Southern Quarterly,* 1985, 23, 157–166.

Painter, Nell Irvin. "Truth, Sojourner (c. 1799–1883)." In Darlene Clark Hine, Elsa Barkley Brown, and Rosalyn Terborg-Penn (eds.), *Black Women in America: An Historical Encyclopedia.* Vol. 2. Brooklyn, N.Y.: Carlson, 1993.

Painter, Nell Irvin. *Sojourner Truth: A Life, a Symbol.* New York: Norton, 1996.

Paris, Peter. "From Womanist Thought to Womanist Action." *Journal of Feminist Studies in Religion,* 1993, 9, 122.

Payne, Daniel A. *History of the African Methodist Episcopal Church.* Nashville, Tenn.: Publishing House of the A.M.E. Sunday School Union, 1891.

Payne, Wardell J. *Directory of African American Religious Bodies.* Washington, D.C.: Howard University Press, 1991.

Peck, Catherine L. "Your Daughters Shall Prophesy: Women in the Afro-American Preaching Tradition." In Ruel W. Tyson Jr. and others (eds.), *Diversities of Gifts: Field Studies in Southern Religion.* Urbana: University of Illinois Press, 1988.

Personal Narratives Group (ed.). *Interpreting Women's Lives: Feminist Theory and Personal Narratives.* Bloomington: Indiana University Press, 1989.

Phillips, Charles H. *The History of the CMEs in America.* Memphis, Tenn.: C.M.E. Publishing House, 1925.

Pierson, Arthur T. *An Unbeliever Convinced.* Los Angeles: Bible House of Los Angeles, 1880.

Pierson, Arthur T. *Many Infallible Proofs: The Evidences of Christianity*. Grand Rapids, Mich.: Revell, 1886.

Pierson, Arthur T. *Woman as a Factor in the World's Evangelization*. Mahwah, N.J.: Funk & Wagnalls, 1895.

Pierson, Arthur T. *The Bible and Spiritual Life*. London: Nisbet, 1908.

Powers, Bernard E., Jr. *Black Charlestonians: A Social History, 1822–1885*. Fayetteville: University of Arkansas Press, 1994.

Price, Charles P. *Ordination of Women in Theological Perspective*. Cincinnati, Ohio: Forward Movement, 1975.

Richardson, Clement. *The National Cyclopedia of the Colored Race*. Vol. 1. Montgomery, Ala.: National Publishing Co., 1919.

Roberts, J. Deotis. *Black Churches and Family Empowerment*. New York: Committee on Ministries with Black Families, National Council of Churches, 1970.

Roberts, J. Deotis. *Opening Closed Doors: Redemption and Reconciliation*. St. Louis, Mo.: Christian Board Publications, 1973.

Roberts, J. Deotis. *A Black Political Theology*. Philadelphia: Westminster Press, 1974.

Ruether, Rosemary Radford. *Liberation Theology: Human Hope Confronts Christian History and American Power*. Mahwah, N.J.: Paulist Press, 1972.

Ruether, Rosemary Radford. *New Woman, New Earth: Sexist Ideologies and Human Liberation*. Boston: Beacon Press, 1975.

Ruether, Rosemary Radford, and Keller, Rosemary Skinner (eds.). *Women and Religion in America*, Vol. 3: *1900–1968*. San Francisco: Harper and Row, 1986.

Ruether, Rosemary Radford, and McLaughlin, Eleanor T. (eds.). *Women of Spirit: Female Leadership in the Jewish and Christian Traditions*. New York: Simon & Schuster, 1979.

Russell, Letty M. *Human Liberation in a Feminist Perspective: A Theology*. Philadelphia: Westminster Press, 1974.

Salem, Dorothy. *To Better Our World: Black Women in Organized Reform, 1890–1920*. In Darlene Clark Hine and others (eds.), *Black Women in United States History*, Vol. 14. Brooklyn, N.Y.: Carlson, 1990.

Sanders, Cheryl J. *Saints in Exile: The Holiness-Pentecostal Experience in African American Religion and Culture*. New York: Oxford University Press, 1996.

Sanders, Cheryl J. "The Woman as Preacher." *Journal of Religious Thought*, 1986, 43(1), 6–23. Reprinted in Gayraud S. Wilmore (ed.), *African American Religious Studies: An Interdisciplinary Anthology*. Durham, N.C.: Duke University Press, 1989.

Scarupa, Harriet Jackson. "Women in Ministry: Challenging Old Assumptions." *New Directions,* Jan. 1996, pp. 6–15.

Schmidt, Jean Miller. "Toward a Feminist Theology in the Wesleyan Tradition: Insights from Nineteenth and Early Twentieth-Century Methodists." In Theodore Runyon (ed.), *Wesleyan Theology Today: A Bicentennial Theological Consultation.* Nashville, Tenn.: Kingswood Books, 1985.

Scruggs, Lawson A. *Women of Distinction.* Raleigh, N.C.: Scruggs, 1893.

Smith, Christine. *Weaving the Sermon: Preaching in a Feminist Perspective.* Louisville, Ky.: John Knox, 1989.

Smith, Jessie Carney. "Lucy Smith (1875–1952)." In Jessie Carney Smith (ed.), *Notable Black American Women,* Vol. 2. Detroit: Gale Research, 1996.

Smith, Jessie Carney (ed.). *Notable Black American Women.* 2 vols. Detroit: Gale Research, 1992, 1996.

Spear, Allan H. *Black Chicago: The Making of a Negro Ghetto, 1890–1920.* Chicago: University of Chicago Press, 1969.

Stringfellow, William. *An Ethic for Christians and Other Aliens in a Strange Land.* Waco, Tex.: Word Books, 1973.

Swift, Wesley F. "The Women Itinerant Preachers of Early Methodism." *Proceedings of the Wesley Historical Society,* 1951–1952, *28,* 89–94; 1953–1954, *29,* 76–83.

Synan, Vinson. *The Holiness-Pentecostal Movement in the United States.* Grand Rapids, Mich.: Eerdmans, 1971.

Terborg-Penn, Rosalyn. "African-American Women's Networks in the Anti-Lynching Crusade." In Noralee Frankel and Nancy S. Dye (eds.), *Gender, Class, Race and Reform in the Progressive Era.* Lexington: University Press of Kentucky, 1991.

Trible, Phyllis. "Depatriarchalizing in Biblical Interpretation." *Journal of the American Academy of Religion,* 1973, *41*(1), 35–42.

Trible, Phyllis. *Two Women in a Man's World: A Reading of the Book of Ruth.* N.p., 1976.

Trible, Phyllis. *God and the Rhetoric of Sexuality.* Minneapolis: Augsburg Fortress, 1978.

Trulear, Dean Harold. "Reshaping Black Pastoral Theology: The Vision of Bishop Ida B. Robinson." *Journal of Religious Thought,* 1989, *46*(1), 17–31.

Tucker, Ruth, and Liefield, Walter. *Daughters of the Church: Women and Ministry from New Testament Times to the Present.* Grand Rapids, Mich.: Zondervan, 1987.

Vick, Marsha C. "Pauli Murray (1910–1985)." In Jessie Carney Smith (ed.), *Notable Black American Women.* Vol. 1. Detroit: Gale Research, 1992.

Walker, Margaret. *Jubilee.* Boston: Houghton Mifflin, 1966.

Walls, William J. *The African Methodist Episcopal Zion Church: Reality of the Black Church*. Charlotte, N.C.: A.M.E. Zion Publishing House, 1974.

Washington, Joseph R., Jr. *Black Sects and Cults*. New York: Anchor Books, 1973.

Weisbrot, Robert. *Father Divine and the Struggle for Racial Equality*. Urbana: University of Illinois Press, 1983.

Weisenfeld, Judith, and Newman, Richard (eds.). *This Far by Faith: Readings in African-American Women's Religious Biography*. New York: Routledge, 1996.

White, Deborah Gray. *Ar'nt I a Woman?* New York: Norton, 1985.

Will, James E. "Ordination of Women." In Hilah F. Thomas and Rosemary Skinner Keller (eds.), *Women in New Worlds: Historical Perspectives on the Wesleyan Tradition*. Nashville, Tenn.: Abingdon Press, 1981.

Williams, Delores S. "Visions, Inner Voices, Apparitions, and Defiance in Nineteenth-Century Black Women's Narratives." *Women's Studies Quarterly*, 1993, *21*, 81–89.

Williams, Fannie Barrier. "The Intellectual Progress of the Colored Women of the United States Since the Emancipation Proclamation." In May Wright Sewall (ed.), *The World's Congress of Representative Women*, Vol. 2. Skokie, Ill.: Rand McNally, 1894.

Williams-Jones, Pearl. "A Minority Report: Black Pentecostal Women." *Spirit: A Journal of Issues Incident to Black Pentecostalism*, 1977, *1*(2), 40.

Wright, Richard R. *The Encyclopaedia of the African Methodist Episcopal Church*. Philadelphia: AME Book Concern, 1947.

Zikmund, Barbara Brown. "The Struggle for the Right to Preach." In Rosemary Radford Ruether and Rosemary Skinner Keller (eds.), *Women and Religion in America*, Vol. 1: *The Nineteenth Century: A Documentary History*. San Francisco: Harper and Row, 1981.

UNPUBLISHED WORKS

Bell, Minerva. "Significant Female Religious Leaders and Factors Leading to Their Success." M.A. thesis, Fairleigh Dickinson University, 1974.

Bird, Phyllis. "The Image of Woman in the Old Testament." Typescript, Temple University, 1972.

Brekus, Catherine A. "Let Your Women Keep Silence in the Churches: Female Preaching and Evangelical Religion in America, 1740–1845." Ph.D. dissertation, Yale University, 1993.

Daniels, David Douglas. "The Cultural Renewal of Slave Religion: Charles Price Jones and the Emergence of the Holiness Movement in Mississippi." Ph.D. dissertation, Union Theological Seminary, 1992.

Dieter, Melvin Easterday. "Revivalism and Holiness." Ph.D. dissertation, Temple University, 1972.

Dodson, Jualynne Elizabeth. "Women's Collective Power in the A.M.E. Church." Ph.D. dissertation, University of California, Berkeley, 1984.

Gaylor, Christine Camille. "The Ordination of Women in the Episcopal Church in the United States: A Case Study." Ph.D. dissertation, St. John's University, 1982.

Goman, Jon Gifford. "The Ordination of Women: The Bible and the Fathers." D.Min. dissertation, School of Theology at Claremont, 1976.

Goode, Gloria Davis. "Preachers of the Word and Singers of the Gospel: The Ministry of Women Among Nineteenth-Century African Americans." Ph.D. dissertation, University of Pennsylvania, 1990.

Hudson, Mary Linnie. "Shall Woman Preach? Or the Question Answered: The Ministry of Louisa M. Woolsley in the Cumberland Presbyterian Church, 1887–1942." Ph.D. dissertation, Vanderbilt University, 1992.

Huyck, Heather Ann. "To Celebrate a Whole Priesthood: The History of Women's Ordination in the Episcopal Church." Ph.D. dissertation, University of Minnesota, 1981.

Marrett, Michael McFarlen. "The Historical Background and Spiritual Authority of the Lambeth Conferences and Their Impact on the Protestant Episcopal Church in the United States of America with Particular Emphasis on the Ordination of Women to the Priesthood." Ph.D. dissertation, New York University, 1980.

Morrison, Susan Murch. "Ministry Shaped by Hope . . . Toward Wholeness: The Woman as Ordained Minister." D.Min. dissertation, Wesley Theological Seminary, 1979.

Mount Sinai Holy Church of America, Inc. "Mount Sinai Training Institute." Typescript, n.d. Ida B. Robinson Collection, Center for African American History and Culture, Temple University, Philadelphia, Pa.

St. Pierre, Simone Marie. "The Struggle to Serve: Towards the Ordination of Women in the Roman Catholic Church." Ph.D. dissertation, University of Manitoba, 1991.

Samuel, James Ray. "Black Theology as a Basis for Holistic Worship in the African Methodist Episcopal Zion Church." D.Min. dissertation, Drew University, 1990.

Sartori, Shirley Larmour. "Conflict and Institutional Change: The Ordination of Women in the Episcopal Church." Ph.D. dissertation, State University of New York, Albany, 1978.

Smith, Herbert Morrisohn. "Three Negro Preachers in Chicago: A Study in Religious Leadership." M.A. thesis, University of Chicago Divinity School, 1935.

Terborg-Penn, Rosalyn. "Afro-Americans in the Struggle for Woman's Suffrage." Ph.D. dissertation, Howard University, 1977.

Travis, J. Ruth. "Preaching Styles of Female Pastors in the African Methodist Episcopal Church, Baltimore, Maryland." D.Min. thesis, United Theological Seminary, 1992.

Wahl, Joseph Anthony. "The Exclusion of Woman from Holy Orders." Ph.D. dissertation, Catholic University, 1959.

THEMATIC INDEX OF SERMONS

Gender Issues

Holiness Doctrine

THE AUTHOR

BETTYE COLLIER-THOMAS is an associate professor in the history depart-
ment and director of the Temple University Center for African American
History and Culture. She is the founding executive director of the Bethune
Museum and Archives Inc., National Historic Site in Washington, D.C.
She has been the recipient of many awards, honors, and recognition. In
November 1994, she received the Conservation Service Award, one of the
highest awards given to a civilian by the Department of the Interior. This
award recognized her singular achievement in the creation and development of the Bethune Museum and Archives. She has received grants from
the National Endowment for the Humanities, the Ford Foundation, and
the Rockefeller Foundation. Currently she is directing research for
"African American Women and the Church: A History," one of four
major documentary religious projects in the nation funded by the Lilly
Endowment.

Collier-Thomas's research has focused primarily on African American
women, popular culture, and religion. She has published more than thirty
articles, is a coeditor of *African American Women and the Vote* (University of Massachusetts Press, 1997), and is the editor of *African American
Christmas Stories: A Heritage* (Henry Holt, 1997).

INDEX